Perspectives on Civil Procedure

Perspectives on Civil Procedure

Geoffrey C. Hazard, Jr.

Sterling Professor of Law
Yale Law School

Jan Vetter

Professor of Law
University of California at Berkeley School of Law

Little, Brown and Company Boston and Toronto

Library of Congress Catalog Card No. 86-81528

ISBN 0-316-35259-4

ALP

Published simultaneously in Canada
by Little, Brown & Company (Canada) Limited

Printed in the United States of America

Contents

Preface *ix*
Acknowledgments *xi*

Chapter 1
The Character of Adjudication **1**

Torstein Eckhoff, The Mediator, the Judge and the Administrator in Conflict-Resolution 1
Lon L. Fuller, The Forms and Limits of Adjudication 15
Abram Chayes, The Role of the Judge in Public Law Litigation 42
Notes and Comments 58
Robert M. Cover, For James Wm. Moore: Some Reflections on a Reading of the Rules 58
Notes and Comments 68
Kenneth E. Scott, Two Models of the Civil Process 68
Notes and Comments 76

Chapter 2
The Institution of a Jury Trial **77**

Fleming James, Jr., Right to a Jury Trial in Civil Actions 77
Notes and Comments 94
Hans Zeisel, . . . And Then There Were None: The Diminution of the Federal Jury 94
Notes and Comments 101
Edward H. Cooper, Directions for Directed Verdicts: A Compass for Federal Courts 102
Notes and Comments 121

Chapter 3
Discovery and the Adversary Process **123**

Wayne D. Brazil, The Adversary Character of Civil Discovery: A Critique and Proposals for Change 123
David L. Shapiro, Some Problems of Discovery in an Adversary System 136
Notes and Comments 152
Jack H. Friedenthal, A Divided Supreme Court Adopts Discovery Amendments to the Federal Rules of Civil Procedure 152
Notes and Comments 155

Chapter 4
Multiparty Controversy **156**

Geoffrey C. Hazard, Jr. & Myron Moskovitz, An Historical and Critical Analysis of Interpleader 156
Benjamin Kaplan, Continuing Work of the Civil Committee: 1966 Amendments of the Federal Rules of Civil Procedure (I) 163
Notes and Comments 180
David L. Shapiro, Some Thoughts on Intervention Before Courts, Agencies, and Arbitrators 180
Kenneth W. Dam, Class Actions: Efficiency, Compensation, Deterrence, and Conflict of Interest 193
Stephen C. Yeazell, From Group Litigation to Class Action, Part II: Interest, Class, and Representation 212
Deborah L. Rhode, Class Conflicts in Class Actions 222
Notes and Comments 241

Chapter 5
Preclusion **243**

John C. McCoid, A Single Package for Multiparty Disputes 243
Notes and Comments 257

Lawrence C. George, Sweet Uses of Adversity: *Parklane Hosiery* and the Collateral Class Action 258
Note, A Probabilistic Analysis of the Doctrine of Mutuality of Collateral Estoppel 272
Notes and Comments 278

Chapter 6
Appeal **279**

Martin Shapiro, Trial Courts and Appellate Courts — Fact-Finding 279
Note, The Finality Rule for Supreme Court Review of State Court Orders 290

Preface

This set of readings is designed to accompany a course on civil procedure. It may be introduced to students at various stages throughout their procedure classes, particularly at the advanced stages. By then, students have learned how to read cases and treatises and will have come to consider the deeper relationships between decisional law and doctrine, on the one hand, and the fundamental dilemmas of procedure on the other. Legal scholarship at its best addresses those relationships. We have compiled a set of materials that we believe reasonably balances comprehensiveness of issues, variation in viewpoint and philosophy, and length.

Neither decisional law nor the rules and statutes governing procedure can fully explain the procedural problems that they address. Courts make law, they do not describe it. Judicial lawmaking demands maintaining institutional reserves of discretion, and requires nesting a new decision in received law insofar as possible, even if that law is muddled or obsolete. It necessitates producing a result even without time or opportunity to think through the matter at hand. Legal scholarship is not subject to these constraints. Of course, legal scholarship does not always succeed in its intellectual ambitions, but even when it does not, it is a mode of thought that law students need to share as much as they need to know cases and rules.

We believe that students benefit from direct encounters with legal scholarship, for much the same reason that we benefit as teachers. It opens one's eyes to aspects of law that courts do not explain and generally do not want to hear. For the latter reason, these aspects usually are also bypassed in treatises, which are designed for citation to courts.

Legal scholarship, in our opinion, must encompass not only theories of justice at a high level of abstraction, but the technical intricacies of a developed legal system. There is a place for Rawlsian or Coasian analysis, or other philosophical inquiry, in the study of all legal subjects, including civil procedure, for the ideas of equality, equity, and transaction cost are essential in comprehending litigation. In the real world, however, these ideas present themselves not in pristine form, but as aspects of highly complex and deeply entrenched social institutions. Hence, we think students benefit best from scholarly works that contemplate the developed law of modern procedure. Our selection is based on that premise.

Geoffrey C. Hazard, Jr.
Jan Vetter

November 1986

Acknowledgments

We would like to thank the authors and copyright holders of the following works, who permitted their inclusion in this book:

Brazil, Wayne D., The Adversary Character of Civil Discovery: A Critique and Proposals for Change, 31 Vand. L. Rev. 1295 (1978). Copyright © 1978 by the Vanderbilt Law Review. Reprinted by permission.

Chayes, Abram, The Role of the Judge in Public Law Litigation, 89 Harv. L. Rev. 1281 (1976). Copyright © 1976 by the Harvard Law Review Association. Reprinted by permission.

Cooper, Edward H., Directions for Directed Verdicts: A Compass for Federal Courts, 55 Minn. L. Rev. 903 (1971). Copyright © 1971 by the Minnesota Law Review. Reprinted by permission.

Cover, Robert M., For James Wm. Moore: Some Reflections on a Reading of the Rules, 84 Yale L.J. 718 (1975). Copyright © 1975 by the author. Reprinted by permission of the author, and The Yale Law Journal Company and Fred B. Rothman & Company from The Yale Law Journal, Vol. 84, pp. 718, 722-728, 730-739.

Dam, Kenneth W., Class Actions: Efficiency, Compensation, Deterrence, and Conflict of Interest, 4 J. Legal Stud. 47 (1975). Copyright © 1975 by the University of Chicago. Reprinted by permission.

Eckhoff, Torstein, The Mediator, the Judge and the Administrator in Conflict-Resolution, 10 Acta Sociologica 148, 156-167, 169-170 (1966). Copyright © 1966 by the author. Reprinted by permission.

Friedenthal, Jack H., A Divided Supreme Court Adopts Discovery Amendments to the Federal Rules of Civil Procedure, 69 Calif. L. Rev. 806 (1981). Copyright © 1981 by the California Law Review. Reprinted by permission.

Fuller, Lon L., The Forms and Limits of Adjudication, 92 Harv. L. Rev. 353 (1978). Copyright © 1978 by the Harvard Law Review Association. Reprinted by permission.

George, Lawrence C., Sweet Uses of Adversity: *Parklane Hosiery* and the Collateral Class Action, 32 Stan. L. Rev. 655 (1980). Copyright © 1980 by the Board of Trustees of the Leland Stanford Junior University. Reprinted by permission.

Hazard, Geoffrey C., Jr. & Myron Moskovitz, An Historical and Critical Analysis of Interpleader, 52 Calif. L. Rev. 706 (1964). Copyright © 1964 by the California Law Review. Reprinted by permission.

James, Fleming, Jr., Right to a Jury Trial in Civil Actions, 72 Yale L.J. 655 (1963). Copyright © 1963 by Mrs. Fleming James. Reprinted by permission of Mrs. Fleming James, and The Yale Law Journal Company and Fred B. Rothman & Company from The Yale Law Journal, Vol. 72, pp. 655-673, 675-676, 679-691.

Kaplan, Benjamin, Continuing Work of the Civil Committee: 1966 Amendments of the Federal Rules of Civil Procedure (I), 81 Harv. L. Rev. 356 (1967). Copyright © 1967 by the Harvard Law Review Association. Reprinted by permission.

McCoid, John C., A Single Package for Multiparty Disputes, 28 Stan. L. Rev. 707 (1976). Copyright © 1976 by the Board of Trustees of the Leland Stanford Junior University. Reprinted by permission.

Note, A Probabilistic Analysis of the Doctrine of Mutuality of Collateral Estoppel, 76 Mich. L. Rev. 612 (1978). Copyright © 1978 by the Michigan Law Review. Reprinted by permission.

Note, The Finality Rule for Supreme Court Review of State Court Orders, 91 Harv. L. Rev. 1004 (1978). Copyright © 1978 by the Harvard Law Review Association. Reprinted by permission.

Rhode, Deborah L., Class Conflicts in Class Actions, 34 Stan. L. Rev. 1183 (1982). Copyright © 1982 by the Board of Trustees of the Leland Stanford Junior University. Reprinted by permission.

Scott, Kenneth E., Two Models of the Civil Process, 27 Stan. L. Rev. 937 (1975). Copyright © 1975 by the Board of Trustees of the Leland Stanford Junior University. Reprinted by permission.

Shapiro, David L., Some Problems of Discovery in an Adversary System, 63 Minn. L. Rev. 1055 (1979). Copyright © 1979 by the Minnesota Law Review. Reprinted by permission.

Shapiro, David L., Some Thoughts on Intervention Before Courts, Agencies, and Arbitrators, 81 Harv. L. Rev. 721 (1968). Copyright © 1968 by the Harvard Law Review Association. Reprinted by permission.

Shapiro, Martin, Trial Courts and Appellate Courts — Fact-Finding, excerpted from Courts: A Comparative and Political Analysis 41-44, 49-56 (1981). Copyright © 1981 by the University of Chicago Press. Reprinted by permission.

Yeazell, Stephen C., From Group Litigation to Class Action, Part II: Interest, Class, and Representation, 27 U.C.L.A. L. Rev. 1067 (1980). Originally published in 27 U.C.L.A. L. Rev. 1067, copyright © 1980, the Regents of the University of California. All rights reserved. Reprinted by permission.

Zeisel, Hans, . . . And Then There Were None: The Diminution of the Federal Jury, 38 U. Chi. L. Rev. 710 (1971). Copyright © 1971 by the University of Chicago Law Review. Reprinted by permission.

Perspectives on Civil Procedure

Chapter 1

The Character of Adjudication

*The Mediator, the Judge and the Administrator in Conflict-Resolution**

Torstein Eckhoff

I. Introduction

Conflicts between people are sometimes resolved by a third party who helps to bring about a reconciliation or makes a decision by which they abide. The conflict-resolver, who in the following will be referred to as the "third party," can be a father or mother who stops a quarrel between children, or a woman who chooses one of two rival suitors, or a court which settles a legal dispute or the United Nations which resolves an international conflict. The purpose of this article is to discuss some of the conditions for attempting such third party intervention and for bringing about positive results. . . .

[The following summarizes the factors or conditions under which the parties may resort to third party intervention. The numbers in parentheses refer to the arrows in Chart 1-1.]

The greater the agreement between the parties concerning normative factors which they consider relevant for the solution, the greater is the probability of their being able to resolve the conflict on their own and the less need is there for bringing in a third party (1).

The greater the common interests of the parties for having the conflict resolved, the more probable is it that they will engage in

* *Source:* 10 Acta Sociologica 148, 156-167, 169-170 (1966).

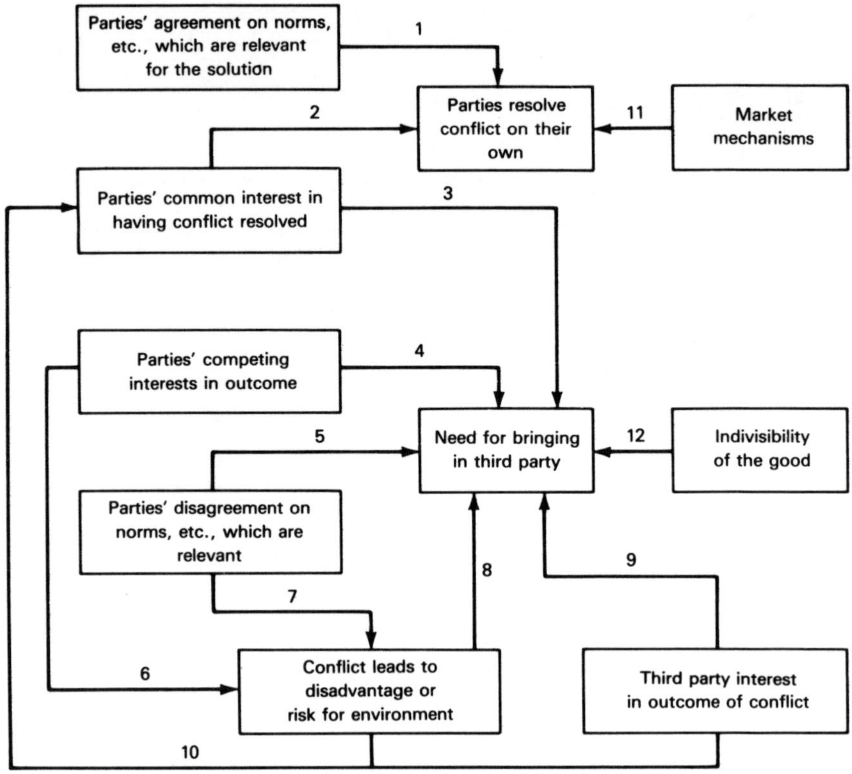

[Chart 1-1]

resolving the conflict *either* on their own, *or,* if that leads to difficulties, by bringing in a third party (2 and 3).

The stronger the competing interests the parties have in the outcome, and the more they disagree on normative factors which they consider relevant, the less probable is it that they will be able to resolve the conflict on their own, and the greater need they have for bringing in a third party, presuming that they have common interests in having the conflict resolved (4 and 5).

The relationship of antagonism between the parties can make their environments interested in having the conflict resolved — if necessary with the help of a third party (6, 7 and 8). The third party may himself be interested in the conflict being resolved (9). His reactions and those of the environment may have the consequence that the parties become more interested in the conflict being resolved (10).

In the diagram it is also indicated that market-mechanisms facilitate conflict-resolution by the parties themselves and reduce the need for third party intervention (11), whereas the circumstance that a disputed good is indivisible operates in the opposite direction (12).

Even if the parties (or their environments) have a *need* to have the conflict resolved by a third party, it is not certain that they [will] find someone suited to undertake the assignment. And if they find someone, it may *cost* so much (in terms of economic expenditures, delays, loss of prestige, etc.) that it does not pay. It is, naturally, also possible to conceive of cases where a third party — either on his own initiative or because the parties or their environments ask him — tries to resolve the conflict but does not succeed. A third party's potentialities for resolving conflicts and the parties' (or others') opinions of his suitability, depend both on characteristics of the conflict and of the third party and the procedure he follows. The connection between these factors will be discussed in the next section. . . .

III. The Mediator, the Judge and the Administrator

Mediation consists of influencing the parties to come to agreement by appealing to their own interests. The mediator may make use of various means to attain this goal. He may work on the parties' ideas of what serves them best, for instance, in such a way that he gets them to consider their common interests as more essential than they did previously, or their competing interests as less essential. He may also look for possibilities of resolution which the parties themselves have not discovered and try to convince them that both will be well served with his suggestion. The very fact that a suggestion is proposed by an impartial third party may also, in certain cases, be sufficient for the parties to accept it. . . . The mediator also has the possibility of using promises or threats. He may, for instance, promise the parties help or support in the future if they become reconciled or he may threaten to ally himself with one of them if the other does not give in. A mediator does not necessarily have to go in for compromise solutions, but for many reasons he will, as a rule, do so. The compromise is often the way of least resistance for one who shall get the parties to agree to an arrangement. . . . [I]t may also contribute to the mediator's own prestige that he promotes intermediate solutions. Therewith he appears as the moderate and reasonable person with ability to see the problem from different angles — in contrast to the parties who will easily be suspected of having been onesided and quarrelsome since they have not managed to resolve the conflict on their own.

In order that both parties should have confidence in the mediator and be willing to cooperate with him and listen to his advice, it is important that they consider him impartial. This gives him an extra reason to follow the line of compromise. . . . For, by giving both parties some support, he shows that the interests of one lie as close to his heart as those of the other. Regard for impartiality carries with it the consequence that the mediator sometimes must display caution in pressing the parties too hard. That the mediator, for instance, makes a threat to one of the parties to ally himself with the opponent unless compliance is forthcoming, may be an effective means of exerting pressure, but will easily endanger confidence in his impartiality. This can reduce his possibilities for getting the conflict resolved if threats do not work and it can weaken his future prestige as a mediator.

The conditions for mediation are best in cases where both parties are interested in having the conflict resolved. The stronger this common interest is, the greater reason they have for bringing the conflict before a third party, and the more motivated they will be for cooperating actively with him in finding a solution, and for adjusting their demands in such a way that a solution can be reached.

If the parties, or one of them, is, to begin with, not motivated for having the conflict resolved, or in any case not motivated to agree to any compromise, such motives must be *created* in him, for instance with the help of threats or sanction. Cases may occur where the parties (or the unwilling one of them), may have a mediator forced upon them, and under pressure of persuasion from him or from the environment, agree to an arrangement. But mediation under such circumstances presents difficulties, among other reasons, because it demands a balancing between the regard for impartiality and the regard for exertion of sufficient pressure. If the conditions for resolving the conflict by a judgment or administrative decision exist (cf. below) these will, as a rule, be more effective procedures than mediation in the cases described here.

That normative factors are considered relevant for the solution, can in certain cases be helpful during mediation. By referring to a norm (e.g., concerning what is right and wrong) the mediator may get the parties to renounce unreasonable demands so that their points of view approach each other. Even if the parties do not feel bound by the norms, it is conceivable that others consider it important that they be followed and that the mediator can therefore argue that a party will be exposed to disapproval if he does not accommodate.

The norms will be of special support for the mediator if the parties are generally in agreement on their content and are willing to submit to them, so that the reason that there is a conflict at all can be traced back to the fact that the norms do not cover all aspects of the difference. The remainder which is not covered will then have the features of a fairly pure conflict of interests where the norms have brought the points of departure nearer one another than they would otherwise have been.

If, however, the parties consider the norms as giving answers to the questions being disputed, but disagree on what the answers are, the possibilities for mediation will, as a rule, be weakened. In the first place, the probability that the conflict will at all be made the object of mediation is reduced, among other reasons, because bringing it before a judge will often be possible and more likely in these cases. Secondly, mediation which has been begun may be made difficult because of the parties' disagreement concerning the norms or the relevant facts. This is the more true the more inflexibly the opinions are opposed to each other and the more value-laden they are. The parties' resistance to compromising on questions of right or truth . . . makes itself felt also when the mediator appears in the arena. Perhaps the presence of a third party will make the parties even more set on asserting their rights than they otherwise would have been. The mediator can try to "de-ideologize" the dispute by arguing that it is not always wise to "stand on one's rights" and that one should not "push things to extremes," but go the "golden middle road." Sometimes he succeeds in this and manages to concentrate attention on the interest-aspects, so that the usual mediation arguments will have an effect. But it may also go the other way. The mediator lets himself be influenced by the parties to see the normative aspects as the most important, and ends up by judging instead of mediating. And even if he does not go so far, his opinions concerning norms and facts may inhibit his eagerness to mediate. In any case, it may be distasteful for him to work for a compromise if he has made up his mind that one of the parties is completely right and the other wrong.

Hoebel's survey (1954) * of conflict-resolution in various primitive cultures confirms the impression that conditions are, generally speaking, less favorable for mediation than for other forms of conflict-resolution when the conflicts are characterized by disagreements about normative factors. Most of the third party institutions he describes have more in common with what I in this article call judgmental and administrative activity than with mediation. The only example in Hoebel's book of the development of a pure mediation institution for the resolution of disputes which have a strongly normative element, is found among the Ifugao-people in the northern part of Luzon in the Philippines. This is an agricultural people without any kind

* A. E. Hoebel, The Law of Primitive Man (1954).

of state-form but with well developed rules governing property rights, sale, mortgage, social status (which is conditional on how much one owns), family relations, violation of rights, etc. Conflicts concerning these relations occur often. If the parties do not manage to solve them on their own, they are regularly left to a mediator, who is called a *mokalun*. This is not a permanent office that belongs to certain persons, but a task to which the person is appointed for the particular case. In practice the *mokalun* is always a person of high rank and generally someone who has won esteem as a headhunter. He is chosen by the plaintiff, but is regarded as an impartial intermediary, not as a representative for a party. The parties are obligated to keep peace so long as mediation is in progress and they may not have any direct contact with each other during this period. The *mokalun* visits them alternately. He brings offers of conciliation and replies to these offers, and he tries, with the help of persuasion, and also generally with threats, to push through a conciliation. If he attains this, he will receive good pay and increased prestige. If the mediation is not successful, the conflict will remain unresolved and will perhaps result in homicide and blood feuds, for the *mokalun* has no authority to make decisions which are binding on the parties.

It is easy to point to features in the Ifugao culture which have favored the growth of such a method of conflict-resolution. On the one hand, there has obviously been a strong need to avoid open struggle within the local society, among other reasons, because the people were resident farmers who had put generations of work into terraces and irrigation works. On the other hand, there was no political leadership and no organized restraining power, and the conditions were therefore not favorable for conflict-resolution by judgment or coercive power. Nevertheless, it is noteworthy that the mediation arrangement functioned so well as it did, considering that it was applied to conflicts where divergent opinions of right and wrong were pitted against each other. It is natural to make a comparison with our present international conflicts, where the conditions are parallel to the extent that the danger for combat actions and the absence of other kinds of third party institutions create a strong need for mediation, but where the mediation institutions so far developed have been far less effective.

The *judge* is distinguished from the mediator in that his activity is related to the level of norms rather than to the level of interests. His task is not to try to reconcile the parties, but to reach a decision about which of them is right. This leads to several important differences between the two methods of conflict-resolution. The mediator should preferably look forward, toward the consequences which may follow from the various alternative solutions, and he must work on the parties to get them to accept a solution. The judge, on the other hand, looks back to the events which have taken place (e.g., agreements which the parties have entered into, violations which one has inflicted on the other, etc.) and to the norms concerning acquisition of rights, responsibilities, etc. which are connected with these events. When he has taken his standpoint on this basis, his task is finished. The judge, therefore, does not have to be an adaptable negotiator with ability to convince and to find constructive solutions, as the mediator preferably should be. But he must be able to speak with authority on the existing questions of norms and facts in order to be an effective resolver of conflicts.

The possibility for judging in a dispute presupposes that the norms are considered relevant to the solution. The norms may be more or less structured. They may consist in a formal set of rules (e.g., a judicial system, the by-laws of an organization or the rules of a game), in customs or only in vague notions of what is right and just. The normative frame of reference in which a decision is placed does not have to be the same — and does not even have to exist — for all those who have something to do with the conflict. What one person perceives as a judgment another may perceive as an arbitrary command. If, however, *none* of those involved (the parties, the third party, the environment) applies normative considerations to the relationship because all consider it a pure conflict of interests, decision by judgment is excluded.

A decision may be a "judgment" (in the sense in which the term is used here) even if the parties do not comply with it. But the greater the possibility that a judgment will be lived up to, the more suitable judgment will be as a method for conflict-resolution, and the better reason will the person who desires a solution have for preferring that procedure. It is therefore of significance to map out the factors which promote and hinder compliance to judgments.

The parties' interests in the outcome play an important role in this connection. If the main thing for them is to have the dispute settled, and it is of secondary importance what the content of the solution is, it will require very little for them to comply with the judgment. If, on the other hand, there are strong and competing interests connected with the outcome, so that submission to the judgment implies a great sacrifice for one or both of the parties, the question of compliance is more precarious.

That one party (voluntarily or by force) submits to a judgment in spite of the sacrifice it means for him, may be due in part to norms and in part to the authority of the judge. There may be many reasons for the parties' respect for those *norms* on which the judge bases his decision, for instance, they may be internalized, or one fears gods' or people's punishment if one violates them, or one finds it profitable in the long run to follow them (e.g., because it creates confidence in one's business activities if one gains a reputation for law-abidance or because it makes the game more fun if the rules are followed). If the parties are sufficiently motivated to comply with the norms and these give exhaustive answers to the question under dispute, then relatively modest demands are made on the *judge's* authority. If he is regarded as having knowledge of the norms and as having ability to find the facts, this will be sufficient to assure that his judgments are respected. Sometimes this is a simple assignment which many can fulfil. We may, for instance, take the case of two chess players who have not yet completely learned the rules of the game and who disagree as to whether it is permissible to castle in the present position. They ask a more experienced player who is present and comply without question to his decision because they consider it obvious that the rules should be followed and know that he is acquainted with them. But there are also cases where insight into norms, and perhaps also ability to clarify the factual relations in the matter, presuppose special expertise which only a few have. The kind of expertise required varies with the nature of the normative ideas. It may be, for instance, that contact with supernatural powers is considered to provide special prerequisites for finding out what is true and right, or it may be life-experience or professional studies. Monopolizing of insight may be a natural consequence of the fact that a norm system is large and cannot be taken in at a glance, but there are also many examples of systematic endeavors on the part of experts to prevent intruders from acquiring their knowledge.

If the parties are not sufficiently strongly motivated to comply with the norms which regulate their mutual rights and duties, or if they do not regard these as giving exhaustive answers to the matter of dispute, the judgment must appear as something more than a conveyance of information in order to command respect. The parties must, in one way or another, be bound or forced to adhere to it. One condition which may contribute to this is that, in addition to the primary norms which define the parties' mutual rights and obligations, there is also a set of secondary norms of adjudication which single out the judge as the proper person to settle the dispute and which possibly also impose upon the parties the duty to abide by his decision. That the judge is in this way equipped with *authority,* is in many cases sufficient reason for the parties to consider themselves bound to live up to his decision. But the establishment of authority often presupposes power, and even if the authority-relationship is established, it may sometimes be necessary to press through a decision by force. The power can reside with the judge, with someone he represents (e.g. the state) or with others who are interested in the decision being respected (e.g., the winning party or his relatives or friends). And it can have various bases: physical or military strength, control of resources on which the parties are dependent, powers of sorcery, etc. How *much* power is necessary depends partly on what other factors promote and hinder compliance, and partly upon the relative strength of the enforcing authority and the disobedient party.

That the parties and others have confidence in the judge's impartiality, promotes compliance to judgments. It strengthens the belief that the decisions he makes are right and it facilitates enforcement by making the application of force more legitimate. As mentioned before, it is also important for the mediator to appear impartial, but the manner of showing impartiality is different for the two kinds of third parties. To a certain extent the judge can display that he gives equal consideration to both parties, for instance, by giving both the same possibilities for arguing and for presenting evidence. But he cannot, like the mediator, systematically endeavour to reach compromises, because the norms sometimes demand decision in favor of one of the parties. If he finds that one party is completely right, he must judge in his favor, and the outcome of the case will not in itself be a testimony to his giving equal consideration to both.

But the judge has other possibilities for appearing impartial. Sometimes his person gives sufficient guarantee. He is, for instance, because of his high rank, his contact with supernatural powers, or his recognized wisdom and strength of character, regarded as infallible, or at least freed from suspicion of partisanship. The privilege of the judge to assume a retired position during the proceedings and not to engage in argumentation with the parties, makes it easier to ascribe such qualities to him than to the mediator. Another significant factor is that there are, as a rule, small possibilities for checking the rightness of a judgment because this presupposes knowledge of both the system of norms and the facts of the particular case. To maintain a belief that certain persons are infallible can, nevertheless, present difficulties, especially in cultures characterized by democratization and secularization. To reduce or conceal the human factor in decision-making will therefore often be better suited to strengthening confidence in the decisions. Letting the judge appear as a "mouthpiece of the law," who cannot himself exert any influence worth mentioning on the outcome of the cases tends to remove the fear that his own interests, prejudices, sympathies and antipathies may have impact on his rulings.

Tendencies to overestimate the influence of the norms, and underestimate the influence of the judge, may also have other functions than strengthening confidence in the judge's impartiality. Firstly, these tendencies contribute to the transmission of authority from the norm system to the individual decisions. Secondly, the conditions are favorable for a gradual and often almost unnoticeable development of a norm system through court practice, so that the resistance to change is reduced. And thirdly, the judge will be less exposed to criticism and self-reproach when he (both in his own and others' eyes) avoids appearing as personally responsible for his decisions. This is important because it might otherwise involve great strain to make decisions in disputes where the parties' contentions are strongly opposed to each other, where there are perhaps great interests at stake for both, and where it may be extremely doubtful who is right. It is therefore not surprising that many techniques have been used in the various judicial systems for the purpose of eliminating, limiting or concealing the influence of the judge. The use of ordeals and drawing of lots in the administration of justice may be mentioned as examples of this, and the same is true for the technique of judicial argumentation which gives the decisions the appearance of being the products of knowledge and logic, and not of evaluation and choice.

Judicial activity and formation of norms serve to support each other mutually. On the one hand, the judge is dependent on normative premises on which he can base his decisions. The greater the relevance attributed to them, and the stronger the ideological anchoring of the norm system, the more favourable are the conditions for conflict-resolution by judgment. On the other hand, the activity of judges can contribute to the spreading of knowledge about norms, to their increased recognition and authority, and to a gradual extension of the norm system to cover new types of conflict situations.

The activity of judging is in these respects quite different from the activity of mediating. As mentioned before, the task of the mediator becomes more difficult the more emphasis the parties place on the normative aspects of the conflict (presupposing that there is disagreement about these, as there usually will be in conflict situations). The mediator, therefore, must try to "de-ideologize" the conflict, for instance, by stressing that interests are more important than the question of who is right and who is wrong, or by arguing that one ought to be reasonable and willing to compromise. The use of mediation in certain types of disputes, may tend to create or reinforce the norm that willingness to compromise is the proper behavior in conflict situations and thereby to reduce the significance of such norms as judges base their decisions on.

The contrasts between the two types of third party intervention make it difficult to combine the role of the judge and the role of the mediator in a satisfactory way. Indeed it does happen that a third party first tries to mediate between the parties and if that does not succeed, passes judgment. Also the reverse is conceivable: that a third party first passes judgment and then proceeds to mediate when he sees that the judgment will not be respected. But in both cases attempts to use one method may place hindrances in the way of the other. By mediating one may weaken the normative basis for a later judgment and perhaps also undermine confidence in one's impartiality as judge; and by judging first, one will easily reduce the willingness to compromise of the party who was supported in the judgment, and will be met by suspicion of partiality by the other.

When the establishment of new third party institutions is sought, for instance, by a legislator who is looking for new ways of settling labour conflicts, or by those who are working for the peaceful adjustment of international conflicts, there may be a dilemma about which way to go. Should one go in for building up the norm system, and for strengthening the normative engagement with the aim of having as many conflicts as possible decided by judgment? Or ought one rather rely on "de-ideologization" and mediation? In considering such questions it is important not to let oneself be led by superficial analogies, but to take account of all the relevant factors. Regarding international conflicts, for instance, one must consider that there is no superior instance which is powerful enough to force a powerful state to obedience. This has the consequence that courts can hardly be effective organs for the resolution of conflicts where substantial interests are at stake. Mediation also presents difficulties, among other reasons because the parties often place great emphasis on the moral and legal aspects of the conflict, and have strongly divergent opinions concerning both norms and (perhaps especially) the relevant facts. But there is good reason to believe that the difficulties in mediation are, after all, easier to overcome and that endeavours should therefore go in the direction of reducing the normative engagement.

The *administrator* has in common with the judge that he *decides* how the conflict should be resolved. He does not, as the mediator, leave this to the parties. But in contrast to the judge, who merely pretends to determine what already *is* right, the administrator establishes an arrangement which has the character of being new. The administrator can indeed give certain consideration to existing normative positions, but his most important concern is what the rights and duties should be in the future. In this respect he has more in common with the mediator than with the judge.

Which considerations the administrator emphasizes in making his decision may otherwise vary. It may be his own interests he seeks to promote, or some organizational or social aim, for instance, to increase a company's sales, to maximize the national product or to strengthen the country's defense-preparedness. It is also possible to conceive of cases where he aims to promote the interests of the parties, but does not want to leave the decision to them because he considers them lacking in insight concerning what is in their best interest or because he knows that they have difficulty in reaching an agreement.

The person who will be able to resolve conflicts administratively must have sufficient power or authority to be able to force his will upon the parties. As mentioned before, this holds also for the judge at times, but for him it is not always necessary and, as a rule, so much will not be required because his decisions have stronger support in normative ideas than do the administrator's.

Sometimes the administrator's power depends on his control of the good about which the parties are disputing. The woman who chooses one of the men who propose to her, and the employer who engages one of the applicants for the position, are examples of this. The power that may be traced to the control one has over a certain good is used up when one gives that good away. Nevertheless, control over goods can sometimes form the basis for permanent power-relationships because it is conceivable that the administrator has enough resources to make many awards.

The administrator's influence may also have other bases, for instance, physical strength, personal leadership qualities, or norms which give him authority to decide over the parties. Several of these factors may be present at the same time and they may also be combined with control over material resources. Sometimes the administrator stands in a permanent relation of superiority to the parties and has many means of power at his disposal. We may, for example, think of the relationship between parents and children, school and pupils, management and employees, institutional staff and inmates, a public agency and its clients, or a state and its citizens.

In such social systems of which I have mentioned examples, the superior has many other tasks in relation to his inferiors besides resolving conflicts between them. And when he must resolve a conflict, he can, because of his position of power, often choose whether he will act as mediator, judge or administrator. For example, if children submit a question of dispute to their father he may say that: "You have to manage to reach an agreement on this yourselves," and restrict himself to mediating between them, or he may act as a judge and decide which of them is right, or in his capacity as administrator, give them an order about what the arrangement should be. Within certain limits the leadership of a company, an institution or a state has corresponding possibilities for choice and will act partly as administrator, partly as judge and partly as mediator in conflicts between inferiors.

Many factors may influence the choice among these procedures. On the one hand, it is of significance whether the superior is interested in the conflict being resolved in a particular direction. The stronger his interest in the outcome is and the less certainty he has that the desired result will be reached through mediation or judgment, the greater reason he has to act as administrator. But on the other hand, the question of costs also plays a role. If the inferiors are opposed to the superior intervening too actively in their differences, or if they have normative ideas which they think ought to be decisive for the solution, it is conceivable that they will react so strongly against being directed that their superior resigns himself to this. He may perhaps have sufficient power to enforce an administrative decision, even if the parties find it arbitrary, but he understands that this will demand so much effort on his part that it does not pay, or he is afraid that it will lead to new conflicts and unpleasantness. It often happens, for instance, that a superior in a company tries to mediate between his inferiors, even though he has authority to decide how the dispute should be resolved. The national authorities sometimes follow a similar practice, for instance, when business organizations or employer- and employee-organizations are in conflict on questions of prices, subsidies or wages. A government may find it wise, in such cases, to content itself with acting as mediator even if it could have resolved the conflict with injunctions or regulations and even if it has an interest in what the solution is. . . .

. . . [I]t may be difficult to combine the role of administrator with that of judge or mediator. Several factors contribute to explaining this. In the first place, conflict-resolution will often be an arduous task for the leadership of an organization. It may be a burden on the administrative apparatus, hinder the execution of other tasks, and create difficulties in relation to inferiors. Moreover, an independent organ will sometimes better be able to resist pressure from the parties, for instance if one of them threatens to make counter-moves that might harm the organization unless he gets support. Such threats can make a greater impression on those who have responsibility for the activities of the organization than on an independent organ. Secondly, from the point of view of the parties it may appear more satisfactory that the conflict is resolved by an independent organ, among other reasons because they have a greater guarantee for the decisions being impartial. This is especially true if the organization itself is a party or has party interests, as for instance in conflicts between a company and its employees or between a state and its citizens. And even if there is no clear party interest, the leadership of the organization may easily be suspected, out of regard for the solution of other tasks, of having interests in the outcome of the conflict which weaken its impartiality. . . .

[The following summarizes the factors or conditions that may influence the parties' choice of mediation, judgment, or administrative decision. The numbers in parentheses refer to the arrows in Chart 1-2.]

Administrative decision is more probable the greater interest the third party has in the outcome (1) and the better the possibilities for enforcing his decision are (2). The stronger the resistance (3 and 4) and the greater the costs (5 and 6) the more is this probability reduced. Interplay among the factors mentioned here may sometimes lead to differentiation within an organization so that its leadership supports with its power of enforcement the decisions that it has left to independent judges.

Factors which counteract administrative decision increase the probability for judgment or mediation (3, 4, 5 and 6), yet in such a way that possibilities for enforcement in certain cases are a presupposition for conflict-resolution by judgment (7). It will normally be a condition for mediation that both parties are interested in having the conflict resolved (8). Otherwise the choice between judgment

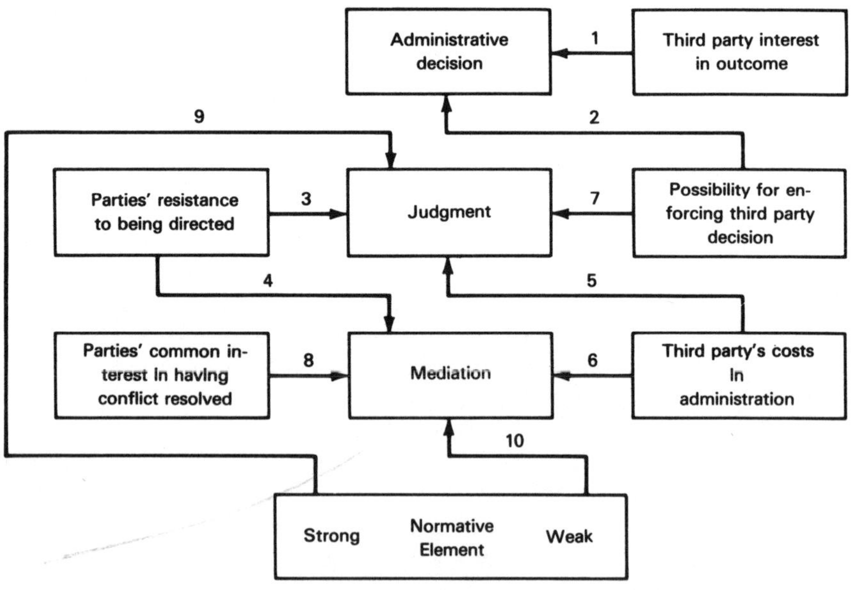

[Chart 1-2]

and mediation is determined primarily by how relevant norms are considered for the solution (9 and 10).

*The Forms and Limits of Adjudication**

Lon L. Fuller

I. The Problems Toward Which This Essay Is Addressed

The subject matter of this essay is adjudication in the very broadest sense. As the term is used here it includes a father attempting to assume the role of judge in a dispute between his children over possession of a toy. At the other extreme it embraces the most formal and even awesome exercises of adjudicative power: a Senate trying the impeachment of a President, a Supreme Court sitting in judgment on the powers of the government of which it is a part, an international tribunal deciding a dispute between nations, a faculty of law — in former centuries — undertaking to judge the rival claims of kings and popes, the Congregation of Rites of the Roman Catholic Church hearing the arguments pro and con in a procedure for canonization.

As the term adjudication is used here its application is not restricted to tribunals functioning as part of an established government. It includes adjudicative bodies which owe their powers to the consent of the litigants expressed in an agreement of submission, as in labor relations and in international law. It also includes tribunals that assume adjudicative powers without the sanction either of consent or of superior governmental power, the most notable example being the court that sat in the Nuremberg Trials.

The problems that are the concern of this paper are those suggested by the two terms of the title, the *forms* and *limits* of adjudication. By speaking of the *limits* of adjudication I mean to raise such questions as the following: What kinds of social tasks can properly be assigned to courts and other adjudicative agencies? What are the lines of division that separate such tasks from those that require an exercise of executive power or that must be entrusted to planning boards or public corporations? What tacit assumptions underlie the conviction that certain problems are inherently unsuited for adjudicative disposition and should be left to the legislature? More generally, to borrow the title of a famous article by Roscoe Pound, what are the limits of effective legal action? — bearing in mind that legislative determina-

* *Source:* 92 Harv. L. Rev. 353, 353-360, 363, 365-372, 374-378, 381-388, 391-395, 397-399, 401-404 (1978).

tions often can only become effective if they are of such a nature that they are suited for judicial interpretation and enforcement.

By the *forms* of adjudication I refer to the ways in which adjudication may be organized and conducted. For example, in labor relations and in international law we encounter a hybrid form called "tripartite arbitration" in which a "public" or "impartial" arbitrator sits flanked by arbitrators appointed by the interested parties. Such a deviation from the ordinary organization of adjudication presents such questions as: What, if any, are its proper uses? What are its peculiar limits and dangers? Other deviational forms present less subtle questions, such as Judge Bridlegoose's decisions by a throw of the dice. In general the questions posed for consideration are: What are the permissible variations in the forms of adjudication? When has its nature been so altered that we are compelled to speak of an "abuse" or a "perversion" of the adjudicative process?

Questions of the permissible forms and the proper limits of adjudication have probably been under discussion ever since something equivalent to a judicial power first emerged in primitive society. In our own history the Supreme Court at an early date excluded from its jurisdiction certain issues designated as "political." This exclusion could hardly be said to rest on any principle made explicit in the Constitution; it was grounded rather in a conviction that certain problems by their intrinsic nature fall beyond the proper limits of adjudication, though how these problems are to be defined remains even today a subject for debate. In international law one of the most significant issues lies in the concept of "justiciability." Similar problems recur in labor relations, where the proper role of the arbitrator has always been a matter in active dispute. . . .

The purpose of this article is to offer an analysis that may be helpful in answering questions like those posed in the preceding paragraphs. Now it is apparent that any analysis of this sort, transcending as it does so many conventional boundaries, will be meaningless if it does not rest on some concept equivalent to "true adjudication." For if there is no such thing as "true adjudication," then it becomes impossible to distinguish the uses and abuses of adjudication. Yet it is unfortunately also true that any suggestion of a notion like "true adjudication" goes heavily against the grain of modern thought. Today it is a mark of intellectual liberation to realize that there is and can be no such thing as "true science," "true religion," "true education," or "true adjudication." "It is all a matter of definition." The modern professional university philosopher is particularly allergic to anything suggesting the doctrine of essence and takes it as a sure sign of philosophic illiteracy when a writer speaks of "the essence of art" or "the essence of democracy."

Yet we must examine critically the implications of this rejection.

Does it imply, for example, that international lawyers are talking nonsense when they discuss the question of what kinds of disputes between nations are suited to decision by a tribunal? Are students of labor relations engaged in mere verbal shadowboxing when they ask how an arbitration should be conducted and what sorts of questions arbitrators are fitted to decide? Do those engaged in discussions of this sort deceive themselves in believing that they are engaged in a rational inquiry? Surely if adjudication is subject to a reasoned analysis in a particular context, there is no a priori reason for supposing that the context cannot be expanded so that adjudication becomes the object of a more general analysis.

A. D. Lindsay once observed that it is scarcely possible to talk intelligently about social institutions without recognizing that they exist *because* and *insofar as* men pursue certain goals or ideals. The ideals that keep a social institution alive and functioning are never perceived with complete clarity, so that even if there is no failure of good intentions, the existent institution will never be quite what it might have been had it been supported by a clearer insight into its guiding principles. As Lindsay remarks, quoting Charley Lomax in Shaw's Major Barbara, there is a certain amount of tosh about the Salvation Army. Surely there is a good deal of tosh — that is, superfluous rituals, rules of procedure without clear purpose, needless precautions preserved through habit — in the adjudicative process as we observe it in this country. Our task is to separate the tosh from the essential. . . .

Accordingly I shall have to begin our inquiry with an attempt to define "true adjudication," or adjudication as it might be if the ideals that support it were fully realized. In doing so I shall of necessity be describing something that never fully exists. Yet it is only with the aid of this nonexistent model that we can pass intelligent judgment on the accomplishments of adjudication as it actually is. Indeed, it is only with the aid of that model that we can distinguish adjudication as an existent institution from other social institutions and procedures by which decisions may be reached.

II. The Two Basic Forms of Social Ordering

It is customary to think of adjudication as a means of settling disputes or controversies. This is, of course, its most obvious aspect. The normal occasion for a resort to adjudication is when parties are at odds with one another, often to such a degree that a breach of social order is threatened.

More fundamentally, however, adjudication should be viewed as a form of social ordering, as a way in which the relations of men to one another are governed and regulated. Even in the absence of any formalized doctrine of stare decisis or res judicata, an adjudicative determination will normally enter in some degree into the litigants' future relations and into the future relations of other parties who see themselves as possible litigants before the same tribunal. Even if there is no statement by the tribunal of the reasons for its decision, some reason will be perceived or guessed at, and the parties will tend to govern their conduct accordingly.

If, then, adjudication is a form of social ordering, to understand it fully we must view it in its relation to other forms of social ordering. It is submitted that there are two basic forms of social ordering: *organization by common aims* and *organization by reciprocity*. Without one or the other of these nothing resembling a society can exist.

These two forms of ordering represent the two basic ways in which men may, by coming together, secure an advantage for all participants. We may illustrate these forms very simply by assuming, first, that two men share an objective which neither could achieve without the aid of the other or could not achieve so easily without that aid. A roadway connects two farms with a highway; it becomes blocked by a boulder. Neither farmer is strong enough to remove the boulder by himself. When the two join forces to remove the boulder we have, obviously, organization or association by common aims. Now let us suppose that our two farmers are to a considerable extent engaged in "subsistence" farming. One of them has a large crop of onions, the other an abundance of potatoes. A trade of a portion of their respective crops may make each richer; to the potato-raising farmer the "last" potato is not so valuable as the "first" onion, and, of course, a surfeit of onions will put the other farmer in the reverse position. Here we have illustrated in its crassest and most obvious form organization or association by reciprocity.

It should be noticed that the conditions which make these two principles of ordering effective are directly opposite to one another. To make organization by reciprocity effective the participants must want different things; organization by common aims requires that the participants want the same thing or things.

In order to bring these forms of ordering into closer relation with adjudication let us now consider briefly *their forms* and *limits*. With respect to reciprocity the form of the relationship may run all the way from a tacit perception of the advantages of an association, scarcely rising to consciousness, to a highly formalized written contract or treaty. Two men find pleasure in one another's company without realizing that the source of that pleasure lies in the fact that they have complementary qualities, so that each needs what the other has to give. There are probably few marriages in which the relations of the spouses are not to some degree organized or directed by the principle of reciprocity. There may, however, be an understandable reluctance to give explicit recognition to this principle, and the acknowledged basis of the relationship may be something closer to a fiction that all aims are shared aims. This may, indeed, be a beneficent fiction; not all the tosh in human relations is harmful. At any rate, whatever reciprocity may underlie any particular marriage, it illustrates the principle of reciprocity in one of its most tacit and informal expressions. At the other end of the scale we might instance a collective labor agreement, every sentence of which was the result of prolonged and explicit bargaining.

Association by common aims also varies over a wide range in the degree of its formality. At the one end of the spectrum, we have the small group, its members all actively sharing and all understanding the same objectives. Such is the case of our farmers uniting to remove a roadblock. At an intermediate point on the scale of formality, we have the voluntary association, the political party, the labor union, and the benevolent society. Here some general aims will commonly be shared actively by most intelligent members; other aims will be promulgated by the leaders which will not in any real sense be shared or even understood by most members; finally, some aims will be pursued by the leaders in the name of the association that will not even be known outside a small circle. In considering this constellation of objectives, it should not be forgotten that it is, in the long run, the actively shared and at least vaguely understood aims that give the association its motive power. Ascending farther along the scale of increasing formality, we finally encounter the nation or the state. Here we have what may be truly called an involuntary association, in the sense that there is no readily available procedure by which the member may resign or effectively disclaim his membership. At the same time he is bound by rules enacted to secure certain objectives whether or not he approves of these objectives or even understands them. The extent to which he and other citizens actively share the objectives pursued by their government is something that varies from nation to nation and over time within a given nation. In times of war the area of actively shared aims normally expands greatly. At other times the area of shared aims may shrink to the point where it embraces merely the negative object of avoiding the disruptions of revolution, of preserving an unsatisfactory status quo. It is possible, in extreme cases, that even this impoverished objective may be shared only by a minority of the citizens, sufficiently organized to impose their will on the majority. At the same time, it is important to recall that without some actual sharing of aims affirmatively entertained, however impoverished the aims and however restricted the sharing, no government is possible. It is for that reason that a government is here considered as a highly formalized variety of organization by common aims.

With respect to the *limits* or the proper provinces of the two basic forms of social ordering, what has just been said sufficiently disposes of organization by common aims. In the case of organization by reciprocity it is obvious that it properly comes into play where an exchange, or something equivalent to it, may enrich both parties. Its proper province lies in that area where divergent human objectives exist. This simple truth is obscured in our complex society, where men and organizations deliberately specialize in order to prepare themselves to enter into relations of reciprocity, as in the case of a factory that expands its earnings and restricts its market by making a highly specialized component part. It may seem silly to say that the sale of a loaf of bread presents a case of "divergent objectives" in the sense that I want the bread more than the twenty cents I pay for it, while the grocer wants my twenty cents more than he wants the bread. Yet the transaction makes no sense in any other terms. Any paradox involved is simply the general one that we cannot truly understand routinized and habitual actions in terms of the actual psychological states that accompany their performance. . . .

III. Adjudication as a Form of Social Ordering . . .

Adjudication, contract, and elections are three ways of reaching decisions, of settling disputes, of defining men's relations to one another. Now I submit that the characteristic feature of each of these forms of social ordering lies in the manner in which the affected party participates in the decision reached. This may be presented graphically as follows:

Form of social ordering	*Mode of participation by the affected party*
Contract	Negotiation
Elections	Voting
Adjudication	Presentation of proofs and reasoned arguments

It is characteristic of these three ways of ordering men's relations that though they are subject to variation — they present themselves in different "forms" — each contains certain intrinsic demands that must be met if it is to function properly. We may distinguish roughly between "optimum conditions," which would lift a particular form of order to its highest expression, and "essential conditions," without which the form of order ceases to function in any significant sense at all.

IV. Adjudication and Rationality

It may be said that the essence of adjudication lies not in the manner in which the affected party participates in the decision but in the office of judge. If there is a judge and a chance to appear before him, it is a matter of indifference whether the litigant chooses to present proofs or reasoned arguments. He may, if he sees fit, offer no argument at all, or pitch his appeal entirely on an emotional level, or even indicate his willingness that the judge decide the case by a throw of the dice. It might seem, then, that our analysis should take as its point of departure the office of judge. From this office certain requirements might be deduced, for example, that of impartiality, since a judge to be "truly" such must be impartial. Then, as the next step, if he is to be impartial he must be willing to hear both sides, etc.

The trouble with this is that there are people who are called "judges" holding official positions and expected to be impartial who nevertheless do not participate in an adjudication in any sense directly relevant to the subject of this paper. Judges at an agricultural fair or an art exhibition may serve as examples. Again, a baseball umpire, though he is not called a judge, is expected to make impartial rulings. What distinguishes these functionaries is not that they do not hold governmental office, for the duties of a judge at a livestock fair would scarcely be changed if he were an official of the Department of Agriculture. What distinguishes them from courts, administrative tribunals, and boards of arbitration is that their decisions are not reached within an institutional framework that is intended to assure to the disputants an opportunity for the presentation of proofs and reasoned arguments. The judge of livestock may or may not permit such a presentation; it is not an integral part of his office to permit and to attend to it.

If, on the other hand, we start with the notion of a process of decision in which the affected party's participation consists in an opportunity to present proofs and reasoned arguments, the office of judge or arbitrator and the requirement of impartiality follow as necessary implications. The logician Frege once took the expression "I accuse" as exemplifying the complex implications contained in the most ordinary language. We may say that the verb "to accuse" presupposes five elements: (1) an accuser, (2) a person accused, (3) a person before whom the accusation is presented, (4) an act charged against the accused, and (5) a principle by which the act may be condemned. The similarity to the analysis here presented is apparent; the fifth element, it should be noted, corresponds to the notion of a *reasoned* argument. Of course, Frege was concerned merely to spell out the implications contained in a phrase, not, as we are here, with the problem of creating and maintaining a social institution that will give effect to those implications.

It may be objected at this point that "reasoned argument" is, after all, not a monopoly of forensic proceedings. A political speech may take the form of a reasoned appeal to the electorate; to be sure, it often takes other forms, but the same thing may be said of speeches in court. This objection fails to take account of a conception that underlies the whole analysis being presented here, the conception, namely, of a form of participating in a decision that is institutionally defined and assured.

When I am entering a contract with another person I may present proofs and arguments to him, but there is generally no formal assurance that I will be given this opportunity or that he will listen to my arguments if I make them. (Perhaps the only exception to this generalization lies in the somewhat anomalous legal obligation "to bargain in good faith" in labor relations.) During an election I may actively campaign for one side and may present what I consider to be "reasoned arguments" to the electorate. If I am an effective campaigner this participation in the decision ultimately reached may greatly outweigh in importance the casting of my own single vote. At the same time, it is only the latter form of participation that is the subject of an affirmative institutional guarantee. The protection accorded my right to present arguments to the electorate is almost entirely indirect and negative. The way will be held clear for me, but I shall have to pave it myself. Even if I am given an affirmative right (for example, under the "equal time" rule of the FCC) I am given no formal assurance that anyone will listen to my appeal. The voter who goes to sleep before his television set is surely not subject to the same condemnation as the judge who sleeps through the arguments of counsel.

Adjudication is, then, a device which gives formal and institutional expression to the influence of reasoned argument in human affairs. As such it assumes a burden of rationality not borne by any other form of social ordering. A decision which is the product of reasoned argument must be prepared itself to meet the test of reason. We demand of an adjudicative decision a kind of rationality we do not expect of the results of contract or of voting. This higher responsibility toward rationality is at once the strength *and the weakness* of adjudication as a form of social ordering.

In entering contracts, men are of course in some measure guided by rational considerations. The subsistence farmer who has a surfeit of potatoes and only a handful of onions acts reasonably when he trades potatoes for onions. But there is no test of rationality that can be applied to the result of the trade considered in abstraction from the interests of the parties. Indeed, the trade of potatoes for onions, which is a rational act by one trader, might be considered irrational if indulged in by his opposite number, who has a storehouse full of onions and only a bushel of potatoes. If we asked one party to the contract, "Can you defend that contract?" he might answer, "Why, yes. It was good for me and it was good for him." If we then said, "But that is not what we meant. We meant, can you defend it on general grounds?" he might well reply that he did not know what we were talking about. Yet this is precisely the kind of question we normally direct toward the decision of a judge or arbitrator. The results that emerge from adjudication are subject, then, to a standard of rationality that is different from that imposed on the results of an exchange.

I believe that the same observation holds true when adjudication is compared with elections. The key to the difference lies again in the mode in which the affected party participates in a decision. If, as in adjudication, the only mode of participation consists in the opportunity to present proofs and arguments, the purpose of this participation is frustrated, and the whole proceeding becomes a farce, should the decision that emerges make no pretense whatever to rationality. The same cannot be said of the mode of participation called voting. We may assume that the preferences of voters are ultimately emotional, inarticulate, and not subject to rational defense. At the same time there is a need for social order, and it may be assumed that this need is best met when order rests on the broadest possible base of popular support. On this ground, a negative defense of democracy is possible; the will of the majority controls, not because it is right, but — well, because it *is* the will of the majority. This is surely an impoverished conception of democracy, but it expresses at least one ingredient of any philosophy of democracy, and it suggests a reason why we demand of adjudication a kind of rationality that we do not expect of elections.

This problem can be approached somewhat obliquely from a different direction by asking what is implied by "a right" or by "a claim of right." If I say to someone, "Give me that!" I do not necessarily assert a right. I may be begging for an act of charity, or I may be threatening to take by force something to which I admittedly have no right. On the other hand, if I say, "Give that to me, I have a right to it," I necessarily assert the existence of some principle or standard by which my "right" can be tested. . . .

Now if we ask ourselves what kinds of questions are commonly decided by judges and arbitrators, the answer may well be, "Claims of right." . . . If, then, we seek to define "the limits of adjudication," a tempting answer would be that the proper province of courts is limited to cases where rights are asserted. On reflection we might enlarge this to include cases where fault or guilt is charged (broadly, "the trial of accusations"), since in many cases it is artificial to treat the accuser (who may be the district attorney) as claiming a right. Though it is not particularly artificial to view the lawbreaker as violating "a right" of the state, to say that when the state indicts the lawbreaker it is claiming a remedial "right" against him does seem to reflect a misguided impulse toward forcing a symmetry between civil and criminal remedies. To avoid any such manipulations of natural modes of thought, let us then amend the suggested criterion to read as follows: The proper province of adjudication is to make an authoritative determination of questions raised by claims of right and accusations of guilt.

Is this a significant way of describing "the limits of adjudication"? I do not think so. In fact, what purports here to be a distinct assertion is merely an implication of the fact that adjudication is a form of decision that defines the affected party's participation as that of offering proofs and reasoned arguments. It is not so much that adjudicators decide only issues presented by claims of right or accusations. The point is rather that *whatever* they decide, or *whatever* is submitted to them for decision, tends to be converted into a claim of right or an accusation of fault or guilt. This conversion is effected by the institutional framework within which both the litigant and the adjudicator function.

Let me spell out rather painstakingly the steps of an argument that will show why this should be so. (1) Adjudication is a process of decision that grants to thé affected party a form of participation that consists in the opportunity to present proofs and reasoned arguments. (2) The litigant must therefore, if his participation is to be meaningful, assert some principle or principles by which his arguments are sound and his proofs relevant. (3) A naked demand is distinguished from a claim of right by the fact that the latter is a demand supported by a principle; likewise, a mere expression of displeasure or resentment is distinguished from an accusation by the fact that the latter rests upon some principle. Hence, (4) issues tried before an adjudicator tend to become claims of right or accusations of fault. . . .

I have suggested that it is not a significant description of the limits of adjudication to say that its proper province lies where rights are asserted or accusations of fault are made, for such a statement involves a circle of reasoning. If, however, we regard a formal definition of rights and wrongs as a nearly inevitable product of the adjudicative process, we can arrive at what is perhaps the most significant of all limitations on the proper province of adjudication. Adjudication is not a proper form of social ordering in those areas where the effectiveness of human association would be destroyed if it were organized about formally defined "rights" and "wrongs." Courts have, for example, rather regularly refused to enforce agreements between husband and wife affecting the internal organization of family life. There are other and wider areas where the intrusion of "the machinery of the law" is equally inappropriate. An adjudicative board might well undertake to allocate one thousand tons of coal among three claimants; it could hardly conduct even the simplest coal-mining enterprise by the forms of adjudication. Wherever successful human association depends upon spontaneous and informal collaboration, shifting its forms with the task at hand, there adjudication is out of place except as it may declare certain ground rules applicable to a wide variety of activities. . . .

V. Adjudication and the Rule of Law

So far a point of crucial importance and difficulty has not been reached in this discussion. It has been repeatedly asserted that adjudication is institutionally committed to a "reasoned" decision, to a decision based on "principle." But what is the source of the "principle" on the basis of which the case is to be argued and decided? Where do the parties and the adjudicator get their respective "reasons"? . . .

It will be useful at this point to consider a kind of paradigm instance of a case-by-case growth of legal doctrine. . . .

Case No. 1. *T* steals *O*'s horse and sells it to *G*, who pays full value for it and has no reason to know it had been stolen from *O*. *O* brings suit against *G* to recover the horse. *Held,* for *O*. One of the deterrents to thievery is the difficulty of disposing of stolen goods. If a purchaser like *G* were able to take goods free of the claim of the true owner, a market for stolen goods would be created and thus an incentive to theft. In any event, it was impossible for *T*, a thief who had no rightful title to the horse, to pass any title to *G;* he who has nothing can give nothing.

Case No. 2. *T* buys a horse from *O* giving as payment a forged note purporting to be that of *X*. *T* knew that the note was forged. After delivering the horse to *T*, *O* discovers that he has been defrauded. He brings suit against *T* to recover the horse. It is argued on behalf of *T* that *O* delivered the horse to him with the intent to confer title; the horse is now *T*'s and *O*'s only remedy is to sue for the price. *Held,* for *O*. The passage of title was vitiated by the fraud of *T;* title throughout remained in *O*.

Case No. 3. The case is similar to Case No. 2, except that after receiving possession of the horse, *T* sold it to *G*, who knew *T* had bought it from *O* but had no reason to know that *T* had worked any fraud on *O*. *O* brings suit against *G* to recover the horse. It is argued on behalf of *O* that title remained in him in accordance with the principle laid down in Case No. 2. Since *T* had no title, he could pass none to *G*. *Held*, for *G*. It would be an intolerable burden on commerce if purchasers of property were compelled to scrutinize the details of a transaction by which the former owner voluntarily delivered it into the hands of the person now offering it for sale. Fraud takes many and subtle forms; if the victim could not recognize it, it is unreasonable to ask of a stranger to the transaction that he ascertain whether it was present. With respect to Case No. 2, all that was said there was with reference to the legal relations between the owner and the defrauder; the court's mind was not directed toward the possibility that a subsequent purchaser, like *G*, might intervene. The principle we are here applying is that if the horse is in the hands of *T* or of someone who knew of his fraud, it may be recovered by *O*. In the hands of an innocent purchaser like *G*, the horse may not be recovered by *O*, for reasons we have already indicated.

Case No. 4. The case is like Case No. 3, except that after buying the horse from *T*, *G* sold it to *K*, who, before he bought the horse from *G*, had been informed of the fraud worked by *T* on *O*. *O* sues *K* to recover the horse. It is argued on behalf of *O* that *K* was not an innocent purchaser, since he knew of *T*'s fraud when he bought the horse. In accordance with the principle laid down in Case No. 3, *O* became entitled to the horse when it came into the hands of *K*. *Held*, for *K*. If the argument made by *O* were accepted, it would be possible for a person in the position of *O* to destroy the value of the title acquired by *G* simply by giving general publicity to the fact that *T* had induced the sale by fraud. Thus the objective of protecting the bona fide purchaser *G* would be defeated, for his property would become unsalable. When the court in Case No. 3 said that *O* could recover the horse from anyone who knew of the fraud of *T*, it did not have in mind the possibility that the horse might have passed previously through the hands of a bona fide purchaser like *G*. When the horse was bought from *T* by *G*, title to it was perfected and was no longer vulnerable to attack by *O*. *G* was then free to sell it to anyone he saw fit.

Case No. 5. This case is like Case No. 4, except that *K* not only knew of *T*'s fraud but had participated in it by forging *X*'s name on the note used by *T* to pay *O* for the horse. *O* sues *K* to recover the horse. *K* rests his defense on the reasoning of Case No. 4; *G* had title to the horse and was free to sell it to anyone he saw fit. If *K* was guilty of any misconduct, that is a question for the criminal law; it ought not to affect his property rights. . . . perhaps it would be well to suspend the series at this point and leave to the reader the burden of decision and the more onerous burden of explanation.

Although the development here traced is considerably neater than anything likely to be encountered in legal history, I assume that lawyers would generally agree that this sort of thing does occur. I assume also it will be agreed that, despite the zigzag pattern which the decisions seem to present, the process illustrated is a "rational" one, falling within the limits of meaningful adjudication. What is the source of this "rational" quality? It seems clear that it derives from the fact that the courts engaged in this development are drawing out the necessary, or at least the reasonable, implications of a regime of private property and exchange.

I suggest more generally that where adjudication appears to operate meaningfully without the support of rules formally declared or accepted in advance, it does so because it draws its intellectual sustenance from the two basic forms of social ordering I have already described. It has done this historically with most notable success in the field where the accepted objective is to develop a regime of reciprocity or exchange. Students of comparative law are often struck by the fact that in the area of commercial transactions courts operating in entirely different environments of legal doctrine will often reach identical or similar results in the decision of actual cases.

But the possibility of a case-by-case development of principle is by no means confined to the field of commercial transactions. For example, the demands of a viable system of federalism are by no means immediately obvious. In gradually discovering and articulating the principles that will make federalism work, the courts may exemplify the process Mansfield had in mind when he spoke of the law "working itself pure." Indeed, just such a development was envisaged by Hamilton in No. 82 of the Federalist Papers, where he wrote:

> The erection of a new government, whatever care or wisdom may distinguish the work, cannot fail to originate questions of intricacy and nicety; and these may, in a particular manner, be expected to flow from the establishment of a constitution founded upon the total or partial incorporation of a number of distinct sovereignties. 'Tis time only that can mature and perfect so compound a system, can liquidate the meaning of all the parts, and can adjust them to each other in a harmonious and consistent *whole*. . . .

If the conception here advanced is sound, it follows that in extending "the rule of law" to international relations, law and community of purpose must develop together. It is also apparent that a community of purpose which consists simply in a shared desire to avoid reciprocal destruction is too impoverished to furnish a proper basis for meaningful adjudication. Where the only shared objective is the negative one of preventing a holocaust, there is nothing that can make meaningful a process of decision that depends upon proofs and reasoned argument. It is of course conceivable that, moved by a desire to prevent such a holocaust, two nations (say, Russia and the United States) might submit a dispute to arbitration, but they would do so in much the same spirit that they might resort to a throw of the dice — unless there were perceived by both some body of principle, however vague, that might control and give rationality to the decision. Such a body of emergent principle would have to derive from one of the two basic principles of order. In practice this would mean that it would have to derive from relationships of reciprocity. Hence a desideratum of overriding importance in the relations of Russia and the United States is the development of every possible bond of reciprocity, every kind of useful exchange, between the two countries. This is essential not merely to promote "understanding" and an atmosphere of good will but to create a community of interest from which adjudication can draw intellectual sustenance. . . .

VI. The Forms of Adjudication

1. *Introduction*

The remainder of this paper will be divided into three main sections: The Forms of Adjudication, The Limits of Adjudication, and Mixed, Parasitic, and Perverted Forms of Adjudication. Of course, all of these topics stand in close relation to one another and some degree of anticipation will be unavoidable.

For example, the limits of adjudication are affected by its forms. Reference has already been made to so-called "tripartite" arbitration. This special and deviant form of adjudication sometimes makes it possible to undertake through an adjudicative process tasks that could not otherwise be handled satisfactorily through adjudication at all. At the same time, this form may impair the effectiveness of adjudication in its more usual employments.

The joining of "mixed, parasitic, and perverted" forms of adjudication in one title should not mislead the reader into thinking that this paper condemns all departures of adjudication from a state of pristine purity. Certain mixed forms are valuable and almost indispensable, though their use is often attended by certain dangers.

In determining whether a deviant or mixed form impairs the

integrity of adjudication the test throughout will be that already stressed repeatedly: Does it affect adversely the meaning of the affected party's participation in the decision by proofs and reasoned arguments?

2. *Is an Adversary Presentation Necessary to Adjudication?*[22]

THE LAWYER'S ROLE AS ADVOCATE IN OPEN COURT

The lawyer appearing as an advocate before a tribunal presents, as persuasively as he can, the facts and the law of the case as seen from the standpoint of his client's interest. It is essential that both the lawyer and the public understand clearly the nature of the role thus discharged. Such an understanding is required not only to appreciate the need for an adversary presentation of issues, but also in order to perceive truly the limits partisan advocacy must impose on itself if it is to remain wholesome and useful.

In a very real sense it may be said that the integrity of the adjudicative process itself depends upon the participation of the advocate. This becomes apparent when we contemplate the nature of the task assumed by any arbiter who attempts to decide a dispute without the aid of partisan advocacy.

Such an arbiter must undertake, not only the role of judge, but that of representative for both of the litigants. Each of these roles must be played to the full without being muted by qualifications derived from the others. When he is developing for each side the most effective statement of its case, the arbiter must put aside his neutrality and permit himself to be moved by a sympathetic identification sufficiently intense to draw from his mind all that it is capable of giving, — in analysis, patience and creative power. When he resumes his neutral position, he must be able to view with distrust the fruits of this identification and be ready to reject the products of his own best mental efforts. The difficulties of this undertaking are obvious. If it is true that a man in his time must play many parts, it is scarcely given to him to play them all at once.

It is small wonder, then, that failure generally attends the attempt to dispense with the distinct roles traditionally implied in adjudication. What generally occurs in practice is that at some early point a familiar pattern will seem to emerge from the evidence; an accustomed label is wanting for the case and, without awaiting further proofs, this label is promptly assigned to it. It is a mistake to suppose that this premature cataloguing must necessarily result from impatience, prejudice or mental sloth. Often it proceeds from a very understandable desire to bring the hearing into some order and coherence, for without some tentative

22. [Under this heading in the original text, Mr. Fuller simply referred the reader to a statement coauthored with John D. Randall entitled Professional Responsibility: Report of the Joint Conference. The Joint Conference on Professional Responsibility was established in 1952 by the American Bar Association and the Association of American Law Schools. The Report appeared in 44 A.B.A.J. 1159 (1958). A few excerpts from the Report, id. at 1160-1161, 1162, 1216, have been inserted into the text.]

theory of the case there is no standard of relevance by which testimony may be measured. But what starts as a preliminary diagnosis designed to direct the inquiry tends, quickly and imperceptibly, to become a fixed conclusion, as all that confirms the diagnosis makes a strong imprint on the mind, while all that runs counter to it is received with diverted attention.

An adversary presentation seems the only effective means for combatting this natural human tendency to judge too swiftly in terms of the familiar that which is not yet fully known. The arguments of counsel hold the case, as it were, in suspension between two opposing interpretations of it. While the proper classification of the case is thus kept unresolved, there is time to explore all of its peculiarities and nuances.

These are the contributions made by partisan advocacy during the public hearing of the cause. When we take into account the preparations that must precede the hearing, the essential quality of the advocate's contribution becomes even more apparent. Preceding the hearing, inquiries must be instituted to determine what facts can be proved or seem sufficiently established to warrant a formal test of their truth during the hearing. There must also be a preliminary analysis of the issues, so that the hearing may have form and direction. These preparatory measures are indispensable whether or not the parties involved in the controversy are represented by advocates.

Where that representation is present there is an obvious advantage in the fact that the area of dispute may be greatly reduced by an exchange of written pleadings or by stipulations of counsel. Without the participation of someone who can act responsibly for each of the parties, this essential narrowing of the issues becomes impossible. But here again the true significance of partisan advocacy lies deeper, touching once more the integrity of the adjudicative process itself. It is only through the advocate's participation that the hearing may remain in fact what it purports to be in theory: a public trial of the facts and issues. Each advocate comes to the hearing prepared to present his proofs and arguments, knowing at the same time that his arguments may fail to persuade and that his proofs may be rejected as inadequate. It is a part of his role to absorb these possible disappointments. The deciding tribunal, on the other hand, comes to the hearing uncommitted. It has not represented to the public that any fact can be proved, that any argument is sound, or that any particular way of stating a litigant's case is the most effective expression of its merits. . . .

These, then, are the reasons for believing that partisan advocacy plays a vital and essential role in one of the most fundamental procedures of a democratic society. But if we were to put all of these detailed considerations to one side, we should still be confronted by the fact that, in whatever form adjudication may appear, the experienced judge or arbitrator desires and actively seeks to obtain an adversary presentation of the issues. Only when he has had the benefit of intelligent and vigorous advocacy on both sides can he feel fully confident of his decision.

Viewed in this light, the role of the lawyer as a partisan advocate appears not as a regrettable necessity, but as an indispensable part of a larger ordering of affairs. The institution of advocacy is not a concession to the frailties of human nature, but an expression of human insight in the design of a social framework within which man's capacity for impartial judgment can attain its fullest realization.

When advocacy is thus viewed, it becomes clear by what principle limits must be set to partisanship. The advocate plays his role well when zeal for his client's cause promotes a wise and informed decision of the case. He plays his role badly, and trespasses against the obligations of professional responsibility, when his desire to win leads him to muddy the headwaters of decision, when, instead of lending a needed perspective to the controversy, he distorts and obscures its true nature. . . .

THE LAWYER AS A GUARDIAN OF DUE PROCESS

The lawyer's highest loyalty is at the same time the most intangible. It is a loyalty that runs, not to persons, but to procedures and institutions. The lawyer's role imposes on him a trusteeship for the integrity of those fundamental processes of government and self-government upon which the successful functioning of our society depends.

. . . Everywhere democratic and constitutional government is tragically dependent on voluntary and understanding co-operation in the maintenance of its fundamental processes and forms.

It is the lawyer's duty to preserve and advance this indispensable co-operation by keeping alive the willingness to engage in it and by imparting the understanding necessary to give it direction and effectiveness. This is a duty that attaches not only to his private practice, but to his relations with the public. In this matter he is not entitled to take public opinion as a datum by which to orient and justify his actions. He has an affirmative duty to helppshape the growth and development of public attitudes toward fair procedures and due process.

3. *May the Arbiter Act on His Own Motion in Initiating the Case?*

In his The Nature and Sources of the Law, John Chipman Gray wrote:

> A judge of an organized body is a man appointed by that body to determine duties and the corresponding rights *upon the application of persons claiming those rights.* It is the fact that such application must be made to him, which distinguishes a judge from an administrative officer. The essence of a judge's office is that he shall be impartial, that he is to sit apart, is not to interfere voluntarily in affairs . . . but is to determine cases which are presented to him. To use the phrase of the English Ecclesiastical courts, the office of the judge must be promoted by some one.

A German socialist critic of "bourgeois law" once caricatured this view by saying that courts are like defective clocks; they have to be shaken to set them going. He, of course, added the point that shaking costs money.

Certainly it is true that in most of the practical manifestations of adjudication the arbiter's function has to be "promoted" by the litigant and is not initiated by itself. But is this coy quality of waiting to be asked an essential part of adjudication?

It would seem that it is not. Suppose, for example, the collision of two ships under circumstances that suggest that one or both masters were at fault. Suppose a board is given authority to initiate hearings in such a case and to make a determination of fault. Such a board might conduct its hearings after the pattern of court proceedings. Both masters might be accorded counsel and a full opportunity for cross-examination. There would be no impairment of the affected parties' full participation by proofs and reasoned argument; the integrity of adjudication seems to be preserved.

Yet I think that most of us would consider such a case exceptional and would not be deterred by it from persisting in the belief that the adjudicative process should normally not be initiated by the tribunal itself. There are, I believe, sound reasons for adhering to that belief.

Certainly it is clear that the integrity of adjudication is impaired if the arbiter not only initiates the proceedings but also, in advance of the public hearing, forms theories about what happened and conducts his own factual inquiries. In such a case the arbiter cannot bring to the public hearing an uncommitted mind; the effectiveness of participation through proofs and reasoned arguments is accordingly reduced. Now it is probably true that under most circumstances the mere initiation of proceedings carries with it a certain commitment and often a theory of what occurred. The case of the collision at sea is exceptional because there the facts themselves speak eloquently for the need of some kind of inquiry, so that the initiation of the proceedings implies nothing more than a recognition of this need. In most situations the initiation of proceedings could not have the same neutral quality, as, for example, where the occasion consists simply in the fact that a corporation had gone two years without declaring a dividend.

There is another reason which justifies the common conception that it is not normal for the adjudicative process to be initiated by the deciding tribunal. If we view adjudication in its widest extension, as including not only the work of courts but also that of arbitrators in labor, commerce, and international relations, it is apparent that the overwhelming majority of cases submitted to adjudication involve the assertion of claims founded directly or indirectly on *contract* or *agreement*. It seems clear that a regime of contract (more broadly, a regime of reciprocity) implies that the determination whether to assert a claim must be left to the interested party.

A contrary suggestion is advanced by Karl Llewellyn in The Cheyenne Way. In answer to the question "Why do we leave it to the affected party whether to assert his claim for breach of contract?" he gives the startling explanation that this is because as a matter of actual experience the motive of self-interest has proved sufficient to maintain a regime of contract. He suggests that if in the future this motive were to suffer a serious decline, then the state might find itself compelled to intervene to strengthen the regime of contract. This curious conception is symptomatic of a general tendency of our times to obscure the role of reciprocity as an organizing principle and to convert everything into "social policy," which is another way of saying that all organization is by common aims (or by the aims that in the mind of the "policymaker" ought to be common).

Any individual contract serves "society" only insofar as society is interested in the individual enrichment made possible by a regime of reciprocity. (Naturally, "individual" here has to be given an extended meaning to include groups and formal entities like the corporation.) If two men discover that by an agreement each can profit by giving up something he values less than the thing he receives in exchange for it, the individuals are enriched by virtue of their own evaluations of the objects of the exchange. If ten days after the agreement is entered there is a change in those evaluations, so that neither party has any further interest in the performance of the agreement, this is as much their affair as was the original agreement. To enforce a contract for a party who is willing to leave it unenforced is just as absurd as making the contract for him in the first place. (I realize, of course, that there are contracts required by law, but this is obviously a derivative phenomenon which would lose all meaning if every human relation were imposed by the state and were called a "contract.")

The belief that it is not normal for the arbiter himself to initiate the adjudicative process has, then, a twofold basis. *First,* it is generally impossible to keep even the bare initiation of proceedings untainted by preconceptions about what happened and what its consequences should be. In this sense, initiation of the proceedings by the arbiter impairs the integrity of adjudication by reducing the effectiveness of the litigant's participation through proofs and arguments. *Second,* the great bulk of claims submitted to adjudication are founded directly or indirectly on relationships of reciprocity. In this case, unless the affected party is deceived or ignorant of his rights, the very foundations of the claim asserted dictate that the processes of adjudication must be invoked by the claimant.

4. *Must the Decision Be Accompanied by a Statement of the Reasons for It?*

We tend to think of the judge or arbitrator as one who decides and who gives reasons for his decision. Does the integrity of adjudication require that reasons be given for the decision rendered? I think the answer is, not necessarily. In some fields of labor arbitration (chiefly, I believe, where arbitration is a facility made available without charge by the state) it is the practice to render "blind" awards. . . .

By and large it seems clear that the fairness and effectiveness of adjudication are promoted by reasoned opinions. Without such opinions the parties have to take it on faith that their participation in the decision has been real, that the arbiter has in fact understood and taken into account their proofs and arguments. A less obvious point is that, where a decision enters into some continuing relationship, if no reasons are given the parties will almost inevitably guess at reasons and act accordingly. Here the effectiveness of adjudication is impaired, not only because the results achieved may not be those intended by the arbiter, but also because his freedom of decision in future cases may be curtailed by the growth of practices based on a misinterpretation of decisions previously rendered.

5. *May the Arbiter Rest His Decision on Grounds Not Argued by the Parties?*

Obviously the bond of participation by the litigant is most secure when the arbiter rests his decision wholly on the proofs and argument actually presented to him by the parties. In practice, however, it is not always possible to realize this ideal. Even where all of the considerations on which the decision rests were touched on by the parties' arguments, the emphasis may be very different. An issue dealt with only in passing by one of the parties, or perhaps by both, may become the headstone of the arbiter's decision. This may mean not only that, had they foreseen this outcome, the parties would have presented different arguments, but that they might also have introduced evidence on very different factual issues.

If the ideal of a perfect congruence between the arbiter's view of the issues and that of the parties is unattainable, this is no excuse for a failure to work toward an achievement of the closest approximation of it. We need to remind ourselves that if this congruence is utterly absent — if the grounds for the decision fall completely outside the framework of the argument, making all that was discussed or proved at the hearing irrelevant — then the adjudicative process has become a sham, for the parties' participation in the decision has lost all meaning. . . .

6. *Qualifications and Disqualifications of the Arbiter*

A full discussion of the questions suggested by this title would lead too far afield for the purposes of this paper. Even a consideration of the comparative efficacy of the various devices intended to guarantee impartiality would require a long chapter.

I shall merely suggest that the problem of securing a properly qualified and impartial arbiter be tried by the same touchstone that has been used throughout — what will preserve the efficacy and meaning of the affected party's participation through proofs and arguments? Obviously, a strong emotional attachment by the arbiter to one of the interests involved in the dispute is destructive of that participation. In practice, however, another kind of "partiality" is much more dangerous. I refer to the situation where the arbiter's experience of life has not embraced the area of the dispute, or, worse still, where he has always viewed that area from some single vantage point. Here a blind spot of which he is quite unconscious may prevent him from getting the point of testimony or argument. By and large I think the decisions of our courts in commercial cases do not represent adjudication at its highest level. The reason is a lack of judicial "feel" for the problems involved. . . .

7. *Must the Decision Be Retrospective?*

In practice both the decisions of courts and the awards of arbitrators are retrospective, both as to their effect on the litigants' rights and their effect as precedents for the decisions of other cases. A paradox is sometimes squeezed from this traditional way of acting, to the effect that courts, in order to avoid the appearance of legislating, cast their legislative enactments in the harshest possible form, making them ex post facto.

The philosophy underlying the retrospective effect of the judicial decision can be stated somewhat as follows: It is not the function of courts to create new aims for society or to impose on society new basic directives. The courts for various reasons analyzed previously are unsuited for this sort of task. Perhaps the most compelling objection to an assumption of any such function lies in the limited participation in the decision by the litigants who (1) represent generally only themselves and (2) participate in the decision only by proofs and arguments addressed to the arbiter. On the other hand, with respect to the generally shared aims and the authoritative directives of a society, the courts do have an important function to perform, that of developing (or even "discovering") case by case what these aims or directives demand for their realization in particular situations of fact. In the discharge of this function, at times the result is so obvious that no one thinks of a "retroactive effect." Theoretically, a court might distinguish between such decisions and those which announce a rule or standard that seems "new," even though it may represent a reasoned conclusion from familiar premises. But if an attempt were made to apply such a distinction pervasively, so that some decisions would be retrospective, some prospective only, the resulting confusion might be much less bearable than the situation that now obtains.

Generally the same considerations apply also to arbitration awards. It is not a matter of "concealing" the legislative nature of the arbitrator's award which makes him give it a retrospective effect. It is rather a conservative philosophy about the proper functions of adjudication, a philosophy which seeks to keep meaningful the adversary presentation, the participation of litigants only through appeals to reason, etc. . . .

9. *How Is Adjudication Affected by the Source of the Arbiter's Power?*

The power to adjudicate may represent a delegated power of government, as in the case of a judge, or it may derive from the consent of the litigants, as in most forms of arbitration. Are these two basically different "forms" of adjudication? Obviously it has been a tacit assumption of this paper that they are not.

On the other hand, this does not mean that the discharge of the arbiter's function is wholly unaffected by the source of his power. In a summary way we may say that the possible advantages of adjudication supported by governmental authority are: (1) The judge is under less temptation to "compromise" than is the contractually appointed arbitrator. (2) The acceptability of the judge's decision may be enhanced by the fact that he seems to play a subservient role, as one who merely applies rules which he himself did not make.

Among the possible advantages of adjudication which derives its power from a contract of the parties are the following: (1) Being unbacked by state power (or insufficiently backed by it in the case of an ineffective legal sanction), the arbitrator must concern himself directly with the acceptability of his award. He may be at greater pains than a judge to get his facts straight, to state accurately the arguments of the parties, and generally to display in his award a full understanding of the case. (2) Being relatively free from technical rules of procedure, the wise and conscientious arbitrator can shape his procedures upon what he perceives to be the intrinsic demands of effective adjudication. Thus, the "due process" which animates his conduct of the hearing may appear to the parties as something real and not something that has to be taken on faith, as allegedly inhering in technical rules that seem quite arbitrary to the layman.

As a special quality of contractually authorized arbitration, which cannot unequivocally be called either an "advantage" or "disadvantage," we may note that the contract to arbitrate may contain explicit or implicit limits upon the adjudicative process itself. The arbitrator often comes to the hearing with a feeling that he must conduct himself in a way that conforms generally to the expectations of the parties and that this restriction is implicit in the contract of submission. Thus, if both parties desire and expect a more "literal" interpretation than the arbitrator himself would prefer, he may feel obligated to adopt an attitude of interpretation that he finds intellectually uncongenial.

VII. The Limits of Adjudication

1. *Introduction*

Attention is now directed to the question, What kinds of tasks are inherently unsuited to adjudication? The test here will be that used throughout. If a given task is assigned to adjudicative treatment, will it be possible to preserve the meaning of the affected party's participation through proofs and arguments?

2. *Polycentric Tasks and Adjudication*

This section introduces a concept — that of the "polycentric" task — which has been derived from Michael Polanyi's book The Logic of Liberty. In approaching that concept it will be well to begin with a few examples.

Some months ago a wealthy lady by the name of Timken died in New York leaving a valuable, but somewhat miscellaneous, collection of paintings to the Metropolitan Museum and the National Gallery "in equal shares," her will indicating no particular apportionment. When the will was probated the judge remarked something to the effect that the parties seemed to be confronted with a real problem. The attorney for one of the museums spoke up and said, "We are good friends. We will work it out somehow or other." What makes this problem of effecting an equal division of the paintings a polycentric task? It lies in the fact that the disposition of any single painting has implications for the proper disposition of every other painting. If it gets the Renoir, the Gallery may be less eager for the Cezanne but all the more eager for the Bellows, etc. If the proper apportionment were set for argument, there would be no clear issue to which either side could direct its proofs and contentions. Any judge assigned to hear such an argument would be tempted to assume the role of mediator or to adopt the classical solution: Let the older brother (here the Metropolitan) divide the estate into what he regards as equal shares, let the younger brother (the National Gallery) take his pick.

As a second illustration suppose in a socialist regime it were decided to have all wages and prices set by courts which would proceed after the usual forms of adjudication. It is, I assume, obvious that here is a task that could not successfully be undertaken by the adjudicative method. The point that comes first to mind is that courts move too slowly to keep up with a rapidly changing economic scene. The more fundamental point is that the forms of adjudication cannot encompass and take into account the complex repercussions that may result from any change in prices or wages. A rise in the price of aluminum may affect in varying degrees the demand for, and therefore the proper price of, thirty kinds of steel, twenty kinds of plastics, an infinitude of woods, other metals, etc. Each of these separate effects may have its own complex repercussions in the economy. In such a case it is simply impossible to afford each affected party a meaningful participation through proofs and arguments. It is a matter of capital importance to note that it is not merely a question of the huge number of possibly affected parties, significant as that aspect of the thing may be. A more fundamental point is that each of the various forms that award might take (say, a three-cent increase per pound, a four-cent increase, a five-cent increase, etc.) would have a different set of repercussions and might require in each instance a redefinition of the "parties affected.". . .

It should be carefully noted that a multiplicity of affected persons is not an invariable characteristic of polycentric problems. This is sufficiently illustrated in the case of Mrs. Timken's will. That case also illustrated the fact that rapid changes with time are not an invariable characteristic of such problems. On the other hand, in practice polycentric problems of possible concern to adjudication will normally involve many affected parties and a somewhat fluid state of affairs. Indeed, the last characteristic follows from the simple fact that the more interacting centers there are, the more the likelihood that one of them will be affected by a change in circumstances, and, if the situation is polycentric, this change will communicate itself after a complex pattern to other centers. This insistence on a clear conception of polycentricity may seem to be laboring a point, but clarity of analysis is essential if confusion is to be avoided. For example, if a reward of $1000 is offered for the capture of a criminal and six claimants assert a right to the award, hearing the six-sided controversy may be an awkward affair. The problem does not, however, present any significant polycentric element as that term is here used.

Now, if it is important to see clearly what a polycentric problem is, it is equally important to realize that the distinction involved is often a matter of degree. There are polycentric elements in almost all problems submitted to adjudication. A decision may act as a precedent, often an awkward one, in some situation not foreseen by the arbiter. Again, suppose a court in a suit between one litigant and a railway holds that it is an act of negligence for the railway not to construct an underpass at a particular crossing. There may be nothing to distinguish this crossing from other crossings on the line. As a matter of statistical probability it may be clear that constructing underpasses along the whole line would cost more lives (through accidents in blasting, for example) than would be lost if the only safety measure were the familiar "Stop, Look & Listen" sign. If so, then what seems to be a decision simply declaring the rights and duties of two parties is in fact an inept solution for a polycentric problem, some elements of which cannot be brought before the court in a simple suit by one injured party against a defendant railway. In lesser measure, concealed polycentric elements are probably present in almost all problems resolved by adjudication. It is not, then, a question of distinguishing black from white. It is a question of knowing when the polycentric elements have become so significant and predominant that the proper limits of adjudication have been reached. . . .

If problems sufficiently polycentric are unsuited to solution by adjudication, how may they in fact be solved? So far as I can see, there are only two suitable methods: *managerial direction* and *contract* (or reciprocity).

The manner in which managerial direction solves polycentric problems is exemplified by the baseball manager who assigns his players to their positions, decides when to take a pitcher out, when and whom to pinch-hit, when and how far to shift the infield and outfield for a particular batter, etc. The relationships potentially affected by these decisions are in formal mathematical terms of great complexity — and in the practical solution of them a good deal of "intuition" is indispensable.

Many problems of economic management are of a similar nature. Substitution of plastic for aluminum in a component part may produce a paper saving of twenty cents on each unit produced but involve the disruption of a longstanding relation with a supplier, the possibility of a strike over the necessary changes in piece rates, though the strike might turn out in the long run to be a good thing, etc. In the solution of some economic polycentric problems, recently developed mathematical methods, like those of Leontief, may reduce the necessity to rely on intuition, though they can never eliminate the element of human judgment.

The other method by which polycentric problems are solved is that of contract or a reciprocal adjustment of each center of interest with those with which it interacts. Thus, an economic market can solve the extremely complex problems of allocating resources, "costing" production, and pricing goods. Whenever the literature of socialism actually deals seriously with those problems the only solution found is the establishment of something akin to a market among the various state enterprises. . . .

The final question to be addressed is this: When an attempt is made to deal by adjudicative forms with a problem that is essentially polycentric, what happens? As I see it, three things can happen, sometimes all at once. *First,* the adjudicative solution may fail. Unexpected repercussions make the decision unworkable; it is ignored, withdrawn, or modified, sometimes repeatedly. *Second,* the purported arbiter ignores judicial proprieties — he "tries out" various solutions in posthearing conferences, consults parties not represented at the hearings, guesses at facts not proved and not properly matters for anything like judicial notice. *Third,* instead of accommodating his procedures to the nature of the problem he confronts, he may reformulate the problem so as to make it amenable to solution through adjudicative procedures.

Only the last of these needs illustration. Suppose it is agreed that an employer's control over promotions shall be subject to review through arbitration. Now obviously an arbitrator cannot decide whether when Jones was made a Machinist Class *A* there was someone else more deserving in the plant, or whether, in view of Jones' age, it would have been better to put him in another job with comparable pay. This is the kind of allocative problem for which adjudication is utterly unsuited. There are, however, two ways of obtaining a workable control over promotions through arbitration. One of these is through the posting of jobs; when a job is vacant, interested parties may apply for promotion into it. At the hearing, only those who have made application are entitled to be considered, and of course only the posted job is in issue. Here the problem is simplified in advance to the point where it can be arbitrated, though not without difficulty, particularly in the form of endless arguments as to whether there was in fact a vacancy that ought to have been posted, and whether a claimant filed his application on time and in the proper form, etc. The other way of accommodating the problem to arbitration is for the arbitrator to determine not who should be promoted but who *has* been promoted. That is, the contract contains certain "job descriptions" with the appropriate rate for each; the claimant asserts that he is in fact doing the work of a Machinist *A,* though he is still assigned the pay and title of a Machinist *B*. The controversy has two parties — the company and the claimant as represented by the union — and a single factual issue, Is the claimant in fact doing the work of a Machinist *A*?

In practice the procedure of applying for appointment to posted jobs will normally be prescribed in the contract itself, so that the terms of the agreement keep the arbitrator's function with respect to promotions within manageable limits. The other method of making feasible a control of promotions through arbitration will normally result from the arbitrator's own perception of the limitations of his role. The contract may simply contain a schedule of job rates and job classifications and a general clause stating that "discharges, promotions, and layoffs shall be subject to the grievance procedure." If the arbitrator were to construe such a contract to give him a general supervision over promotions, he would embark himself upon managerial tasks wholly unsuited to solution by any arbitrative procedure. An instinct toward preserving the integrity of his role will move him, therefore, to construe the contract in the manner already indicated, so that he avoids any responsibility with respect to the assignment of duties and merely decides whether the duties actually assigned make appropriate the classification assigned by the company to the complaining employee. . . .

In closing this discussion of polycentricity, it will be well to caution against two possible misunderstandings. The suggestion that polycentric problems are often solved by a kind of "managerial intuition" should not be taken to imply that it is an invariable characteristic of polycentric problems that they resist rational solution. There are rational principles for building bridges of structural steel. But there is no rational principle which states, for example, that the angle between girder *A* and girder *B* must always be 45 degrees. This depends on the bridge as a whole. One cannot construct a bridge by conducting successive separate arguments concerning the proper angle for every pair of intersecting girders. One must deal with the whole structure.

Finally, the fact that an adjudicative decision affects and enters into a polycentric relationship does not of itself mean that the adjudicative tribunal is moving out of its proper sphere. On the contrary, there is no better illustration of a polycentric relationship than an economic market, and yet the laying down of rules that will make a market function properly is one for which adjudication is generally well suited. The working out of our common law of contracts case by case has proceeded through adjudication, yet the basic principle underlying the rules thus developed is that they should promote the free exchange of goods in a polycentric market. The court gets into difficulty, not when it lays down rules about contracting, but when it attempts to write contracts.

*The Role of the Judge in Public Law Litigation**

Abram Chayes

In our received tradition, the lawsuit is a vehicle for settling disputes between private parties about private rights. The defining features of this conception of civil adjudication are:

(1) The lawsuit is *bipolar*. Litigation is organized as a contest between two individuals or at least two unitary interests, diametrically opposed, to be decided on a winner-takes-all basis.

(2) Litigation is *retrospective*. The controversy is about an identified set of completed events: whether they occurred, and if so, with what consequences for the legal relations of the parties.

(3) *Right and remedy are interdependent*. The scope of the relief is derived more or less logically from the substantive violation under the general theory that the plaintiff will get compensation measured by the harm caused by the defendant's breach of duty — in contract by giving plaintiff the money he would have had absent the breach; in tort by paying the value of the damage caused.

(4) The lawsuit is a *self-contained* episode. The impact of the judgment is confined to the parties. If plaintiff prevails there is a simple compensatory transfer, usually of money, but occasionally the return of a thing or the performance of a definite act. If defendant prevails, a loss lies where it has fallen. In either case, entry of judgment ends the court's involvement.

(5) The process is *party-initiated* and *party-controlled*. The case is organized and the issues defined by exchanges between the parties. Responsibility for fact development is theirs. The trial judge is a neutral arbiter of their interactions who decides questions of law only if they are put in issue by an appropriate move of a party.

* *Source:* 89 Harv. L. Rev. 1281, 1281-1302, 1304, 1307-1316 (1976).

This capsule description of what I have called the traditional conception of adjudication is no doubt overdrawn. It was not often, if ever, expressed so severely; indeed, because it was so thoroughly taken for granted, there was little occasion to do so. Although I do not contend that the traditional conception ever conformed fully to what judges were doing in fact, I believe it has been central to our understanding and our analysis of the legal system.

Whatever its historical validity, the traditional model is clearly invalid as a description of much current civil litigation in the federal district courts. Perhaps the dominating characteristic of modern federal litigation is that lawsuits do not arise out of disputes between private parties about private rights. Instead, the object of litigation is the vindication of constitutional or statutory policies. The shift in the legal basis of the lawsuit explains many, but not all, facets of what is going on "in fact" in federal trial courts. For this reason, although the label is not wholly satisfactory, I shall call the emerging model "public law litigation."

The characteristic features of the public law model are very different from those of the traditional model. The party structure is sprawling and amorphous, subject to change over the course of the litigation. The traditional adversary relationship is suffused and intermixed with negotiating and mediating processes at every point. The judge is the dominant figure in organizing and guiding the case, and he draws for support not only on the parties and their counsel, but on a wide range of outsiders — masters, experts, and oversight personnel. Most important, the trial judge has increasingly become the creator and manager of complex forms of ongoing relief, which have widespread effects on persons not before the court and require the judge's continuing involvement in administration and implementation. School desegregation, employment discrimination, and prisoners' or inmates' rights cases come readily to mind as avatars of this new form of litigation. But it would be mistaken to suppose that it is confined to these areas. Antitrust, securities fraud and other aspects of the conduct of corporate business, bankruptcy and reorganizations, union governance, consumer fraud, housing discrimination, electoral reapportionment, environmental management — cases in all these fields displays in varying degrees the features of public law litigation.

I. The Received Tradition

The traditional conception of adjudication reflected the late nineteenth century vision of society, which assumed that the major social and economic arrangements would result from the activities of autonomous individuals. In such a setting, the courts could be seen as an adjunct to private ordering, whose primary function was the resolution of disputes about the fair implications of individual interactions. The basic conceptions governing legal liability were "intention" and "fault." Intentional arrangements, not in conflict with more or less universal attitudes like opposition to force or fraud, were entitled to be respected, and other private activities to be protected unless culpable. Government regulatory action was presumptively suspect, and was tested by what was in form a common law action against the offending official in his private person. The predominating influence of the private law model can be seen even in constitutional litigation, which, from its first appearance in Marbury v. Madison,[17] was understood as an outgrowth of the judicial duty to decide otherwise-existing private disputes.

Litigation also performed another important function — clarification of the law to guide future private actions. This understanding of the legal system, together with the common law doctrine of stare decisis, focused professional and scholarly concern on adjudication at the appellate level, for only there did the process reach beyond the immediate parties to achieve a wider import through the elaboration of generally applicable legal rules. So, in the academic debate about the judicial function, the protagonist was the appellate judge (not, interestingly enough, the appellate *court*), and the spotlight of teaching, writing, and analysis was almost exclusively on appellate decisions. In practice, the circle was even more narrowly confined to the decisions of the United States Supreme Court, the English high courts (though decreasingly so in recent years), and a few "influential" federal and state appellate judges. As to this tiny handful of decisions subjected to critical scrutiny, the criterion for evaluation was primarily the technical skill of the opinion in disposing of the case adequately within the framework of precedent and other doctrinal materials, so as to achieve an increasingly more systematic and refined articulation of the governing legal rules.

In contrast to the appellate court, to which the motive power in the system was allocated, the functions of the trial judge were curiously neglected in the traditional model. Presumably, the trial judge, like the multitude of private persons who were supposed to order their affairs with reference to appellate pronouncements, would be governed by those decisions in disposing smoothly and expeditiously of the mine-run of cases. But if only by negative implication, the traditional conception of adjudication carried with it a set of strong notions about the role of the trial judge. In general he was passive.

17. 5 U.S. (1 Cranch) 137, 177 (1803).

He was to decide only those issues identified by the parties, in accordance with the rules established by the appellate courts, or, infrequently, the legislature.

Passivity was not limited to the law aspects of the case. It was strikingly manifested in the limited involvement of the judge in factfinding. Indeed, the sharp distinction that Anglo-American law draws between factfinding and law declaration is itself remarkable. In the developed common law system, these were not only regarded as analytically distinct processes, but each was assigned to a different tribunal for performance. The jury found the facts. The judge was a neutral umpire, charged with little or no responsibility for the factual aspects of the case or for shaping and organizing the litigation for trial.

Because the immediate impact of the judgment was confined to the parties, the traditional model was relatively relaxed about the accuracy of its factfinding. If the facts were not assumed as stated in the pleadings or on the view most favorable to one of the parties or determined on the basis of burdens or presumptions, they were remitted to a kind of black box, the jury. True, some of the law of evidence reflects an active suspicion of the jury. And if the evidence adduced would not "rationally" support a finding for one party or the other, the case could be taken from the jury. But the limits of rationality are inevitably commodious. Even law application, unless there was a special verdict (never much favored in this country), was left to the jury's relatively untrammeled discretion. Indeed, one of the virtues of the jury was thought to be its exercise of a rough-hewn equity, deviating from the dictates of the law where justice or changing community mores required.

The emphasis on systematic statement of liability rules involved a corresponding disregard of the problems of relief. There was, to be sure, a good deal of discussion of measure of damages, as a corollary to the analysis of substantive rights and duties. Similarly, the question of the availability of specific performance and other equitable remedies came in for a share of attention. But the discussion was carried forward within the accepted framework that compensatory money damages was the usual form of relief. Prospective relief was highly exceptional in the traditional model and was largely remitted to the discretion of the trial judge. . . .

Besides its inherent plausibility in the nineteenth century American setting, the traditional model of adjudication answered a number of important political and intellectual needs. The conception of litigation as a private contest between private parties with only minimal judicial intrusion confirmed the general view of government powers as stringently limited. The emphasis on the appellate function, conceived as an exercise in deduction from a few embracing principles themselves induced from the data of the cases, supplied the demand of the new legal academics for an intellectual discipline comparable to that of their faculty colleagues in the sciences, and for a body of teachable materials. For practitioners and judges, the same conception provided a professional methodology that could be self-consciously employed. Most importantly, the formulation operated to legitimate the increasingly visible political consequences of the actions of a judiciary that was not politically accountable in the usual sense.

II. The Public Law Litigation Model

Sometime after 1875, the private law theory of civil adjudication became increasingly precarious in the face of a growing body of legislation designed explicitly to modify and regulate basic social and economic arrangements. At the same time, the scientific and deductive character of judicial lawmaking came under attack, as the political consequences of judicial review of that legislation became urgent. . . .

A. *The Demise of the Bipolar Structure*

Joinder of parties, which was strictly limited at common law, was verbally liberalized under the codes to conform with the approach of equity calling for joinder of all parties having an "interest" in the controversy. The codes, however, did not at first produce much freedom of joinder. Instead, the courts defined the concept of "interest" narrowly to exclude those without an independent legal right to the remedy to be given in the main dispute. The definition itself illustrates the continuing power of the traditional model. . . .

. . . The proponents of "efficiency" argued for a more informal and flexible approach, to the end that the courts should not have to rehear the same complex of events. This argument ultimately shifted the focus of the lawsuit from legal theory to factual context — the "transaction or occurrence" from which the action arose. This in turn made it easier to view the set of events in dispute as giving rise to a range of legal consequences all of which ought to be considered together.

This more open-ended view of the subject matter of the litigation fed back upon party questions and especially intervention. Here, too, the sharp constraints dictated by the right-remedy nexus give way. And if the right to participate in litigation is no longer determined by one's claim to relief at the hands of another party or one's potential liability to satisfy the claim, it becomes hard to draw the line determining those who may participate so as to eliminate anyone who is or might be significantly (a weasel word) affected by the outcome — and the latest revision of the Federal Rules of Civil Procedure has more or less abandoned the attempt.

The question of the right to intervene is inevitably linked to the question of standing to initiate litigation in the first place. The standing issue could hardly arise at common law or under early code pleading rules, that is, under the traditional model. There the question of plaintiff's standing merged with the legal merits: On the facts pleaded, does this particular plaintiff have a right to the particular relief sought from the particular defendant from whom he is seeking it? With the erosion of the tight structural integration of the lawsuit, the pressure to expand the circle of potential plaintiffs has been inexorable. Today, the Supreme Court is struggling manfully, but with questionable success, to establish a formula for delimiting who may sue that stops short of "anybody who might be significantly affected by the situation he seeks to litigate."

"Anybody" — even "almost anybody" — can be a lot of people, particularly where the matters in issue are not relatively individualized private transactions or encounters. Thus, the stage is set for the class action. . . . Whatever the resolution of the current controversies surrounding class actions, I think it unlikely that the class action will ever be taught to behave in accordance with the precepts of the traditional model of adjudication. The class suit is a reflection of our growing awareness that a host of important public and private interactions — perhaps the most important in defining the conditions and opportunities of life for most people — are conducted on a routine or bureaucratized basis and can no longer be visualized as bilateral transactions between private individuals. From another angle, the class action responds to the proliferation of more or less well-organized groups in our society and the tendency to perceive interests as group interests, at least in very important aspects. . . .

B. *The Triumph of Equity*

One of the most striking procedural developments of this century is the increasing importance of equitable relief. It is perhaps too soon to reverse the traditional maxim to read that money damages will be awarded only when no suitable form of specific relief can be devised. But surely, the old sense of equitable remedies as "extraordinary" has faded.

I am not concerned here with specific performance — the compelled transfer of a piece of land or a unique thing. This remedy is structurally little different from traditional money-damages. It is a one-time, one-way transfer requiring for its enforcement no continuing involvement of the court. Injunctive relief, however, is different in kind, even when it takes the form of a simple negative order. Such an order is a presently operative prohibition, enforceable by contempt, and it is a much greater constraint on activity than the risk of future liability implicit in the damage remedy. Moreover, the injunction is continuing. Over time, the parties may resort to the court for enforcement or modification of the original order in light of changing circumstances. Finally, by issuing the injunction, the court takes public responsibility for any consequences of its decree that may adversely affect strangers to the action.

Beyond these differences, the prospective character of the relief introduces large elements of contingency and prediction into the proceedings. Instead of a dispute retrospectively oriented toward the consequences of a closed set of events, the court has a controversy about future probabilities. Equitable doctrine, naturally enough, given the intrusiveness of the injunction and the contingent nature of the harm, calls for a balancing of the interests of the parties. And if the immediate parties' interests were to be weighed and evaluated, it was not too difficult to proceed to a consideration of other interests that might be affected by the order.

The comparative evaluation of the competing interests of plaintiff and defendant required by the remedial approach of equity often discloses alternatives to a winner-takes-all decision. An arrangement might be fashioned that could safeguard at least partially the interests of both parties, and perhaps even of others as well. And to the extent such an arrangement is possible, equity seems to require it. Negative orders directed to one of the parties — even though pregnant with affirmative implications — are often not adequate to this end. And so the historic power of equity to order affirmative action gradually freed itself from the encrustation of nineteenth century restraints. The result has often been a decree embodying an affirmative regime to govern the range of activities in litigation and having the force of law for those represented before the court.

At this point, right and remedy are pretty thoroughly disconnected. The form of relief does not flow ineluctably from the liability determination, but is fashioned ad hoc. In the process, moreover, right and remedy have been to some extent transmuted. The liability determination is not simply a pronouncement of the legal consequences of past events, but to some extent a prediction of what is likely to be in the future. And relief is not a terminal, compensatory transfer, but an effort to devise a program to contain future consequences in a way that accommodates the range of interests involved.

The interests of absentees, recognized to some extent by equity's balancing of the public interest in individual suits for injunction, become more pressing as social and economic activity is increasingly organized through large aggregates of people. An order nominally addressed to an individual litigant — the labor injunction is an early example — has obvious and visible impact on persons not individually before the court. Nor must the form of the action be equitable: A suit against an individual to collect a tax, if it results in a determination of the constitutional invalidity of the taxing statute, has the same result for absentees as a grant or denial of an injunction. Statutory construction, for example of welfare or housing legislation, may have a similar extended impact, again even if the relief is not equitable in form. Officials will almost inevitably act in accordance with the judicial interpretation in the countless similar situations cast up by a sprawling bureaucratic program. We may call this a stare decisis effect, but it is quite different from the traditional image of autonomous adjustment of individual private transactions in response to judicial decisions. In cases of this kind, the fundamental conception of litigation as a mechanism for private dispute settlement is no longer viable. The argument is about whether or how a government policy or program shall be carried out.

Recognition of the policy functions of litigation feeds the already intense pressure against limitations on standing, as well as against the other traditional limitations on justiciability — political question, ripeness, mootness and the like. At the same time, the breadth of interests that may be affected by public law litigation raises questions about the adequacy of the representation afforded by a plaintiff whose interest is narrowly traditional.

Again, as in private litigation, the screw gets another turn when simple prohibitory orders are inadequate to provide relief. If a mental patient complains that he has been denied a right to treatment, it will not do to order the superintendent to "cease to deny" it. So with segregation in education, discrimination in hiring, apportionment of legislative districts, environmental management. And the list could be extended. If judicial intervention is invoked on the basis of congressional enactment, the going assumption is that the statute embodies an affirmative regulatory objective. Even when the suit is premised on constitutional provisions, traditionally regarded as constraining government power, there is an increasing tendency to treat them as embodying affirmative values, to be fostered and encouraged by judicial action. In either case, if litigation discloses that the relevant purposes or values have been frustrated, the relief that seems to be called for is often an affirmative program to implement them. And courts, recognizing the undeniable presence of competing interests, many of them unrepresented by the litigants, are increasingly faced with the difficult problem of shaping relief to give due weight to the concerns of the unrepresented.

C. *The Changing Character of Factfinding*

The traditional model of adjudication was primarily concerned with assessing the consequences for the parties of specific past instances of conduct. This retrospective orientation is often inapposite in public law litigation, where the lawsuit generally seeks to enjoin future or threatened action, or to modify a course of conduct presently in train or a condition presently existing. In the former situation, the question whether threatened action will materialize, in what circumstances, and with what consequences can, in the nature of things, be answered only by an educated guess. In the latter case, the inquiry is only secondarily concerned with how the condition came about, and even less with the subjective attitudes of the actors, since positive regulatory goals are ordinarily defined without reference to such matters. Indeed, in dealing with the actions of large political or corporate aggregates, notions of will, intention, or fault increasingly become only metaphors.

In the remedial phases of public law litigation, factfinding is even more clearly prospective. As emphasized above, the contours of relief are not derived logically from the substantive wrong adjudged, as in the traditional model. The elaboration of a decree is largely a discretionary process within which the trial judge is called upon to assess and appraise the consequences of alternative programs that might correct the substantive fault. In both the liability and remedial phases, the relevant inquiry is largely the same: How can the policies of a public law best be served in a concrete case?

In public law litigation, then, factfinding is principally concerned with "legislative" rather than "adjudicative" fact. And "fact evaluation" is perhaps a more accurate term than "fact-finding." The whole process begins to look like the traditional description of legislation: Attention is drawn to a "mischief," existing or threatened, and the activity of the parties and court is directed to the development of on-going measures designed to cure that mischief. Indeed, if, as is often the case, the decree sets up an affirmative regime governing the activities in controversy for the indefinite future and having binding force for persons within its ambit, then it is not very much of a stretch to see it as, *pro tanto,* a legislative act. . . .

The courts, it seems, continue to rely primarily on the litigants to produce and develop factual materials, but a number of factors make it impossible to leave the organization of the trial exclusively in their hands. With the diffusion of the party structure, fact issues are no longer sharply drawn in a confrontation between two adversaries, one asserting the affirmative and the other the negative. The litigation is often extraordinarily complex and extended in time, with a continuous and intricate interplay between factual and legal elements. It is hardly feasible and, absent a jury, unnecessary to set aside a contiguous block of time for a "trial stage" at which all significant factual issues will be presented. The scope of the fact investigation and the sheer volume of factual material that can be exhumed by the discovery process pose enormous problems of organization and assimilation. All these factors thrust the trial judge into an active role in shaping, organizing and facilitating the litigation. We may not yet have reached the investigative judge of the continental systems, but we have left the passive arbiter of the traditional model a long way behind.

D. *The Decree*

The centerpiece of the emerging public law model is the decree. It differs in almost every relevant characteristic from relief in the traditional model of adjudication, not the least in that it *is* the centerpiece. The decree seeks to adjust future behavior, not to compensate for past wrong. It is deliberately fashioned rather than logically deduced from the nature of the legal harm suffered. It provides for a complex, on-going regime of performance rather than a simple, one-shot, one-way transfer. Finally, it prolongs and deepens, rather than terminates, the court's involvement with the dispute.

The decree is also an order of the court, signed by the judge and issued under his responsibility (itself a shift from the classical money judgment). But it cannot be supposed that the judge, at least in a case of any complexity, composes it out of his own head. How then is the relief formulated?

The reports provide little guidance on this question. Let me nonetheless suggest a prototype that I think finds some support in the available materials. The court will ask the parties to agree on an order or it will ask one party to prepare a draft. In the first case, a negotiation is stipulated. In the second, the dynamic leads almost inevitably in that direction. The draftsman understands that his proposed decree will be subject to comment and objection by the other side and that it must be approved by the court. He is therefore likely to submit it to his opponents in advance to see whether differences cannot be resolved. Even if the court itself should prepare the initial draft of the order, some form of negotiation will almost inevitably ensue upon submission of the draft to the parties for comment. . . .

. . . Thus, the formulation of the decree in public law litigation introduces a good deal of party control over the practical outcome. Indeed, relief by way of order after a determination on the merits tends to converge with relief through a consent decree or voluntary settlement. And this in turn mitigates a major theoretical objection to affirmative relief — the danger of intruding on an elaborate and organic network of interparty relationships.

Nevertheless it cannot be supposed that this process will relieve the court entirely of responsibility for fashioning the remedy. The parties may fail to agree. Or the agreement reached may fail to comport with the requirements of substantive law as the judge sees them. Or the interests of absentees may be inadequately accommodated. In these situations, the judge will not, as in the traditional model, be able to derive his responses directly from the liability determination, since, as we have seen, the substantive law will point out only the general direction to be pursued and a few salient landmarks to be sought out or avoided. How then is the judge to prescribe an appropriate remedy?

If the parties are simply in disagreement, it seems plausible to suppose that the judge's choice among proposals advanced by the *quondam* negotiators will be governed by his appraisal of their good faith in seeking a way to implement the constitutional or statutory command as he has construed it. The interest in a decree that will be voluntarily obeyed can be promoted by enforcing a regime of good faith bargaining among the parties. Without detailed knowledge of the negotiations, however, any attempt to enforce such a regime can rest on little more than an uneasy base of intuition and impression. . . .

For these reasons, the judge will often find himself a personal participant in the negotiations on relief. But this course has obvious disadvantages, not least in its inroads on the judge's time and his pretentions to disinterestedness. To avoid these problems, judges have increasingly resorted to outside help — masters, amici, experts, panels, advisory committees — for information and evaluation of proposals for relief. These outside sources commonly find themselves exercising mediating and even adjudicatory functions among the parties. They may put forward their own remedial suggestions, whether at the request of the judge or otherwise.

Once an ongoing remedial regime is established, the same procedure may be repeated in connection with the implementation and enforcement of the decree. Compliance problems may be brought to the court for resolution and, if necessary, further remediation. Again, the court will often have no alternative but to resort to its own sources of information and evaluation.

I suggested above that a judicial decree establishing an ongoing affirmative regime of conduct is *pro tanto* a legislative act. But in actively shaping and monitoring the decree, mediating between the parties, developing his own sources of expertise and information, the trial judge has passed beyond even the role of legislator and has become a policy planner and manager. . . .

. . . Litigation inevitably becomes an explicitly political forum and the court a visible arm of the political process.

III. A First Appraisal

A. *Trial Balance*

One response to the positive law model of litigation would be to condemn it as an intolerable hodge-podge of legislative, administrative, executive, and judicial functions addressed to problems that are by their nature inappropriate for judicial resolution. Professor Lon Fuller has argued that when such functions are given to the judiciary they are parasitic, in the sense that they can be effectively carried out only by drawing on the legitimacy and moral force that courts have developed through the performance of their inherent function, adjudication according to the traditional conception. A certain limited amount of such parasitism can be accommodated, but too much undermines the very legitimacy on which it depends, because the nontraditional activities of the judiciary are at odds with the conditions that ensure the moral force of its decisions. . . .

. . . [W]e have invested excessive time and energy in the effort to define — on the basis of the inherent nature of adjudication, the implications of a constitutional text, or the functional characteristics of courts — what the precise scope of judicial activity ought to be. Separation of powers comes in for a good deal of veneration in our political and judicial rhetoric, but it has always been hard to classify all government activity into three, and only three, neat and mutually exclusive categories. In practice, all governmental officials, including judges, have exercised a large and messy admixture of powers, and that is as it must be. That is not to say that institutional characteristics are irrelevant in assigning governmental tasks or that judges should unreservedly be thrust directly into political battles. But such considerations should be taken as cautionary, not decisive; for despite its well rehearsed inadequacies, the judiciary may have some important institutional advantages for the tasks it is assuming:

First, and perhaps most important, is that the process is presided over by a judge. His professional tradition insulates him from narrow political pressures, but, given the operation of the federal appointive power and the demands of contemporary law practice, he is likely to have some experience of the political process and acquaintance with a fairly broad range of public policy problems. Moreover, he is governed by a professional ideal of reflective and dispassionate analysis of the problem before him and is likely to have had some experience in putting this ideal into practice.

Second, the public law model permits ad hoc applications of broad national policy in situations of limited scope. The solutions can be tailored to the needs of the particular situation and flexibly administered or modified as experience develops with the regime established in the particular case.

Third, the procedure permits a relatively high degree of participation by representatives of those who will be directly affected by the decision, without establishing a *liberum veto.*

Fourth, the court, although traditionally thought less competent than legislatures or administrative agencies in gathering and assessing information, may have unsuspected advantages in this regard. Even the diffused adversarial structure of public law litigation furnishes strong incentives for the parties to produce information. If the party structure is sufficiently representative of the interests at stake, a considerable range of relevant information will be forthcoming. And, because of the limited scope of the proceeding, the information required can be effectively focused and specified. Information produced will not only be subject to adversary review, but as we have seen, the judge can engage his own experts to assist in evaluating the evidence. Moreover, the information that is produced will not be filtered through the rigid structures and preconceptions of bureaucracies.

Fifth, the judicial process is an effective mechanism for registering and responding to grievances generated by the operation of public programs in a regulatory state. Unlike an administrative bureaucracy or a legislature, the judiciary *must* respond to the complaints of the aggrieved. It is also rather well situated to perform the task of balancing the importance of competing policy interests in a specific situation. The legislature, perhaps, could balance, but it cannot address specific situations. The bureaucracy deals with specific situations, but only from a position of commitment to particular policy interests.

Sixth, the judiciary has the advantage of being nonbureaucratic. It is effective in tapping energies and resources outside itself and outside the government in the exploration of the situation and the assessment of remedies. It does not work through a rigid, multilayered hierarchy of numerous officials, but through a smallish, representative task force, assembled ad hoc, and easily dismantled when the problem is finally resolved.

The foregoing enumeration is admittedly one-sided. It surely does not warrant unqualified endorsement of the public law litigation model in its present form. For one thing, the returns are not all in, and those we have show varying degrees of success. Legislative apportionment, although bitterly opposed as an arena of judicial intervention, seems to have worked out reasonably well. School segregation, on the other hand, seemed obviously appropriate for judicial reform under the Constitution, but the results are at best mixed. And some heralded efforts at management of state institutions may turn out to be pretty thorough-going failures. . . .

B. The Problem of Interest Representation

. . . Public law litigation, because of its widespread impact, seems to call for adequate representation in the proceedings of the range of interests that will be affected by them. At the stage of relief in particular, if the decree is to be quasi-negotiated and party participation is to be relied upon to ensure its viability, representation at the bargaining table assumes very great importance, not only from the point of view of the affected interests but from that of the system itself. As noted above, the tendency, supported by both the language and the rationale of the Federal Rules of Civil Procedure, is to regard anyone whose interests may be significantly affected by the litigation to be presumptively entitled to participate in the suit on demand. In a public law system, persons are usually "affected" by litigation in terms of an "interest" that they share with many others similarly situated, whether organized or unorganized, that is to say, as members of an "interest group." Participation of those affected by the decision has a reassuringly democratic ring, but when participation is mediated by group representatives, often self-appointed, it gives a certain pause.

Professor Richard Stewart . . . perceptively develops these misgivings about the theory and practice of interest representation. . . .

[Stewart's] main thrust . . . is that in a proceeding with broad public impacts, whether judicial or administrative, there are no very reliable criteria for identifying the affected interests, apart from the decibel level of the protest. The fundamental objection, of course, is not to the participation of those who perceive themselves as affected and can make a plausible showing on that point. . . .

The real problem that emerges from Professor Stewart's analysis is the inevitable incompleteness of the interest representation. What about those who do not volunteer — most often the weak, the poor, the unorganized? A first response is that these groups are unlikely to be better off in any other process to which the policy issue might be remitted for decision. On this score, neither the judiciary nor the administrative agencies, it seems to me, need entertain feelings of inferiority to the typical bureaucratic decision or local governing board action, or even to the operation of "de-regulated" private activity. And to retreat to the notion that the legislature itself — Congress! — is in some mystical way adequately representative of all the interests at stake, particularly on issues of policy implementation and application, is to impose democratic theory by brute force on observed institutional behavior.

Moreover, a number of techniques are available to the judge to increase the breadth of interests represented in a suit, if that seems desirable. He can, for example, refuse to proceed until new parties are brought in, as in the old equity procedure, where the categories of necessary and proper parties converged. In class actions, the judge may order such "notice as may be required for the protection of members of the class or otherwise for the fair conduct of the action," [133] including "sampling notice" designed to apprise the judge of significant divisions of interest among the putative class, not brought to light by its representatives. And that notice is supposed to be reasonably calculated to inform absentees of their potential interest in the litigation, which is more than can be said of notification of administrative proceedings in the Federal Register. The judge can also appoint guardians *ad litem* for unrepresented interests. And as we have seen, he can and does employ experts and amici to inform himself on aspects of the case not adequately developed by the parties. Finally, the judge can elicit the views of public officials at all levels. . . .

Even if one could be reasonably confident of the capacity of the court to construct ad hoc a kind of mini-legislature for the situation in litigation, I take it an even more fundamental query remains. In reaching a decision, what weight is to be assigned to the interests represented? A part of the answer may be found in the suggestion that the decision, or at least the remedy, involves a species of negotiation among the parties. But on this issue, the argument is familiar and powerful that Congress, whatever its makeup, is the institution authoritatively empowered in our system to balance incommensurable political values and interests. Here we confront, finally, the question of the legitimacy of judicial action in public law litigation. . . .

The two principal parties to the debate and their positions have grown familiar to the point of caricature. The "Classical" view saw the courts as performing the objective — even "scientific" — function of deducing legal consequences from agreed first principles. The Realists, after challenging and eventually undermining their predecessors' "pretentions" to objectivity, substituted a more pliable view of judicial

133. Fed. R. Civ. P. 23(d)(2).

method: "reasoned elaboration" or "the inner morality of law" or adherence to "neutral principles." But both schools accepted the traditional conception of adjudication and the premise that the limits of proper judicial action inhered in and could be derived from it.

As the traditional model has been displaced in recent years, therefore, questions of judicial legitimacy and accountability have reasserted themselves.

The fundamental ground of traditional reservations about constitutional adjudication is that the courts may be called upon to act counter to the popular will as expressed in legislation. In this respect, constitutional litigation in the new mode differs to some extent from the characteristic activity of the courts under the due process clause in the early part of the century. In the economic due process cases the courts acted to frustrate legislatures "speak[ing] the present will of the dominant forces in the state," and, beyond that, to withdraw altogether vast realms of policy from the reach of legislative action. Public law litigation is at once more and less intrusive: more, because it may command affirmative action of political officers; less, because it is ordinarily limited to adjusting the *manner* in which state and federal policy on education, prisons, mental institutions, and the like is carried forward. Its target is generally administrative rather than legislative action, action that is thus derivative rather than a direct expression of the legislative mandate. Moreover, one may ask whether democratic theory really requires deference to majoritarian outcomes whose victims are prisoners, inmates of mental institutions, and ghetto dwellers. Unlike the numerical minorities that the courts protected under the banner of economic due process, these have no alternative access to the levers of power in the system.

These observations will, no doubt, fail to dispel the uneasiness that American political and legal thinkers have always felt at the power of courts to frustrate, or to order, action by elected officials. For it cannot be denied that public law litigation explicitly rejects many of the constraints of judicial method and procedure in which we have characteristically sought respite from the unease. Now, I do not deny that the law, like other creative and performing arts, encompasses a recognizable (and teachable) technique; and this technique plays an important part in the development of the medium and in the criticism and evaluation of its practitioners. But in the law, as elsewhere, technical virtuosity has never been a guarantee of acceptable performance. . . .

More fundamentally, our transformed appreciation of the whole process of making, implementing, and modifying law in a public law system points to sources other than professional method and role for the legitimacy of the new model lawsuit. As we now begin to see it, that process is plastic and fluid. Popular participation in it is not alone through the vote or by representation in the legislature. And judicial participation is not by way of sweeping and immutable statements of *the* law, but in the form of a continuous and rather tentative dialogue with other political elements — Congress and the executive, administrative agencies, the profession and the academics, the press and wider publics. Bentham's "judge and company" has become a conglomerate. In such a setting, the ability of a judicial pronouncement to sustain itself in the dialogue and the power of judicial action to generate assent over the long haul become the ultimate touchstones of legitimacy. . . .

NOTES AND COMMENTS

Eckhoff and Fuller seem concerned about identifying the defining features of adjudication. These features are seen also as conditions of the efficacy of courts, or at least of their optimal functioning as such. For Fuller, these may also be regarded as conditions of legitimacy. Chayes's sympathetic exposition of contemporary "public law litigation" presents a picture sharply at odds with Fuller's account of adjudication. What would count as evidence confirming or refuting Fuller's view? If he is correct, isn't there something important gone wrong with courts carrying on public law litigation?

Does public law litigation as described by Chayes come within Fuller's description of polycentric disputes? Fuller, of course, thought these disputes especially unsuitable for adjudication but capable of resolution by either negotiation or managerial discretion. If the cases described by Chayes were typically settled, as his account suggests they would be, would that tend to support Fuller's description of adjudication? What would induce the adverse parties in such cases to negotiate settlements?

For James Wm. Moore: Some Reflections on a Reading of the Rules *

Robert M. Cover

We have become so transfixed by the achievement of James Wm. Moore and his colleagues in creating, nurturing, expounding and

* *Source:* 84 Yale L.J. 718, 722-728, 730-739 (1975).

annotating a great trans-substantive code of procedure that we often miss the persistent and inevitable tension between procedure generalized across substantive lines and procedure applied to implement a particular substantive end. There are, indeed, trans-substantive values which may be expressed, and to some extent served, by a code of procedure. But there are also demands of particular substantive objectives which cannot be served except through the purposeful shaping, indeed, the manipulation, of process to a case or to an area of law. What follows is by no means an attempt to denigrate or undermine the ongoing trans-substantive achievement of the Federal Rules of Civil Procedure. Rather it is an exploration to rediscover the feel of a tension. . . .

I ask the reader's indulgence for an excursion into the past, though I promise a return to the considerations of current procedure. It is useful to test our intuition about the substance-oriented manipulation of procedure in a remote context where, hopefully, we may assume a degree of unanimity among readers about substance. The first rough sketch of my intuition thus emerges from . . . cases involving the issue of whether particular persons were or were not slaves.

Robinson v. Smyth [16] was decided by the English Court of Common Pleas in 1799; it is short enough to reproduce in its entirety:

> Shepherd Serjt. moved to put off the trial in this case on account of the absence of a material witness. He stated that the action was brought for wages supposed to be due to the Plaintiff as a seaman, upon a voyage from the West Indies to London, and that the defence to be established by the evidence of the absent witness, was that the Plaintiff was slave to the Defendant who had paid a valuable consideration for him.
>
> Sed per Curiam. This is an odious defence, to which the Court will give no assistance. If the Defendant were to offer to put it on the record, we should not give him a day's time. It is as much a denial of justice as the plea of alien enemy, which is always discouraged by the Court.
>
> Shepherd took nothing by his motion.

This case seems a most troubling one despite (or, rather, because of) the admirable sentiment against slavery expressly stated as a ground for the exercise of discretion. . . .

. . . [T]he case is troublesome because of the nature of the justification, a manipulation of a procedural component to an admirable (from our moral perspective) substantive end. Needless to say, we would be at least as troubled by a case in which the same procedural amenities were withheld from a black person petitioning for freedom because the jurisdiction held freedom suits in disfavor.

16. Robinson v. Smyth, 1 Bos. & Pul. 454, 126 Eng. Rep. 1007 (C.P. 1799). . . .

Having reached the conclusion that it is the (admirable) substantive justification for the procedural step in *Robinson* that is troublesome rather than the procedural step itself, we must concede that there are many examples of substantive justification for procedural steps which do not trouble us in the same way. Indeed, the next . . . opinions from the slavery [era] are, to a greater or lesser extent, justifiable instances of such manipulations.

Within a month of *Robinson,* the Virginia Supreme Court of Appeals considered a question of standing in Pleasants v. Pleasants;[18] the issue was whether to permit a person who had already been discharged as executor of an estate to petition a court of equity in order to compel legatees to free slaves who had passed to them under a will. The will directed the beneficiaries to set the slaves free "when the laws should allow of it." The Virginia Act of 1782, permitting manumission, was passed after the executor had been discharged. The Virginia court allowed the petitioner to present the slaves' claims to freedom, despite its certainty that he did so neither in his capacity as executor nor as heir at law. . . .

Finally, consider the United States Supreme Court case of Mima Queen v. Hepburn,[23] more particularly, Justice Duvall's dissenting argument. Plaintiffs, Negroes held in servitude, claimed descent from a free maternal ancestor and sought to introduce . . . hearsay to prove that fact. The lower court refused to admit such evidence and the Court, per Chief Justice Marshall, affirmed. Marshall asserted that whatever the rules governing admissibility of evidence might be, they must be trans-substantive:

> [T]he rule then, which the Court shall establish in this cause will not, in its application, be confined to cases of this particular description, but will be extended to others where rights may depend on facts which happened many years past.

Justice Duvall's dissent, the only one he wrote in 24 years on the Court, contains both an argument from established hearsay principles and an argument from the special favor he supposes freedom suits ought to enjoy. He reports that the Maryland courts had admitted such hearsay in freedom suits on "the same principle, upon which it is admitted to prove a custom, pedigree and the boundaries of land." But Duvall goes on to argue that the rationale for admission of hearsay in freedom suits is still stronger since "[i]t will be universally admitted that the right to freedom is more important than the right of property." He then considers the litigation plight of plaintiffs in freedom suits and concludes:

18. 6 Va. (2 Call) 319, 6 Va. (2 Call 2d ed.) 270 (1799). . . .
23. Mima Queen v. Hepburn, 11 U.S. (7 Cranch) 290 (1813). . . .

> And people of color from their helpless condition under the uncontrolled authority of a master, are entitled to all reasonable protection. A decision that hearsay evidence in such cases shall not be admitted, cuts up by the roots all claims of the kind, and puts a final end to them, unless the claim should arise from a fact of recent date, and such a case will seldom perhaps never, occur.

I am horrified by the Supreme Court's failure to adopt Duvall's position. . . .

Robinson seems to me to sit outside the limits of continuum of more to less acceptable manipulations of process. It is thus particularly important to understand what is disturbing in it. The difficulty seems to me fourfold. First, the case seems to further no consistent, coherent substantive policy, given what is presumed to be the operative rule of law to be applied. Since slavery is presumed to be an acceptable defense to the action for wages, we are confronted by the use of process as a means of undermining the formal rule of law. Now qualification or mitigation of substance through process is not unusual or necessarily problematic. But it usually takes the form of imposing presumptions or allocating burdens to structure the usual litigation risks of uncertainty in a fashion which recognizes a substantive preference. What is highly unusual about *Robinson* is that it ignores this route altogether in undermining the rule of law; it purposefully refuses to permit uncertainty to be reduced. And it does so without any reference to cost or efficiency criteria which may, in many situations, acceptably impose a limit on the amount of trouble or expense we are prepared to undertake to reduce uncertainty.

The only sense that can be made of the combination of the substantive rule of law in this case with the procedural ruling and its articulated justification is that slavery is to be formally recognized, but the holding of this form of interest is to be purposefully rendered insecure. It might be noted that this kind of objective, if it can be justified at all, is usually justified as a "transition" stage in the development of substantive law. It suggests a position of disequilibrium which, when resolved, will eventuate in a more stable substantive configuration that will presumably not need, and should not use, such manipulation of procedural components to achieve its ends. In a sense this type of justification is itself a recognition of the character of the process as a departure from a norm, as problematic.

The second disturbing characteristic of *Robinson* inheres in its failure to achieve equality of treatment of litigants. . . .

The third problem in *Robinson* inheres in the unpredictable character of the justification when applied to process. That a claim or defense is "disfavored" does not generate any plausible or predictable pattern of impact on process. If the "disfavored" rubric will justify failure to extend time to secure an absent witness, it may, but need not, eventuate in a predilection to dismiss pleadings for trivial errors, a careful scrutiny of testimony for trivial inconsistencies, an enlargement of privileges to exclude testimony which would support the disfavored claim, a narrowing of privilege to permit testimony against the disfavored claim, etc. Indeed, the sum effect of calling an action disfavored seems to be that lightning may strike at any time or in any way; we know only which party it will strike.

Finally, *Robinson* is troublesome because the court chooses to make a point of the lack of procedural justification for the decision. There are a broad variety of procedural desiderata and a decision often involves a choice among them. While a decision such as the one I suggest as an acceptable alternative implicitly sets off one procedural value against another, the Court of Common Pleas expressly failed to do so. It may be justifiable, once a trade-off between process values is inevitable, to make the choice in one direction rather than another because of the substantive end that will thereby be served; in any event, such a form of decision appears less nakedly as a disregard for a process value. But it seems intuitively troublesome to ignore these values altogether.

The other . . . cases considered above present fewer difficulties of exposition than did *Robinson*. In *Pleasants* the court is confronted with a problem of remote participatory rights, the issue of access to litigation for those against or for whom a decree will not run. Indeed, one may go further in terms of our present rules governing participation and stress that Pleasants himself would have neither been injured nor benefited as a practical matter if his participation had been denied. The conferral of rights of participation upon those whose interest is remote or, in a sense, gratuitous, must represent in large part a judgment about the likelihood of a particular form of litigation taking place without such participation, and about the desirability of encouraging such litigation. It is difficult to imagine how such judgments can be made in a trans-substantive fashion. One might wish to encourage litigation in order to deter a certain kind of conduct (by structuring litigation risks and making adverse results more likely) or in order to protect a certain class of persons considered particularly vulnerable to some specified form of predatory conduct. But those judgments must be made on an individual basis for each substantive question. . . .

. . . *Mima Queen* involved a still different form for the introduction of substantive preferences. We acknowledged a trans-substantive value of reliability which was furthered by the general hearsay rule. We also acknowledged, however, the likely existence of certain litigation plights which were the inevitable consequence of an unrelaxed application of the rule. As Justice Duvall pointed out, the plight of petitioners for freedom such as Mima Queen constituted an instance of such an unenviable plight. But the issue of whether to relieve such petitioners of that problem may well and properly involve trading off the disutility of "improperly" adjudicating someone a slave because no evidence save hearsay exists as to the freedom of an ancestor against the disutility of possible incorrect adjudications of freedom on the basis of unreliable evidence. The availability-reliability tension is a common one between two process goals.

A brief summary of the positions assumed thus far may be in order. First, there is something problematic about manipulation of a procedural component to undermine the ostensible and articulated rule of law; it appears as a purposeful, result-oriented refusal to permit process to play its accustomed role of reducing uncertainty with no countervailing procedural objective to justify that refusal. Second, beyond the basic participatory rights of those immediately affected by outcomes, scope of litigation can be determined only with respect to substantive goals. Purposeful manipulation of the scope of participation to achieve substantive ends is permissible and appropriate. But there is additional force to the argument to expand remote participatory rights where the litigation plight of a potential litigant is especially vulnerable. That plight and our reaction to it may be (but need not necessarily be) related to our substantive preferences and values. Third, the consequences of uncertainty and the characteristics that certainty need attain before it is satisfactory to assess consequences are substance-related. It is in no sense offensive to my intuition that a single factor be or not be considered sufficient to support an inference even if that decision be made in a patently counter-probabilistic fashion. This intuition is simply a part of my somewhat broader sense that there are some consequences which entail a desire to be more certain about our premises than the single factor inference would warrant. Fourth, it is likewise permissible and possibly desirable to consult our substantive preferences when trading off reliability against availability of evidence. . . .

. . . It is extraordinary that our legal system holds a divided view of procedure: Our norms for minimal process, expressed in the constitutional rubric of procedural due process, are generally conceded to constitute a substance-sensitive calibrated continuum in which the nature of the process due is connected to the nature of the substantive interest to be vindicated; yet our primary set of norms for optimal procedure, the procedure available in our courts of general jurisdiction, is assumed to be largely invariant with substance. It is by no means intuitively apparent that the procedural needs of a complex antitrust action, a simple automobile negligence case, a hard-fought school integration suit, and an environmental class action to restrain the building of a pipeline are sufficiently identical to be usefully encompassed in a single set of rules which makes virtually no distinctions among such cases in terms of available process. My point is not that the Federal Rules are not workable over such a broad range. But it may be worth asking in what sense that codification works well because of its trans-substantive aspiration, and in what sense it works in spite of it. . . .

A. The Limits of Generality: Remote Participatory Rights in the Contemporary Setting

In recent years courts have had to consider a modest variety of schemes which can permit or encourage the participation of litigants whose interests are remote or who seek to represent interests not their own. . . .

The class action has constituted the most widely noted and most problematic case for construction of the Federal Rules. Commentators could hardly fail to note the variety of contexts in which the remedial clout purchased by the class action has far-reaching effects on substantive law. Some . . . have argued for a cautious approach to the application of the Rule [23] to antitrust laws because of the inhibiting effect on legitimate business activity of both the increased likelihood of private litigation and the possibility of enormous recoveries. Others have argued that the private class action should be embraced precisely because it is a form of private enforcement, which may well be more efficient and cheaper in deterring unwanted and illegal activity than public enforcement. But with the single significant exception of truth in lending cases, courts have not analyzed class action cases as presenting problematic questions of substantive law: of antitrust, securities regulation or environmental policy. Rather, they have treated the text of the trans-substantive rule as more or less controlling on the issue of its availability.

Some opponents of the class action have argued that it is precisely the characteristics noted above that make application of the rule problematic under the Rules Enabling Act, a statute which provides that the rules not "abridge, enlarge or modify" substantive rights of parties. The first section of this article leads to the conclusion that the manipulation of procedural tools to effectuate substantive objectives is by no means undesirable and often seems necessary. . . . But there is a way of reading the Enabling Act which neither renders it a dead letter, as courts have tended to do, nor construes it as a bulwark against change. Such a reading would start with the premise suggested above, that absent a trans-substantive structure of rules, courts must often justify decisions about procedure with a combination of substantive and procedural objectives and values. The Rules Enabling Act might then be read to mean that the courts, in applying the Federal Rules of Civil Procedure or any subsequently enacted similar body of rules, may not forsake their responsibility to justify substantive impact in terms of substantive values. It would not be enough to point to Rule 23; one would have to justify invoking it. . . .

. . . In imposing a limitation on the power to alter substantive rights *through* the Federal Rules, Congress was not concerned with the danger of explicit remedial creativity accompanied by substance-oriented justifications. Rather it was concerned lest the power granted to regulate procedure enlarge the power of the courts to make substantive law. So long as courts make explicit their substance-oriented justifications for procedural steps, they will place themselves in precisely the same position they occupy with respect to (nonconstitutional) questions of standing, equitable relief, or any other remedial characteristic. . . .

B. The Problem of Ad Hoc Application

The model of decisionmaking under the Federal Rules that I have suggested hardly constitutes a cure-all for our procedural ills. For in the past several years the application of the Federal Rules of Civil Procedure to federal habeas corpus actions has worked along just such a model with, at best, mixed results. Far from precluding use of tools such as interrogatories for purposes of discovery, the Supreme Court has simply turned the question into one of case-by-case determination of whether the needs of effective adjudication of the particular issue warrant the use of such a tool. In Harris v. Nelson,[51] the Court stated:

> We conclude that, in appropriate circumstances, a district court, confronted by a petition for habeas corpus which establishes a prima facie case for relief, may use or authorize the use of suitable discovery procedures, including interrogatories, reasonably fashioned to elicit facts necessary to help the court to "dispose of the matter as law and justice require."

Most important for our purposes is the Court's reasoning concerning the *source* of authority for discovery, such as it may be, in habeas corpus:

> Clearly, in these circumstances [the absence of specific congressional guidance on methods of "securing facts"], the habeas corpus jurisdiction

51. 394 U.S. 286 (1969).

> and the duty to exercise it being present, the courts may fashion appropriate modes of procedure, by analogy to existing rules or otherwise in conformity with judicial usage. . . . Their authority is expressly confirmed in the All Writs Act, 28 U.S.C. §1651. This statute has served since its inclusion, in substance, in the original Judiciary Act as a "legislatively approved source of procedural instruments designed to achieve 'the rational ends of law.' "

Justice Harlan's dissent in *Harris,* though prompted by his satisfaction on the record that the discovery sought in the instant case was not necessary to a fair hearing, also raised in stark form the difficulty inherent in a case-by-case approach to procedure.

> If discovery procedures are developed case by case, there will at least be a very long period during which procedures will differ from district to district. . . . It is unlikely that the rules thus generated will be the best that could have been devised. . . .

In some sense Harlan has certainly been proven correct. One cannot re-invent a procedural system for every case. And the question of what is to be presumptively or generally available may be best settled by rule. But where the only or primary issues at stake are substantive, justifications in substantive terms may be necessary.

Sero v. Preiser[57] . . . is an example. In that case the Second Circuit upheld a habeas corpus class action on behalf of "more than 500" New York state prisoners who had received special four-year sentences as young adults for misdemeanors which would have entailed shorter sentences if treated as adult crimes. The places and conditions of confinement for those "young adult" (16 to 21 years old) offenders were the same as for adult offenders.

In upholding the class action the court grounded its authority in the All Writs Act and found the content of its procedural tool by analogy to Rule 23. But it went further:

> A number of other persuasive justifications enforce our conclusion that the class action was appropriately used in this case. Because many of those serving reformatory sentences are likely to be illiterate or poorly educated, and since most would not have the benefit of counsel to prepare habeas corpus petitions, it is not improbable that more than a few would otherwise never receive the relief here sought on their behalf.

This invocation of the litigation plight of young, poor prisoners is highly reminiscent of the justification for the holding in *Pleasants* and for Justice Duvall's dissent in *Mima Queen.*

Why, indeed, may the All Writs Act (or alternatively, some notion of a residual constitutional power of a court) not be read to provide the same flexibility of process for ordinary civil actions to which the

57. 506 F.2d 1115 (2d Cir. 1974).

Federal Rules apply as that provided for habeas corpus? The significance of that question may be demonstrated by contrasting *Sero* with the opinion of the Supreme Court in Eisen v. Carlisle & Jacquelin.[59] In *Eisen* the Court, eschewing constitutional grounds for its decision, ruled that actual notice must be sent to all known or readily ascertainable class members in a 23(b)(3) action, even if the cost of such notice would be so high as effectively to preclude the action being brought. The Court grounded its opinion in the language of Federal Rule 23(c)(2):

> [T]he Court shall direct to the members of the class the best notice practicable under the circumstances, including individual notice to all members who can be identified through reasonable effort.

Eisen is remarkable for its absolute silence on the issue of the impact that this ruling would have on substantive issues of antitrust and securities law enforcement. Instead of considering a vague term, "practicable," as an invitation to inject substantive preferences, the Court treats the Rules notice provision as a clear legislative command which is binding and susceptible to only one resolution. I must stress that my criticism of *Eisen* does not go to the result. It may be eminently reasonable (though I doubt it) to refrain from the use of such a procedural device in terms of antitrust policy. But it seems absurd to refrain from a remedy which *may* make sense in substantive terms because of lack of individualized notice to persons who cannot conceivably be harmed thereby as a practical matter. In *Eisen* both economic considerations and the statute of limitations made it a virtual certainty that no individual actions would conceivably be brought if the class action failed. Thus a class member would lose no viable litigation opportunity even if notice failed to reach him, while the defendants' securing of a res judicata bar would constitute no better barrier to subsequent law suits than that afforded by cost barriers to individual suits and the statute of limitations.

If the All Writs Act may serve as a repository of power to create the process needed by a particular case or substantive interest, *absent* a rule or body of rules, why could it not serve equally to provide a basis for modification of rules where they do exist? Such a scheme would neither destroy the Federal Rules of Civil Procedure nor violate some notion of separation of powers. Indeed, just as *Sero* and *Harris* have hardly shaken the normal presumption that habeas corpus petitioners' actions will have no recourse to discovery or class actions, so an application of the All Writs creative power to modify the Federal Rules in extraordinary circumstances such as *Eisen* would not alter the presumptive applicability of the Rules as they stand. As to separation of powers, I have already argued that the most problematic

59. Eisen v. Carlisle & Jacquelin, 417 U.S. 156 (1974).

character of the Federal Rules of Civil Procedure under the Rules Enabling Act emerges from letting the mere fact of a rule's existence control the promotion (or lack thereof) of substantive values. The use of the All Writs Act to implement substantive values is simply a device for avoiding such a bind.

NOTES AND COMMENTS

A "trans-substantive" code of procedure could reflect a conception that procedure is a kind of transparent medium for the display of the substantive considerations implicated in litigation. On this view adjudicative procedures would be neutral as between substantive positions. Cover partly rejects this conception. He believes that procedure should sometimes be "manipulated" to serve substantive ends. But he also believes that there are some values that "resist substantive-oriented manipulation." Is there any way of distinguishing between justified and unjustified manipulations, that is not just a function of substantive preferences?

*Two Models of the Civil Process**

Kenneth E. Scott

. . . [W]hat is the purpose of imposing civil liability on a person, and how should the rules governing civil actions be shaped toward achieving that end?

I

A. The Conflict Resolution Model

One possible view of the civil process is a Conflict Resolution Model that sees civil process primarily as a method of achieving peaceful settlement of private disputes. If *A* has acted in a way that injures or threatens to injure *B*, *B*'s resort to force in order to forestall the injury or obtain redress is undesirable, if for no other reason, because violence has a tendency to escalate and to injure innocent bystanders in the process. So in the interests of preserving the peace,

* *Source:* 27 Stan. L. Rev. 937, 937-945 (1975).

society offers through the courts a mechanism for the impartial judgment of personal grievances, as an alternative to retaliation or forcible self-help. The services of the court system are furnished free or at nominal cost to the disputants in order to make the alternative of recourse to the courts more attractive.

This model has only weak implications for the precise content of the legal rules whereby judgment is rendered. To facilitate acceptance of the outcome and resort to the process, the rules should be seen as "fair" in terms of prevailing community values, but notions of what is fair may vary a great deal from one era or society to another. Such variations are of only secondary importance; it is more important for society that the dispute be settled peaceably than that it be settled in any particular way. Indeed, in such applications of the model as arbitration or grievance proceedings, the award may stand by itself, without any opinion undertaking to explain the outcome in terms of rules at all.

The Conflict Resolution Model quite naturally leads to emphasis, first, on the extent to which the plaintiff has been harmed, for that is correlated with the possibility that he may resort to means of redress leading to violence, and second, on compensating him if he is determined to be in the right. Conversely, if his grievance is less intense, concern with giving him a judicial remedy is much less; if he is content to grumble and let it pass, society feels no threat. Hence this model is strongly inclined to let sleeping dogs lie. It does not welcome anyone stirring up trouble or "fomenting litigation," and it takes a dim view of officious intermeddlers. Seeking out persons who are unaware that they have a cause of action or unlikely to litigate a claim or pursue any other remedy, and persuading them to file suit, burdens the courts with matters beyond their proper function and wastes the judicial subsidy on trivia. Champerty and maintenance are genuine abuses of their position by members of the bar, who should be forced to look elsewhere for their subsistence.

B. *The Behavior Modification Model*

A Behavior Modification Model, on the other hand, sees the courts and civil process as a way of altering behavior by imposing costs on a person. Not the resolution of the immediate dispute but its effect on the future conduct of others is the heart of the matter. Consistency and predictability of outcome, therefore, assume an importance that they do not possess in the Conflict Resolution Model.

The implications of the Behavior Modification Model are at their most powerful if coupled with a view of the substantive rules of civil liability as designed to contribute to economic efficiency. If a person negligently injures another, the law of torts requires him to pay for the damages he has caused; if he breaches his agreement, contract law requires him to make whole the person who has relied on it. As a result he is led to take appropriate precautions to avoid injury and to make appropriate judgments about honoring agreements; and consequently, the social loss from such conduct is minimized.[2] The imposition of legal liability is, in economists' jargon, a way of making a person "internalize" or take into account the costs of his actions, thereby inducing appropriate levels of care and performance toward others. But this Essay is not principally concerned with the correctness or justification of the substantive rules of civil liability. Whatever their actual merits may be, if legal rules are seen as attempts to alter public behavior in ways that have been deemed desirable, the civil sanction contributes toward that end by depriving one who violates them of his gains or by imposing on him the costs occasioned by his violation.

The Behavior Modification Model, then, focuses on the defendant, not on the plaintiff. The fact that the cost imposed on the defendant takes the form of a payment to the plaintiff is significant only in that it affords the needed incentive for the plaintiff to bring the action and activate the machinery. The real concern is to confront the defendant (and the rest of society) with the right set of costs for different behavioral choices rather than to compensate the plaintiff for his harm or effect a wealth redistribution in the name of equity.

Nonetheless, the incentive to the plaintiff is an aspect of the model's operation that may not be ignored. In particular, the plaintiff's incentive causes difficulty in the class of situations where the costs of the defendant's conduct, while large in the aggregate, are not concentrated on a few but are widely shared in amounts that are in general fairly small. Air pollution provides familiar examples, as does the field of consumer protection. Despite subsidization of the court system (which this model would not generally call for), the private costs of litigation are still substantial. Especially in a system which does not charge the winner's attorneys' fees to the loser, few individuals will sue to recover modest amounts. And even if one person did sue, an award of merely his own damages would not impose the proper total amount of costs on the defendant.

If the Behavior Modification Model is not to prove ineffectual in cases where damages are widely spread, a way to surmount the incentive gap has to be found. The creation of an administrative

2. This assumes that social costs and the private damages to the plaintiff are the same, which is not always the case.

agency charged with the duty of enforcing the legal rules in these situations is one solution that has been tried. But a statutory instruction is not the same as an incentive for efficient enforcement, as continuing dissatisfaction with the performance of administrative agencies has led a growing number to perceive. Furthermore, agency resources are limited by the political process; in an area in which by definition the stakes for the defendants are large while the theoretical plaintiffs are numerous and only moderately concerned, it is not difficult to predict what will be the balance of pressures exerted on the political process and the agency.

Another device that has evolved to meet this need is the private representative action. In the stockholder's derivative suit or the class action, one plaintiff may sue on behalf of, and seek a judgment in the amount of aggregated damages for, the entire group. This procedure in no way changes the size of the plaintiff's individual recovery, which is still inadequate. If the device is to function effectively, therefore, the incentive must lie elsewhere, and of course in fact it does — in the recovery of sizeable fee awards by plaintiff's counsel if successful.

II

These two models, like all models, are abstractions from reality; they bring together and organize certain aspects of the civil process as it exists and of our attitudes toward it. They are not the only models which could be constructed and they do not purport to capture all of a complex world. In practice, judges and decisions may reflect a blend of both models, in varying proportions. Nonetheless, it may be enlightening to consider their separate implications for a number of actual problems and cases.

A. *Consumer Class Actions*

In its most primitive form, the class action is justified on grounds of simple judicial economy. On occasion there exist a number of cases involving common issues of law and fact and often a common defendant, for example, cases involving injuries resulting from a train wreck. Such actions might well be tried separately under either model, but if the commonality is sufficient, there is a saving of time and cost for everyone in trying them together, through joinder or through a class suit where joinder is impractical.

The kind of class action for monetary damages previously discussed, however, is in a different category; it consists of cases that could not be maintained in any other form and it therefore has nothing to do with judicial economy. Two . . . cases, Daar v. Yellow Cab Co.[5] and Eisen v. Carlisle & Jacquelin,[6] illustrate the point. In *Daar,* the plaintiff alleged that the defendant Los Angeles cab company had stepped up all of its mileage meters in order to overcharge taxicab passengers, resulting in effective rates above those established by the city public utilities commission. Plaintiff sued on behalf of the thousands of taxicab passengers overcharged during the 4-year period open under the statute of limitations. Under the Behavior Modification Model there is no question that this is a proper suit. Such a suit imposes on the defendant an amount of damages corresponding to his illegal overcharges (which plaintiff alleged could be calculated in the aggregate by applying the overcharge percentage to the trip and mileage information in defendant's records) and thereby removes the incentive to exceed legally established rates. Under the Conflict Resolution Model, on the other hand, this is a quite artificial and unnecessary suit because the loss to the great majority of individual passengers would be so trifling — a few cents on the dollar — that almost none would bother to pursue the matter for himself.

The fact that there are a large number of class members, many with trifling damages, leads to the recurring question of what disposition should be made of that portion of the judgment that remains after awarding counsels' fees. The standard answer is that, for equitable compensatory reasons, it goes to the injured class. The costs of filing a claim and proving the amount of personal damage are, of course, a great deal less than the cost of conducting the entire litigation. Therefore, one would expect a great many more class members to appear as claimants than as litigants or intervenors at an earlier stage of the action. But the claimants who turn out will not necessarily amount to the whole class, and indeed there would be no way on earth to identify every person who paid for a Los Angeles taxicab ride between 1960 and 1964.

In a case like *Daar,* what follows from the fact that the total damages can be estimated and collected from the defendant without ever knowing or receiving claims from all of the persons injured, and perhaps without ever exhausting the recovery? Under the Behavior Modification Model, nothing follows — the primary objective of imposing the appropriate amount of liability on the rule-breaker has been achieved, there was a sufficient incentive for the plaintiff's attorney to bring the suit, and any surplus remaining after payment of readily identifiable claims might as well go to any designated worthy

5. 67 Cal. 2d 695, 433 P.2d 732, 63 Cal. Rptr. 724 (1967).
6. 479 F.2d 1005 (2d Cir. 1973), *vacated and remanded,* 417 U.S. 156 (1974).

cause.[8] But under the Conflict Resolution Model, an unidentifiable class and a surplus recovery after claims constitute major embarrassments: why was the suit brought in the first place, if not to redress grievances that were not only identifiable but also large enough to be potentially troublesome? The answer is, of course, to enrich the attorney, which according to conventional wisdom is ethically shocking.

The choice in *Daar* was clear, and so was the decision. The California Supreme Court in a unanimous opinion held that there can be an ascertainable class, bound by the judgment, even though it is not possible to identify all of its individual members. And the court was evidently less troubled by the possibility of an unclaimed recovery than by the prospect that, "absent a class suit, defendant will retain the benefits from its alleged wrongs."

But while California appears to have opted for the Behavior Modification Model in its approach to class actions, the federal courts seem to be moving in the other direction. In *Eisen* the plaintiff sued the two New York Stock Exchange member firms which executed all orders for less than 100 shares ("odd lots"), claiming that they had agreed in violation of the antitrust laws to fix the commission or "differential" which they charged for this service. The class consisted of all those who had bought or sold odd lots on the New York Stock Exchange over a 4-year period from 1962 to 1966; its size was estimated at approximately 6 million people, of whom only about 2¼ million could be identified by name.

Essentially, *Eisen* was like *Daar* — a suit to recover illegal overcharges collected in small amounts from a large group. While many in the group could never be identified or expected to come forward to obtain a small rebate, since the treble damages to which the average class member would be entitled were estimated to $3.90, it was alleged that the aggregate damages could be calculated from the volume of transactions shown by defendants' records and might amount to as much as $120 million.[12] If there were a surplus in the judgment ultimately collected over attorneys' fees awarded and claims actually filed, the district court indicated that it would follow a "fluid recovery"

8. The State of California, as amicus curiae, suggested itself. 67 Cal. 2d at 715 n.15, 433 P.2d at 746 n.15, 63 Cal. Rptr. at 738 n.15. When the case was settled, however, the entire amount of $1.4 million (less $200,000 in attorneys' fees) was used to lower taxi rates in Los Angeles for a period of 8 years.

12. . . . Whether treble damages are appropriate depends upon the probability of successful detection and suit for this type of violation. Where the existence of an infraction of the legal rule and the identity of the violator will almost always be known to the injured party, as in a breach of contract, imposing actual damages is a reasonably correct deterrent. But where the violation goes undetected much of the time, as in a secret price-fixing agreement, the penalty when caught would have to be correspondingly increased to achieve the same expected value of the deterrent.

approach in which the surplus would be used until consumed to reduce the current odd-lot commission, thereby benefiting odd-lot traders in general as the nearest practical approximation for the injured class.

But the attitude of the United States Court of Appeals for the Second Circuit was very different from that of the California Supreme Court. To quote from Judge Medina's opinion:

> [S]tatements about "disgorging" sums of money for which a defendant may be liable, or the "prophylactic" effect of making the wrongdoer suffer the pains of retribution and generally about providing a remedy for the ills of mankind, do little to solve specific legal problems. The result of this approach is almost always confusion of thought and irrational, emotional and unsound decisions. In cases involving claims of money damages all litigation presumes a desire on the part of the judicial establishment to make the wrongdoer pay for the wrongs he has committed, but to do this by applying settled or clearly stated principles of law, rather than by some process of divination.

Having disposed of the claims of the Behavior Modification Model as an exercise in emotionalism, the opinion went on:

> As soon as the evidence on the remand disclosed the true extent of the membership of the class and the fact that Eisen would not pay for individual notice to the members of the class who could be identified, and the evidence further disclosed that the class membership was of such diversity and was so dispersed that no notice by publication could be devised by the ingenuity of man that could reasonably be expected to notify more than a relatively small proportion of the class, a ruling should have been made forthwith dismissing the case as a class action. . . . The fact that the cost of obtaining proofs of claim by individual members of the class and processing such claims was such as to make it clear that the amounts payable to individual claimants would be so low as to be negligible also should have been enough of itself to warrant dismissal as a class action.

In other words, the only justification for a lawsuit is to compensate the injured party, and if that cannot be achieved the suit should be thrown out.

This plaintiff-compensation attitude toward the function of civil damage suits affected the way the court interpreted the requirement of Rule 23(c)(2) of the Federal Rules of Civil Procedure that the members of the class be given "the best notice practicable under the circumstances, including individual notice to all members who can be identified through reasonable effort." [16] The Second Circuit held that all members of the class who could be identified, some

16. The purpose of the notice is to enable the members of the class to protect their rights personally, if they prefer, by opting out of the class or participating in the suit directly. Under the circumstances of *Eisen*, neither would be likely.

2¼ million people, had to be sent individual mail notice at the outset of the action, at a cost of $315,000. This decision overturned the ruling of the trial judge that it would be sufficient to give individual mail notice to the larger potential claimants, such as institutions and persons with 10 or more transactions, and inform the rest of the class by a process of random selection and newspaper publication, at a total cost of $22,000.[18]

This reading of Rule 23(c)(2) subordinates the rule's general standard of what is "practicable under the circumstances" to the subsequent reference to individual notice, although as a matter of language and grammar the word "including" could easily be read as subordinating individual notice to practicality. . . .

After placing the most costly — and useless — obstacle of an individual notice requirement in the path of a very large class whose members are known, the Second Circuit also took care of the class that has many unidentifiable members. In a sweeping pronouncement it stated: "We hold the 'fluid recovery' concept and practice to be illegal, inadmissable as a solution of the manageability problems of class actions and wholly improper. . . .

The Supreme Court opinion in *Eisen* did not display the extreme hostility toward the consumer class action that marked Judge Medina's opinion, and it did not reach the issue of whether the fluid-recovery approach may be used to render a class action manageable. It did, however, uphold the Second Circuit on the crucial individual-notice requirement, founding its position on the "unambiguous requirement of Rule 23," which, as noted, is unambiguous only if the word "practicable" is ignored. The Supreme Court also held that the notification cost must be borne by the plaintiff rather than allocated between plaintiff and defendant as the district court had done.

Viewed in terms of the Behavior Modification Model, the Supreme Court, by its *Eisen* construction of the federal notice requirement, has increased the costs of many class actions to no purpose, and has thereby made the deterrence of socially undesired behavior through private court actions less likely and efficient. Apart from the fact that the notice cost is excessive, its imposition on the plaintiff is not itself objectionable, provided it is treated as part of counsel's risky investment in the suit and appropriately compensated in the event plaintiff succeeds.[23] But consumer class actions will not have

18. . . . The district court also held a mini-hearing on the merits and then allocated the notification cost between defendants (90 percent) and plaintiff (10 percent), an innovation that both the Second Circuit and the Supreme Court held was unauthorized.

23. The Court's opinion notes that a plaintiff with only $70 at stake would not pay even the more reasonable notice cost of $22,000, which is correct but continues to indulge the fiction that such actions are maintained by plaintiff rather than by counsel. . . .

been completely crippled so long as the Supreme Court does not adopt the Second Circuit's position that fluid-recovery techniques may not be employed.

NOTES AND COMMENTS

Scott maintains that "[t]he implications of the Behavior Modification Model are at their most powerful if coupled with a view of the substantive rules of civil liability as designed to contribute to economic efficiency." If procedure is to be guided by substantive rules of liability, why isn't the model equally powerful when the substantive policy is not "economic efficiency" but instead is redistribution of wealth, maintaining the status quo, or something else?

Chapter 2

The Institution of a Jury Trial

Right To A Jury Trial In Civil Actions *

Fleming James, Jr.

I. The Constitutional Right To Jury Trial

The federal Constitution guarantees the right to jury trial in civil actions in federal courts, and nearly every state constitution contains a similar guaranty. While there are some differences among these provisions, they have been given an essentially uniform effect for the purpose under discussion here. They do not extend but preserve the right of jury trial as it existed in English history at some past time, either in 1791 when the seventh amendment was adopted or, in the case of the states, at the date of the first state constitution. And at such times not all civil matters were tried to a jury. Issues in actions at law were so tried, with some exceptions; issues in suits in equity were not, unless the chancellor in his discretion sent an issue to a jury for an advisory verdict.

Many new rights and remedies have, of course, been created since the adoption of the federal and state constitutions. In devising new remedies the legislature has considerable latitude to determine whether they shall carry a right to jury trial. The legislature may even abolish a common law remedy, such as the former action by a servant against his master for injuries caused by the latter's negligence, and substitute for it an entirely new system of compensation for all

* *Source:* 72 Yale L.J. 655, 655-673, 675-676, 679-691 (1963).

industrial injuries to be administered by a board or commission which will determine factual disputes without resort to either court or jury. But there are probably limits beyond which a legislature may not go. If a legislature creates a right to be redressed by an action which is analogous to a common law action (e.g., for a penalty such as treble damages, or for compensatory damages caused by wrongful death), it probably may not deprive the parties to the action of a right to jury trial, unless the new right is given against the sovereign and therefore involves a waiver of sovereign immunity. Where the legislature says nothing about how a new remedy is to be tried, the courts fit it into the nearest historical analogy to determine whether there is a right to jury trial.

One other aspect of the constitutional guaranty of jury trial should be noted. It has been uniformly construed as a right which may be waived by the parties. Statute or court rule may therefore prescribe reasonable conditions for obtaining jury trial, such as timely demand, and may provide that failure to take these steps constitutes a waiver.

The federal courts and most state courts hold that there is no constitutional barrier to legislative or judicial extension of jury trial to issues which were formerly equitable. A few state constitutions provide for an extension of jury trial beyond those issues allotted to a jury by history; few others have construed their constitutions as guaranteeing the right of *nonjury* trial of equitable issues.

A. The Historical Test

Thus, most constitutions preserve the right to jury trial upon what may be called a historical test. The question then arises whether this freezes the right absolutely as it was in England in 1791 (for example), or whether it has some elasticity so as to accommodate extensions or contractions of jury trial and, if so, what the limits of this elasticity may be. . . .

Before the adoption of the constitutions the line between law and equity (and therefore between jury and nonjury trial) was not a fixed and static one. There was a continual process of borrowing by one jurisdiction from the other; there were less frequent instances of a sloughing off of older functions. An instance of the latter may be seen from early petitions asking the Chancellor to grant ordinary legal remedies because of the corruption or political impotence of the regular courts, a branch of equity jurisdiction that withered and died in the fifteenth century.

In the course of time many matters and issues worked over into law from equity. The growth of general assumpsit, "especially that implied contract, so highly beneficial and useful, of having undertaken to account for money received to another's use," had already become in Blackstone's time a legal action "almost as universally remedial as a bill in equity." Many matters such as duress, fraud, illegality, and perhaps even payment of a specialty, which had once been cognizable only in equity, were familiar defenses to a legal action by the end of the eighteenth century.

On the other hand, chancellors came to try an ever-growing number of issues which once they had left to be tried at law. There was a time, for instance, when equity was reluctant to grant specific performance where the existence of the contract was disputed; the parties, it was thought, should settle such disputes at law. Later equity courts had no hesitation about deciding for themselves whether there was a contract. Again the notion developed that if a ground for equitable relief existed, equity would not stop with the granting of equitable relief but would (at least if plaintiff wished) decide all aspects of the controversy, and this would often include issues which were ordinarily for the law courts. Thus, if a plaintiff sought reformation of a contract for mutual mistake, the chancellor, if he found mutual mistake, would not only reform the contract but also try any remaining issues which would determine whether damages should be awarded for breach of the contract as reformed, and decree payment of the proper amount. Ordinarily, where the ground for equitable relief failed, the bill would be dismissed and the parties left to seek in the common law courts whatever legal remedies remained. But in 1786 an equity court decided not to dismiss the bill but to retain jurisdiction for the granting of legal relief where the ground for equitable relief (specific performance) failed only because of defendant's wrongful conduct after the suit was begun. This granting of substituted legal relief in equity enjoyed a limited expansion after that.

The borrowing by each jurisdiction from the other was not accompanied by an equivalent sloughing off of functions. This led to a very large overlap between law and equity. Many facts — fraud in the inducement, for instance — might have been presented and decided either at law or in equity, depending on the context in which they arose. It also meant that the rubric which precluded equitable relief when the remedy at law was adequate ceased to have any claim to universal or even general validity, although it continued to be applied in some situations. Blackstone noted that every bill in equity suggested the inadequacy of legal remedy, but continued: "But he who should from thence conclude that no case is judged of in equity where there might have been relief at law, and at the same time casts his eye on the extent and variety of the cases in our equity reports, must think the law a dead letter indeed."

This process of borrowing continued in American jurisdictions, to some extent at least, even after the constitutions were adopted. The issue of fraud in the inducement as a defense to an action on a specialty worked over into law during the nineteenth century. During the same century courts of equity came to try disputed issues of contract *vel non* (in specific performance), nuisance *vel non* (in suits to enjoin nuisances), and even, in some states, title *vel non* (in suits to enjoin trespasses). The notion of substituted legal relief in equity enjoyed, as we have seen, a limited extension during the nineteenth century. For the most part these steps were taken without any indication that the courts were aware of the constitutional problems which the steps involved. . . .

At no time in history was the line dividing equity from law altogether — or even largely — the product of a rational choice between issues which were better suited to court or to jury trial. There is little to suggest that the chancellor's initial choice of a procedure borrowed from canon law reflected a considered rejection of jury trial. Rather, the choice between law and equity frequently was made upon considerations of other factors. For when equity procedure took shape it differed from the procedure at law in several important respects. Evidence in equity was produced largely by sworn pleadings and written depositions taken upon written interrogatories, rather than by testimony taken orally and subject to oral cross-examination, all in the presence of the trier of fact. At law the parties to an action were neither competent nor compellable to testify, whereas in equity each party could offer his own sworn statements and also "probe the conscience" of his adversary by propounding written interrogatories, which had to be answered under oath. The chancellor used specific remedies which were not available to the law courts, and the chancellor could handle multiple parties and the possibility of multiple suits in a way that the law courts had not developed. The procedure of each tribunal had to be taken as a package, and each procedure had substantial limitations which the other did not share. . . .

. . . To put it colloquially, jury trial (or court trial) was often merely the tail of the dog under a system where you had to take the whole dog.

The extensions of equity jurisdiction noted above were also motivated in part by considerations having little or nothing to do with the merits or flaws of jury trial. They reflected rather the concern of equity to mitigate the hardships of the dual system. An equity suitor who was relegated to his legal remedy would always face the expense and delay of starting all over again; and he might also risk loss of his legal rights through the running of a statute of limitations or inability to obtain jurisdiction over a defendant.

In addition to these considerations, it is familiar learning that the allocation of a dispute to either law or equity was often made on the basis of considerations relevant to the long political struggle between the King and Parliament in England. These considerations had little to do with the efficient administration of justice. And while the jury occasionally became a symbol and a bone of contention in this struggle, yet here, too, many factors other than the mode of trial often dominated the allocation of subject matter.

It would be a mistake, of course, to suppose that chancellors were never concerned with the jury trial problem in taking or refusing jurisdiction. One reason often given for assuming equitable jurisdiction over an accounting was the difficulty of the case for a jury. The issue of mutual mistake in written instruments may well have been kept from juries out of fear that they might be too ready to upset, on uncritical emotional grounds, the stability which written instruments ought to represent. On the other hand, when equity courts refused to try disputed questions of legal title in suits to enjoin trespasses, the appropriateness of trying such a dispute to a jury was often stressed.

B. Modern Application of the Historical Test

Under a merged procedure, few if any of the differences between law and equity continue to have any vitality, except the question of mode of trial. No longer must an entire set of procedural incidents be taken as a package, either legal or equitable. A single court is charged with applying the whole law of the land and drawing from it whatever is appropriate to any civil action. All trials are conducted by oral examination of available witnesses in court. Parties are competent and compellable to testify upon any issue. There is no reason, apart from history, why sharply disputed issues of fact in an action seeking specific performance of a contract should not be tried to a jury if that mode of trial is thought preferable. And no other reason to keep a court from assigning a complicated building contract case for court trial if the issues are deemed to be beyond the competence of the jury.

The considerations discussed above tend to show that the historical test of jury trial right embodied in our constitutions is probably not well-adapted to the merged or united procedures of the present day. It carries too much of the deadwood of the past. A critical use of history may be an excellent guide to present problems, but a critical use takes account of changes in conditions as well as similarities. The historical constitutional test is with us, however, and probably will remain so, because men are unlikely to agree on any basic changes. If that is so, then the above considerations argue in favor of an elastic construction of the historical test by the courts in order to accommodate further shifts of the kind and along the lines of those which were continually taking place in the very period of history to which the constitutions refer. And if such shifts are to be countenanced at all, the courts should judge them on the basis of considerations which have vitality in terms of modern judicial administration and not in terms which had relevance only under the divided procedure.

The arguments for a static historical test are (1) its greater protection of the jury trial right from inroads by active courts which would restrict the right; (2) the curb it would put upon equally active courts bent on enlarging the scope of jury trials; and (3) its greater certainty. Since the value of jury trial in civil cases today is a hotly disputed issue and since both the constitutions and the codes embody a judgment that it should be neither expanded (by any general procedural system) nor contracted at all, much can be said for a static historical test.

It is submitted, nevertheless, that there should be some room for change from a pattern made nearly two centuries ago. . . .

II. The Jury Trial Problems Inherent in a United or Merged Procedure

A. *The Choice of Mode of Trial at Common Law*

The jury trial problem as we know it today is a product of the united procedure; it had no counterpart under the old system. . . . [O]nce it was conceded or determined that a case was in the proper court, the mode of trial to be had followed nearly automatically. For trial of the issues made by the pleading, a jury was all a law court had to offer. Except for a discretionary advisory jury, court trial was all that equity would afford. This simplicity was purchased, however, at the price of much hardship and waste by way of double actions to get complete relief and frequent dismissals of meritorious claims brought to the wrong forum.

Any true merger of law and equity avoids these hardships of the old system. To do so it provides that all relief, legal and equitable, may be sought in a single action; moreover, it must be sought in a single action where it arises out of a single transaction or occurrence. Thus many a civil action of today comprises more than any action could before the merger. When this aspect of merger is coupled with a constitutional guaranty of jury trial geared to the old system, and a decision not to extend the scope of jury trial, complex problems arise.

B. The Provisions for Mode of Trial in Merged Systems . . .

. . . [T]he Federal Rules of Civil Procedure . . . seek to embody the historical test. . . . [T]he architects of the united procedures took a neutralist position with respect to jury trial. Like the constitutions, they sought to preserve it where it previously existed. But they did not intend their procedural reform to extend jury trial any more than the framers of the constitutions intended the guaranty of jury trial to extend its scope.

The historical test, though widely accepted as the basis for solution, poses certain problems. Some of them are purely practical; one goes much deeper. On the practical level, it appears that history is sometimes equivocal. Moreover even where history is clear, analogies drawn from the divided procedure cannot be matched exactly with the situations that arise under a merged procedure, so that the precise application of history is hard or even impossible. . . .

The deeper difficulty with the historical test is that it tends to foreclose renewed and continuing judicial inquiry into the suitability of different types of issues for jury trial in a modern context. . . .

C. The Types of Situations in Which Jury Trial Problem Is Presented

1. CIVIL ACTIONS WHICH ARE COUNTERPARTS OF FORMER LAW ACTIONS OR EQUITY SUITS

Many suits today are, from summons to judgment, no more than the counterpart of a former action at law. The typical personal injury suit furnishes a ready example. Other suits present throughout only such facts and claims as would clearly have been cognizable in equity. A suit to foreclose a mortgage is a good illustration. In cases like these there is no greater jury problem today than there was under a divided procedure. Such right exists where it did before, and not otherwise. . . .

The problems peculiar to a united procedure are presented by that peculiar product of union, the civil action that contains more in the way of claims or defenses than any suit could have contained in the old days. The case may be one where a plaintiff injects both legal and equitable claims, or where an equitable defense or counterclaim is interposed to an action presenting only legal issues, or vice versa. And there may be combinations of these situations in a single action.

2. CIVIL ACTIONS WHERE PLAINTIFF INJECTS BOTH LEGAL AND EQUITABLE CLAIMS

a. Historical patterns

There were several different situations under the former procedure where a suitor needed both equitable and legal relief to get complete redress for his injury. There were other types of situations where the suitor had a choice of remedies. There were still others where he had only one remedy but mistakenly pursued the other. The differences among these were important because different patterns of trial and trial sequence were applied.

In one class of cases a suitor had to resort to equity first to get any relief, or to get full relief. Where an instrument to which *A* and *B* were parties did not, as it was written, support any legal claim by *A* and *A* also claimed that the writing failed by mutual mistake to embody the actual agreement of the parties, which would support *A*'s legal claim if it had been embodied in the instrument, then *A* could get nowhere in a court of law unless and until equity decreed a reformation of the instrument. This was not the kind of mistake which the common law would remedy; it would simply enforce the instrument as written. If the chancellor found mutual mistake, he would not only decree reformation but would also settle any remaining issues pertinent to *A*'s right to relief under the instrument as reformed and award relief. At least the chancellor would do all that if *A* asked him to. If the chancellor found no mutual mistake he would dismiss the bill, leaving the parties to any remedy they might have at law. In the illustration put, that would be none; but there were cases where either the equity plaintiff, *A*, or his adversary, *B*, would have some legal remedy under the instrument as written. In this type of case if *B* sued *A* at law under the instrument as written, the chancellor would enjoin the prosecution of this legal action until the question of mutual mistake had been determined.

Let us call this pattern of behavior Pattern I. In it the equitable issue would always be tried first and tried without a jury.[79] Neither of the parties had a choice about this nor did the equity court have any real discretion since a temporary injunction against prosecution of the law action would issue as a matter of course. Moreover, the equitable issue (mutual mistake) was one which law courts did not recognize. Finally, if the equitable issue was decided in favor of *A*, there would be no second suit and thus no jury trial of any issue.

79. Unless, of course, the defendant at law was unaware of the pendency of the law suit, or of his own equity, or for some other reason failed to resort to equity before judgment in the action at law. It was the issuance of injunctions in such situations that precipitated the Coke-Ellsmere struggle and finally established the ascendancy of equity.

At the opposite pole was a class of cases in which equity refused to give relief unless and until a preliminary legal issue had been determined at law by a jury, yet where equitable relief was needed for plaintiff's complete protection. Where *A* claimed that *B*'s structure encroached on *A*'s land but *B* also claimed title to the land under the structure, equity would not order the structure removed until the title dispute was settled at law. If *A* won the law action, equity would order *B* to remove the structure if it was impractical for the sheriff to remove it under a writ of execution. . . .

Let us call this pattern of behavior Pattern II. In it, equity would refuse to try the legal issue; and the legal issue would always be tried first. If the trial was won by *A*, he still would often need a second suit in equity to get complete relief. Thus there would be two trials, one to a jury, and one to a court alone on those issues which pertained to the propriety of equitable relief. Again, neither party had any choice in the matter, and the courts had no discretion.

Between these two fairly clear-cut patterns lay a host of others in many of which either kind of relief depended on the resolution of an issue which either tribunal would try (with its own mode of trial). Thus *B*'s violation of *A*'s statutory right (e.g., to a patent or copyright) might entitle *A* to an injunction, to compensatory damages, and to a penalty. The right to any relief would turn on whether *B* violated the statute. *A* might get a determination of that issue without a jury in an equity suit, seeking an injunction and perhaps compensatory damages as incidental to an injunction. Or he might get such determination in an action at law for damages or for the penalty. . . .

In another class of cases *A* also had a choice, but it was a more limited one. Breach of certain kinds of contracts (e.g., to convey land) would entitle the injured party to either specific performance (with incidental damages for delay of performance, and the like) or to damages for breach (measured on the assumption that the contract would not be performed). Here *A* could in no case get both forms of relief — he had to elect one or the other. His election would govern the mode of trial of issues, such as making of the contract, performance of conditions precedent, breach, and the like, which would be presented in a claim for either kind of relief. . . .

b. Modern patterns

The application to the current scene of Patterns I and II has not given much trouble. There is not, and should not be, in these cases any talk of the court's discretion in directing the order of trial of the issues. If any fidelity to history whatever is observed, the equitable issue will be tried first in Pattern I, the legal issue in Pattern II. . . .

In the third group of cases . . . (which is too heterogeneous to be called a pattern) there is a common issue, or set of issues, which is determinative of both forms of relief and which either law or equity would try under some circumstances. Here again pre-merger patterns of judicial behavior are helpful in determining the mode of trial of the common issue.

In cases such as patent or copyright infringement, where plaintiff is entitled to cumulate legal and equitable remedies, he had an option as to the mode of trial which excluded any option by defendant or any discretion by the court. Plaintiff exercised this option by seeking his remedies in separate suits, and bringing them in the order he chose. Today under merger, plaintiff must seek in a single suit all relief arising out of a single group of operative facts; thus the traditional manner of exercising his option is no longer available. But it would be inconsistent with the preservation of his jury right, embodied in both the constitutions and the charters of the merged procedures, to take away the substance of the option. The problem is simply one of finding a substitute method of exercising it which is consistent with the other objectives of merger. It has been suggested that this method may be the drafting of the complaint in separate counts for the legal and equitable relief. But this seems to put undue stress on form. The best solution, it is submitted, is to let plaintiff express his choice of jury trial by simply claiming it in the way provided by statute or rule. . . .

The defendant had no choice of mode of trial in the situation under discussion. The only justification for giving him any choice today would be a desire to extend, rather than merely preserve, his jury trial right. Nevertheless a federal court of appeals has held that a defendant is entitled to jury trial of the common issue in such a case; the Supreme Court has recently cited this decision, apparently with approval. Both these cases disapproved earlier decisions which left the mode of trial to the trial court's discretion, a ruling which is equally indefensible historically and could result in curtailing the plaintiff's constitutional right (as well as in extending the defendant's). . . .

3. CIVIL ACTION INVOLVING EQUITABLE DEFENSE TO A LEGAL CLAIM

a. Historical pattern

Certain matters, cognizable in equity, would defeat a legal claim but were not recognized at law and could not, therefore, be successfully pleaded in an action at law. If *A*, the obligor on a specialty, claimed that he was induced by fraud to execute it in favor of *B*, he could not interpose that fraud in *B*'s legal action on the specialty. To get relief, *A* would have to go into equity and seek cancellation of the specialty for the fraud. Equity would then enjoin the prosecution of the law suit temporarily until the question of fraud was determined. If the chancellor found fraud, he would decree cancellation of the specialty and make permanent the injunction against *B*'s prosecution of the law action. Thus there would be no jury trial of any issue. The equitable issue would be tried first and dispose of the whole case, or where there were residual legal issues (as where the instrument was reformed rather than cancelled), equity would dispose of them as incidental to the equitable relief. It will be noted that the equitable relief, though always affirmative in form (cancellation, rescission, etc.) in most cases had only the effect of defeating the law action. If, on the other hand, the chancellor found no fraud, he would dismiss the equity suit, dissolve the temporary injunction, and leave the parties to their claims and defenses in the legal action. This pattern will be recognized as being essentially a variant of Pattern I, described above.

One thing more should be noted before we leave history. Many matters which were cognizable only in equity in remote times came to be recognized as defenses by courts of law — worked over into law as we say — in the course of time. After this process had become complete, equity would typically refuse to enjoin the law action and grant relief, stating that the remedy at law was adequate. The equity plaintiff in any illustration could plead the matter as a defense in the law action.

b. Modern patterns

The prevailing pattern in merged procedures faithfully follows the historical pattern except that all steps occur in a single civil action and there is no injunction. When *B* sues *A* upon the legal claim, *A* affirmatively pleads in that action the matter that would have been the subject of a separate suit in equity before the merger. What was accomplished by the temporary injunction under the old procedure is done under the new by a simple order that the equitable issues tendered by the answer (or counterclaim) be tried to the court and tried first. Since, as we have seen, a temporary injunction would issue as a matter of course in such a situation, there should be no room for judicial discretion today in the matter of trial sequence. And if the equitable issue is determined in *A*'s favor, there is no historical basis for awarding *B* a jury trial on any residual legal issues.

4. CIVIL ACTION WHEREIN COMPLAINT PRESENTS EQUITABLE ISSUES AND COUNTERCLAIM PRESENTS LEGAL ISSUES

a. Historical patterns

Where *A*'s equitable claim against *B* had no factual connection with *B*'s legal claim against *A*, then each claim would require a separate action with its own mode of trial.[159] Where there is a factual connection between the two claims so that they present one or more common issues of fact the problem was more complicated. There were at least two situations where this might have been the case.

In one situation, the equity plaintiff *A* sought what we may call actual or substantial equitable relief such as foreclosure of a mortgage, specific performance of a contract, an injunction against conduct (other than prosecuting a law suit) or the like. In the other type, *A* sought relief which, though in personam and coercive in form, was in effect a declaration of rights which would dispose of a potential legal claim by *B* against *A* on grounds which would have been available at law to defeat *B*'s claim if *B* pursued it by legal action. In such a case *A* was a putative defendant at law, and he sought in equity simply to defeat the law action on grounds cognizable at law. Equity jurisdiction was sometimes based on the fact that *A*'s defense (or some other right or interest of *A*) might be prejudiced by delay in the commencement of *B*'s legal action — either because that action was premature or because *B* was free to delay it for tactical reasons.[160] Equity jurisdiction was sometimes based on the desire to prevent a multiplicity of legal actions.

In either type of situation described in the previous paragraph, *B* might have a legal claim against *A* arising out of the same operative facts (indeed in the second type *B* would always have such claim). In the first type of situation *B* would have a choice whether to interpose his claim in the equity suit or to save it for a separate action at law. The latter choice might entail defeat in the equity suit, but if *B* was willing to pay that price he could have jury trial of the legal issues presented by his own claim. Suppose, for example, that *A*, a contractor, sought to foreclose a mechanics' lien for the amount he claimed due for the installation of a heating plant for *B*, owner of the building. If *B* had a claim for breach of contract because of defective installation of the plant (including, perhaps, consequential damages in excess of the amount claimed by *A*), *B* could use his claim to defeat or diminish the amount for which foreclosure was sought (in which

159. Unless defendant sought to use his damage claim as a set-off against plaintiff's equitable claim, according to the principles formerly prevailing in equity. . . .

160. American Life Ins. Co. v. Stewart, 300 U.S. 203 (1937), presents a typical situation. Here a life insurance policy would become incontestable, by its terms, "two years from its date of issue," except for nonpayment of premium. The insured had died but the beneficiary was in a position to postpone her suit until after the policy had become incontestable. The insurance company, claiming fraud by the insured in the application for the policy, sued for cancellation of the policy before it became incontestable. The court cited many federal and state decisions sustaining equitable relief in similar situations. . . .

case the issues concerning *A*'s performance would be tried to the court alone). Or *B* could fail in the equity suit to controvert *A*'s performance, suffer foreclosure for the amount claimed by *A* and then sue *A* at law for damages for breach of contract. His former pleading (failure to deny *A*'s performance) would be admissible against him as an admission, but the former decree would not preclude him from taking a new position and explaining to the jury why he had done so. It would not be res judicata or collateral estoppel and it would not preclude *B* from later resort to law.

In the second situation described, where *A* sought equitable relief principally to defeat a contemplated law action by *B*, equity would sometimes enjoin the bringing or prosecution of a law action subsequently brought by *B;* sometimes it would not. This would depend upon all the circumstances and would rest to a considerable extent in the discretion of the chancellor. An example would be a suit by an insurer to cancel an insurance policy for fraud in the application, where the policy by its terms was to become incontestible on this ground after two years of its issuance, where the insured had died within the two years, and where the beneficiary would have had a longer time for bringing suit than the period of contestibility, and he had not yet brought suit. Fraud would be a defense to a legal claim brought within the contestible period, and so an issue triable to the jury. But the insurer needs protection against the possibility of delay by the beneficiary beyond that time — hence its resort to equity. Suppose now that after the equity suit was brought and still within the contestible period the beneficiary did bring his legal action. The way was then clear for the insurer to make its defense of fraud at law. But the beneficiary could still defeat this defense by withdrawing his law action (which he could do without prejudice) and bringing it again after the policy had become incontestible.

When faced with this later, but still timely, suit by the beneficiary, equity did not dismiss the insurer's suit (since there had been ground for equitable relief when it was brought). Rather, it did one of two things: it either retained the case on its docket until the insurer's defense was actually tried by jury in the law action, or it enjoined the prosecution of the law action and proceeded to try the fraud issue itself. The matter was said to rest within the jurisdiction of the trial court[165] and the Supreme Court enumerated the following factors as appropriate guides for the exercise of such discretion:

> There would be many circumstances to be weighed, as, for instance, the condition of the court calendar, whether the insurer had been precipitate or its adversaries dilatory, as well as other factors. In the

165. American Life Ins. Co. v. Stewart, 300 U.S. 203 (1937). . . .

> end, benefit and hardship would have to be set off, the one against the other, and a balance ascertained.[166]

This situation, which involves an issue which was traditionally cognizable in either law or equity, is to be sharply distinguished from what we have described above as Pattern I and its variants, wherein the threshold issue is by tradition of exclusively equitable cognizance.

b. Modern patterns

It was widely stated under the Codes that the interposition of a legal counterclaim in an equitable action constituted a waiver by defendant of any right to jury trial he might otherwise have on the issues tendered by the counterclaim. Any such rule — which pits one objective of a merged procedure (economy of litigation) against another (preservation of jury trial) — is unfortunate. And where the counterclaim is compulsory, a rule which attaches the consequence of waiver to its interposition would probably be unconstitutional. Under later provisions for merger, like those of the Federal Rules, it is clear that the filing of a counterclaim — whether permissive or compulsory — does not constitute a waiver of jury trial. . . .

If there is no waiver in this situation, the question comes down largely to one of whether the common issue is to be tried by the court or the jury. . . .

Where *A* seeks what we have called actual or substantial equitable relief, *B* can no longer preserve his legal claim for a jury by saving it out of the equity suit. The provision for compulsory counterclaim prevents that. This fact should not, however, deprive *B* of his jury right. The best solution, and the simplest, would be to let him exercise his option today by simply claiming jury trial in the way provided by statute or rule. This treatment would parallel that accorded *A* when he must join legal and equitable claims in the same complaint. . . .

5. CIVIL ACTION FOR DECLARATORY JUDGMENT . . .

Beginning with the 1920s a good many statutes were passed which provided broadly for actions seeking declaratory judgments with or without coercive relief in all types of situations, including those in which equity had given relief and those in which it had not, and including those in which plaintiff sought simply to establish his nonliability under a claim against him as well as those in which he sought some affirmative relief.

The framers of declaratory judgment acts, like the framers of merged systems of procedure, took a neutralist position toward jury

166. American Life Ins. Co. v. Stewart, *supra* n. 165, at 216.

trial, seeking neither to contract nor to expand it. The courts worked out an essentially simple test for jury trial, quite consistent with this legislative intent. Where the declaratory judgment action did not fit into one of the existing patterns for equitable relief, but was, so to speak, an inverted law suit, then the parties had a right to jury trial. Where the declaratory judgment was the counterpart of a suit in equity, there was no such right. This simple and consistent pattern has been disrupted, for the federal courts, by the decision in Beacon Theatres v. Westover.[182]

In this action Fox, operator of a movie theatre in San Bernardino, California, sued Beacon, operator of a drive-in theatre 11 miles from San Bernardino, seeking a declaration that Fox was not liable to Beacon for treble damages under the antitrust laws and an injunction *pendente lite* to prevent Beacon from suing Fox and its distributors under these acts. The controversy arose over first-run clearances. Fox alleged that it had long been operating under contracts with distributors granting it exclusive rights to show first-run pictures in the "San Bernardino competitive area"; that when Beacon built its drive-in it notified Fox that it considered these contracts to be violations of the antitrust laws and threatened treble damage suits thereunder; that these notices and threats against Fox and its distributors gave rise to "duress and coercion" which deprived Fox of its valuable property right to negotiate these contracts. Threat of irreparable harm was charged.

Beacon answered and counterclaimed for treble damages. A common issue of the complaint and counterclaim was the reasonableness of the clearances granted to Fox, which depended, in part, on the existence of competition between the two theatres. Beacon made timely demand for jury trial of all the issues. The trial court, however, viewed the complaint as essentially equitable and ordered the issues tendered by it (including the common issue) to be tried by the court before jury trial of the issues tendered by the counterclaim. . . .

The Supreme Court reversed. The holding itself is not radical. Fox may have been simply trying to circumvent Beacon's jury right by "jumping the gun" with an equitable action; the district court's exercise of discretion may have been so questionable as to border on abuse. But on the assumptions which the Court made (existence of a common issue and of grounds for equitable relief) the decision represented an *extension* of defendants' jury trial right. Traditionally this had depended (in this context) upon the chancellor's discretion; now it is made a matter of right upon issues tendered both by an equitable claim and by a legal counterclaim.

Even this departure from the historical pattern is not radical, but the grounds given for it are cloudy and ambiguous and susceptible

182. 359 U.S. 500 (1959).

of an interpretation which would go far to abolish the historical test altogether and extend jury trial over most of the former domain of equity.[189]

For one thing, the Court argues, injunction against defendant's lawsuit is not needed for plaintiff's full protection under the merged procedure; and the remedies open to plaintiff under the Federal Rules make his remedy at law adequate, thereby undercutting his need for equitable relief. This of course is true in a sense, not only here but in a fairly wide class of cases wherein the main thrust of the equity suit was to defeat a potential legal claim on grounds cognizable at law. The Court mentions "such equitable remedies as Bills of Peace, *Quia Timet* and Injunction" in this connection. Interpleader (where the grounds of the adverse claimants' claims are legal) would be another example, reformation still another. In all such cases modern systems substitute direct procedures for the cumbersome and circu-

189. Further cloudy and ambiguous reasoning is added by the Court's later opinion in Dairy Queen, Inc. v. Wood, 369 U.S. 469 (1962). Here again the actual decision is not radical, though, again, it points to something of an extension of jury trial right. The action was brought by owners of the trademark Dairy Queen against licensees of the trademark, for alleged breaches of the licensing contract by (1) failure to make the payments it called for, and by (2) continuing to use the trademark and collect money for that use after its right to do so had terminated by the first breach. The complaint sought a declaration that the contract was null and void, an accounting of profits illegally obtained since the first breach, and a permanent injunction restraining defendant from using the trademark within the area of the exclusive license and from executing sublicensing agreements to others which would thus infringe plaintiff's rights. . . . Defendants admitted the contract and claimed that there had been a novation under which there was no breach. Defendant also claimed that plaintiffs, because of violations of the antitrust laws, had come into court with unclean hands. . . .

The District Court regarded the complaint as one claiming equitable relief and struck defendant's demand for jury. . . .

Defendant, licensee, then sought mandamus to compel the district judge to vacate this order. The Court of Appeals denied this request without opinion, but the Supreme Court reversed this judgment and indicated that the writ should issue. . . .

The Court held that "insofar as the complaint requests a money judgment it presents a claim which is unquestionably legal.". . . And since "the factual issues related to the question of whether there has been a breach of contract," are presented by this legal claim as well by the claims for equitable relief "the legal claims involved in the action must be determined prior to any final court determination of respondents' equitable claims.". . .

The reasoning of the majority opinion delivered by Mr. Justice Black, purported to rest on history, but it ignored half the historical picture. Reliance was placed on two cases decided under the former procedure in which the Supreme Court had upheld the right to jury trial of the issue of debt *vel non* where unsecured contract creditors sought equitable aid in collecting their claims. Scott v. Neely, 140 U.S. 106 (1891); Cates v. Allen, 149 U.S. 451 (1893). These decisions were said to scotch the notion that legal issues may be tried without a jury because they are "incidental" to equitable issues. . . . This notion, it was suggested, was a latter-day gloss, introduced by courts which had lost their way in the merged procedure created by the federal rules.

The Court concludes from this its reaffirmation of the broad principle in *Beacon* "that where both legal and equitable issues are presented in a single case, 'only under the most imperative circumstances . . . can the right to a jury trial of legal issues be lost through prior determination of equitable claims.' ". . .

itous injunction against lawsuits.[192] But these beneficial short cuts of the blended procedures have not generally been looked on as *legal* remedies in a sense which would disrupt the historical pattern of jury trial. Rather they have been regarded as aimed at improving judicial administration *without* disturbing the previous balance between jury and nonjury trial.

Even more disturbing is the Court's treatment of the Declaratory Judgment Act as providing a *legal* remedy which "necessarily affects the scope of equity." As we have seen, the remedy provided by this Act is available in a wide variety of situations covering nearly the whole spectrum of what used to be law and equity. It would be a proper vehicle for tendering issues which have traditionally been exclusively equitable as well as issues, like those in *Beacon Theatres,* which might appear in either a legal or equitable context and were sometimes tried to a jury. A claim of mutual mistake, for an accounting between partners, for a trust accounting or for advice by a trustee, to name only a few examples, could all be presented by an action for declaratory judgment. Indeed it is hard to think of an equitable claim that might not be. To be sure, coercive relief would often be needed for complete protection, but the Court recognized this possibility also in *Beacon Theatres* and showed that it could be taken care of by a temporary injunction pending jury determination of the issues of fact and by permanent injunction thereafter, if that was needed. Presumably, then, the "legal remedy" would be inadequate only in a case where *permanent* equitable relief would be needed before a jury could determine factual issues — a rare case indeed. . . .

III. Conclusion . . .

. . . No one has explicitly suggested re-examination of the whole matter with a view to determining what issues or types of issues are best fitted for court trial or jury trial. If all were *tabula rasa,* and some solon were trying to devise an ideal system for the administration of justice, he would probably approach the jury trial problems with just such an inquiry in mind. And it may well guide the future course of those charged with amending or recasting constitutions or, within narrower compass, of legislators. But as a guide for *judicial,* as opposed to political, action in the matter any such test meets serious difficulties. For one thing the constitutions themselves, as we have seen, impose a different test (namely an historical test which was never guided, even in the making, by the consideration here suggested as ideal). Furthermore, even if the matter is left to the people acting through

192. Or, where an injunction is actually needed it may always be granted on a temporary basis until the legal claim is determined by a jury. . . .

their legislators, they lack any scientific way of telling what issues are best suited for jury or for court trial, and there is no general agreement (among judges, among politicians, within the profession, or in the community at large) about the matter or even about the underlying premises that should be assumed in making the evaluation.

NOTES AND COMMENTS

In discussing Beacon Theatres v. Westover toward the end of his article, James remarks that the grounds of the decision "are cloudy and ambiguous and susceptible of an interpretation which would go far to abolish the historical test altogether and extend jury trial over most of the former domain of equity." He refers to Dairy Queen v. Wood, which he analyzes in article n.189, in similar terms: Many observers concluded, especially after the later case of Ross v. Bernhard, 396 U.S. 531 (1970), that the Supreme Court indeed meant to extend jury trial over a great deal of at least the former domain of equity. *Beacon Theatres* would thus be subject to the criticism that it was wrong, but not that it was ambiguous.

The Chayes excerpt, *supra* Chapter 1, describes the growth of "public law litigation" as representing "the triumph of equity" and speaks of a shift in factfinding responsibility away from the jury and toward the judge. To what extent is an interpretation of the Seventh Amendment strongly favoring jury trial, as in *Beacon Theatres, Dairy Queen,* and *Ross,* compatible with public law litigation as described by Chayes? The attitude of the present Court toward the Seventh Amendment is unclear.

. . . And Then There Were None: The Diminution of the Federal Jury *

Hans Zeisel

Goneril: Hear me, my lord. What need you five-and-twenty? ten? or five?
Regan: What need one?

King Lear, Act II, Scene IV

Juries with less than twelve members, of course, are not foreign to our experience. Some state courts try small civil claims and minor

* *Source:* 38 U. Chi. L. Rev. 710, 710-712, 715-724 (1971).

criminal cases before six-member juries; four states even try noncapital felony cases before juries that have fewer than twelve members. Despite this background, experimentation with the jury was previously confined to the states. Until the present time, the federal jury appeared to be immutable.

The reasons presently given for reduction of the size of federal civil juries are to expedite jury trials and to lessen their cost. With respect to the latter, the Chief Justice has estimated that contracting the size of federal civil juries to six would result in an annual savings of four million dollars. While this may seem to be a substantial sum, it is only 2.4 percent of the total federal judicial budget, and little more than a thousandth part of one percent of the total federal budget.

With respect to minimizing delay, the smaller jury would merely decrease the time required for impaneling. Although there are no data available on the time consumed in impaneling juries, we do have accurate data indicating that federal district court judges spend eight percent of their total working time in trying civil jury cases. Estimating that impaneling the jurors takes, on the average, about ten percent of the trial time, one discovers that only eight-tenths of one percent of the federal district judges' total working time is presently consumed by impaneling civil juries. On first impression, it might seem that reducing the twelve jurors to six would save half of that impaneling time. But in many federal courts the jurors are examined primarily by the judge, who directs most of his questions to all jurors at the same time. In this situation the savings would be minimal, since it takes no more time to ask a question of twelve jurors than to ask it of six. In any event, we are discussing an amount which is less than half of the impaneling time — at best four-tenths, more likely three-tenths, of one percent of the judge's working time.

Thus, neither the amount of money nor the amount of time that would be saved can adequately explain and justify the reform recommended by the Chief Justice. However, when viewed in the broader context of the other proposals to limit the functioning of the jury, the decision of the federal district courts to adopt the six-member jury appears as a significant step toward a drastic reduction of the American jury system in general. Under these circumstances, this initial reform deserves careful scrutiny on its own merits. . . .

History . . . might have embodied more wisdom than the Court would allow. It might be more than an accident that after centuries of trial and error the size of the jury at common law came to be fixed at twelve. A primary function of the jury was to represent the community as broadly as possible; yet at the same time, it had to remain a group of manageable size. Twelve might have been, and might still be, the upper limit beyond which the difficulty of self-management becomes insuperable under the burdensome condition of a trial. On this view, twelve would be the number that optimizes the jury's two conflicting goals — to represent the community and to remain manageable. . . .

II. Six-Member Civil Juries in a Stratified Community

The jury system is predicated on the insight that people see and evaluate things differently. It is one function of the jury to bring these divergent perceptions and evaluations to the trial process. If all people weighed trial evidence in the same manner, a jury of one would be as good as a jury of twelve because there would never be any disagreement among them. In fact, we know the opposite to be true, if not from observation of our community then from the performance of our juries. Two-thirds of all juries find their vote split in the first ballot in a criminal case.[34] We have no comparable data on the liability vote of the civil jury, but we do know that the evaluation of damages usually covers a broad range.

There is, therefore, good reason to believe that the jury, to some extent, brings into the courtroom the differences in perception which exist in the community. To see how the six-member jury performs this function in comparison with a twelve-member jury, it will be useful to begin with a simple model of a stratified society. We shall assume that 90 percent of the community share identical viewpoints and that the remaining 10 percent have a different viewpoint. Even a jury of twelve, of course, is too small to represent all community views, but it can be shown that the smaller the size of the jury, the less frequently it even approaches community representation.

Juries, especially federal juries, are chosen by lottery from the pool of available jurors. Suppose, now, we were to draw 100 twelve-member juries and 100 six-member juries from a population that had a 10 percent minority. Of the 100 twelve-member juries, approximately 72 would have at least one representative of that minority; while of the 100 six-member juries, only 47 would have one. It is clear, then, that however limited a twelve-member jury is in representing the full spectrum of the community, the six-member jury is even more limited, and not by a "negligible" margin.

Whether this difference in degree of community representation results in a difference in civil verdicts is, of course, even more important. To explore this question we will slightly complicate our stratification model of the community. We know from experience and from many careful studies that the values different people place on the

34. H. Kalven, Jr. & H. Zeisel, The American Jury 487 (1966).

TABLE [2-1]
Community Evaluation of Personal Injury Claim

	Fraction of community	*Dollar evaluation*
	1/6	1,000
	1/6	2,000
	1/6	3,000
	1/6	4,000
	1/6	5,000
	1/6	6,000
Average	1/1	3,500

harm done in a personal injury case are likely to diverge considerably. Table [2-1] assumes that with respect to the evaluation of a particular claim the community is divided into six groups of equal size. We shall make a further assumption, very close to reality, that whatever the composition of the jury, the damages it awards will lie around the average of the evaluations of all individual jurors. Again, we shall simulate 100 random selections of the two types of juries — the twelve-member and the six-member jury. This time, however, we shall be interested in the average of the individual evaluations of all members of any given jury. Thus, we shall record a twelve-member jury consisting of 6 persons who would evaluate an injury at $1,000, and 6 who would evaluate the same injury at $2,000, as $1,500 — the average of 6 × $1,000 + 6 × $2,000. Table [2-2] indicates the relative spread of these averages around the middle value for all juries of $3,500.

It is easy to see that the six-member juries show a considerably wider variation of "verdicts" than the twelve-member juries. For instance, 68.4 percent of the twelve-member jury evaluations fall between $3,000 and $4,000, while only 51.4 percent of the six-member jury evaluations fall in this range. Almost 16 percent of the six-member juries will reach verdicts that will fall into the extreme levels of more than $4,500 or less than $2,500, as against only a little over 4 percent of the twelve-member juries. The appropriate statistical measure of this variation is the so-called standard deviation.[37] The actual distribution pattern will always depend on the kind of stratification that is relevant in a particular case, but whatever the circumstances, the six-member jury will always have a standard deviation that is greater by about 42 percent. This is the result of a more general principle that is by now well known to readers of such statistics as public

37. The standard deviation is the square root of all squared deviations from the group average.

TABLE [2-2]
Percent Distribution of the Average Evaluation by 100 Randomly Selected Juries

Interval	*Twelve-member*	*Six-member*
$1,000-1,499	—	0.1
$1,500-1,999	0.1	1.4
$2,000-2,499	2.0	6.4
$2,500-2,999	13.7	16.4
$3,000-3,499	34.2	25.7
$3,500-3,999	34.2	25.7
$4,000-4,499	13.7	16.4
$4,500-4,999	2.0	6.4
$5,000-5,499	0.1	1.4
$5,500-6,000	—	0.1
Totals	100.0	100.0

opinion polls — namely, that the size of any sample is inversely related to its margin of error.[38]

Lest it be thought that standard deviation is merely part of a statistician's game that has no counterpart in reality, it will be useful to provide the appropriate translation of the term into lawyer's language. It is the measure of the gamble the lawyer takes when he goes to trial. The "gambling" notion is seldom made explicit because normally each case is tried only once, but lawyers are quite conscious of the degree to which jury verdicts may vary. To obtain a measure of this variability, trial lawyers were asked to think about their next civil case and to estimate how they would expect ten different juries to decide.[39] These estimates show, as a rule, a considerable amount

38. A reduction of the size of a sample by ½ increases the margin of error by the square root of 2 / 1, or simply of 2 — that is, by a factor of 1.42, or by 42 percent.

39. Data collected by the University of Chicago Jury Project, on file at the University of Chicago Law School. The following is an excerpt from the questionnaire and a sample answer:

> Which, in your estimate, will be the most likely award in this case after trial?
>
> $25,000
>
> Of course, you cannot be certain that this will be the verdict. If you had to try this case ten different times before ten different juries, you would expect some variation in the verdicts. What do you think these verdicts would look like?

$ 0	$ 20,000	$ 25,000	$ 25,000
$ 35,000	$ 35,000	$ 50,000	$100,000
$100,000	$100,000		

Another way of providing an estimate of the variability of jury verdicts would be to allow properly selected extra-juries — for instance by observation of closed-circuit television screens — to try the same case after simulated deliberations.

of variation, which should not come as a surprise since a case goes to the jury on the very ground that reasonable men may differ in its resolution. Whatever the extent of the "gamble" incurred through the twelve-member jury, we must expect that it will be significantly greater with a six-member jury.[40]. . .

In addition to the tendency to be less representative and to produce more varied damage verdicts, the six-member jury is likely to yield fewer examples of that treasured, paradoxical phenomenon — the hung jury.[42] Hung juries almost always arise from situations in which there were originally several dissenters. Even if only one holds out, his having once been the member of a group is essential in sustaining him against the majority's efforts to make the verdict unanimous. Fewer hung juries can be expected in six-member juries for two reasons: first, as discussed earlier, there will be fewer holders of minority positions on the jury; second, if a dissenter appears, he is more likely to be the only one on the jury. Lacking any associate to support his position, he is more likely to abandon it.

. . . [As stated in] The American Jury [*supra* at n.34]:

> Nevertheless, for one or two jurors to hold out to the end, it would appear necessary that they had companionship at the beginning of the deliberations. The juror psychology recalls a famous series of experiments by the psychologist Asch and others which showed that in an ambiguous situation a member of a group will doubt and finally disbelieve his own correct observation if all other members of the group claim that he must have been mistaken. To maintain his original position, not only before others but even before himself, it is necessary for him to have at least one ally.

The distinction is crucial in this respect: If it is only the *proportion* that matters, then one versus five is the equivalent of two versus ten; but if the original companionship of an ally is essential, then one versus five is far less likely to produce a hung jury than two versus ten. As stated previously, the probability of having at least one member of a minority (which comprises 10 percent of the population) on the twelve-member jury is 72 out of every 100, as against 47 on six-member juries. The discrepancy is aggravated by the fact that the expectation of having *more than one* minority member on

40. The juries in our model have not undergone voir dire challenges which, when conducted by competent counsel, would tend to eliminate the extreme value positions. Nevertheless, it is fair to assume that such challenges would affect both types of juries equally and consequently would not eliminate the differences between them.

42. The hung jury is treasured because it represents the legal system's respect for the minority viewpoint that is held strongly enough to thwart the will of the majority. The paradox lies in the fact that the hung jury is only tolerable in moderation; too many hung juries would impede the effective functioning of the courts.

the twelve-member jury is 34 out of every 100, as against only 11 on six-member juries. . . .

III. Criminal Six-Member Juries and Majority Verdicts

Neither the reduction of the size of the criminal jury nor the adoption of majority verdicts are presently being considered by the federal courts. Yet it is not premature to explore the consequences that would accompany these two changes. . . .

With respect to the abandonment of the unanimity rule, there is again considerable experience in the state courts. Many states allow majority verdicts in civil trials before both twelve- and six-member juries; some states permit such verdicts in minor criminal trials, and two states allow majority verdicts even in felony trials for noncapital offenses. The important element to observe is that the abandonment of the unanimity rule is but another way of reducing the size of the jury. But it is reduction with a vengeance, for a majority verdict requirement is far more effective in nullifying the potency of minority viewpoints than is the outright reduction of a jury to a size equivalent to the majority that is allowed to agree on a verdict. Minority viewpoints fare better on a jury of ten that must be unanimous than on a jury of twelve where ten members must agree on a verdict.

An example will elucidate this proposition. Suppose we again assume a minority position held by 10 percent of the population, and that two sets of juries are drawn: 100 twelve-member juries and 100 ten-member juries. In Table [2-3] are the frequencies with which the minority view can be expected to be represented.

Looking first at the 100 twelve-member juries, we expect to find 38 juries with one minority representative, 23 with two, and 11 with three or more. If these twelve-member juries must be unanimous to reach a verdict, the majority will have to reckon with at least one minority member in 38 + 23 + 11 = 72 out of the 100 cases. If these juries are permitted to reach a verdict by agreement of ten jurors, then the majority will be able simply to disregard the minority position in 38 + 23 = 61 of the 72 cases. Only in the 11 cases in which we must expect three or more minority jurors will they be able to influence the verdict.

Let us now turn to the ten-member juries. Here only 39 + 19 + 7 = 65 of the 100 juries are expected to have at least one minority member. But if we assume that the ten-member jury must be unanimous, then the ten-member jury will give the 10 percent minority a chance to influence the verdict almost six times as frequently (65:11) as in the case of the twelve-member jury with majority rule. . . .

TABLE [2-3]
Expected Number of Minority Jurors*
on 100 Randomly Selected Juries

Number	*Twelve-member*	*Ten-member*
None	28	35
One	38	39
Two	23	19
Three or more	11	7
Totals	100	100

* Representing 10 percent of the population.

IV. Conclusion

We have shown that the change in verdicts that might be expected from the reduction of the twelve-member jury to six members is by no means negligible. We have also considered another potential modification of the federal jury, the majority verdict, and the possible combined application of both. However, the thrust of this article must not be misread. Its purpose is not to advocate any of the possible forms of federal juries. It pleads neither for the twelve-member jury nor for the smaller one, neither for the unanimity requirement nor for the majority verdict. All these solutions are possible, as is shown by the variety of rules adopted by our states. The legal systems of most countries do not have any jury trials; to be sure, their mode of selecting judges differs radically from ours.

The purpose of this article, rather, is simply to make clear that all these modifications make for differences in adjudication that appear to be negligible only to superficial scrutiny. Both in the short and in the long run our judicial system has many options, but every solution has its own balance sheet of advantages and costs. What is necessary is that we, and with us the United States Supreme Court, see both with equal clarity.

NOTES AND COMMENTS

It is often thought that a jury should meet at least two criteria: It should be impartial, and it should be drawn from a cross-section of the community. At the same time it is accepted that each jury does not have to be representative of the community.

Zeisel's criticism goes to the second of these two points. He shows that constituting juries of less than twelve persons has the consequences that minority viewpoints are less likely to be represented on any particular jury, and that when minority viewpoints do appear they are likely to have fewer representatives than on juries of twelve. Why is this important? If the jury is impartial, what difference does it make whether it is representative of the community? Or do "impartial" and "representative" refer to the same thing: a jury is regarded as impartial *because* it is representative?

It could be argued that the jury's job is to find the truth and that the "truth" is simply the consensus of the community with regard to a particular matter. But even on this view it is still not clear why there is a separate requirement that the jury be impartial or why no particular jury needs to be representative. It is now unconstitutional deliberately to exclude from juries, for example, blacks or women, as was done over much of the country until recently. It is said that juries that include blacks or women may decide cases differently than juries that are all-white or male. This may seem very plausible. But if so, don't the same questions apply — that is, why a requirement that each jury be impartial but no requirement that any particular jury be representative?

Which of the following standards should govern? (1) That no group should be deliberately excluded from jury service; (2) that deliberate efforts should be made to insure that groups historically excluded from jury service be represented over a series of juries in proportion to their numbers in the community; (3) that jury panels be selected from the community by technically random methods.

Directions for Directed Verdicts: A Compass for Federal Courts *

Edward H. Cooper

Directed verdicts, and their hang-fire cousins judgments notwithstanding the verdict,[1] are among the most fundamental tools used

* *Source:* 55 Minn. L. Rev. 903, 903-911, 916-934, 937, 941-944, 946-948, 955, 957-962 (1971)

1. Since the standards for entering judgment notwithstanding the verdict are the same as the standards for directing a verdict, the discussion throughout will refer only to directed verdicts. Appellate courts are increasingly insisting on the advantages of obtaining an actual verdict, . . . so in practice it is likely that more and more of the rulings actually will occur in the form of grant or denial of judgment notwithstanding the verdict. The primary advantages of allowing the jury to return its own verdict are that the jury may very well reach the result the judge thinks is

by judges to control juries. Exercise of this control in an individual case inherently involves a large measure of careful judgment, tailoring general principles of deference to jury freedom to the unique facts before the court. . . . [T]he appropriate exercise of judicial control . . . properly depends heavily on the nature of the factual uncertainties and legal rules involved in all the evidence in specific cases: general statements of deference to the jury cloak widely different degrees of deference according to the perceived consequences of possible jury error. . . .

I. Generalities of Purpose and History

A. The Basic Problem

Juries are admittedly, even vauntedly, tyros at the task of adjudication. And the adjudicatory task set for them is one of immense intellectual challenge. The central difficulty of recreating historic data — of "finding" facts which often have never been known and which cannot be known with certainty at the time of decision — requires a literally unattainable combination of experience, intuition, understanding and luck, no matter who is trying the case. Jurors additionally are charged with the burden of comprehending instructions on the law, often involving concepts which boggle the minds of students, confuse experienced practitioners, and narrowly divide the opinions of outstanding judges. Application of uncertainly com-

---

required, thereby sparing the need to make what may be a difficult determination of the appropriateness of a directed verdict, and that, if the trial judge should chance to be wrong in his determination that the case is appropriate for judicial disposition, the results of the first trial can be salvaged if it is otherwise free from reversible error.

Direction before the jury has a chance to return a verdict, however, has advantages which ensure its continued employment. The more obvious advantages lie in the direction of "efficiency" — the directed verdict obviates the need for argument, instructions, and what may be lengthy jury deliberation. Some cases may call so clearly for a directed verdict that these advantages easily outweigh the potential advantages of judgment notwithstanding the verdict; at the extreme are cases disposed of by directed verdict on the basis of opening statements of counsel at trial. . . . An advantage more difficult to evaluate is that direction before the jury has had an opportunity to deliberate changes the nature of the confrontation between judge and jury. Although the directed verdict is a clear exercise of a control which might have been avoided by awaiting rendition of the verdict, there is an offsetting uncertainty whether the control has functioned so as to do anything more than expedite a result which any jury would inevitably reach anyway. Judgments notwithstanding the verdict, on the other hand, place the fact of control in stark relief — the jury's actual verdict has been superceded by an exercise of judicial power. Long-run acceptability of our combined judge-jury system of adjudication may well be best served by retaining, and using, both options.

prehended law to imperfectly induced or deduced fact is a final chore of no mean demands. The jury, moreover, must perform these separate duties so as to produce a unanimous result. Difficult as the task is, a verdict ordinarily is produced, and ordinarily it is effective to terminate the lawsuit. The merciful obscurity of the verdict commonly alleviates the embarrassment which might result from any detailed knowledge of a jury's chosen means of discharging its duties. Many cases remain, however, in which either the prospect of a particular verdict or its actual rendition is in itself enough to impugn the jury's performance. Directed verdicts are the basic means for controlling jury performance in such cases.[4] This control is exercised, as it must be, by the only other public participants in the litigation — the judges, trial and appellate.

The contemporary problem of directed verdicts is the problem of developing and enforcing the standards limiting this power of judicial control. Since judges are experts in adjudication by training and experience, at least as compared to jurors, it might be urged that the limits on their power of control should be wide. The extreme reach of such power, short of simply abolishing any effective jury function, would allow a judge to dictate the result whenever he prefers one outcome of the suit to another. This extreme has never been approached in formal statement and probably has seldom been realized in actual application. Indeed, judges instead have veered a zigzag pattern, at times approaching rather close to the opposite extreme, at which the jury is denied the right to dispose of a case only when there is literally nothing to support the position of one party.

Such strict limits on the judicial power to control jury verdicts have been developed in large measure because of the preferred position assigned to the jury by Constitution and tradition. The preservation of jury trial by the seventh amendment[5] includes the basic division of functions ascribing the task of factfinding to the jury and the task of lawgiving to the judges. The immediate result of this division is that judges have assumed a very narrow role in limiting

4. The same function could conceivably be discharged solely by exercise of the power to grant repeated new trials until some jury should return a verdict in agreement with the views of the judge. The obvious unfairness of such a procedure to the parties, and the heavy burden an unseemly parade of successive trials would impose on the institution of jury trial, have persuaded virtually everyone that the power to grant new trials is not alone sufficient to the needs of jury control.

5. "In Suits at common law, where the value in controversy shall exceed twenty dollars, the right of trial by jury shall be preserved, and no fact tried by a jury, shall be otherwise reexamined in any Court of the United States, than according to the rules of the common law." U.S. Const. amend. VII.

jury factfinding, acting to control the jury only when a factual determination opposed to that made by the judge is, in some varying and uncertain sense, very probably wrong.

Factfinding freedom, further, has had the additional consequence of carrying with it a largely unintended, but unavoidably high, degree of jury freedom with respect to following and applying the law. This consequence has followed because no one has been able to devise a system for limiting the jury to its primary factfinding chore. In most cases, the variety of factual issues and the number of possible combinations of findings make it impossible even for judge and litigants to frame adequately detailed, alternative specific findings, much less ask the jury to generate such findings on its own. Simple examination of a respectable set of findings of fact prepared by a judge trying a case without a jury, and reflection on the number of implicitly rejected alternative findings, should demonstrate the complexity of the task involved. Even if such findings could somehow be prepared with adequate completeness in the heat of litigation, asking jurors to reach unanimous acceptance of such findings, instead of simple concurrence in the general justice of a general verdict, or a partly degeneralized special verdict, could impose unwise loads on the system. Since the jury's findings of fact thus cannot be adequately communicated to the judge, the alternative has been accepted that the judge must communicate his learning in the law to the jury. Without any system to check on the jury's understanding of the judge's instructions, or on their application of the instructions to the unknown facts they have found, the result is that for all practical purposes the jury has a large degree of freedom to misunderstand, misapply or wilfully ignore the law.

The vital justification for the institution of directed verdicts is found in the need to provide at least some minimal device for preserving the integrity of the legal rules given by the judges. (It need hardly be added that very often the legal rules transmitted by the judges have their ultimate source in legislative, rather than judicial, rulemaking.) At some point, undefinable in the abstract, it must become clear that a particular jury verdict would represent not a finding of facts which justify that result in terms of the legal rules authoritatively prescribed for the jury but a failure, for whatever reason, to apply the legal rules to the facts as they "must have been" found. . . .

One of the major shortcomings of the directed verdict as a device for preserving the integrity of legal rules is that it depends upon the preliminary determination that the jury "must" find the facts in a certain way; whenever it cannot be said, within the accepted limits of judicial reticence, that the jury *could* not find facts sufficient to warrant invocation of a particular legal rule, the jury is given its factfinding, law-applying chore without any means of determining whether it has so found the facts or has instead worked an intentional or unintentional change in the law. Under current approaches, directed verdicts simply cannot be used to ensure rigid obedience to the law by jurors. Matters are complicated further, moreover, by the fact that, despite the bromide that judges decide the law, juries have an avowed function in generating little "one-case" rules of law in many areas — refining the standard of reasonable care is simply the most common example — and often are urged to have as well a clandestine function of improving the law as given by the judges to keep it more in tune with current community values. Even if directed verdicts could be used to ensure rigid obedience to the law, in short, courts would not always wish to use them so. . . .

B. History

1. JURY AS JUDGES OF FACT

"Preservation" of the right of jury trial has been taken to mean that the measure of the right should be sought in the practices of the common law courts at the time of adoption of the seventh amendment in 1791.[8] . . . The basic historic difficulty posed by directed verdict practices is that there had not emerged, by 1791, either the detail or more than the approximate substance of a parallel method of judicial control. . . .

2. METHODS OF CONTROL

. . . [T]here did exist in 1791 a practice of "directing" juries as to the verdict which should be returned. Although it is not entirely clear, apparently the direction was simply a particularly clear way of combining instructions on the law with advice on the facts — the jury was told, in effect, that the court was of the view that, on the facts shown at trial as combined with the law, one party or the other was entitled to recover. While the jury was apparently thought to be under a duty to obey the instruction, the remedy for disobedience was a new trial. . . .

New trials were given not only as a sanction for failure to follow the court's directions, but more importantly, also on the ground that

8. See, e.g., Dimick v. Schiedt, 293 U.S. 474, 476 (1935).

the verdict was against the evidence at trial. While this device was well established by 1791, its differences from the directed verdict are so apparent as to need no further elaboration.

The third primary method of control in well-established use in 1791 was the demurrer to the evidence. . . . The consequence of demurring to the evidence was to deprive the demurring party of any chance to have the case considered by the jury; by demurring, he admitted the truth of his opponent's case, and all that his opponent's proof reasonably tended to prove, and posed the question of law whether upon the facts as thus admitted his opponent was entitled to recover. The admission was binding — the answer to the question of law was the end of the case. Under modern practice, of course, denial of a motion for directed verdict does not end matters but simply paves the way for a jury determination. The jury remains perfectly free to find facts quite different from those the court is obliged to assume in passing on the motion. . . .

4. EFFECTIVE DIRECTED VERDICT PROCEDURE

The Supreme Court resolved the problem raised by the lack of precise common law precedent for the modern directed verdict procedure in the masterful, if slightly slippery, opinion in Galloway v. United States.[36] The primary basis for the decision is found in the Court's statement of the proper method of applying the seventh amendment preservation of jury trial. . . . [T]he Court ruled that the vital aspect of jury trial is that the jury be allowed to perform the factfinding part of adjudication. Procedural reforms designed to facilitate the jury's factfinding function, or to improve it, are not invalidated by the fact that they may limit the jury's freedom or desire to find the facts arbitrarily or ignorantly, or to disregard the law. Common law precedent for preventing jury consideration of an issue which lacks adequate evidential support exists in the demurrer to the evidence. Directed verdicts simply continue this function without the penalty that the movant must sacrifice the right to a jury determination of the facts in his favor if the judge is unable to say that the jury must so find them. . . .

Constitutional permission of directed verdicts simply sets the stage for the major inquiry. Everyone knows that the Constitution allows directed verdicts, even if no one can quite say why; no one knows any articulable standards defining the constitutional limits of such judicial control. Statements of the appropriate standards have

36. 319 U.S. 372 (1943).

varied widely over the course of the past century or so. Practice in applying the standards varies as widely at the present time. . . .

5. GENERAL STANDARDS

a. In Statement . . .

The original method of statement, as might be expected, was that as the directed verdict was a means of accomplishing essentially the same result as the demurrer to the evidence, its availability should be "tested by the same rules." However nicely this may seem to respond to the historic orientation of the right to jury trial, it really answers very little because of the obscurity of the tests used on the demurrer. . . .

Closely associated with this reference of standards to the demurrer to the evidence is the common supposition that nineteenth century courts followed a "scintilla" rule which required a case to be submitted to the jury if there was any evidence whatever to support the position of the party opposing the motion for directed verdict. There is no question that most courts soon abandoned any such rule in favor of a broader, if variously phrased standard based upon the inquiry whether there was evidence "upon which a jury can *properly* proceed to find a verdict for the party producing it." This in turn soon yielded to frequent statements that a verdict might appropriately be directed whenever the trial court would be obliged to set aside a contrary verdict as against the weight of the evidence.

Statements today remain as varied, even among federal appellate courts, as they have been over the course of history. . . .

The most common current approach is often dubbed the "substantial evidence" test and is stated in terms close to those recently employed by the Fifth Circuit: directed verdict motions should be denied "if there is substantial evidence opposed to the motions, that is, evidence of such quality and weight that reasonable and fair-minded men in the exercise of impartial judgment might reach different conclusions." [59] A concise statement of the attitude taken in approaching this question may be borrowed from an opinion of the Fourth Circuit, requiring that

> the evidence must be considered in the light most favorable to the party against whom the directed verdict or the judgment n.o.v. is asked, . . . any conflict in evidence must be resolved in his favor and . . . every conclusion or inference that can be legitimately drawn therefrom in his behalf must be drawn.[60]

59. Boeing Co. v. Shipman, 411 F.2d 365, 374-375 (5th Cir. 1969) (en banc). . . .
60. McClure v. Price, 300 F.2d 538, 543 (4th Cir. 1962).

In essence, this approach represents an attempt to limit the jury to its factfinding function by inquiring what is "reasonable." Traditional respect for the jury and its constitutional benison requires that it be allowed to find whatever facts are reasonably suggested by the evidence. The impossibility of defining reasonableness requires that the scope of freedom be left large. But at some point the possibility that twelve jurors may find the facts "unreasonably," and the much greater probability that twelve jurors can misunderstand or happily ignore the law, permits and requires judicial control. The general statements ordinarily adopted by the courts are simply a way of stating that the fundamental tenet of control must be one of minimum interference.

b. Procrustean or Multifarious Standards?

The fundamental dilemma of judicial control in its application is that of reconciling the principle of minimum interference with the obdurate need for some measure of control. . . . But there are broader difficulties as well, including the crucial uncertainty whether the same degree of minimum interference is uniformly appropriate regardless of the nature of the case, or whether judges should feel freer to interfere in some cases than in others. . . .

Among the reasons for favoring jury trial, one of the most troublesome in terms of directed verdict standards is the desire to have the jury effect some improvement in the law, at least for particular cases, notwithstanding rejection of a general policy of jury lawgiving freedom. . . . [I]n many cases, the directed verdict standard appropriately includes an allowance for reasonable jury lawmaking as well as reasonable jury factfinding.

. . . It should be obvious that however difficult it may be to reach any abstract definition of the appropriate jury contribution, it may vary enormously from case to case. Jurors are thought to have so much to contribute to the evaluation of many kinds of behavior that they are accorded avowed lawmaking functions in determining what is "reasonable" in the light of common experience in an enormous variety of common transactions. Jurors probably have very little indeed to contribute to an evaluation of the "obviousness" of a patented improvement in computer circuitry.

A third major function of the jury lies in improving the acceptability of adjudication. . . . This function may be particularly important in the not inconsiderable number of cases which are not really capable of rational decision — a jury can terminate the case with a blessedly oracular verdict which requires no embarrassing explanations.

Various other roles are occasionally assigned to the jury. One is that of protecting litigants against venal or simply incompetent judges. Another is that jury service is a valuable means of educating citizens; yet another is that the jury is the most commonly available means of participating in the workings of democratic government.

Taking these various jury functions as a springboard, it should be possible to restate a variety of considerations which counsel that no attempt should be made to find in the seventh amendment a rigid prescription of a single standard of judicial deference applicable to all jury-tried cases alike.

First is the fact that history, formally recognized as the primary measure of the seventh amendment right, simply does not provide any meaningful guidance in measuring the sufficiency of a case for jury determination. Second, and closely related, is the simple fact that it would be impossible to implement a uniform standard in a uniform manner, no matter how it were stated. Courts historically have been unable to fashion a uniform standard; courts today are equally helpless. Third, there are a great many other devices of jury control which could be used to shape the result desired by the judge, often with considerable effect. Rulings on the admissibility of evidence, comments on the evidence, the way instructions are framed, the judge's own mien and behavior during trial and a host of other tools are available to influence the jury. There is little effective appellate control over a broad range of trial court behavior in these areas. Forcing adoption of a single directed verdict standard might force trial judges to wield their other controls with more vigor, perhaps leading in some cases to results which would not be accepted under proper standards as a directed verdict but which are accepted as the verdict of the jury, even though the jury was artificially forced along a path which would not otherwise have been followed. Finally, apart from such negative reasons, there are excellent reasons for supposing that the nature of the jury's sound contribution varies enormously across the spectrum of cases triable as of right to a jury. . . .

One of the currently popular areas focusing interest on the question of uniform standards involves litigation under the Federal Employers Liability Act. Supreme Court opinions dealing with the sufficiency of an injured worker's case for jury consideration have opened a wide vista of jury speculation, both in the area of fact and in the area of legal evaluation of the facts found. Many circuit courts of appeal have announced that the directed verdict standards found in FELA cases are unique and do not control other cases. . . . FELA cases involve special reasons for allowing juries a wide discretion in fact inference and in law application. The principle of compensation without fault for industrial accidents is widely accepted;

the antiquated reliance on principles of negligence in the FELA is tolerated only because the negligence principle has been so far attenuated in its application by judges and juries alike (and perhaps because jury awards are more attractive in the eyes of injured workmen or their unions and lawyers than scheduled benefits). The consequence of a mistaken denial of recovery for the injured plaintiff is disaster; the consequence of a verdict imposing liability after dispensing with any real requirement of negligence is that one more easily anticipated cost is added to the many costs of railroading. Although it sometimes may seem that railroads are less than ideally situated for absorbing or redistributing extra costs, there can be no question that they are far better situated than their injured workmen. That the seventh amendment is appropriately applied to preserve this area for jury justice does not mean that it is appropriately applied to require allowing an equivalent scope of jury freedom in areas where it may be more capricious or arbitrary.

II. Specifics of Credibility, Inference, and Application

A. Introduction

General statement of a principle of minimum interference with jury functions is scant help in addressing a concrete problem. Although in the end there is no magic formula for disposing of a real, living case, there are various general problems which at least admit of further analysis. The most convenient framework for approaching these problems breaks them down into three main areas following a model of rational disposition of adversary litigation conducted along our traditional lines. First, the trier must determine what testimony he believes. Second, taking the testimonial facts so established, it is frequently necessary to go beyond them in the half-logical, half-intuitive process of "inferring" other facts which have not been the subject of direct testimony. Finally, once all of the facts have been puzzled out in one way or the other, it is necessary to plug those facts into the applicable legal rules or standards to determine the outcome of the case. Discussion will largely focus on these three steps as if they were separate stages. But it is obvious that they are not separate, even in theory. Tentative belief in a testimonial fact, for instance, may ultimately be rejected because it is thought inconsistent with the inferences drawn from other testimonial facts or even because the inferences it suggests by itself are thought unreasonable. Likewise, the strength of the belief in any particular testimonial proposition will influence the nature of the consequences drawn from it — a fact strongly believed may often carry much further than one believed only as the least unlikely in an array of improbable alternatives. Likewise, the requirements of the legal rules will shape the direction of the inference processes and may even have some justifiable impact on the determination of facts, direct or inferential.

Beyond this theoretical interdependence of the steps suggested, it is clear that jury decisional processes seldom follow any such model. Determination of a case is apt to be considerably more direct and simple. Nonetheless, the model is of considerable aid in approaching directed verdict problems because it forces attention into the paths necessary to implement the principle of minimum intrusion in as reasoned a manner as possible. . . .

B. *Credibility*

The right to determine the credibility of witnesses lies at the core of the jury's factfinding function. If there is a conflict in direct testimony, it is clear that the jury must be allowed to determine which witnesses to believe, even if it chooses to believe a single witness of dubious credentials in preference to twenty witnesses of unassailed integrity. . . .

1. UNCONTRADICTED, UNIMPEACHED, UNINTERESTED TESTIMONY

It is important in setting the framework for a discussion of the jury's role with respect to the credibility of uncontradicted, unimpeached, uninterested testimony to be certain that the case is one in which there is no implied contradiction to be found in the circumstances surrounding the matter of direct testimony. All of the discussion of this issue will assume that there is no such contradiction. As a model of such a case, there may be assumed a collision between two cars. Each car was driven by a lone driver; neither driver survived the crash. Examination of the remains of the cars has indicated no hint of mechanical malfunction in either. The debris left by the impact was scattered in such a way that no one claims that the location of the point of impact can be inferred from it. One witness, a highway patrolman, testifies to the event. He testifies that he had followed the car driven by the defendant's decedent for a distance of two miles along a straight highway under ideal driving conditions, that the car was being driven at a very high rate of speed and that it had twice veered from one side of the road to the other. This car had been on its own side of the road for approximately a mile before the moment of the accident; immediately before the collision, however, it swerved directly into the oncoming lane of traffic and collided with the car driven by the plaintiff's decedent.

Several courts have said that a jury should be allowed to disbelieve the sole witness. Many more have made it clear that the jury must accept his testimony. It is submitted that the majority rule is correct, for a wide variety of reasons which, because they are essentially negative, may be appreciated most easily after examining the contrary arguments.

Two major arguments can be advanced in support of the minority rule that the jury should be allowed to determine the credibility of *all* direct testimony. The first is that much direct testimony, no matter how sincerely believed, is simply wrong. In a single apt phrase, "the testimony of any witness describes the combination of himself and the event.". . . One simple possibility, for instance, is that the patrolman in the example case saw the accident as he did only because he had anticipated it when he saw the approaching car.

The inability of human observers to record, retain and relate perfectly given the best of will is subject to the further difficulty that human will may itself add further distortions, either through outright lying or through a more or less unconscious process of discarding and supplementing memories until they have been accommodated to the presently desirable contours. . . .

The second major argument advanced in support of allowing jury freedom to reject uncontradicted, unimpeached testimony of an uninterested witness is that the jury should be able to rely on the demeanor of the witness. In the jargon of the social sciences, "there is frequently posited a relationship between the manner of a witness' verbal, gesticulative, facial, and gross postural behavior and the conclusions . . . [the] jury . . . draws from his testimony." Presumably such demeanor "evidence" is logically relevant in two different ways — first as a basis for determining whether the witness is consciously trying to depart from the truth, and second as an index of his probable ability to know and tell the truth.

. . . Is a jury, then, likely to make fewer mistakes if it is allowed free rein to reject uncontradicted testimony which is not at odds with any known facts, and which is given by an uninterested witness who has not been impeached in any way, than if it is required to accept such testimony? Several considerations suggest that more, not fewer, mistakes would result. . . .

. . . [W]hat the psychologists have found so far is that, as compared to persons making judgments based on recordings or transcripts of the same testimony, persons making judgments on the basis of observation of the "witnesses" form significantly *less* accurate judgments. In short, the much-despised cold record of appellate review actually may be the least distorted of all possible bases for judgment. . . .

In short, there are many reasons for hesitating to put much confidence in the ability of juries to discover the truth by discerning evaluation of witness demeanor. The jury's main factfinding advantages lie in the contribution of a variety of everyday experience in the world; ordinary experience seems to offer little help in the adjudicatory task of assessing credibility. . . .

2. INTERESTED TESTIMONY

. . . No one would champion a rule which requires belief of anything an interested witness might say.

Beginning from this point, the initial problem to be faced in differentiating the rules to be applied to interested testimony lies in determining when a witness should be considered to be interested. It might be held that all willing witnesses are interested, simply because they identify with the side which has trusted them by offering their testimony. Presumably such a level of interest is too low to be taken into account. Likewise, the general interest any witness has in maintaining his own sense of integrity and consistency by repeating in court testimony he has previously given should not be enough to warrant departure from the rules which apply to disinterested witnesses. Although little more should be required, it remains difficult to know where to suggest a line. It would be possible to urge that any shared community of interest, even on a very general and abstract plane, should be enough; social, economic, political, ethnic, sexual, and other "classes" could be constructed, for instance, which would frequently separate the litigants from each other and assign the crucial witness to some class in common with the party favored by his testimony. The possibility of bias and the resulting distortions of testimony cannot be denied. Nonetheless, "interest" at such levels of abstraction would often involve too low a level of danger to justify altering the permissible scope of jury freedom. There may remain situations of such intense group consciousness that they should be taken to place a witness in the interested category. Similarly, more particular forms of involvement between a witness and a party or issue involved in the actual case should readily be found to invoke the rules applied to interested witnesses. Simple friendship, for instance, involves sufficient pressures to warrant such treatment. . . . Unhappily, the only general guide that can be offered is that the courts are seeking to enforce the general directed verdict approach of attempting to discover what a reasonable jury might reasonably do in circumstances where no more definite rule can be laid down. . . .

. . . As a first approximation, indeed, it may be accepted that in all situations where it would be easy for the opposing party to offer at least some contradictory evidence if the interested testimony were untrue, the interested testimony should be accepted if no such showing is attempted.

Beyond the cases of failure to adduce easily available evidence lie cases of strong circumstantial corroboration. In one compelling case, Mexican sellers of sisal testified that they would not have sold to the bankrupt purchasing firm if they had realized it had acquired the name of the firm they had formerly dealt with. Corroboration was found in the fact that under Mexican law it would have been illegal to sell to the bankrupt if the facts had been known. . . .

3. CIRCUMSTANTIAL CONTRADICTION

Directly contradictory testimony almost always raises a jury question. Circumstantial contradiction can likewise make it clear that the credibility of testimony which is not directly contradicted should be left to the jury, even though it is otherwise unimpeached and emanates from a disinterested witness. Inferences from the circumstances established by the testimony of others, or of the witness himself, may conflict either with the direct testimony or with inferences which can be drawn from it. Probably all courts would today accept the proposition that such conflict is sufficient to make the credibility of the direct testimony a jury question at some point far short of rendering the testimony inherently improbable. So too the one-time notion that circumstantial evidence is not sufficient to raise a jury question when there is contradictory direct testimony seems properly abandoned, at least in the federal courts. . . .

4. COROLLARIES AND MISCELLANY

a. Directing for Proponent

In large part, the permissibility of directing a verdict for a party bearing the burden of persuasion is controlled by the rules just canvassed. To the extent that the case is made out by oral testimony which the jury is not at liberty to disbelieve, a verdict may be directed. . . .

Questions of appropriate inferences and law application are apt to be involved in a proponent's motion as well, particularly where a directed verdict is sought on a major issue such as liability. Because of this admixture, it is common to find in the cases the statement that a verdict may be directed for the party having the burden of persuasion only when the evidence is "overwhelming.". . .

b. Evidence Considered

. . . The court must, at a minimum, consider all of the evidence favorable to the party opposing the motion which the jury may believe, and must in addition consider all of the unfavorable evidence which the jury must believe. . . .

C. *Inference*

Terse statements . . . of the jury's function may be found in the observations that courts simply lack the ability to say whether two or more reasonable inferences are equal, or that the very fact that inferences seem equal to a judge is strong evidence that other reasonable men might rationally regard one as more probable than the other. A more elaborate statement of the justification would focus on the reasons for deference to the jury. The process of inference, after all, is one which must depend not only on the matters in evidence but also on application to the evidence of general knowledge of life at loose and in the large. Much of the value of the jury is thought to lie precisely in bringing such general knowledge to bear on problems with a collective earthy wisdom which a single, often cloistered judge cannot command. . . .

. . . It should be apparent, even without example, that very little can be said in the abstract about the best method for determining the strength of the inferential possibilities, or probabilities, suggested by the evidence in a particular case. . . . Decision must rest on an evaluation of the degree of uncertainty, the gains from correct decision, and the losses from mistaken decision. Much of this evaluation, however, is at least formally provided for judge or jury by legal rules for resolving uncertainty, cast in the form of rules as to the burdens of production and persuasion. If the standard of proof embodied in the "preponderance of the evidence" requirement applied to most issues is equated, as it often is, with any probability greater than fifty percent, there is an implied judgment about the relative losses resulting from a mistaken verdict for the proponent of the issue (here identified, for simplicity, as the plaintiff) and from a mistaken verdict for the defendant. The judgment, simply, is that a mistaken denial of recovery to a deserving plaintiff is just as costly as a mistaken imposition of liability on an innocent defendant. . . .

On the plane of description of actual decisional processes, one of the obvious failings of the determinations implicit in the model just sketched is that it builds on the premise inherent in most legal rules that a choice must be made between only two possible decisions — a "yes" decision in which a determination of liability is accompanied by an effort to award a full measure of damages or other relief, or a "no" decision in which a determination of no liability results in a denial of any relief whatever. Judges as well as juries, however, often resolve uncertainty in a quite different way, compromising between a full "yes" or "no" answer by rendering a judgment for partial relief corresponding to an inability to reconcile an uncertain evaluation of the "facts" with an absolute decision either way. The bets of justice can be hedged just as other bets. It may very well be argued that this sort of decision making often represents an optimal adjustment to uncertainty, superior to the flat choice required by a legal theory which superstitiously chooses to ignore the fact that legal administration is incapable of discovering absolute truth. . . .

A more fundamental practical difficulty with the "more probable than not" approach to the resolution of indecision is that it suggests the possibility of a precision which is simply unattainable. It may very well be more helpful to juries to tell them to decide by a balance of the probabilities than by a preponderance of the evidence; it seems wildly unlikely that the calculus of jury decision can ever lead to a determination that the probability of liability is 0.50, or 0.51. Instead, instructions on the burden of proof are designed to assist the jury in reaching a conclusion where they feel that their uncertainty is too high to justify a resolution of the controversy submitted to them. This assistance is in part simply a caution that care should be taken and in part a reassurance that there is an acceptable general rule for disposing of cases where reason fails. It is not an assistance which can narrow the frequently broad range of uncertainty within which a jury may justifiably find itself unable to reach a unanimous decision either way. Even more clearly, it is not an assistance which amounts to an effective control of the actual level of probability a jury will require as a predicate for a finding of liability. . . .

. . . Acceptance of the equal probability basis for decision rests, as noted, on the assumption that the loss resulting from a mistaken decision for the party bearing the burden is equal to the loss resulting from a mistaken decision for the other party. This assumption is unsound. There is no reason to suppose that the importance of the respective losses is equal, and little reason to suppose that courts are incapable of developing rules on some other basis. . . .

. . . Stated most baldly, the proposition is that in some circumstances a plaintiff should be allowed to recover on a showing amounting to less than a preponderance of the evidence because a mistaken denial of recovery is so disastrous that its possibility overwhelms the stronger probability that the decision is mistakenly imposing liability on the defendant. The converse proposition may be true as well, of course; because it is implicit in the decisions imposing a standard of proof higher than a simple preponderance of the evidence, there is less need of justification, but it should be noted that the same phenomenon may occur when the burden of proof is the ordinary one. . . .

The first illustration . . . may be borrowed from a real case. The plaintiff, an employee in an automobile service center, was badly injured by the explosion of a tubeless tire he was mounting on a wheel rim. Evidence is available that between 75 and 80 percent of the tires sold at the center are manufactured by the defendant. If there is no other evidence that the tire involved in this particular incident was manufactured by the defendant, should the case be allowed to go to the jury? The court said it should not. Very often this approach may be justified on the ground that it should be possible for the parties to find something beyond the bare statistic, and they should be encouraged to do so. But suppose there really is nothing more to be done — the plaintiff can show that he was unconscious after the accident and that diligent attempts to identify the tire made since the accident have failed. If there is a temptation to allow that case to go to the jury, is the temptation as strong if the plaintiff can show only that he was hit by a taxicab and that the defendant owns four of the five taxicabs licensed to operate in the town where the accident occurred? Whatever the reaction to these possibilities, what of the case where the defendant manufactured only 45 percent of the tires?

One range of uncertainty, in short, is that concerning the identity of the actor involved in the transaction affecting the plaintiff. The hazards of mistaken identification are so great, resulting in the imposition of liability on a defendant who had no connection whatever with the incident involved, that courts are very reluctant indeed to allow jury resolution of uncertainty even when there is a very persuasive showing that the plaintiff's requested resolution is indeed more probable than not.

A second range of uncertainty may involve the question whether an identified actor has done anything which the law recognizes as the basis for imposing liability. It might be shown, for instance, that the defendant manufactured all of the tires sold at the service center; that with all due diligence nothing could be found out about the reason for the explosion of this particular tire, because the carcass has disappeared; and that on the 100 occasions on which tires of this model, made by this defendant, have exploded, 55 of the explosions resulted from a defect in the tire and 45 resulted from carelessness of the person mounting the tire. Most courts would be uncomfortable about allowing such a case to go to a jury. . . .

Further down the scale of importance come cases in which there is a clearly sufficient showing as to the identity of the actor and a similar showing as to liability-incurring conduct, but uncertainty as to the causal connection between the conduct and the injury. In one newly famous case, a claimant sought workmen's compensation benefits on the ground that her husband's death from cancer was caused by his fall from an ice cream truck. This claim was supported by expert testimony which the court accepted as establishing a "mathematical likelihood that the employee's death was causally related to his accident." Nonetheless, it was found insufficient. Whether or not most courts would agree with this particular example, it illustrates a category of uncertainty whose mistaken resolution most would agree is less serious than the categories just examined.

One final category may be offered. Assessment of damages, given a sufficient showing of the identity of the defendant, his wrongful conduct and its causal connection with the plaintiff's claimed injury, is an area in which courts allow jury determination on the basis of very slender showings. In part this approach is a result of necessity; once the possibility of periodically reviewed serial awards is rejected, for instance, measurement of future damages must often depend on such probability calculations as life expectancy. In part, however, this approach results from a quite explicit determination by the courts that once the fact of liability is established it is better to err on the side of mistaken overcompensation than on the side of mistaken undercompensation.

The perhaps incomplete ranking of uncertainties just offered is one way of testing the proposition that courts should allow jury resolution of greater or smaller levels of uncertainty according to the nature of the consequences resulting from a mistaken decision. Another way of testing the proposition may be found in examining a few cases for examples of other policies, attached to particular areas of the law, which may likewise affect the desirable degree of jury freedom to speculate. . . .

. . . As a single example, there may be offered a case in which an insured changed the beneficiary on his life insurance policy from his former wife to his paramour. There was ample showing that the insured was in a state of psychosis and alcoholism leaving him susceptible to the exertion of undue influence and that the new beneficiary had excellent opportunity to exert it. Nonetheless, the court ruled that, absent any direct showing of attempted influence, it was erroneous to submit the issue to the jury. It would be difficult to say that only an unreasonable jury could infer the exercise of undue influence; the justification for the ruling seems to lie rather in the importance of stability in such matters and in the danger of jury prejudice in choosing between paramour and one-time wife.

Inferential freedom may likewise be narrowed because of the

involvement of judicially favored or disfavored rights. The strong current favor for free expression, for instance, has led to an obvious narrowing of the scope of permissible inference in determining whether there has been a showing of the "actual malice" required to support a defamation action brought by a public figure. Judicial disfavor of the defense of contributory negligence, on the other hand, seems the only acceptable justification for a recent decision refusing to allow a jury to infer, on the basis of a showing that the deceased driver's blood-alcohol content was such that he would not be in any condition to drive, that the passengers in the car were guilty of contributory negligence in riding with him.

The foregoing examples have been offered in an attempt to demonstrate that directed verdict standards are properly framed to allow or deny jury disposition of inferential uncertainties on the basis of criteria other than the reasonableness of a determination that the legally required findings are more probable than not. . . . Judges may nonetheless do well to continue to bury these considerations under a blanket of just such generalities. Reticence may be justified in part because litigation continues to serve a witch-doctor function, and it would lose much of its perhaps dwindling acceptability if it were frankly confessed that ordinarily courts cannot really know what happened once upon a time and are prepared to act in states of ignorance which vary according to individual circumstances. . . .

D. *Law Application*

It was urged above that the need to ensure proper application of the law provides the primary justification for the institution of judicial control through directed verdicts. Paradoxically, one of the justifications for limiting the scope of judicial control is found in the importance of the jury's contributions in applying or even modifying the law.

Much of the jury's contribution to law application needs no explication. The law of negligence has long been accepted as the outstanding illustration of an area in which courts are unable to formulate detailed rules in advance but must instead rely on a general standard. Application of this general standard involves generation of a unique rule, good only for the particular case in which it is generated. Juries, with their supposed broad fund of common knowledge of the ways of hypothetical reasonably prudent people, are given a broad freedom to develop this particular one-case rule with the hope that they may do a better job than the judges can do. Directed verdict practice is shaped accordingly.

In civil cases, this sense of the importance of the jury's contribution is apt to run deepest in tort litigation, where there is often a close affinity to parallel criminal prohibitions and a significantly lower level of danger to predictability and stability. Directed verdict practices doubtless do reflect such notions, in spasmodic and uncertain fashion, by encompassing some allowance for jury tempering of the law.

The factors involved in admitting this sort of flexibility into the law application process frequently may overlap the factors explored in the parallel area of inference freedom. More leeway may be given if the plaintiff is badly injured and in great need, if the defendant enjoys a capacity for spreading losses which the law does not take into account, and so on. But there are crucial differences between jury freedom in applying the law, when such freedom is not built into the legal rules themselves, and jury freedom in drawing factual inferences.

. . . However [it is] difficult to announce that the permissible degree of jury freedom depends in part on the extent to which the court is concerned with preserving the integrity of the particular legal rules involved, whether initially created by judges or legislatures. . . .

. . . Jury ignorance and prejudice are left free to run rampant when it becomes a question of allowing jurors to disregard legal rules whose foundation they can understand only dimly, if at all. Justice by plebiscite can be an unredeemably ugly monster. . . .

Finally, jury departure from the law must remain a spasmodic and uncertain thing. Some juries will, presumably, loyally adhere to the court's instructions to follow the law pronounced by the court. The result may at times accord with the strength of the individualized factors making it just to depart from the general law; it may often degenerate into a capriciously different treatment of cases which should be treated alike. On a longer range view, moreover, the possibility of relying on jury justice may operate to retard the emergence of desirable new legal doctrines which judges would be forced to adopt if they were not free to throw responsibility for achieving justice over to the jury.

NOTES AND COMMENTS

Cooper suggests, especially in discussing FELA cases, that directed verdict practice may vary from one sort of case to another. In some types of cases, the latitude given the jury may be such that judges allow juries in effect to modify the substantive law that formally remains in place. This could occur where juries systematically resolve factual conflicts or apply general standards such as the negligence test, so as to produce a certain outcome. For example, juries might award compensation for injured plaintiffs in negligence cases regardless of defendant's degree of fault — and judges might tacitly collaborate with them by denying motions for directed verdicts where such motions could justifiably be granted.

Compare these situations with another kind of case. Very broadly speaking, federal law forbids discriminating in the sale or rental of housing on grounds of race. There is a right to a jury trial in cases claiming such discrimination. If a judge believes that the same racial prejudice the statute was enacted to combat is influencing jury verdicts against plaintiffs, how should he deal with a plaintiff's motion for directed verdict? A motion for new trial?

Should procedural law aim for a kind of transparence or neutrality that avoids unacknowledged substantive change? If it does aim to transform substantive outcomes, should it openly acknowledge that aim?

Chapter 3

Discovery and the Adversary Process

The Adversary Character of Civil Discovery: A Critique and Proposals for Change *

Wayne D. Brazil

The thesis I explore is that the adversary character of civil discovery, with substantial reinforcement from the economic structure of our legal system, promotes practices that systematically impede the attainment of the principal purposes for which discovery was designed. The adversary structure of the discovery machinery creates significant functional difficulties for, and imposes costly economic burdens on, our system of dispute resolution. Because these difficulties and burdens are an inevitable consequence of adversary relationships and competitive economic pressures, they cannot be removed by the kind of limited, nonstructural discovery reforms that have been made in the past and are once again under consideration. To come to terms with these problems will require an assault on their sources; effective reform consequently must include institutional changes that will curtail substantially the impact of adversary forces in the pretrial stage of litigation. . . .

The purposes that modern civil discovery is designed to accomplish are crucial to a system of dispute resolution committed to justice. In its seminal opinion about the scope of discovery, the United States

* *Source:* 31 Vand. L. Rev. 1295, 1295-1299, 1303-1304, 1311-1326, 1328-1331 (1978).

Supreme Court declared that "[m]utual knowledge of *all* the relevant facts gathered by both parties is essential to proper litigation."[8] Discovery is designed to serve as the principal mechanism by which such "[m]utual knowledge of all the relevant facts" will be achieved.[9] . . .

Minimal reflection reveals a fundamental antagonism between the goal of truth through disclosure and the protective and competitive impulses that are at the center of the traditional adversary system of dispute resolution. While drafters and early proponents of the rules of discovery were not oblivious to that antagonism, they seem to have assumed that the rules themselves would reduce the size of the litigation arena in which adversary instincts and tactics would predominate. They apparently believed the discovery machinery would reduce the role of adversary pressures and tactics in the pretrial process of gathering relevant evidentiary data. . . .

Instead of reducing the sway of adversary forces in litigation and confining them to the trial stage, discovery has greatly expanded the arenas in which those forces can operate. It also has provided attorneys with new weapons, devices, and incentives for the adversary gamesmanship that discovery was designed to curtail. Rather than discourage "the sporting or game theory of justice," discovery has expanded both the scope and the complexity of the sport. Modern discovery also has removed most of the decisive plays from the scrutiny of the court. Because so many civil cases are settled before trial and because the conduct of attorneys is subject only to fitful and superficial judicial review during the discovery stage, much of the decisive gamesmanship of modern litigation takes place in private settings. . . .

V. Discovery's Psychological and Institutional Environment

. . . Attorneys in litigation have five primary objectives: (1) to win; (2) to make money; (3) to avoid being sued for malpractice; (4) to earn the admiration of the professional community; and (5) to develop self-esteem for the quality of their performances. These objectives are not born simply of cynicism and selfishness. They are institutionalized commands that emanate from a system of combat within a competitive economic structure. It is not difficult to perceive that these goals make the purposes of discovery for individual litigators quite different from the purposes which the architects of the discovery system contemplated.

8. Hickman v. Taylor, 329 U.S. 495, 507 (1947) (emphasis added).
9. Id. at 501.

The pursuit of victory psychologically dominates all other objectives of litigation. . . . This preoccupation with winning is not simply a product of competitive instincts or self-selected personality traits; it cannot be dismissed as a peculiarity that is congenital to the personalities of the kinds of people who become litigators. It is, rather, compelled by professional prescriptions and reinforced by strong economic pressures and incentives. The rules of professional responsibility, for example, impose no direct obligation on counsel to pursue the truth or voluntarily to disclose information that might help establish the truth. Instead, these rules command the advocate to vest his primary loyalty in his client, to resolve all litigation doubts in the client's favor, and to pursue as vigorously as possible the client's best interests. These commandments of fealty to client and the absence of ethical directives to make full disclosures or to pursue justice result in a professional ethic that compels advocates to pursue the best resolution possible for their clients without regard to the merits of the dispute. To act otherwise is to court professional and economic disaster. . . .

The means employed by litigators to achieve victory for their clients regularly involve manipulating people and the flow of information in order to present their clients' positions as persuasively and favorably as possible. This manipulation may involve any or all of the following general techniques: *not disclosing* evidence that could be damaging to the client or helpful to an opposing party; *not disclosing* persuasive legal precedents that could be damaging to the client; *undermining* or deflating persuasive evidence and precedents that are damaging to the client and are introduced by opposing counsel, by such means as upsetting or discrediting honest and reliable witnesses or by burying adverse evidence under mounds of obfuscating evidentiary debris; *overemphasizing* and presenting out of context evidence and precedents that appear favorable to the client; *pressuring* or cajoling witnesses, jurors, and judges into adopting views that support the client's position; *deceiving* opposing counsel and parties about the weaknesses of the client's case and the strengths of opposing cases; *aggravating and exploiting* to the fullest extent possible vulnerabilities of the opposing party and counsel that have nothing to do with the merits of a given dispute by such means as intimidating an anxious opponent, spending a poor opponent into submission, or "soaking" in settlement an opponent who has public image problems or who for other reasons cannot endure the risk and public exposure of a trial. None of these techniques is illegal or violates the letter of the ethical rules of the profession. Indeed, the refusal to resort to at least some of these devices may be construed as a breach of an attorney's obligation "to represent his client zealously within the bounds of the law."

Pressure from clients to cut litigation costs probably is not sufficient to discourage attorneys from resorting to expensive, obfuscating tactical devices that seem to promise a competitive advantage. There are several reasons such economic pressure from clients will remain largely ineffective as a means of controlling litigation costs and discouraging adversarial maneuvering during discovery. One is the ever-present and increasingly intense fear of malpractice. . . .

. . . For the lawyer being paid by the hour, there is a great economic temptation to protract and complicate discovery. Most clients, furthermore, are completely incapable of determining which tactical ploys by attorneys are wise and justified and which are simply ways to increase the attorney's fee. . . .

VI. The Use of Specific Discovery Tools to Limit and Distort the Flow of Information . . .

A. The Investigation Stage

The first major component of the pretrial process of gathering and organizing evidentiary data consists of private investigations by counsel. The conduct of such investigations generally is not governed by the formal rules of discovery. Nonetheless, the character and quality of discovery depends so much on the investigative processes that precede and parallel it that discovery cannot be intelligently evaluated without examining these processes. Litigators shape the strategy and tactics of their discovery on the basis of their investigations.

One primary purpose of investigation is to form a preliminary evaluation of the strengths and weaknesses of the client's case. The criteria applied by counsel during such evaluations have little to do with truth and justice. Counsel generally are less concerned about the merits of the case, per se, than they are about such factors as the discoverability, admissibility, and persuasiveness of the evidence; the political, psychological, and economic resources available; the vulnerabilities of the parties and their attorneys; and the potential extent of damages. Of the many factors involved in a preliminary evaluation that can affect discovery, the one with perhaps the most far-reaching implications is the attorney's conclusion regarding whether the case will be settled before trial. The strategy and tactics of discovery that are appropriate for such a case can be quite different from those that are appropriate for a matter that is likely to go to trial.

Counsel's conclusions about the likelihood of settlement may determine which of two different tactical approaches will dominate their discovery plans and decisions. Discovery whose clear purpose is to prepare for trial should be designed to identify and evaluate all the data that the trier of fact might consider. During trial discovery, counsel seek to uncover and confront in intricate detail the full scope of their opponent's case. The litigators' discovery goals in this context are to reduce to an absolute minimum the chances of being surprised during trial and to prepare themselves to rebut and undermine their opponent's evidence. Counsel have no interest in disclosing any more than they must about their client's case, but their objective vis-à-vis their opponent is full disclosure.

The objectives of litigators during the kind of discovery that is oriented toward settlement are strikingly different. Settlement discovery is essentially a process of record building. It is a private trial without judge, jury, or the rules of evidence. Counsel's goal is to build in their opponent's mind the most favorable impression possible of their client's case in order to secure the best settlement. To build this favorable impression, counsel will attempt to manipulate the flow of information about both sides of the dispute. Litigators in this situation are not interested in openly exploring the strength of the evidence against their client. Instead, they will attempt to avoid devices that might alert their opponent to the existence of such evidence. Settlement discovery is designed to emphasize all the data that is favorable to counsel's client and to undermine the credibility and create doubts about the admissibility of the evidence that supports the opposing party. In short, the primary purpose of such discovery efforts is not education but persuasion. . . .

One function of investigation, then, is to gather the information that is necessary to define the strategic purposes of, and the tactical means for, manipulating the flow of information during discovery or trial. Toward that end, investigating litigators must identify all the evidence that is favorable to their clients and determine how to use this material. If, for example, an attorney has concluded that a matter is likely to go to trial and, thereafter, interviews witnesses who have favorable testimony to offer, he probably will take statements from them but will not notice their depositions. The lawyer will disclose the witnesses' identity only if clearly compelled to do so and will hope to surprise his opponent with this testimony at trial. By contrast, a litigator engaged in settlement discovery probably would take statements from such witnesses and notice their depositions as part of his record-building strategy. The litigator's treatment of any favorable documents and other tangible evidence that his investigation uncovered would follow a similar pattern. If a trial is foreseeable the lawyer will try to save these materials for surprise, but if settlement is likely his goal will be to decide how and when to present the favorable evidence so as to maximize its dramatic impact on opposing counsel and parties.

The investigating litigator is also concerned about identifying and deciding what to do with evidence that is damaging to his client. Unlike favorable evidence, there is rarely any reason voluntarily to disclose damaging information. When deciding what to do with damaging evidence, therefore, counsel's primary objective is to devise means to reduce the likelihood that the evidence will be discovered. The litigator, for example, may begin preparing his client to interpret narrowly all inquiries that seem directed toward sensitive material and to guard aggressively against providing any more information during discovery than is clearly and properly demanded.

If investigation results in locating a nonparty witness whose testimony would be damaging, one of counsel's first efforts will be to ascertain the likelihood that the witness will be discovered by the opponent and will testify at trial. If there is a real chance that the damaging witness will not be discovered by the opposition, counsel probably will take a statement, for possible use in impeachment and in preparation of other witnesses, and will hope the opponent never learns about the witness or his testimony. If it is likely that the opposing attorney will discover the witness, the investigating lawyer will take a detailed statement and will conduct an aggressive search for ways to assault the witness' credibility and to counter his testimony. If the investigating attorney assumes the case will be settled, he will not notice the deposition of the hostile witness and will attempt to negotiate the settlement before the opponent learns about the damaging testimony. If the matter appears likely to go to trial, however, and the witness will probably be called, the investigating attorney will notice the witness' deposition and will use it to explore fully not only the damaging testimony but also ways to influence, impeach, intimidate, confuse, pressure, disarm, and deflate the witness.

Counsel's responses to damaging documents and other tangible evidence uncovered during private investigations will follow a similar pattern. If possible, the attorneys will try to acquire control over the evidence and to prevent their opponents from discovering it. In addition to attempts to mislead opposing counsel by creating false, diversionary leads and generating obfuscating clouds of irrelevant information, there are several more clearly ethical devices available for use in concealing damaging evidence.

If counsel's private investigation reveals that their client has major and potentially discoverable problems, they not only must fashion a strategy to reduce the chances of those problems being discovered, but also must consider ways to terminate the litigation before the severity of those problems makes escape by their client very expensive. One tactical approach to this problem is to initiate discovery that is designed to evaluate the resources and psychological staying power of opposing parties and their counsel. If the investigating lawyer discovers a vulnerability, he will feel considerable pressure to exploit it for the purpose of establishing an early, favorable settlement. He may consider, for example, trying to smother a relatively impecunious adversary with extensive discovery costs. Another strategy employed by litigators whose clients have serious problems is to focus intensive early discovery efforts on reducing the size of, or undermining the evidentiary support for, the opposition's damage claims. If counsel can use aggressive discovery to create doubts in an opponent's mind about the strength of his damage claims, they may be able to orchestrate a settlement before their opponent discovers the full extent of their client's difficulties. . . .

(1) INTERROGATORIES AND DOCUMENT PRODUCTIONS . . .

In settlement discovery, sophisticated counsel draft interrogatories, requests for production of documents, and requests for admissions that are calculated to build a record that is most favorable to their client. They are careful not to frame questions that will encourage their opponent to investigate in areas that are likely to yield evidence that is damaging to the propounding counsel's client. Similarly, propounding attorneys will try to avoid questions that will compel their opponent to review the positive aspects of his case or encourage him to do additional analytical thinking or legal research that will improve his preparation. Even in trial-oriented discovery, counsel drafting interrogatories attempt to frame questions that do not reveal their theory of the case, their view of the evidence, their tactical plans, or the aspects of the dispute that cause them the greatest concern. In short, the drafting litigator is constantly under pressure not to initiate discovery that could help educate the opponent. The search process for relevant data is thus circumscribed by the fear that offensive discovery efforts will disclose something new and useful to opponents. This fear distorts the process of information acquisition until settlement is secured.

The preceding examples are relatively subtle ways in which adversary pressures distort and complicate what could be a more straightforward and less expensive pursuit of information. It is the less subtle distortions of the process of drafting interrogatories, however, that are most commonly perceived as abuses of the discovery process. That the ABA's Special Committee proposed only one major change in the rules governing the propounding of interrogatories and that this change would consist of limiting to thirty the number of interrogatories which a party may serve without a special showing of need, suggests that the abuse of this discovery tool that most concerns today's bar is the practice of propounding a burdensome number of written questions to party opponents.

Many litigators feel compelled to use written interrogatories as weapons for purely tactical purposes if doing so might promote their client's interests and generate greater fees for themselves. Some attorneys serve lengthy sets of "canned" interrogatories if they perceive some advantage to be gained by psychologically or economically harassing an opposing party or counsel. Litigators also may use interrogatories to pressure or manipulate opposing counsel into doing such initial case preparation as factual investigation and legal research and analysis that properly should be undertaken by the propounding counsel and paid for by that counsel's client. One additional abuse of interrogatories about which lawyers frequently have complained is the "fishing expedition," which involves serving numerous and far-reaching questions, not for the purpose of obtaining information about matters already in dispute, but in order to search for evidence that might support new types of claims, uncover competitors' business secrets, or harass an opponent into a favorable settlement. . . .

Like interrogatories, requests for documents and for admissions suffer from obvious abuses. Demands for document production, for example, can be used to impose great economic burdens upon or to harass or intimidate opposing parties and lawyers, to disrupt normal business operations or professional schedules, to steal trade secrets, or to fish for evidence to support new claims. Moreover, the pressures generated by such abusive tactics can be exploited to coerce a settlement that bears no relation to the merits of the dispute.

The disfunctional effects that adversary pressures have on discovery are even more obvious in the ways litigators respond to interrogatories, demands for documents, and requests for admission. The principal goals of the responding attorney tend to be completely adversarial: to provide as little information as possible, and to make the process of acquiring that information as expensive and difficult as possible for the opposing party and lawyer. To do otherwise might be considered a breach of the ethical obligation owed to a client, thereby exposing counsel to the risk of a malpractice suit. Volunteering information rather than resisting its production may also deprive the litigator of opportunities to demonstrate his adversarial skills and to increase the size of his fee.

There are many standard devices used by litigators to resist the disclosure of information and to mislead the opponent through their responses to interrogatories, requests for admissions, and demands for documents. The responding adversary's first impulse is to construe all inquiries and requests as narrowly as possible, thereby limiting the amount of useful information that must be divulged. . . .

The narrow reading of inquiries and demands is by no means

the only semantic ploy that litigators use to frustrate the discovery efforts of opponents. An aggressive counsel also will refuse to respond to written requests that are not free of virtually all ambiguity, imprecision, overbreadth, irrelevance, or other technical deficiency. Counsel's instinct is to object to the form or substance of any discovery request whenever an objection is arguably reasonable and if failure to respond might secure some competitive or self-serving economic advantage. Here, as elsewhere in litigation, institutional rules and pressures invite counsel to conclude that doubts must be resolved against disclosure, and that opponents must be forced to expend as much of their resources as possible to obtain data favorable to their cause.

Nor will litigators necessarily answer a request even after they have construed it as narrowly as possible and have objected to every arguable technical deficiency. Responding counsel's next line of defense is built on the use of privileges and the work product doctrine. Conscientious litigators will scrutinize every probe from an adversary to determine whether it is directed at material that is arguably shielded from disclosure. Counsel also will evaluate every item of information they feel constrained to divulge to determine whether its disclosure may constitute a waiver of any privilege possibly held by their client.

Counsel can manipulate privileges and the work product doctrine with especially pernicious effects when responding to requests for documents. The first stage of such manipulation may consist of efforts to include as many documents as possible within the arguable scope of some privilege or the work product doctrine. These efforts will be especially intense with regard to documents that could damage a client's position. Next, counsel will omit any reference in their response to documents they have decided might be considered privileged or might fall within the work product doctrine. The lawyers' hope, of course, is that their opponent will either forget to press for information about the withheld documents or will assume the privileges in fact apply. In other words, responding counsel will identify the withheld documents only if their opponent or the court so compels. Moreover, if compelled to identify withheld documents, the information counsel will submit will be as meager as possible. At each stage in what can become a tortuous and very expensive process, resisting counsel hope the opponent will abandon pursuit of the damaging material. It is worth emphasizing that these tactics of resistance fall short of such overtly unethical conduct as destroying or hiding incriminating documents.

When responding to document production demands, litigators sometimes resort to the obstructive device of burying significant documents in mounds of irrelevant or innocuous materials. This practice is sufficiently widespread to have provoked an unusually explicit condemnation in the report by the ABA's Special Committee for the Study of Discovery Abuse. One of the proposed changes in Rule 34 would compel a party responding to a document production request to produce its documents "as they are kept in the usual course of business or . . . [to] organize and label them to correspond with the categories in the request. . . ."

An additional obstructionist purpose can be served by burying crucial documents in mounds of irrelevant material — a massive document production forces opponents to spend a great deal of time and money copying and ferreting through the produced papers. The Special Committee's proposal would help deter only deliberate efforts to disguise and disorganize documents; it would do nothing to curb the massive overproductions that are designed to exert economic pressure on parties making requests. Nor would the proposal reduce the considerable pressure exerted on responding attorneys to find some excuse not to produce any material that might weaken their client's position.

If the tactics discussed above fail to conceal damaging information, counsel may feel constrained to refuse to respond to interrogatories or document production requests until compelled to do so. The first ploy is to ignore the original discovery probe and its deadline. At least among seasoned litigators the fear of sanctions for missing one deadline is not great. If the opposing attorney then presses for a response, the next defensive maneuver is to make excuses, play up sympathies, and seek extensions. When the deadline for the first extension approaches, additional extensions are sought. Such self-conscious and systematic efforts at procrastination impose additional financial strains on opponents, may undermine their will to pursue the litigation, and give the defensive attorney time to negotiate a favorable settlement before the damaging evidence is disclosed.

Unfortunately, the economics and tactics of adversary litigation occasionally make calculated, systematic resistance of the kind described above virtually inevitable. Especially in major commercial litigation, the stakes may be so high and the economic benefits to be gained by delay so great that litigators intent on serving the best interests of their clients, will feel compelled to resist discovery by every available ploy short of wilful bad faith. Each day's profit from a legally vulnerable operation, or each day's interest on the money that might be lost in a judgment, could far exceed the cost of counsel's delaying services and any likely sanctions imposed for failing to cooperate fully in discovery.

(2) DEPOSITIONS

Like the written tools of discovery, oral depositions can be used not only to gather data about events and witnesses but also as adversarial weapons designed to place burdens on opponents and to manipulate the flow of information. The manipulative and competitive purposes for which depositions can be used generally begin evolving during counsel's private investigation into the background of the dispute. It is during this stage of the litigation that the attorney frequently decides who to depose and for what purpose. It is also during this stage that the litigator will begin identifying the persons whom he will try to prevent from being deposed. Such people may include percipient witnesses or, perhaps more frequently, experts who have been retained by parties or lawyers to form opinions about some aspect of a case. The incentive to resist efforts by an opponent to depose experts is especially strong when the experts have reached conclusions that are equivocal or damaging to the party on whose behalf they were retained. Such conclusions are at least occasionally reached, even though some lawyers attempt to manipulate their experts psychologically and to orchestrate the flow of information to the experts in order to maximize the likelihood of receiving favorable opinions.

A very recent California case [100] offers a striking example of resistance by counsel to the taking of depositions of experts who have reached damaging conclusions. The action was for personal injuries that plaintiff alleged were caused by a defective tire-changing machine or by a defective tire. The machine manufacturer's investigator concluded, not surprisingly, that the injury was attributable to a defect in the tire. That defendant consequently designated its investigator as an expert who would testify at trial. Apparently the tire manufacturer's counsel found this expert's probable testimony persuasive and dangerous. After reading the expert's report, counsel for the tire manufacturer entered an agreement with its codefendant that it would indemnify the machine manufacturer for any liability for plaintiff's injuries provided the expert was withdrawn as a witness, the expert's report was withheld from plaintiff's counsel, and plaintiff's attorney was not permitted to depose the expert. In the ensuing litigation plaintiff's counsel sought an order requesting that the expert be made

100. Williamson v. Superior Court of Los Angeles, 582 P.2d 126, 148 Cal. Rptr. 39 (1978). For another relatively recent example of attorneys attempting to use the work product doctrine to prevent the deposition of an expert who had formed a potentially very damaging opinion, see Petterson v. Superior Court of Merced County, 39 Cal. App. 3d 267, 114 Cal. Rptr. 20 (1974).

available for deposition. Counsel for the machine manufacturer insisted that because he was professionally obligated to pursue the best interests of his client, he should be permitted to use his expert's opinion in whatever manner seemed most likely to produce the best result at trial for his client. The majority of the justices of the California Supreme Court rejected this argument and concluded that the purported indemnification agreement was an illegal conspiracy among defendants to suppress relevant evidence. After a battle that went through three levels of the judiciary, plaintiff was granted an opportunity to depose the expert.

Such wholesale resistance is, of course, not the only discovery problem associated with depositions. Depositions, like other discovery devices, are expensive and thus can be used to exert economic pressure on opposing parties and counsel. An aggressive litigator bent on straining the resources and testing the will of an adversary can notice numerous depositions and can prolong each examination for extended periods. Because depositions can be used to require the presence of the deponent for lengthy periods of time, they also have great adversarial potential for harassing and embarrassing adverse parties or witnesses and for disrupting their lives and businesses. . . .

Another tactic employed during settlement-oriented depositions that limits even more severely the ascertainment of truth is the skillful determination of which questions not to ask. Before a deposition is taken, conscientious litigators frequently have identified the key weaknesses of their case from a source to which their opponent is denied access: their client. Armed with what often may be exclusive information about their client's vulnerabilities, litigators will structure their questions so as to avoid those areas of the witness' knowledge that might be damaging and to emphasize testimony that strengthens their client's position. If their efforts result in a transcript that on balance is helpful, they will do nothing to impair the credibility of the witness. If, however, opposing counsel somehow has identified weaknesses or stumbled into damaging areas of testimony, resourceful litigators will do all they can to destroy the credibility of the witness or to camouflage the significance of the testimony. With both sides of a dispute so intent on exposing only what is favorable to their client, and therefore shaping their questions to elicit only selected portions of the evidence, there is no assurance that the depositions will disclose all the potentially relevant information the witness may have. Again, fortuity rather than institutional design is truth's most consistent ally.

Aggressive litigators can also limit and distort the flow of information during discovery through the manner in which they prepare their clients and witnesses to be deposed. The adversarial objective of attorneys whose clients or witnesses are being deposed is to limit to the greatest extent possible the information divulged. To maximize their control over the flow of information from their clients, attorneys may conduct mock depositions in which they pose dangerous questions to their clients and coach them as to the least troublesome answers. Short of such rehearsals, attorneys can instruct their clients in the art of nondisclosure. A recitation of the standard admonitions attorneys give their clients before depositions graphically illustrates how preoccupied litigators can be with resisting disclosure: (1) never volunteer information or help attorneys who are posing questions; (2) ignore the long silences and expectant faces attorneys will use to pressure you into continuing to speak; (3) answer questions with the fewest words and least elaboration that is consistent with self-serving consistency; (4) never interrupt the examining attorney before he has completed a question (to do so might provide an answer to a question the attorney had not thought to ask); (5) never edit or help clarify a confusing question (instead, simply say you do not understand); (6) always pause before answering in order to think and to give your attorney an opportunity to object; and (7) always listen carefully to your attorney's objections because they may contain directives or clues about how to respond to a line of questions. The purpose of such instructions to witnesses obviously is not to ensure that all the relevant information they have will be disclosed during their depositions.

Counsel may use many other devices to regulate and restrict the evidence their client or witness provides during deposition. Counsel can assert privileges whenever they arguably apply and can direct the witness not to answer questions that might invade protected spheres. They also may attempt to pressure the examining attorney into abandoning sensitive areas of inquiry by aggressively interposing disruptive objections to the form or relevance of questions. Counsel even may try to delay indefinitely the taking of their witness' deposition or to manufacture excuses to limit the scope of permissible questions. Such tactics will communicate quickly to an opponent that he will have to work very hard, withstand unpleasant pressures, spend considerable money, and seek aid from the bench if he intends to pursue what may or may not be fruitful lines of inquiry. My point here is not simply that such obstructionist devices are available and employed, but that the intense competitive pressures of the adversary system make resort to them a constant temptation. Indeed, some lawyers might argue that a thoroughgoing adversarial professionalism commands the use of such obstructive devices whenever they appear to promise significant advantages for a client.

Some Problems of Discovery in an Adversary System *

David L. Shapiro

Pretrial discovery plays a central role in civil litigation. Indeed, so central is that role that some "experienced" litigators have seldom emerged from the tunnel of discovery into the daylight of trial in open court. . . .

. . . Professor Brazil has argued that the present adversary character of civil discovery systematically encourages obstruction of the goals of discovery and that substantial changes in the pretrial environment must be made if those goals are to be achieved.[3] He would "curtail substantially" the role of the adversary system at the pretrial stage, preserving it in its present form primarily for the "dialectical evaluation of the relevant evidence" at the trial itself.

He may be right. Surely, there is considerable tension between the apparent duty of the lawyer, in response to discovery requests, to reveal information, opinion, and even belief, and the duty and desire of that same lawyer to represent his client zealously and effectively. Perhaps such tension may be found in every corner of litigation, both civil and criminal. But it may well be more acute in the civil arena, where the client is not entitled to stand mute in the dock, and especially in the realm of discovery, where the lawyer may be asked to act as investigator, counselor, advocate, witness, and officer of the court all at the same time.

But a drastic change in the nature of litigation of the sort suggested by Professor Brazil would be hard to legislate and even harder to implement. Is it possible, then, that at least some of the difficulty may be due not to the inevitability of conflict between the goals of discovery and the nature of the adversary system, but rather to a gap between the theory and practice of discovery? Is it also possible that the present rules, and even the sonorous tones of Hickman v.

* *Source:* 63 Minn. L. Rev. 1055, 1055-1085, 1088, 1090-1092 (1979).

3. Brazil, The Adversary Character of Civil Discovery: A Critique and Proposals for Change, 31 Vand. L. Rev. 1295 (1978). Professor Brazil catalogs a number of techniques, many of which go beyond the concepts of pushing and tripping, that he claims are used "to limit and distort the flow of information." Id. at 1315-1331. The core of his proposed changes includes shifting the lawyer's obligation before trial away from the client's interest and "toward the court"; imposing a duty on counsel to investigate thoroughly the factual background of disputes; imposing a "duty" on counsel and client to disclose "voluntarily" all relevant information and evidence (how can there be a duty to volunteer?); narrowing the scope of the attorney-client privilege and the work product doctrine; expanding the role of the court in supervising discovery; and requiring "judicial review of, or participation in, all settlements that exceed a specified dollar amount." Id. at 1349.

Taylor,[9] do not speak to practitioners and judges with a sufficiently clear voice? If so, there may be hope for reducing the conflict without so thorough an overhaul of the system itself.

I put to one side problems of unduly burdensome discovery demands and excessive delay caused by clearly frivolous objections and just plain stalling. Such problems are serious but can, I believe, be dealt with by proper judicial management within the present structure. Quite apart from these problems, it seemed feasible to probe the gap between theory and practice, and to test the clarity of the present rules, by asking practicing lawyers to respond to a hypothetical case that raises at least some of the hard questions. . . .

. . . I came up with the following:

1. You represent *A*, executor of *B*, in a Superior Court action for negligence arising out of an automobile accident at a highway intersection in the state. The intersection contained a stop sign at all access roads. *B* died in the accident and *C*, a passenger in the car *B* was driving, stated to you in an interview that *B* did not come to a full stop before entering the intersection. *C* too has since died, from causes unrelated to the accident, and none of the other witnesses you have spoken to claims to have seen *B* enter the intersection. You have no reason to doubt the correctness of *C*'s statement. *D*, the defendant in the action, has alleged contributory negligence as a defense and has submitted the following interrogatory to *A* under Rule 33 of the state rules of civil procedure:

> Did *B* come to a full stop before entering the intersection where the accident in suit occurred?

What should be the response to this interrogatory?

2. The facts are as stated in question 1, but the interrogatory submitted by *D* reads as follows:

> If you have any information about whether or not *B* came to a full stop before entering the intersection where the accident in suit occurred, please state: (a) the nature of that information; and (b) your opinion with respect to whether or not *B* came to a full stop at that time.

What should be the response to this interrogatory?

3. The facts are as stated in question 1, but instead of an interrogatory under Rule 33, *D* submits the following request for admission under Rule 36:

> *B* did not come to a full stop before entering the intersection where the accident in suit occurred.

9. 329 U.S. 495 (1947). . . .

What should be the response to this request?

4. Assume that *C*'s statement in question 1 was not made in an interview with you but was made to *A* a few days after the accident and before a lawyer was consulted. *A* has no reason to doubt the correctness of *C*'s statement.

(a) Would your answer to question 1 be different? If so, how?
(b) Would your answer to question 2 be different? If so, how?
(c) Would your answer to question 3 be different? If so, how?

This case was examined by several colleagues who differed on the appropriate responses to the questions but who agreed on their intrinsic interest. It was then sent to 200 practicing lawyers in Massachusetts and another 200 in Maine. . . .

The responses showed a good deal of variation among the lawyers involved. These variations were generally more notable within each state than between them. . . .

I. Interrogatories in an Adversary System

A. *Responses to the Questionnaire*

Questions 1, 2(a), 2(b), 4(a), and 4(b) all raise issues of the appropriate response to interrogatories addressed to a party under Rule 33.[21] Those responses will therefore be summarized before the issues raised by the hypothetical case are discussed. . . .

Of the 110 responses [to question 1 — the interrogatory asking whether *B* came to a full stop] only twenty-two (20 percent) contained a statement or even a hint (through a reference to hearsay, privilege, or work product, for example) that there was a *C* who had said something on the subject.[23] Also, nine of the 110 responses (8 percent) were explicit refusals in whole or in part to answer on the basis that any information constituted lawyer's work product, or more loosely, was privileged.[24]

Question 4(a) asked whether the answer to question 1 would be different if *C*'s statement had been made to *A* before a lawyer was consulted. . . . Twenty respondents (18 percent) said that the

21. Fed. R. Civ. P. 33. The federal discovery rules will be used in this discussion since . . . the rules in Maine and Massachusetts match the federal in all relevant respects and federal decisions are frequently relied on in interpreting those rules.

23. These 22 include . . . five . . . who stated, in answer to the interrogatory, that *B* did not come to a full stop.

24. These include two . . . who stated they had no personal knowledge.

answer would change, and ten actually moved in the direction of greater disclosure, from . . . (other limited answers or refusals to answer) to . . . (I am informed [by *C*] that *B* did not stop). . . . References to work product or privilege, for example, were dropped, and in some cases other justifications for a limited answer were substituted. In one case the statement "I don't know" was changed to "I don't know of personal knowledge." The number of instances in which there was a statement or at least a hint that there was a *C* who had said something on the subject rose from twenty-two to thirty-five (32 percent of the total of 110 responses).

Question 2(a) contained an interrogatory asking for the nature of any information bearing on the question of whether *B* came to a full stop. . . . In all, seventy-nine responses (72 percent) either stated, or hinted through objections or otherwise, that there was a *C* who had said something relevant; twenty-one responses (19 percent) gave no such hint, with some of these even expressly stating that there was no information; and ten (9 percent) were too ambiguous to classify. There were thirty respondents (27 percent) who expressly relied on the work product doctrine or "privilege," in whole or in part, as a basis for refusal to answer.[26]

. . . [O]f the . . . responses to the inquiry whether the answer to question 2(a) would be different if *C*'s statement had been made to *A* before a lawyer had been consulted . . . [s]ixty respondents (55 percent) said that it would, with a virtual disappearance of the work product objection from the answers, and a general shift in the direction of disclosure. Twelve respondents changed their answer but did not move in the direction of greater disclosure, and I concluded that after all the changes, there were only five respondents — down from twenty-one initially responding in this category in answer to question 2(a) — who gave no hint that there was a *C* who had said something relevant.

Question 2(b) was an interrogatory asking for an opinion about whether *B* had come to a full stop. It was the most unorthodox of the questions and . . . it was treated by many respondents as being naive or even in singularly bad taste. A total of nineteen respondents (17 percent) relied on the work product doctrine or "privilege" as a basis for complete or partial refusal to answer or to express an opinion. . . .

26. There were, in addition, 13 responses . . . disclosing only that a statement had been made to *A*'s attorney . . . which implicitly relied on the work product doctrine for failure to make any further disclosure. A work product claim also appeared to underlie other limited responses.

B. The Work Product Issue

It is worth at least passing notice that, with one or two possible exceptions, there were no respondents who indicated that *A* should be consulted as to the proper response to interrogatories that were directed to *A* and that *A* would have to answer under oath. This may have been due in part to the way in which the questions were asked and in part to the fact that the questions were hypothetical ones in which *A* was not even a name, just a letter. But it also may reflect an awareness that, unlike questions asked a witness at trial or on deposition, written interrogatories are, in a significant sense, directed to the lawyer. It is expected that the lawyer, after whatever consultation with the client he deems necessary, will draft the answers for the client to sign and swear to.

Whether or not this assumption of responsibility is appropriate in all instances, it is certainly proper for the lawyer and not the client to decide on the extent to which a work product objection should be made. The work product doctrine, after all, is not one that clients can be expected to know much about. Indeed, it has managed to evade the grasp of lawyers, judges, and commentators ever since the Court in Hickman v. Taylor first decided that the discovery rules did not really mean what they seemed to say. Moreover, Rule 33 specifically states that, while answers are to be signed by the party, objections are to be signed by the lawyer.[32]

In the present problem, a substantial number of lawyers, though far from a consensus, raised an explicit work product objection to the interrogatories, especially in responding to question 2(a).[33] And I suspect that many others would defend their failure to disclose more than they did on work product grounds. Thus here, as in many other instances in which discovery is resisted, a close look at the work product objection is required. For reasons canvassed more fully below, there seems little doubt that, in the absence of a valid work product objection, *C*'s out-of-court statement should be dis-

32 Fed. R. Civ. P. 33(a).

33. . . . In those instances in which a claim of "privilege" was made, it was generally clear that the real basis of the claim was work product. In a few instances, the respondent did appear to be relying on the lawyer-client privilege, which, under the generally accepted definition of that privilege, is inapplicable on the facts stated in the hypothetical case. See, e.g., 4 Moore's Federal Practice §26.57(2), at 26-200 to -201 (2d ed. 1979) (The "interrogated party cannot avoid an answer on the ground that the names were learned by counsel in the course of investigation . . . Nor may the interrogated party . . . plead personal ignorance of the names on the ground that they were known only to his attorney." (Footnotes omitted)).

closed.[34] — at least it should be if the right question is asked. . . .

While express or implied work product objections were frequent when *C*'s statement had been made to the lawyer, they were virtually nonexistent when the statement was made to *A*, the client. This is somewhat surprising since the protection afforded "trial preparation materials" by Rule 26(b)(3) extends to materials prepared in anticipation of litigation "by" a party as well as for him.[36] Perhaps the respondents simply assumed that an individual unrepresented by counsel is not acting in anticipation of litigation, or, more likely, that no matter how the rule is worded, its central purpose is to protect lawyers and those acting under their direction.

There is one other possible explanation for the general failure to invoke the work product doctrine to shield from disclosure *C*'s statement to *A:* Rule 26(b)(3) — the rulemakers' codification of *Hickman* — is addressed *only* to "documents and tangible things," not to whatever might be inside the head of the party or his lawyer. But of course, this explanation would also eliminate any basis for a work product objection to disclosure of *C*'s oral statement if made to *A*'s lawyer. And, as noted, that objection was frequently made.

What is the significance of the limitation of Rule 26(b)(3)'s protection to documents and tangible things? *Hickman* itself was not so limited; the lawyer Fortenbaugh and his client resisted both production of documents and disclosure of their recollection of oral statements made by witnesses. The Court not only upheld this resistance but also appeared to bestow a higher degree of immunity on witnesses' oral statements than on their signed, written statements, whether those oral statements were reflected in a lawyer's memorandum or not:

> But as to oral statements made by witnesses to Fortenbaugh, whether presently in the form of his mental impressions or memoranda, we do not believe that any showing of necessity can be made under the circumstances of this case so as to justify production. Under ordinary conditions, forcing an attorney to repeat or write out all that witnesses have told him and to deliver the account to his adversary gives rise to grave dangers of inaccuracy and untrustworthiness. No legitimate purpose is served by such production. The practice forces the attorney to testify as to what he remembers or what he saw fit to write down regarding witnesses' remarks. Such testimony could not qualify as evidence; and to use it for impeachment or corroborative purposes would make the attorney much less an officer of the court and much more an ordinary witness. The standards of the profession would thereby suffer.

34. . . . In view of the conclusion reached below that the substance of *C*'s statement to *A*'s lawyer is not protected by the work product doctrine, I have not considered whether sufficient need can be shown under Fed. R. Civ. P. 26(b)(3) to compel disclosure.

36. Fed. R. Civ. P. 26(b)(3).

The point was underscored by Justice Jackson's concurrence. He would have set a low threshold for production of witnesses' signed statements but a virtually insuperable barrier to disclosure of oral statements: "I can conceive of no practice more demoralizing to the Bar than to require a lawyer to write out and deliver to his adversary an account of what witnesses have told him."

But *Hickman* was not simply a vindication of the adversary role of the lawyer. Rather it was an adroit compromise between the felt necessities of that role and the pressures toward candor and disclosure generated by the new discovery rules. Like most compromises, the decision contained ambiguities and unresolved inconsistencies. In addition to delivering a panegyric to the discovery rules as "one of the most significant innovations of the new Federal Rules of Civil Procedure," clearing the way "for the parties to obtain the fullest possible knowledge of the issues and facts before trial," the Court stressed that "[a] party clearly cannot refuse to answer interrogatories on the ground that the information sought is solely within the knowledge of his attorney." The Court also waxed quite specific in describing the application of the discovery rules to the case at hand:

> Interrogatories were directed toward all the events prior to, during and subsequent to the sinking of the tug. Full and honest answers to such broad inquiries would necessarily have included *all pertinent information gleaned by Fortenbaugh through his interviews with the witnesses*. . . .
>
> . . . Searching interrogatories directed to Fortenbaugh and the tug owners, production of written documents and statements upon a proper showing, and direct interviews with the witnesses themselves all serve to reveal the facts in Fortenbaugh's possession to the fullest possible extent consistent with public policy.[41]

Thus the distinction, however tenuous and unworkable it might be, seemed to lie between information or facts uncovered by the lawyer in investigation, which were unprotected and which could be obtained through interrogatories, and the content of a witness' oral statement, which could not be obtained, at least in the absence

41. . . . The opinion at another point, however, equated "written materials" in the lawyer's files with "facts" and indicated that the "facts," like the written materials, could be obtained only on a proper showing:

> We do not mean to say that all written materials obtained or prepared by an adversary's counsel with an eye toward litigation are necessarily free from discovery in all cases. Where relevant and nonprivileged facts remain hidden in an attorney's files *and where production of those facts is essential to the preparation of one's case*, discovery may properly be had.
>
> . . . (emphasis added). Compounding the ambiguity, the opinion went on to suggest that such a showing of necessity could be made even on the rather flimsy ground that a document "might be useful for purposes of impeachment or corroboration.". . .

of an extraordinary showing. Witnesses' written statements, and presumably their contents, were also given protection, though to a lesser and ill-defined degree. This distinction gave trouble to the lower federal courts, which varied in their interpretation of *Hickman*, but which in the main made a valiant effort to compel disclosure of "facts" while protecting oral and written statements themselves.

Was this distinction jettisoned by the 1970 amendments in favor of a distinction protecting *only* documents and tangible things? . . . [T]he Advisory Committee's Note stressed that the broad protection afforded "mental impressions, conclusions, opinions, or legal theories of an attorney or other representative" was given only to documents:

> Rules 33 and 36 have been revised in order to permit discovery calling for opinions, contentions, and admissions relating not only to fact but also to the application of law to fact. Under those rules, a party and his attorney or other representative may be required to disclose, to some extent, mental impressions, opinions, or conclusions. But documents or parts of documents containing these matters are protected against discovery by this subdivision. Even though a party may ultimately have to disclose in response to interrogatories or requests to admit, he is entitled to keep confidential documents containing such matters prepared for internal use.

The ambiguities in *Hickman* and in the 1970 codification are reflected in the approaches of the leading commentators on the rules. Professors Wright and Miller, for example, approve of the view that if a document is protected from discovery, an interrogatory calling "for such complete information about the document as to be equivalent to furnishing the document itself" would be improper. But their emphasis throughout is upon the limitation of Rule 26(b)(3) to documents and things, and upon the discoverability, under *Hickman* and the 1970 amendments, of facts and information obtained in investigation. Professor Moore's approach seems quite different. After conceding that "information" in the hands of the lawyer is subject to discovery, he notes that the *Hickman* rationale applied "with special force to discovery of mental impressions of the attorney, as illustrated by the recollections of oral interviews with witnesses sought by the plaintiff in that case." Since Rule 26(b)(3) deals only with documents, "it leaves the 'work product' doctrine unchanged in this regard. Discovery of such material by any method is therefore limited to that rare case which Justice Murphy [writing for the Court in *Hickman*] mentioned but did not describe." At another point, Professor Moore states that while it is permissible to get "the facts that have been learned," work product protection extends "to the substance of the matter that has [been] written down." Finally, the decisions since the 1970 amendments dealing with this problem are infrequent and inconclusive.

Much of the difficulty stems from the ambiguity of the distinction between facts and information, on the one hand, and the content of oral or written statements on the other. To return to our hypothetical example, *C* has told *A*'s lawyer that *B* did not come to a full stop. Can it be said that the work product doctrine does not give even qualified protection against disclosure of the "fact" of whether or not *B* stopped but does give virtually absolute protection against disclosure of the lawyer's "mental impression" of *C*'s statement? Or,Obm Professor Moore notwithstanding, is the substance of the statement (though perhaps not its precise language) to be included within the scope of the "fact" that must be disclosed?

Note also that, in many instances, requiring *A* only to state whether or not *B* came to a full stop will be of little help to *D: A* is quite likely to say that he does not know, if his only information is a statement of one now unavailable. The instances will at best be rare in which *A* is, in effect, willing to stipulate to a damaging and critical fact on that basis. On the other hand, *D* may be very interested in knowing of *C*'s statement — its substance as well as its existence — whether or not *A* is willing to accept the truth of that statement. If *C* made the statement to *A*'s lawyer, he may have made it to someone else under circumstances that would make it admissible despite the hearsay rule. Or the statement may have contained a lead to other evidence that is admissible.

Even if the work product doctrine gives protection against disclosure of *C*'s statement, *D* may be able to make a showing sufficient to compel production. But, given that the work product doctrine slows down the process of discovery and sometimes requires judicial intervention to resolve disputes, one may well question whether the doctrine should be applicable at all. . . . [A]ny apprehension about making *A*'s lawyer a witness could be resolved by not permitting the material discovered to be used at trial "for any purpose." Any legitimate fear about probing the lawyer's mental processes, I submit, relates not to asking a lawyer to recall what a witness told him, but requiring the lawyer to evaluate the accuracy of what he was told in a way that might strain his conscience, or his role as an advocate, to the breaking point. Finally, requiring disclosure of the substance of what the lawyer was told is no more likely to discourage effective investigation than the existing requirement that the "statement" of a party or a witness must be furnished simply on the request of that party or witness.

The idea that the "fact" is not protected but the content of the statement is — if that is the idea — seems to have things upside down. There is little if any reason to give work product production to the substance of the statement itself. And there should, of course, be no prohibition of a party's acknowledging the occurrence or nonoccurrence of an event on the basis of a statement made by a third person to his lawyer. But it is difficult to see how the lawyer can effectively represent his client and at the same time maintain his integrity if he can be required by an adversary to evaluate the truth of what he has been told and if the client can then be forced to adopt that evaluation in answering an interrogatory.

There is no clear consensus of either theory or practice on this problem. The theory, as embodied in Rule 26(b)(3), seems to lean toward disclosure by limiting work product protection to documents. The practice, if the results of the questionnaire are any indication, seems to lean toward using the work product protection to justify not disclosing oral statements made to a lawyer. One reason for the variation in practice may well be the ambiguity of the rule. Perhaps, then, the soundest way to narrow this gap is to make it more clear that the present work product protection afforded by the rules applies only to documents, but to extend the protection of the lawyer's mental impressions and opinions to any evaluation of witness credibility, whether or not embodied in a document. . . . I believe the client should be able to stand mute when asked, in effect, for his lawyer's evaluation of a witness' credibility.

C. *Answering the Interrogatories*

If the work product doctrine does not shield the substance of *C*'s statement from disclosure, even if made to a lawyer, how should the interrogatories be answered? . . .

. . . I believe the appropriate answer to the interrogatory in question 2(a) [posed at the beginning of this article], regardless of whether *C*'s statement was made to *A* or to the lawyer, should include a summary of *C*'s statement and an identification of its source. A number of those responding to the questionnaire did not disclose either fact, even when *C*'s statement was made directly to *A*. But there were many who referred to the statement (permitting a follow-up question), and an even larger number who revealed its nature and source. It is clear from the rules themselves, and well established in the cases, that the inadmissibility of *C*'s statement is not in itself a bar to its discovery. . . .

A more difficult problem is posed by the interrogatory in question 1: Did *B* come to a full stop? I have already indicated my view that, if *C*'s statement was made to the lawyer, the work product doctrine should preclude any compelled disclosure of the lawyer's evaluation of *C*'s credibility. And assume for the moment that if *C*'s statement had been made to *A*, *A* would similarly not be required to evaluate its accuracy. Is it then proper simply to answer "I do not know," or words to that effect, as so many respondents did?

I think not. In the first place, there is substantial authority for the view that if the party interrogated does not know the answer to a question, he must specify in some detail the effort he has made to find out. Such detail in this case should probably include a reference to *C*'s statement and its contents, though it might also add that *C* is dead and that other witnesses interviewed were unable to corroborate or refute that statement.

Moreover, failure to disclose information relevant to the question is, in my view, a failure to answer the question. Every interrogatory of this type — which asks directly about the fact and not for information relating to the fact — is in substance a two-part question: (1) what information do you have that relates to this fact? and (2) what is your evaluation of that information? Assuming that the discoveree is unable or for some proper reason unwilling to answer the second part of the question with a clear statement, that should not shield him from answering the first. . . .

Once *A* has disclosed the content of *C*'s statement and its source, the issue is whether *A* must go on to state whether he accepts *C*'s statement as correct, either in response to the specific interrogatory in question 2(b) or in answer to the second implicit component of the interrogatory in question 1. Although a few respondents did state *A*'s conclusion on the subject in response to both interrogatories — surprisingly, without any indication that the decision might be left to *A* — a majority declined to do so in both instances, and many protested that the interrogatory in question 2(b) was improper, irrelevant, or beyond the scope of legitimate discovery because the answer could not constitute evidence or lead to admissible evidence.

But is the interrogatory in question 2(b) so plainly improper? Does it do any more than make specific the implication present in any question about a fact: that the person questioned is being asked for his opinion about the fact? It is true that a lay witness ordinarily cannot be asked for an opinion at trial if he is not competent to testify on the basis of personal observation.[75] But there is no reason why that limitation should be imposed at the discovery stage if some

75. See Fed. R. Evid. 601, 701.

legitimate purpose of discovery will be served by compelling an answer. Certainly most of the things we believe to be true, including many which we believe beyond all doubt, involve matters that we would not be competent to testify about at a trial.

Furthermore, the rulemakers in 1970 made an effort, especially with respect to Rule 33 interrogatories, to render the fact-opinion distinction irrelevant: "An interrogatory otherwise proper is not necessarily objectionable merely because an answer to the interrogatory involves an opinion or contention that relates to fact or the application of law to fact. . . ."[76] The effort is laced with reservations, however. The interrogatory may not be "otherwise proper." And even if it is, the rule, in stating that a request for an opinion is not "necessarily" objectionable "merely" on the basis that it calls for an opinion, uses adverbs that rarely find their way into statutes and rules.

The issue . . . should turn on whether any valid purpose of discovery would be served by requiring an answer. It is true, as a number of respondents pointed out, that given *A*'s incompetence to testify that *B* did or did not come to a full stop, *A*'s opinion about that fact may be inadmissible in evidence. Moreover, once *A* has revealed the information available to him, it is difficult to see how *A*'s opinion can in itself lead to any admissible evidence. Despite the language of Rule 26(b)(1),[79] however, those two possibilities do not exhaust the purposes of discovery. Another important purpose, though it appears to have been among the least realized in practice, is to narrow the issues. At least if *A* is willing to admit to an opinion, and perhaps if he can be so compelled, the effect will likely be to narrow the issues when the case comes to trial.[82]

There is a difference, however, between the instance in which *C* has spoken directly to *A* and the one in which *C* has spoken to *A*'s lawyer. Assuming that *C*'s statement is the only available information on the question whether *B* came to a full stop, any opinion *A*

76. Fed. R. Civ. P. 33(b).

79. "It is not ground for objection [to discovery] that the information sought will be inadmissible at the trial if the information sought appears reasonably calculated to lead to the discovery of admissible evidence." Fed. R. Civ. P. 26(b)(1).

82. In our hypothetical case, an admission that *B* did not stop, even if equivalent to an admission of contributory negligence, presumably could not furnish a basis for summary judgment because of the comparative negligence rule in force in the jurisdictions. It would, however, facilitate proof at the trial by eliminating the need for testimony on the question of whether or not *B* stopped. In a similar case in a state in which contributory negligence was a complete defense, a late filed answer to a request for admissions was deemed untimely, and the requested facts were taken to be admitted, allowing summary judgment to be granted on the basis of that admission. Morast v. Auble, 164 Mont. 100, 105-106, 519 P.2d 157, 159-160 (1974).

might have in the latter instance is necessarily based on the report and evaluation of his lawyer. If the statement of an opinion were required in this instance, it would more likely be the opinion of the lawyer than that of the client.

II. Requests for Admission in an Adversary System

A. Responses to the Questionnaire

The third question in the questionnaire contained a request for an admission that *B* did not come to a full stop. Although only five of the responses to that question could be construed as an admission, the range of all responses . . . was surprisingly wide. . . .

B. Preliminary Issues

The request for admission is among the least used of the principal discovery devices. In fact, since it is singularly ill-suited to the obtaining of information, it is thought by some not to be a discovery device at all. But . . . the request for admission has some extraordinary advantages when the requester's objective is to facilitate proof or to narrow the issues. If the request is not objectionable, there must be an admission, a denial, or an explanation of why the party can do neither. Thus . . . the "closed-ended" nature of the inquiry makes its purpose clear and equivocation difficult. And its ability to pinpoint a particular matter makes the request to admit more useful than an allegation in a pleading even when a responsive pleading is required. If there is an explanation for the failure of litigants to make more frequent use of this valuable device, perhaps it lies in the inconsistency between a rule compelling an adversary to stipulate to certain propositions and some of the tenets of the adversary system.

In our survey, there were only a very few respondents who made or hinted at a work product objection to the request for admission even when the sole source of information was *C*'s statement to *A*'s lawyer. . . .

A work product objection seems soundly based in the instance in which *A*'s lawyer has obtained the statement from *C* during an investigation in preparation for trial. . . . Subjective evaluations of credibility — of sincerity, perception, and memory — are involved in determining the underlying correctness of those statements. To require a response to a request for admission in such a case, when the witness statements have been obtained by the lawyer in anticipation of litigation, calls, in my view, for precisely the kind of inquiry into the lawyer's mental processes that the work product doctrine ought to protect. Work product protection can, of course, be waived, and I am not suggesting that an admission or denial based on the lawyer's evaluation of *C*'s credibility is in any sense improper if it is made in good faith. But, a lawyer cannot be expected to function effectively as an advocate if he can be compelled by the adversary to state his evaluation of a witness' credibility and if the client can be bound and subject to sanctions as a result.[98] . . .

. . . [O]nce the fact of *C*'s statement has been disclosed to the defendant,[101] the lawyer's belief that *C* was telling the truth, no matter how soundly based that belief might be, should not preclude *A* from resisting the defense of contributory negligence by all available legal means. *A* should not have to find a lawyer who did not speak to *C*, or who does not believe him, in order to resist defendant's allegations.

The work product issue aside, there seems to be no basis for an objection to the request for admission, and in fact very few lawyers made one in response to the questionnaire. Whatever the propriety of a refusal to admit because any opinion of *A* or his lawyer is based on hearsay, or for similar reasons, it seems clear, at least since 1970, that an objection based on such grounds would not be sustained.[102] The request is proper in form and goes to a matter that is a proper subject for admission or denial. . . .

C. *Answering the Request*

To obviate any work product objection, assume that *C*'s statement was made to *A* before any lawyer was consulted and before litigation was more than a speck on the horizon. The problem, then, is how to respond if *A* has "no reason to doubt" the truth of *C*'s statement — a phrase that is only a feeble attempt to capture in a few words the locus of a state of mind that may range from absolute certainty to total disbelief.

Had the question of the appropriate response arisen before the 1970 amendments to Rule 36, a conscientious researcher would have found the rule unhelpful and the cases in considerable disarray. . . . Professor Finman in 1962 advocated an expansive approach to Rule

98. Indeed, the ABA Code of Professional Responsibility DR 7-106(C)(4) makes it a breach of professional ethics for a lawyer to state his evaluation of a witness's credibility at trial. . . . Such a statement, whether favorable to the client or not, is seen as clashing with the lawyer's role as advocate rather than judge.

101. The fact of *C*'s statement should be disclosed if an interrogatory has been submitted under Rule 33. . . .

102. See Fed. R. Civ. P. 26(b)(1).

36. He argued that . . . "The obligation to admit should exist whenever a party is convinced that a proposition is true, regardless of the factors which led to his conviction. Whether belief is based on personal observation or information furnished by others, a proposition that is not disputed should be conceded." Revision of Rule 36 was proposed by Professor Finman to make these duties clear.

The amendments to Rule 36 in 1970 were plainly, indeed explicitly, influenced by Professor Finman's proposals, and language in some respects tracking those proposals was adopted. Thus the rule now appears to provide that if, after the necessary inquiry, a party has arrived at the requisite degree of certainty that a proposition is true, that proposition should be admitted. That the proposition is one relating to an opinion or conclusion, or to a central issue in the case, is no basis for refusal to admit or for objection.

Although the statement of the rule may be clear, I am still puzzled about how the necessary degree of certainty is to be defined. . . .

Whatever the requisite degree of certainty, let us assume that *A* has arrived at it, and tells his lawyer so. Should the proposition then be admitted, a course followed by only 10 (9 percent) of the respondents to the questionnaire? Does it matter that *A*'s belief is based on inadmissible evidence, that there may be no other credible evidence on the question, and that the adversary has the burden of proof? Nothing in Rule 36 itself expressly states that it does, but there is a cryptic provision that, subject to the provisions of Rule 37(c), a matter does not have to be admitted if it "presents a genuine issue for trial." [119] . . .

. . . I do not think, however, that in every case a party must admit a proposition when he reasonably believes it to be true, if there is a substantial chance that the party with the burden will be unable to prove it at trial. . . .

. . . But I would try to make it clearer than the rules do now that a refusal to admit may be proper, in some instances, regardless of the discoveree's belief or the reasonableness of that belief.

III. Conclusions and Some Modest Suggestions . . .

1. Rule 26 should be revised to make it clear that the protection afforded a lawyer's mental impressions and opinions extends beyond

119. Fed. R. Civ. P. 36(a): A party who considers that a matter of which an admission has been requested presents a genuine issue for trial may not, on that ground alone, object to the request; he may, subject to the provisions of Rule 37(c), deny the matter or set forth reasons why he cannot admit or deny it.

the impressions and opinions recorded in documents and includes, at the least, the lawyer's evaluation of the credibility of witnesses. I recognize that the problem of drafting here is a difficult one, and that there are substantial reasons for requiring the disclosure of a lawyer's contentions, and even of certain opinions, at the pretrial stage. But a party should not be required to answer an interrogatory, or to make an admission, if the answer or admission must be based on the lawyer's assessment of witness credibility. . . .

2. Rule 26 should be further revised to make it clear that work product protection does not extend to the substance of witness statements when sought as an answer to an interrogatory under Rule 33. Here, short of abolishing work product protection of written statements altogether, I would resolve the ambiguity in *Hickman*, and the conflicting signals emanating from the 1970 amendments, in favor of expansive discovery. While it might be pushing too far to allow without hindrance a request for the precise language of a witness' written (or oral) statement, any interrogatory calling for the substance of such a statement ought to be appropriate. For those who are concerned about making the lawyer a witness, it may be necessary to bar any use of the answer except as a lead to other evidence, and to preclude compelling a lawyer to testify at trial about what he was told in a pretrial interview.

3. Rule 33 should be revised to make it clear that a party, whether natural or artificial, who is unable after reasonable inquiry to give a complete answer to an interrogatory should furnish any relevant information that is available. Whatever the state of the case law, it appears that there are too many lawyers who will answer the question "Did *B* stop?" with only an "I don't know," or words to that effect, when they have relevant information that is plainly beyond any protection of privilege or work product.

This proposed change is a critical one. It is quite possible that the present rule speaks with sufficient clarity on this point and that the problem, as Professor Brazil suggests, is a structural one. But I remain guardedly hopeful that the adversary system can accommodate this degree of compelled disclosure, at least when the question asked is not too sweeping.

4. Finally, Rule 36 should make it clearer than it now does that, regardless of what a party believes or should believe, he is not required to make an admission if there is reasonable ground for concluding, on the basis of all admissible evidence known to him, that the proponent who is seeking the admission may not prevail at trial.

NOTES AND COMMENTS

Is it realistic to expect litigants to treat the discovery phase of a case as a collaborative, disinterested search for the truth of the matter while the trial remains an arena for self-interested, competitive behavior? If discovery standards clearly oblige adversaries to disclose damaging information, what consideration would induce self-interested, competitive adversaries to comply with these obligations?

A Divided Supreme Court Adopts Discovery Amendments to the Federal Rules of Civil Procedure *

Jack H. Friedenthal

The Policy Issues Implicated by a Call for Limitations on the Scope of Discovery

A. *Discovery as a Means to Ascertain if a Suspected Case Does in Fact Exist*

At the heart of the controversy over the scope of discovery is the question whether a potential plaintiff should be entitled to bring an action solely on a good faith belief that a valid cause exists, without hard evidence that it does. The issue is hardly a new one. It has arisen time and again in a variety of contexts ever since the federal rules were introduced with their concept of notice pleading, where a plaintiff need only make "a short plain statement of a claim," rather than the "statement of facts setting forth a cause of action" then required by the codes of most states.

The modern form of notice pleading has been challenged primarily on behalf of defendants in civil actions. It is always to a defendant's advantage to require the plaintiff to pinpoint its case specifically and in detail. First, if the case is based primarily on speculation, the plaintiff may be unable to allege sufficient facts to sustain the complaint and the action can be dismissed immediately. Second, even if the complaint is sufficient, it necessarily narrows the range of facts that the plaintiff will be allowed to discover and to prove at trial. If plaintiff's attorney has erred at the pleading stage as to the specific facts by which a valid case for his client could be established, defendant can thwart successful prosecution of the action by keeping out vital facts

* *Source:* 69 Calif. L. Rev. 806, 815-819 (1981).

on the ground that they were not pleaded and, hence, are not relevant.

Once it became clear that the battle for a return to the code formulation of pleading was irretrievably lost, other devices were utilized to raise the same issue in different contexts. For example, there have been attempts to convert the pretrial conference mechanism into a second pleading, so that the desired specificity could be introduced into the process, albeit at a later stage. And defendants frequently argue, occasionally with success, that certain types of cases are so unique that they should be dismissed in the absence of specific pleading of detailed facts showing that a right to relief exists. . . .

It is not surprising to find that the battle over specificity has shifted from pleading to discovery. The relationship between the policy of pleading and that of discovery is obvious. The very purpose of permitting pleadings based upon good faith speculation must be to permit plaintiffs to employ the discovery provisions to determine whether a valid case in fact exists. If plaintiff had the resources and ability to ascertain all the facts without resort to the formal discovery process, there would be no need, of course, to permit any but the most specific allegations. Conversely, it would not matter that general pleadings sufficed if discovery could nevertheless be curtailed, thus preventing or hindering plaintiffs from ascertaining if, and on what facts, valid claims exist.

From a theoretical point of view, the current practice of allowing general pleadings and extensive discovery cannot seriously be challenged. There seems to be little reason why litigants should be prevented from establishing legitimate claims in actions in which the admissible facts are to be found only in the files and minds of opposing parties. Similarly, the Supreme Court should not give in to charges of abuse by lawyers who, rather transparently, are merely acting as lobbyists for their particular clientele. The practical problems, however, are not so easily treated. There are cases in which extensive discovery results in costs well out of proportion to the dispute. Nevertheless, lawyers push on with their inquiries — not so much to build their fees, as is sometimes suggested, but to ensure that after the case is completed the lawyers will not be subjected to malpractice claims following the sudden appearance of favorable, hitherto undiscovered documents or testimony. The fact that some clients can afford such extensive discovery does not alter the fact that it often wastes both time and money.

The inherent difficulty with proposals to limit the scope of discovery, however, is that they apply to every case, including those in which discovery will cover a broad base but will not necessarily be extensive and costly, those in which costly, time-consuming discovery is justifiable, and those in which limits should legitimately be imposed.

There is but one obvious solution. Trial judges must be willing to concern themselves on a case-by-case basis to determine when a litigant has gone too far. It is not a question of scope so much as a question whether a party has raked over the ground again and again to the point that the cost of additional depositions or other discovery would be too high a price to pay for the remote chance that the procedure would yield any additional information of value.

Even before the most recent rules amendments, trial courts had substantial power to control abuses. That power has now been increased by the new discovery conference provision. Although discovery conferences certainly involve costs to the litigants, court appearances to argue about the validity of specific discovery requests are also expensive. Thus, even if one could agree on the legitimacy of an across-the-board limitation on the scope of discovery, the cost of court appearances to apply such a limitation might outstrip its advantages. The Special Committee itself recognized this problem even while proposing to alter the scope of discovery by requiring it to be relevant to "issues" pleaded rather than to "the subject matter" of the case: "Determining when discovery spills beyond 'issues' and into 'subject matter' will not always be easy." If a case-by-case determination must be made, at least it should be made in an efficient, informal setting.

B. Discovery as a Catalyst for the Growth of Substantive Remedies

Arguments regarding the scope of discovery typically have not dealt with the role discovery has played in the evolution of substantive law. It is clear, however, that over the years developments in areas such as products liability, employment discrimination, and consumer protection have been the result at least partly of broad-ranging discovery provisions. For example, lawyers would not have pushed in the courts and in the legislatures for expanded causes of action hinged on proof that defendants knew or should have known of a product's danger, if such proof were normally unavailable. The ability of plaintiffs' attorneys to obtain a corporate defendant's records, to depose corporate employees, and to send searching interrogatories has had a substantial impact in particular areas of law, and is one important factor in the dramatic increase in cases filed.

This growth in litigation was largely unforeseen when the discovery rules were first introduced. There was no conscious monitoring of the long-term effects on substantive law that might result. Had there been, courts and legislators might well have taken different approaches. Perhaps special tribunals or administrative panels would have been used to try certain types of cases; liability or damages might have been limited or curtailed. Instead, development has taken place along traditional common law lines to a point where courts today are heavily burdened by plaintiffs who sometimes treat the judicial system as if it were a gigantic slot machine. It is therefore understandable that defendants and their attorneys argue for discovery limitations; in a sense, they are "victims" of the discovery process.

Nevertheless, it seems clear that this concern with expansive liability is not an appropriate reason for limiting the general scope of discovery. Valid claims for relief from recognized injuries should not be thwarted by altering procedural rules to make it impossible for plaintiffs to obtain hard evidence. If the results of a particular substantive doctrine are unsatisfactory, the answer is to face the matter squarely and change that substantive doctrine, its proof requirements, or its remedies.

NOTES AND COMMENTS

Friedenthal points out that relaxed pleading standards and wide scope for discovery are not neutral as between plaintiffs and defendants, but are favorable to plaintiffs. If there are changes in substantive law in a certain direction, as by substituting strict liability for negligence to the benefit of plaintiffs, isn't it predictable that procedural law would change in ways that facilitate the substantive change? Could such changes enlarge the substantive effect beyond that intended by the legislature or justified by "sound policy"?

Chapter 4

Multiparty Controversy

An Historical and Critical Analysis of Interpleader *

Geoffrey C. Hazard, Jr. & Myron Moskovitz

The essential idea of interpleader seems simple enough: A person confronted with conflicting demands that he do or pay something ought not to be liable twice.[1] In medieval and renaissance England the typical case was that of a bailee holding chattels as security for the performance of a promise by one bailor to another and in doubt whether the promise had been performed, and therefore in doubt as to whom to make redelivery. In the nineteenth century the cases most typically arose out of commercial transactions, for example where a carrier, broker, or warehouseman found himself holding goods claimed on the one hand by a seller attempting to rescind and on the other by the creditors of a buyer who had become insolvent. Today, the standard case of interpleader is the insurance company confronted by rival claimants to the proceeds of a life insurance policy. . . .

* *Source:* 52 Calif. L. Rev. 706, 750-762 (1964).

1\. . . . Rule 22 of the Federal Rules of Civil Procedure, the most widely adopted current formulation of the interpleader rule, in principal part provides . . . "Persons having claims against the plaintiff may be joined as defendants and required to interplead when their claims are such that the plaintiff is or may be exposed to double or multiple liability."

A. *The Basic Model*

We may begin by reflecting on the simplest case, that of a holder of a tangible object of personal property confronted with two claimants who demand it.

The stakeholder in such a situation has a dilemma, as we quickly recognize. He seems to deserve a procedural device by which to escape. It does not follow as quickly as might be supposed that the stakeholder should have a remedy. In fact, there are similar predicaments from which the law does not provide an escape. A debtor has no procedure to which he can resort — short of bankruptcy — to determine which creditor to pay now and which to pay later, though a conscientious debtor would surely feel anxiety about the fairness of a choice he might make in such circumstances. . . . [I]t is not the existence of a dilemma before the stakeholder that is the basis of interpleader. . . .

Nor is the threat of multiple litigation facing the stakeholder a sufficient basis for interpleader. Everyone theoretically stands subject to the threat of litigation, even baseless litigation. The accident that one person becomes the target of simultaneous suits does not of itself justify the unusual procedure of drawing them all into one proceeding. Moreover, *even if the suits relate to the same transaction, and there is a possibility that they might have inconsistent outcomes,* we submit that the conditions would not exist that have impelled the interpleader remedy. Take the case of multiple suits by passengers against a railroad following a trainwreck. There would be a plurality of actions, in some sense asserting "the same claim," which render the railroad "doubly vexed" and in which the possibility exists that some would result in verdicts for and others against the plaintiffs. A case can be made that all such claims should be determined in a single proceeding, a case whose components include the conservation of judicial and party time and energy and the achievement of consistency in adjudication. Conservation of judicial and party resources is an economic objective that has weight, perhaps weight sufficient in the absence of seriously competing considerations to call decisively for reduction of multiparty claims to a single proceeding. Consistency in adjudication is a value of a somewhat different order. In part it is simply aesthetic, the quest for symmetry in the system's results. In more important part, the urge to consistency is one phase of the search for equality in treatment that is pervasive, if never fully realized, in a legal order. One way to conduce to similarity of result in similar cases is to decide them simultaneously before a single tribunal, which in fact occurs in interpleader.

Indeed, so weighty are the values of conservation of resources and consistency of result that they could be held to justify a single proceeding whenever it appears that several claims are asserted which could be decided inconsistently. Especially is this so contemporarily, when we have come to accept the idea of big lawsuits as routine if not the norm. And if one were to take the literal meaning of Federal Rule 22 as the essential definition of interpleader, this would be the stopping point of the inquiry, for that Rule *says* that interpleader may be had where the middleman "is or may be exposed to double or multiple liability.". . .

. . . We submit that there is something more to interpleader, a deeper basis of concern about the middleman's position than considerations of economy and equality. . . .

The principal point to be recognized is that the middleman does not simply confront a dilemma — the debtor with two creditors does that — nor does he simply face "double or multiple liability" — the railroad with the trainwreck is in that position. Rather, the middleman that interpleader seeks to help is a man facing a dilemma that is *caused by* the fact that the law (incipiently if not yet actually) is addressing him with conflicting commands. In the simple case of the stakeholder in possession of, say, a watch, if claimant *A* and claimant *B* each demand the watch, the stakeholder has a dilemma of a practical nature and perhaps a moral one as well. But if *A* and then *B* successfully establish in a court of law that they are each entitled to possession of the watch, and if no procedure exists for reconciling the results, the middleman is confronted with two commands one of which he must violate.

This is not only a grave matter, it is a subversion of the very basis of the legal order. It is intolerable that a legal system should come down at the point of application to tell someone that he has orders such that he cannot help but disobey. . . .

B. *Variations from the Model*

The possibility of conflicting legal commands, it seems to us, is the basis for the archetype, the standard case, of interpleader. The next step is to consider variations from the model. The first variation is presented if we suppose that one of the two claimants would be denied the remedy of restitution of the object and be given compensatory damages in lieu. In this variation there is no obstacle to enforcing both orders, for the middleman though he cannot in material fact give the watch to both *A* and *B* nevertheless can give it to *A* and reach in his pocket for money of equal value to pay *B*. The extremity of contradictory legal orders is avoided, and so the case for interpleader in this situation is not quite so compelling.

Surely, however, it is compelling enough. The damages remedy afforded *B* is intelligible only if it is understood as a compensatory substitute for actual restitution of the watch. The reason why the substitution is necessary is because the law with the other hand had directed that the watch be given to *A*. Since it cannot be given to both, the middleman is compelled to put up his own money as compensation to *B* for an injury that the law ordered him to commit. This is little different from an expropriation of the middleman's property, and we should suppose on that account is a proper case for interpleader. . . .

The next variation from the original model is to suppose that the claims of *A* and *B* relate not to a tangible object but to an obligation on the part of the middleman. The simplest case is where the middleman comes under obligation to *A* and then *B* suggests that on account of some dealing between *B* and *A*, the middleman's obligation is now due *B*. This is the case, for example, of an insurance annuity in favor of *A* the proceeds of which allegedly have been assigned by *A* to *B*. . . .

. . . We can properly treat the obligation as *a* thing similar to *a* watch only if *A* and *B* each affirms that (1) he claims on a policy in the amount of 2000 dollars, *and* (2) there is only one such policy, *and* (3) that policy is no. 1234.

. . . But it is also possible that even though *A* and *B* each thinks there is only one policy, in fact they have in mind different policies. Only if they each identify a single obligation-creating event as the predicate of their claim can we safely speak of there being one obligation. Both *A* and *B* have to *contend* congruently before we may safely assimilate the case to that where the claims relate to a single tangible object. . . .

When the claimants start from this kind of common ground, the case is a proper one for interpleader. In such a case we may justifiably assimilate the middleman's obligation to a thing and grant interpleader for the same reasons that support interpleading of claims to a watch. Unless there is a proceeding in which the inconsistent affirmations of *A* and *B* can be resolved consistently, the middleman stands to suffer an expropriation.

Indeed, for just this reason interpleader in such a situation was held to be not merely appropriate but obligatory under the due process clause. This was [exemplified] in Western Union Telegraph Co. v. Pennsylvania.[171] The Commonwealth of Pennsylvania brought an es-

171. 368 U.S. 71 (1961).

cheat proceeding to recover sums deposited with the telegraph company for transmission as money orders. The sums in question had gone uncollected by the addressees and unreclaimed by the senders. It was held that Pennsylvania could not hold the company liable for these sums in the face of proceedings by New York (and other states) to recover the same amounts, for this would subject the company to the risk of having to pay twice and thus deprive it of its property. The State of New York could not be made party to the Pennsylvania proceedings, on account of sovereign immunity, nor Pennsylvania a party to New York proceedings, so neither state could enter a judgment that would acquit the company against the claim of the other. The Supreme Court invited an original proceeding before it between the states, the company no doubt to be joined as a party. This amounts to interpleader.

Two further points need to be made at this stage of the analysis. The first is that a proper case for interpleader is made when the claimants' claims are congruent (and inconsistent) in *any* material respect, and not merely when they are congruent in *all* respects. Indeed, it is strictly speaking impossible for the claims to be precisely the same, for each claimant at some point or other (in pleading or in proof) has to show what events occurred that entitle him rather than his rival to recover the object or obligation in question. A claim consists of a linked series of propositions which in conjunction are a legally recognized predicate for granting the claimant judicial relief. At least one of the links will have to connect the particular claimant with the object or obligation, and this link differentiates the respective claims from each other. . . .

The second point to be mentioned at this stage is that the logic of interpleader is essentially the same as the logic of the necessary parties rule. That rule, which appears in formulations of varying precision and felicity,[178] requires that all persons be joined in a suit who ought to be parties if the court is to render a judgment that will dispose of the controversy without prejudice to the practical interests of persons concerned with the transaction in question. The necessary parties rule permits the court, on its own motion or at the suggestion of a party, to bring in the third person. In the typical necessary parties situation, the third person is a claimant of the property or obligation that is in suit. He is brought in so that the person holding the property or owing the obligation, ordinarily the defendant in the original suit, will not later be squeezed by an inconsistent adjudication. To use the nomenclature we have used so far, it is a case where *A* sues Middleman and Middleman then demands that

178. E.g., Fed. R. Civ. P. 19; Cal. Code Civ. Proc. §389, N.Y. CPLR §1001.

B be brought in as a necessary party. Interpleader is a case where, relying on same considerations of fairness, Middleman initiates the legal proceedings by joining *A* and *B* and demanding that they interplead. It may be added, finally, that intervention is likewise parallel in its logic: That is a case where *A* sues Middleman and *B* takes the initiative to enter the suit by applying for intervention. Three rules have grown where one could do.

We now may take a further step away from the model, one that carries us very nearly to the end of our journey. This is where the middleman has an obligation which under its terms he may discharge by paying *either A* or *B*. The simplest case is a promissory note payable jointly to *A* and *B* or to a partnership, where payment to any of the obligees is a performance discharging the obligation. A more complicated but modernly more important type of case is where a liability insurance carrier is confronted with claims against its insured that exceed the limits of the policy. In this type of case, the middleman does not face the risk of paying twice, for he is acquitted upon payment. There is a risk, however, that the members of the group may be treated disproportionately, for if the first to come forward is fully served, there may be nothing left for the tail-enders. It is unfair that a group similarly situated be treated dissimilarly, and especially that preference among them be shown to the hoggish. There is still more at stake in the typical case of the liability policy, for the claims in such a situation, being personal injury claims, are indeterminate in amount in advance of settlement or adjudication. Because settling one share cuts down the pie available for another, the settlement process easily breaks down into a circular interdependency. Interpleader invites supervision of settlement, and enhances the possibility that trials may be avoided to fix the shares.

The case for interpleader here certainly is not as strong as in the original model, nor even in the variations previously considered. There is neither the risk that the legal system will order the impossible, nor that its orders will by their inconsistency work an unjust exaction. The risk is that if the law stands aside and lets private dispositions proceed in their own way, someone who has a legal right on a par with another — a claim to a share — will be left empty-handed in the payout. It may well be inappropriate, indeed almost surely would be inappropriate, for the law to insist that the obligor in such a situation see to a fair-sharing as a condition to being discharged of his obligation. Interpleader accordingly should not be required. But if the obligor is bothered by the prospect that he may work a disproportion if he proceeds by himself and if he on that account asks official aid to effect an equitable distribution of the proceeds of his obligation, it would seem that this is a sufficient case for interpleader.

C. *The "First Stage" of Interpleader*

The basic model with which we began involved no question that the claimants were seeking "the same thing," a watch. The variations from the model were similar in that they all involved cases where the claims were "the same" in the qualified sense that they each contained at least one common link. . . .

The problem that then arises is this: What if the middleman contends that there is a single obligation but one or more of the claimants disagrees, and asserts that there are two (or more) obligations? The case is not one of which we can say at the point of beginning that there is a risk that the middleman may have unjustly to pay twice, because for all we know he ought rightly to pay twice — there may indeed have been two watches or two insurance policies.

In the basic model it was established *in advance of any adjudication*, by the common assent of the parties, that there was a single predicate for the middleman's obligation to *A* or to *B*. Where there is a dispute whether there is a single predicate or multiple predicates, until this dispute is resolved it cannot be ascertained whether the middleman will have to pay twice and, if so, whether it will be unjust that he do so. In short, we cannot say whether it is a proper case for interpleader.

In the absence of some sort of special procedures, the solution to this problem was fairly simple but not entirely satisfactory. The claims would proceed separately against the middleman, and he would defend one or both on the ground that the obligation sued on was owed to another. If he succeeded in both defenses, he would have a windfall; if he succeeded in one, he would be relieved of the obligation to pay twice, whether justly so being another matter. If he lost both, it *could be* that justice had triumphed, for he might well have had two obligations and simply been trying to play one off against the other. But it is also possible that in losing both he would have been made the victim of inconsistent dispositions.

The nub of the problem was the absence of any procedure to invite the trial tribunal to consider the possibility that the middleman was right in contending that there was only one obligation, however confused he might be as to whom he owed it. The evidence in the trial of one claim would not ordinarily be admissible in the trial of the other; the verdict in the first would never be admissible; and the proof-taking as a whole could not be exactly the same where in each trial one claimant was a party and the other at most only a witness. With these discrepancies between the hearings, the result could be reached in each case that there was only one claim but that it was due the plaintiff in the case at hand.

A solution is to provide a preliminary trial to determine whether the middleman's contention that he has only one obligation is well-founded. This is what Professor Chafee called the "first stage" of interpleader, though strictly speaking it would perhaps be more appropriate to call it a preliminary to interpleader. . . .

What needs to be said here is only that the rationale supporting such a procedure is much weaker than that which underlies interpleader itself. The injustice it obviates is contingent, not certain. Moreover, even without the procedure the middleman has a fighting chance to escape by making a good defense to the actions by the claimants. But of course he has that chance without interpleader even in the case of the basic model: He might be successful in defending the replevins of the watch and, indeed, wind up with a timepiece for himself. The Chancellors thought that chance was inadequate in the model case and in consequence fashioned interpleader to help the middleman out of his predicament. That reasoning seems to carry far enough to justify a "first stage" for interpleader where the middleman contends that he has only one obligation.

Finally, we may give brief consideration to the situation where the middleman disputes the *amount* of his obligation, which long ago gave rise to the idea of a "bill in the nature of interpleader." This actually involves tacking on an additional preliminary inquiry, a pre- "first stage" hearing, and is covered in general by the analysis that has been already developed.

At its outer limit, this is the case where the plaintiff in interpleader denies that he owes anything at all, a middleman who in effect denies that there is anything of which he is in the middle. His request for interpleader is thus conditional on his losing an initial contention that he owes nothing. His next contention, which ordinarily follows a fortiori, is that if he owes anything, he only owes it once, i.e., the same contention made by the interpleader plaintiff in the "first stage" that he has only one obligation. At this point the two situations are identical and the analysis heretofore applies.

Continuing Work of the Civil Committee: 1966 Amendments of the Federal Rules of Civil Procedure (I) *

Benjamin Kaplan

This article will summarize and comment upon various amendments of the Federal Rules of Civil Procedure, effective on July 1,

* *Source:* 81 Harv. L. Rev. 356, 356, 358-366, 370-371, 375-381, 383, 384-394, 397-398, 400-403, 405 (1967).

1966, which were sponsored by the Advisory Committee on Civil Rules. . . .

I. Problems of Parties

A. *Compulsory Joinder of Parties: "Joinder of Persons Needed for Just Adjudication"*

1. *Equity practice before the Federal Rules.* The old equity practice on joinder of parties has been assiduously studied and well-described by Professor Hazard. He shows that until the late eighteenth century equity sought to secure joinder in the suit of all the persons interested in the underlying controversy, but many times tolerated the absence of an interested person when it was shown that his joinder was impossible, or impractical, or involved undue complication. Full joinder was desirable because it tended to obviate multiple litigations and inconsistent adjudications; but it was not made an absolute condition of maintaining a suit because the chancellors apprehended that doing an incomplete job in a litigation would often be better than doing no job at all. Hazard goes on to report that chancery's attitude began to change in the late 1700s under the influence of the heady slogans of "doing perfect justice" and "making complete decrees." It began to be held that there were persons who sustained such relationships to any given controversy that in their absence a court not only should not, but, forsooth, could not proceed. Moreover, these relationships, so it was thought, could be described according to their essence in abstract terms. It will soon appear that there was a fallacy in the idea of a court's lack of power to proceed *inter praesentes* because some other person was absent, and some naive self-delusion in the reliance on disembodied categories.

Fell v. Brown,[15] a judgment by Lord Chancellor Thurlow in 1787, exemplified the "new" corrupted practice. The lore of that case was imported into this country by Joy v. Wirtz,[16] a decision by Justice

15. 2 Bro. C.C. 276, 29 Eng. Rep. 151 (Ch. 1787). Here a second mortgagee sought an accounting of rents and profits against a first mortgagee in possession. Thurlow was inclined to dismiss the bill when it appeared that the deceased mortgagor's heir was out of reach in America. . . .

16. 13 F. Cas. 1172 (Nos. 7553-7554) (C.C.D. Pa. 1806). This was an attempt to set aside for mistake a release of claims given by a number of creditors to their debtor; one of the creditors could not join as a party plaintiff because that would have destroyed diversity of citizenship. . . .

The *Joy* case used the characterization of "united" interests, 13 F. Cas. at 1172, later to figure in the Field Code, ch. 438, §119, [1849] Laws of N.Y. 639, and the Federal Equity Rules, Equity R. 37, 226 U.S. 627, 659 (1912).

Washington on circuit. A formula was finally set out in Shields v. Barrow.[17]

Barrow, a citizen of Louisiana, in 1836 sold his plantations in Louisiana to Shields, also a citizen of Louisiana, for $227,000 payable in installments, evidenced by notes. The notes were endorsed by six persons, four citizens of Louisiana and two citizens of Mississippi. Purchase money up to $107,000 was paid, the rest defaulted. In 1842 a compromise was agreed to by Barrow, Shields, and the six endorsers. The original transaction was to be undone, the plantations were to be returned to Barrow, Barrow was to retain the $107,000 already paid, and the six endorsers were to execute notes in varying amounts aggregating $32,000. (A tough proposition for the debtors: the panic of 1837 had intervened.) The settlement was carried out to the point where Barrow went into possession of the plantations and discontinued litigation previously begun, and the endorsers executed the new notes.

Barrow then claimed that he had been induced to enter the compromise by fraud. He started the present rather unattractive suit in the Federal Circuit Court for Louisiana, joining only the two Mississippi parties, and seeking rescission of the compromise and a recovery on the defendants' original obligations as endorsers. The question in the Supreme Court was whether the suit could be maintained in the absence of the other interested persons whose joinder would destroy diversity. The Court ruled that it could not be maintained. Justice Curtis, in a passage endlessly repeated in later cases, said there were three classes of parties to a bill in equity. Besides formal parties, there were:

> 2. Persons having an interest in the controversy, and who ought to be made parties, in order that the court may act on that rule which requires it to decide on, and finally determine the entire controversy, and do complete justice, by adjusting all the rights involved in it. These persons are commonly termed necessary parties; but if their interests are *separable* from those of the parties before the court, so that the court can proceed to a decree, and do complete and final justice, without affecting other persons not before the court, the latter are not indispensable parties. 3. Persons who not only have an interest in the controversy, but an interest of such a nature that a final decree cannot be made without either *affecting that interest*, or leaving the controversy in such a condition that its final termination may be wholly inconsistent with equity and good conscience.

If "affecting that interest" in the foregoing statement is taken in a practical sense, and if "separable" is taken in the same way, then we have a reasonable if painfully condensed thought. A decree

17. 58 U.S. (17 How.) 130 (1855).

between *P* and *D* may have effects upon an absent person *X*. These may range from possible remote stare decisis implications in putative later litigation by *X* against *P*, *D*, or even a fourth person *Y*, all the way to severe material injury to *X* as in certain instances where *D* is holding a limited fund in disputed shares for *P* and *X*, and the *P-D* decree may invade the fund and deprive *X* of adequate recourse. We can speak of *X*'s interest in the *P-D* controversy as "inseparable" if the practical effect on *X* is severe, and "separable" if it is not, although the words are not happily chosen for the purpose. Whether the court ought to proceed in *X*'s absence is seen as a pragmatic question in which the detriments to *X* are weighed and the court at the same time is not unmindful of any hardships to *P* arising from a dismissal of the action. This reading of Shields v. Barrow would produce a sensible pattern.

But without apologetic interlineation, the famous statement is rather empty. "Separable" is not really informing. The "affecting" phrase probably contributed to the jurisdiction-fallacy recurrent in the cases. For it lent itself not only to the practical interpretation but also to a distinctively legal interpretation — i.e., binding in the sense of res judicata. In the following caricature . . . let "affected" shift from the legal to the practical meaning: "(1) *X* cannot be affected by a judgment rendered in a case in which he is not a party. (2) *X* is not a party. (3) He would be affected by a judgment rendered in this action. (4) Therefore no judgment can be rendered." What has been lost in the shuffle here is that, though in the common personal action there is no jurisdiction or power to enter a judgment legally binding on the absent person *X*, there is jurisdiction or power as against the duly joined *D*; the question is whether it should in all the circumstances be exercised.

The *Shields* case set a poor example in slighting the specifics of the situation, including possible consequences of and alternatives to dismissal of the action. Thus the Court left unmentioned that the plaintiff Barrow might possibly lack access to any court in which all parties could be joined, so that dismissal of the instant suit might leave him remediless. If the suit was allowed to proceed and went to judgment on the merits against Barrow, the controversy might be disposed of for all practical purposes. Nor was it clear that any awkwardness would arise if Barrow succeeded against the defendants appearing in the action, especially if he collected in full and thereupon surrendered the property. There was also the possibility of conditioning a judgment for Barrow upon his obtaining a similar decree against the other debtors in another court. To sum up, then, one cannot say that Shields v. Barrow was incorrectly decided, for factors not mentioned by the Court might show that the judgment of dismissal was practically justified; but one can say that it is not shown to have been correctly decided.

Thorough examination of the later course of decision led Professor Reed to say: "The result of Shields v. Barrow was to embed in American procedural law the now familiar division of required parties into categories (necessary and indispensable — a classification not inherently bad) and a shoddy and unimaginative method of its application to individual cases." For the criterion of separability of rights, sometimes transmogrified into a criterion of whether rights were "joint" or "common," or whether the absent person was "united in interest" with those present, turned out usually meaningless or unhelpful and sometimes misleading as a measure of "indispensability.". . .

2. *The original Federal Rule 19.* Rule 19, as adopted in 1938 (it remained unchanged up to 1966), did not avoid the defects and frustrations of the courts' treatment of the required joinder problem during the previous century. Like the *Shields* case, the rule could be read compatibly with the original and better equity tradition, but there was little in its language or mood positively to induce the courts to change their indurated habits. . . .

Judge Hays thought Rule 19 "embodies and continues [the] unfortunate approach" that "the failure to join indispensable parties is 'jurisdictional'. . . ." This criticism was perhaps not merited if the rule was closely read; but subdivision (b) used the word "jurisdiction" five times and in more than one sense, and courts might easily lose track. The jurisdiction-fallacy could in fact be described in various decisions under the rule.

3. *Reforming Rule 19.* The critical literature and the reforms in Michigan and New York had indicated the direction of desirable amendment of Rule 19. Avoiding excessive abstraction and eliminating fuzziness as to jurisdiction, the new rule must describe those who, ideally, should be joined in the action, and then set out useful guides for deciding whether to dismiss or continue the action if complete joinder is not feasible because of an obstacle such as inability to effect service of process. Consideration of the interests to be served by enlarging a lawsuit to bring in additional parties — those of the public in preventing repetitive litigation, of the existing parties in having the litigious situation fully treated and averting later exposure to double liability, and of the potential party in avoiding practical prejudice by reason of the decision of the cause in his absence — consideration of these factors led to a meaningfully compendious description of "Persons to be Joined if Feasible" adopted in subdivision (a) of the rule as amended. The better reasoned cases were rich in suggestions about the second basic problem, how to determine whether "in equity and good conscience" the court should quit or

go ahead when it appears that a particular absentee cannot be forced into the lawsuit. New subdivision (b) has a nonexhaustive list of relevant factors: first, the degree of practical prejudice to the parties or the absentee by reason of the judgment likely to be entered in the action; second, the extent to which that prejudice can be reduced by the shaping of relief or other measures (for example, recalling the fraud cases, by giving damages in lieu of rescission); third, the adequacy of the eventual judgment as to those who are parties; fourth, the recourse open to the plaintiff in another forum if the instant action is dismissed. In elaboration of the second factor, the Advisory Committee's Note observes that it will sometimes be open to the absentee without undue hardship to appear or intervene voluntarily in the action and thus fend off practical prejudice to himself by reason of the judgment.[36] It is not improper, and may make good sense, for a party or the court to notify the absentee informally of the pendency of the action so that he may consider what to do. His inaction with knowledge may be pertinent to the issue of maintaining the action or dismissing it. Similarly a joined party may be in a position to take steps for his own protection against exposure to "double" liability in a subsequent suit by an absentee.

With the disappearance of the bugaboo of jurisdiction, it should be easier for the courts to accept that a decision as to dismissal for nonjoinder need not invariably be made instantly on the pleadings, but may be postponed until the facts of the case are better understood, for the joinder question is necessarily related to those facts. Similarly it should now be clear that when this question arises at the appellate stage, it is wrong to decide it without regard to what has occurred in the action after the pleading stage.

. . . [T]he complaint was heard that the way to solve the Rule 19 problem was not to amend the rule, but to cut down the situations where joinder was infeasible. Put another way, where a litigation may touch scattered persons, the law should relax requirements of

36. Fed. R. Civ. P. 19, Advisory Comm. Note, 39 F.R.D. 92 (1966). When joinder of a person is infeasible because of waivable requirements of venue or service of process, there is not likely to be any formal obstacle to his voluntarily appearing or being admitted as an intervenor. But when joinder would have ousted subject matter jurisdiction (as by destroying diversity of citizenship), a formal difficulty has been thought to arise if the absentee seeking to appear or intervene is properly characterized as "indispensable" to the action. Ordinarily an intervenor "of right" has been conceived to have an ancillary position in the lawsuit and hence excused from having to satisfy independently the requirements of subject matter jurisdiction; but it has been said that this does not hold with regard to an "indispensable." See Chance v. County Bd. of School Trustees, 332 F.2d 971, 973-974 (7th Cir. 1964) ("[a] contrary view would provide an easy means to evade diversity jurisdictional requirements"); . . . Johnson v. Middleton, 175 F.2d 535, 537 (7th Cir. 1949); C. Wright, Federal Courts 286 (1963). The changes in Rules 19 and 24 will affect the incidence of this doctrine. Note also the vast expansion in recent years of the ideas of "ancillary" and "pendent" jurisdiction and the recent avowal that "complete" diversity is not constitutionally prescribed. . . .

process, subject matter jurisdiction, and venue and allow all hands to be brought in, and thus avoid the question whether it is wise to go ahead in such-and-such a person's absence. Certainly there is much to be said for relaxing the formal requirements in those cases, and the American Law Institute's study of jurisdiction has already made important proposals on just that line. The necessary steps, however, could not all be taken by rule; some require statutory revision, as the ALI model shows. . . .

B. Class Actions

Chancellors who were prepared on practical grounds to hold that joinder of an interested person could be excused when he was outside the jurisdiction or otherwise unamenable, might hold on a similarly expedient view that when the interested persons were so numerous as to make joinder of all impracticable some might stand in judgment as representatives of all. Secondly, the class action probably reaches back to bills of peace with multiple parties. When numerous persons stood in the same position toward an adversary so that there was potentially a large number of essentially identical lawsuits, equity might in effect allow a consolidation of the expected actions and clear up the entire situation through a bill of peace. The requirement of a "separate equity" for such a bill was increasingly seen to be artificial; the possibility of multiple repetitive litigations itself began to appear a good ground of equitable relief. But then, as Professor Chafee said, "[t]he very identity of interests which made it easy to bring everybody in, also made it somewhat superfluous to do so."

1. *Federal equity practice and original Federal Rule 23.* Until quite late in the game there does not appear to have been much anxiety about classifying or limiting representative actions by reference to the abstract nature of the rights or duties involved. Thus Federal Equity Rule 38 of 1912 said merely: "When the question is one of common or general interest to many persons constituting a class so numerous as to make it impracticable to bring them all before the court, one or more may sue or defend for the whole." Here the emphasis fell on community or solidarity of interest among the members of the class deriving from the existence of a common question. If we add numerousness of the class (as the rule did) and fair representation of the class by parties in court (as the rule suggested), we begin to see an outline of basic prerequisites of a class action. When, however, the time came to write Rule 23 on class actions effective in 1938, simple statement was discarded: a drive for more sophisticated analysis and a strategic effort at solution of collateral issues, such as that of subject matter jurisdiction for class actions, combined to produce a text burdened with a categorization of rights at a high

pitch of abstraction. The chief draftsman, Professor Moore, consulted an earlier analysis by Story, but the new master somewhat exceeded the old in the refinements of the nomenclature by which he sought to arrange or carve up the field.

Rule 23(a) started well enough by requiring such numerousness of the class as to make joinder of all members infeasible, and such a selection of parties from the class as to assure adequate representation of all. But then "the character of the right" to be asserted for or against the class must be "joint" or "common" or "secondary" — this was the category of class actions which came to be called "true"; or the right must be "several" with the action directed to the adjudication of claims affecting specific property — the "hybrid" category; or the right must be "several," with a common question of law or fact affecting the right and common relief sought — the "spurious" category. Somewhere amid these definitions could no doubt be found all the actions ever considered class actions. The draftsman's object, however, was not merely to achieve completeness of coverage, but to adumbrate important differences of treatment and result as among the types of action. Originally, indeed, Professor Moore would have added expressly to his text a subdivision "Effect of Judgment," declaring that the judgment in true actions was conclusive on the class; in hybrid actions, conclusive upon the appearing parties and upon all claims whether or not presented insofar as they affected the property; and in spurious actions, conclusive only upon the appearing parties. He also proposed that another subdivision state "Requisites of Jurisdiction": where jurisdiction of the class action was founded upon diversity of citizenship, only the citizenship of the original parties would matter; where a certain amount in controversy was essential to jurisdiction, the "aggregate claim" of or against the class could be availed of in a true action, but not so for a hybrid or spurious action where the amount would have to be satisfied separately with respect to each original party. Intervenors, according to Professor Moore, need not independently satisfy jurisdictional requirements even in the spurious action, but could rest on the jurisdiction made out for the main action.

The Advisory Committee of that day ultimately declined to promulgate the proposed subdivision dealing with subject matter jurisdiction, which is understandable enough. It declined also to rule on "effects": "The Committee consider it beyond their functions to deal with the question of the effect of judgments on persons who are not parties." It would indeed have been awkward to attempt to predetermine in a blanket way the binding effects of class action judgments. Having thus refused to pronounce upon the consequences of the typing of class actions as true, hybrid, and spurious, the Advisory Committee nevertheless accepted the typing itself. And Professor

Moore's unofficial views on binding effect and other matters as elaborated in his treatise have certainly been influential.

Neither the earlier Federal Equity Rules nor state code provisions had paid any attention to the details of the procedural management of class actions. Rule 23 as adopted followed suit, except for details in subdivision (c) about court approval and notice with respect to dismissal or compromise of class actions. Management questions, including notably the general question of the desirability of providing some notice or information to class members, came to the fore in the professional appraisals of Hansberry v. Lee,[84] decided in 1940. A few lot owners in a development brought an action in a state court of Illinois on behalf of themselves and others similarly situated to enforce against four recalcitrant lot owners a race-restrictive covenant which by its terms was to have come into force when ninety-five percent of the frontage joined in the agreement. The parties to the action stipulated that the required percentage had signed the agreement; the issue litigated was whether intervening neighborhood changes had made the agreement inequitable and unenforceable; and judgment went for the plaintiffs. Later other lot owners brought a second action in the state court to enforce the agreement against still other lot owners. The question was whether the first judgment was binding in the second action, for it could now be shown by independent proof that only fifty-four percent had signed — the stipulation had been mistaken. The state court ruled that the point was concluded, but the Supreme Court reversed, holding that the plaintiffs in the first action did not represent the present defendants or their predecessors in interest and that the state's contrary ruling had deprived the defendants of due process. Justice Stone's discussion intertwines fairness or adequacy of representation of the class with other procedural safeguards. It was plausible to suppose that where claimed inadequacy of representation was the nub of a collateral attack on a class judgment, the question whether members had been informed of the action and thereby had a chance to object to the representation would be distinctly relevant. Informal notice might be thought owing to class members as a matter of "common decency" quite apart from any constitutional necessity. But further, at least where the homogeneity or "solidarity" of the class was open to some question, notice could bear directly on a court's authority to render a judgment with full binding effect on the class. The question of notice, however, was hardly dealt with in Rule 23.

2. *Ambiguities of original Federal Rule 23*. In the wash of more

84. 311 U.S. 32 (1940). One needs to be reminded that *Hansberry* was decided in the era before Shelley v. Kraemer, 334 U.S. 1 (1948).

than a quarter-century's experience, Rule 23 did not come out very well. First, as to the categories. They were confusing. We are reminded of the trouble with the terminology of old Rule 19. At least when not subverted by statute, the words "joint" and "common" perhaps still have some firm meaning as applied to real and personal property, connoting undivided interests in the same thing with varying rights of survivorship, severance, and the like. "Several" perhaps still has a useful meaning as descriptive of exclusive rights in a particular or severed piece of real or personal property. But apart from these cores of possible intelligibility, the terms "joint," "common," and "several" have little or no clear and ascertainable meaning in or out of the context of class actions. . . .

It would have been an argument for retaining the categories, had they been helpful in solving the problem of binding effect. On the whole they were not helpful and on occasion they seemed to distract attention from the real issues. Some cases classified by the courts as spurious seemed suitable, at least on surface inspection, for judgments having full binding effect. . . .

On the other hand, there were instances of courts classifying actions as true or attributing consequences to them seemingly following from such a classification where the net results appeared sound but it was hard to see why the rights were not "several.". . . Professor Wright summed up: "Where the case is such that a class suit can be brought, some courts have thought it 'true,' others have thought it 'spurious,' while most have simply called it a class action.". . .

The class-action device, then, had become snarled. It was a sign of the breakdown of the systematics of the rule that doctrine was growing up which, in class actions taken to be of the nonbinding type, would permit nonjoined members of the class to appear or intervene *after* the merits had been determined favorably to the class. So in Union Carbide & Carbon Co. v. Nisley [113] a majority of the Tenth Circuit Court of Appeals held that absent members of a plaintiff class could take advantage of a favorable interlocutory determination of antitrust liability against the defendants and come in after that determination to present their individual claims for money damages. To some critics this procedure, heretical though it might be, commended itself as a not unfair means of settling controversies involving a large number of small claimants similarly situated. To others the procedure was distasteful as being "one-way," as lacking "mutuality": for it was assumed that members of the class could remain outside the action if the determination were adverse to their interests and in that event they would not be bound. From another quarter, finally, came strong insistence that only by a perverse anomaly could there

113. 300 F.2d 561 (10th Cir. 1961), *petition for cert. dismissed,* 371 U.S. 801 (—).

be such a thing as a class action that did not run fully for or against the class; thus the essential task was to redefine the conditions for maintaining the fully effective action.

3. *Formulation of revised Federal Rule 23.* Despondency over the inadequacies of Rule 23 had led Professor Chafee, among others, to recommend what would have been in effect a return to Federal Equity Rule 38 of 1912, that is, a general formulation in terms of "common question," to which there would have been added provisions regarding the procedural management of the lawsuit, where Rule 23 was plainly deficient. Such a reform would have relieved the courts of the painful exercise of jumping through the hoops of the categories of Rule 23(a), but it would not have been helpfully informative; it would have remitted to case-by-case judicial development a subject and a set of problems on which there had now been large if checkered experience, and which ought to be capable of restatement in a rule providing more than minimal guidance to courts and litigants. The Advisory Committee, at any rate, thought a further effort should be made. They perceived, as lawyers had for a long time, that some litigious situations affecting numerous persons "naturally" or "necessarily" called for unitary adjudication. The problem was how to elaborate this insight while avoiding the pitfalls of abstract classification on the style of 1938. Approaching Rule 23, then, in much the same spirit in which it was considering Rule 19, the Committee strove to sort out the factual situations or patterns that had recurred in class actions and appeared with varying degrees of convincingness to justify treatment of the class *in solido*. The revised rule was written upon the framework thus revealed, after a preliminary analysis which resulted in shearing away and dealing separately with the special situations of derivative actions and actions relating to unincorporated associations.

The Committee started with the well-agreed proposition that there is no basis for a class action unless the class is so numerous as to make individual joinder impracticable, questions of law or fact exist common to the class, and the representative parties are proper champions of the class. These "prerequisites" to any class action are set out in new subdivision (a), a somewhat improved version of the text of the rule of 1912 and of the opening language of the 1938 rule.

What needs to be added to make a "natural" class action? The key to the answer, or to a part of it, was to consider, in relation to varying states of fact, the difficulties that could arise if litigations were carried on, one by one, with individual members of the class. If such repetitious litigations might confront the party opposing the class with adjudications establishing for him inconsistent or incompatible standards of action, then a class action with a single adjudication is evidently in order. This is the substance of new subdivision (b)(1)(A). It takes in cases where the party is obliged by law to treat the members of the class alike (a utility acting toward customers; a government imposing a tax), or where the party must treat all alike as a matter of practical necessity (a riparian owner using water as against downriver owners). The party is saved by a class action from being forced into a "conflicted" position. In new subdivision (b)(1)(B) the Committee took up a vantage point within the class, and spied out situations where lawsuits conducted with individual members of the class would have the practical if not technical effect of concluding the interests of the other members as well, or of impairing the ability of the others to protect their own interests. In the *Ben-Hur* case,[124] . . . the association was either validly reorganized or not: in the nature of the case the adjudication, if attempted at all, must as a practical matter extend to the whole class of certificate holders. The same holds for an action to compel a corporation to declare a dividend and for other kinds of actions seeking to fix the rights of security holders. And an action by one of a numerous group of claimants attacking a fund insufficient to satisfy the demands of all claimants may illustrate that impairment of the ability of other members to protect their rights in the fund, which suggests that the class-action device should be put to work. It will be noted that the criteria so far mentioned resemble those used in new Rule 19; the resemblances are not accidental but logical. Next comes new subdivision (b)(2), building on experience mainly, but not exclusively, in the civil rights field. Here individual lawsuits, even if they could conceivably avoid untoward effects comparable to those following from separate actions in (b)(1) situations, would nevertheless be inadequate and inefficient. When the party opposing a class had acted on grounds apparently applying to the whole group, a representative suit should be available to secure for the class any appropriate injunctive or declaratory relief. So (b)(2) provides.

The most interesting problem in the law of multiple parties, however, is tendered by the recurrent cases where a party's act or omission has radiated outward to affect a large number of people, yet there are no such clear indicia for use of class actions as in the prior examples. Not all these cases call for class treatment, but some do. New subdivision (b)(3) tries to distinguish; and it is well at the outset to say that the cases which will pass through the screen of (b)(3) and qualify as class actions are not simply the spurious cases of former Rule 23 with a discreet suppression of the old soubriquet. The object is to get at the cases where a class action promises important

124. [Supreme Tribe of Ben-Hur v. Cauble, 255 U.S. 356 (1921).]

advantages of economy of effort and uniformity of result without undue dilution of procedural safeguards for members of the class or for the opposing party. The new provision invites a close look at the case before it is accepted as a class action and even then requires that it be specially treated.

After any necessary hearings the court must have made an express finding that common questions not only exist but "predominate" over questions touching only individual members of the class. For a class action loses attractiveness as the individual questions are seen to have such scope or variety as to overload the action. The court must also have found expressly that a class action is "superior" to other means of disposing of the particular set of quarrels. For . . . the procedural alternatives are hardly confined to the class action, on the one side, and individual uncoordinated lawsuits, on the other; there are often other possibilities ranging from use of a model action to consolidation or coordination of the numerous individual actions for all or selected purposes.

The rule sets out a number of matters pertinent to the (b)(3) findings, and among them "the interest of members of the class in individually controlling the prosecution or defense of separate actions." This interest can be high where the stake of each member bulks large and his will and ability to take care of himself are strong; the interest may be no more than theoretic where the individual stake is so small as to make a separate action impracticable. But even when the action is found by the court to lie within (b)(3), individual preference is still allowed to operate, and in a somewhat novel manner. Any member of a (b)(3) class may, under new subdivision (c)(2), "opt out" by informing the court that he requests exclusion; he is then untouched by the action and fends for himself. By inaction, he accepts representation. If unwilling to rely entirely on the representative party, the class member may enter an appearance in the action through counsel.[137] By the ordinary procedure he can of course, go further and, upon a proper showing, move to intervene. The machinery which touches off the possibility of election is an informing (though informal) notice which the court is required by (c)(2) to direct to members of the class, including individual notice to those members who can be identified by reasonable effort. This notice, besides helping

137. I read this "appearance" as entitling counsel to receive the papers in the action to enable him to follow the case with a view to deciding, e.g., whether he should move to intervene. If "appearance" is read as enabling the class member to be admitted automatically into the action as a party, it would stand in odd contrast to intervention in the action under Rule 24, which is not automatic and requires a showing. Interpretation is, however, made less important because the appearance could in all events be limited under Rule 23(d)(1), just as intervention may be limited. . . .

to democratize the procedure for members of the class, joins with other features of the new rule in helping to justify the ultimate extension of the judgment in (b)(3) cases to all members of the class, except those who requested exclusion from the action: recall Hansberry v. Lee with its suggestion that the validity of class adjudication is related to the fairness of the procedural forms through which the adjudication is attained.

The Advisory Committee forecast that cases of fraudulent misrepresentations or antitrust violations affecting numerous persons would be likely, although not by any means sure candidates for class treatment under subdivision (b)(3). . . . On the other hand, the Committee stated that litigation arising from "mass accidents" injuring numerous persons would ordinarily not be appropriate for class handling. What makes against a class action here is not the fact that after determination of common questions the individual claimants might have to come in and prove their damages, for such follow-up proceedings will occur in various (b)(3) actions. The point rather is that in accident cases the realities of litigation will often suggest that the class procedure is not "superior" to more commonplace devices; in some of these cases, moreover, individual questions of liability and defense will overwhelm the common questions.

It is implicit in what has been said that the anomaly of a class action covering only the particular parties does not survive under the new rule. Subdivision (c)(2) makes clear that the judgment in any class action maintained as such extends to the class (excluding opters-out in (b)(3) cases), whether or not favorable to the class. This is a statement of how the judgment shall read, not an attempted prescription of its subsequent res judicata effect, although looking ahead with hope to that effect.

The revised rule is rounded out with a provision entitled "Orders in Conduct of Actions" listing a number of discretionary steps available to the court for the better management of class actions generally. Among them are orders requiring, "for the protection of the members of the class or otherwise for the fair conduct of the action," that notice be given to some or all members of the class informing them of any event in the action, or of their opportunity to speak their piece on the adequacy of the representation, or to intervene in the action. Here the Committee was responding to Professor Chafee's remark, echoed by others, that class members "ought to be informed as well as represented." Finally, the new rule broadens the old in requiring notice to members, in such manner as the court directs, as a condition of dismissal or compromise of any class action; the old rule made the notice mandatory for true actions but discretionary for hybrid and spurious actions. . . .

It was suggested that the judgment in a (b)(3) class action, instead of covering by its terms all class members who do not opt out, should embrace only those individuals who in response to notice affirmatively signify their desire to be included (others might perhaps be included if considered essential by the court). It is unfair to a defendant opposing the class, so the argument goes, to subject him to possible liability toward individuals who remain passive after receiving notice or who may, indeed, have had no notice of the proceeding: under the previous law, some, perhaps many, of those persons might simply have foregone any claims against the defendant; they might in fact have remained ignorant of having any possible claims. Running through this argument was the idea that litigation should be a matter for distinct action by each individual. . . .

. . . [R]equiring the individuals affirmatively to request inclusion in the lawsuit would result in freezing out the claims of people — especially small claims held by small people — who for one reason or another, ignorance, timidity, unfamiliarity with business or legal matters, will simply not take the affirmative step. The moral justification for treating such people as null quantities is questionable. For them the class action serves something like the function of an administrative proceeding where scattered individual interests are represented by the Government. In the circumstances delineated in subdivision (b)(3), it seems fair for the silent to be considered as part of the class. Otherwise the (b)(3) type would become a class action which was not that at all — a prime point of discontent with the spurious action from which the Advisory Committee started its review of Rule 23. . . .

C. *Intervention*

According to new Rule 19(a) on compulsory joinder, the likelihood that the disposition of an action will, as a practical matter, impair a third person's ability to protect an interest which he claims in the subject of the litigation, is a reason for having that person joined in the action. Indeed, if for some formal reason he cannot be joined, a question is raised under Rule 19(b) whether the action should not be dismissed. Suppose, in the circumstances mentioned, the third person, without waiting to be rung into the action by a party, himself demands admission to it as an intervening party. It seems to follow as a counterpart to Rule 19 that he has a plausible case for intervention.

Old Rule 24(a)(3) showed an understanding of the point in providing for intervention "of right" when the "applicant" (the intending intervenor) was "so situated as to be adversely affected by a distribution or other disposition of property which is in the custody of the court." The trouble was that the language was too much hedged about, for an applicant might be severely affected in a practical sense by the outcome of an action even though it did not involve property in custody. Quite understandably, some courts read Rule 24(a)(3) without literal attention to the requirement regarding property.

A further provision for intervention of right appeared in 24(a)(2): "when the representation of the applicant's interest by existing parties is or may be inadequate and the applicant is or may be bound by a judgment in the action." This was intended to permit a beneficiary, say, to come into an action in which his fiduciary was appearing for him when the fiduciary suffered a conflict of interest or other disqualification; and the same applied to a member of a class coming into a class action to challenge and improve the representation. But if "bound" in the text of the rule was taken to mean that the applicant, though he remained outside the lawsuit, would be concluded by the judgment as a matter of strict res judicata, then a kind of dilemma or stymie could occur. In regard to a class action, Hansberry v. Lee taught that where a member of the class to which the judgment supposedly extended had been "represented" by purported champions with interests antagonistic to his own, he might establish that fact in a subsequent proceeding in which the judgment was sought to be used against him, and the judgment would then be held not to bind him. Now consider a class member who attempted to anticipate the occasion for collateral attack by intervening in the class suit to claim such a lack of sound representation. If the representation was in fact defective the judgment in the action would not "bind" under *Hansberry*, and, in strictness, intervention should be denied under Rule 24(a)(2); but if the representation was in fact satisfactory, there was no predicate at all for intervention. In 1961 the Supreme Court appeared to read 24(a)(2) in this crippling way in the case of Sam Fox Publishing Co. v. United States; [171] disfavor of private interventions in government antitrust suits, however, may have influenced the result. The Government in a Sherman Act proceeding had secured a consent decree against ASCAP, an unincorporated association. It now proposed a modification of the decree further to regulate the internal affairs of ASCAP by improving the systems of electing the governing board and distributing revenues to members. Sam Fox, a small publisher-member of ASCAP, tried to intervene of right, claiming that the proposals did not go far enough for the protection of the smaller members and that the representation of such members in the action was inadequate because the board, purportedly representing the members of the association as a class, was dominated

171. 366 U.S. 683 (1961). . . .

by the big fish. The Supreme Court, in denying intervention of right, gave weight to the reasoning outlined above.

Lower courts were somewhat incredulous about the dilemmatic interpretation of the rule and showed a distinct tendency to balk at it. This interpretation had, indeed, some of the perverseness of the jurisdiction-fallacy discussed under rule 19. But whatever might be said about the literal meaning of Rule 24(a)(2), common sense suggested that any real question of the adequacy of representation ought to be thrashed out within the action itself, rather than indefinitely deferred.

To sum up, subdivision (a)(3) of Rule 24 needed some extension, and the "binding" language had to be excised from subdivision (a)(2). The Advisory Committee undertook only these reforms. They were accomplished by writing a new composite subdivision (a)(2) which states that an applicant qualifies for intervention of right when he claims "an interest relating to the property or transaction which is the subject of the action" and "disposition of the action may as a practical matter impair or impede his ability to protect that interest" — the language to this point is analogous to that of new Rule 19(a)(2)(i) — "unless the applicant's interest is adequately represented by existing parties." It might be objected that the "unless" clause is *de trop* because the applicant should be his own judge of whether his interest is being adequately represented; but that would break in rudely on ideas of fiduciary representation and contribute, besides, to a cluttering of lawsuits with multitudinous useless intervenors. On the other hand, the question of representation and its adequacy, released from specific connection with res judicata, is to be decided without fetishes of form — thus representation may be adequate even though it is not formal — and with due attention to the character of the litigation and to its condition at the time of the application to intervene.

. . . The changed wording of the rule was intended (besides overcoming *Sam Fox*) to drive beyond the narrow notion of an interest in specific property. But the interest spoken of in the new rule finds its own limits in the historic continuity of the subject of intervention and in the concepts of new Rule 19, to which intervention looks for analogy. New Rule 24(a)(2) invites us to see that the practical consequence to the applicants of being denied intervention is that they cannot stop a settlement nor, if dissatisfied with the decree entered after contest, press their contentions on appeal; they are remitted, instead, to subsequent independent private actions in which it would be hard (although not impossible) to induce the courts to grant them better relief than was accorded by the settlement. This factor can weigh for intervention; it is a matter for consideration from case to case.

NOTES AND COMMENTS

What accounts for the structure that Rule 23(b) gives to the class action? Class actions described by 23(b)(3) are separated from those falling within subsections (b)(1) and (b)(2) in that absent members of (b)(3) classes are to receive "the best notice practicable under the circumstances" and have the opportunity to opt out of the action, unlike members of the other classes. Thus the rule preserves the right of (b)(3) class members to litigate independently (subject to the chance that "the best notice practicable" does not reach them), while the rule denies this right to absent members of (b)(1) and (b)(2) classes. When members of (b)(3) classes opt out and litigate separately, the result may be that similarly situated persons are treated differently — some class members may lose while others win. The effect of denying a right to opt out in (b)(1) and (b)(2) cases is to insure that similarly situated persons will be treated alike, once the cases are certified as such. What explains this difference in treatment?

Some Thoughts on Intervention Before Courts, Agencies, and Arbitrators *

David L. Shapiro

I. Introduction

A Civil action, in the Anglo-American tradition, has usually been thought of as a private controversy between plaintiff and defendant. Although outsiders were sometimes permitted to take part in order to protect their interests, they were more often regarded by the court and the parties as undesired intermeddlers who should be required to protect themselves — if they could — by bringing a lawsuit of their own. Indeed after courts of admiralty, and later of equity, recognized intervention as a proper means of asserting an interest in property in the custody of the court, there remained considerable uncertainty for many years about whether, and to what extent, intervention could be permitted in a routine action at law.

But in recent decades the increased complexity of litigation and the growing number of cases involving the public interest or a wide variety of private interests have been accompanied by a steady change in the attitude toward intervention. Both intervention of right and

* *Source:* 81 Harv. L. Rev. 721, 721-724, 726-727, 729-744, 746-752, 754, 757, 761-763 (1968).

permissive intervention were given new vitality in the federal system by adoption of Rule 24 of the Federal Rules of Civil Procedure in 1938, and subsequent amendments have broadened their scope. The most recent pronouncement of the Supreme Court in Cascade Natural Gas Corp. v. El Paso Natural Gas Co.,[5] interpreting the 1966 amendment to Rule 24 before scarcely a district court had been able to look at it, may have expanded the right to intervene beyond the dreams, or nightmares, of the draftsmen of that amendment. The question now has shifted to whether in public or private litigation we have gone too far in welcoming those who wish to participate in, and perhaps obstruct, the course of the proceedings. . . .

An example . . . may help to crystallize the questions posed when a person seeks to intervene in a proceeding. . . .

The Justice Department brings an action against company *A* under section 7 of the Clayton Act,[14] challenging the acquisition by *A* of company *B*. After negotiation, the parties prepare for approval of the court a consent decree which requires divestiture of *B* by *A* over a period of several years, defines the properties to be conveyed to *B*, and sets forth the permissible relations between *A* and *B* prior to divestiture. Company *C*, a competitor of *A*'s, seeks to intervene in the proceeding, alleging that the terms of the divestiture leave *A* too strong and *B* too weak and give *A* too much time to divest. In addition, some of *A*'s dealers seek to intervene, alleging that the decree will leave *A* too weak and will deprive them of an opportunity to deal in *B*'s products when divestiture occurs. Is it sufficient to permit *C* and *A*'s dealers to communicate these views to the parties and perhaps to the court as amici curiae? [16] Must they also be given an opportunity for full participation as parties, including the right to engage in discovery, to introduce evidence, to cross-examine, to block a settlement, and to appeal from the entry of a decree? What weight is to be given the Justice Department's argument that intervention will only produce unnecessary delay and unduly interfere with its task of effectuating antitrust policy in the public interest? . . .

II. Some Basic Issues

A. *Intervention v. Initiation*

Perhaps it should go without saying, but it must be understood that there is a difference between the question whether one is a

5. 386 U.S. 129 (1967).

14. 15 U.S.C. §18 (1964).

16. There may be a difference between *C* and *A*'s dealers in that *C* is seeking to strengthen the decree, and thus arguably to represent a broad public interest, while *A*'s dealers are seeking to weaken it. . . .

proper plaintiff or defendant in an initial action and the question whether one is entitled to intervene. Thus, to decide whether a particular action may be brought by this plaintiff against this defendant may require a determination of whether the controversy is ripe for adjudication, whether the parties before the court are the real parties in interest, and whether the interests asserted are sufficient to mobilize the judicial machinery. When one seeks to intervene in an ongoing lawsuit, these basic questions have presumably been resolved; the disposition of the request, then, should focus on whether the prospective intervener has a sufficient stake in the outcome and enough to contribute to the resolution of the controversy to justify his inclusion. In the federal courts, at least, this distinction in some instances may be of constitutional dimensions. *A* may not have a dispute with *C* that could qualify as a case or controversy, but he may have a sufficient interest in *B*'s dispute with *C* to warrant his participation in the case once it has begun, and the case or controversy limitation should impose no barrier to his admission.

The difference suggested here is most evident in the case of one who seeks to intervene on the side of the defendant in civil litigation. When property owners sue to enjoin a railroad from maintaining storage tracks in a residential neighborhood, a local businessman who is heavily dependent on the use of that trackage may have an important interest to protect and much to contribute to the court's understanding of the case, even though he has no claim that could be asserted against any of the parties and they have none that could be asserted against him.

This difference can also exist when the intervention is on the plaintiff's side. Under Title IV of the Landrum-Griffin Act, only the Secretary of Labor can initiate an action to set aside a union election, but it need not follow that the complainant who starts the machinery of the Secretary in motion may never intervene to protect his interest once a case is filed. That determination may well turn on a number of factors quite separate from his standing to sue, including the nature of his interest and the adequacy of the protection afforded that interest by existing parties.

I believe the suggested distinction has important implications in determining the content of intervention. When one is granted intervention, either as of right or in the exercise of discretion, it does not necessarily follow that he must be granted all the rights of a party at the trial and appellate levels, including full rights of discovery and cross-examination, the ability to veto a settlement of the case, and the right to appeal from a final decision. It is both feasible and desirable to break down the concept of intervention into a number of litigation rights and to conclude that a given person has one or some of these rights but not all. . . .

B. Defining the "Interest" of the Applicant for Intervention

At the heart of almost every intervention case is the nature and extent of the applicant's interest in the proceeding. Statutes will occasionally grant an "interested person" or a "party in interest" a right to intervene in administrative or judicial proceedings without defining what that interest should be. The amended version of Rule 24(a) is a bit more ambitious; it creates a right to intervene — unless an applicant's interest is adequately represented by existing parties — when he "claims an interest relating to the property or transaction which is the subject of the action and he is so situated that the disposition of the action may as a practical matter impair or impede his ability to protect that interest. . . ." This language indicates that one must have more of a stake in the proceeding than simply a concern with the general precedent value of the decision in wholly unrelated litigation, but beyond that the boundaries of Rule 24(a) are uncertain. Any effort to read the rule narrowly will have to contend with the decision of the Supreme Court in the *El Paso* case. That case involved a decree of divestiture entered by the trial court, pursuant to a stipulation by the parties, following a decision by the Supreme Court that the acquisition of Pacific Northwest Pipeline Corporation by El Paso Natural Gas Company violated the Clayton Act. On appeal from the district court's denial of intervention in the decree proceedings, the Court held: (1) that the state of California and a large industrial user of natural gas in California had a right to intervene . . . and (2) that on remand a customer of Pacific Northwest was entitled to intervene . . . because of its "interest" in seeing that the company to be created by the divestiture was viable and able to supply its requirements. Just why this interest is sufficient to warrant intervention — or how the case is to be distinguished from hundreds of others in which suppliers, customers, or competitors of a party to the action are "interested" in the outcome — is left to conjecture. . . .

. . . I have discovered that it is not particularly helpful to divide the cases into those involving intervention of right and permissive intervention, or those involving an interest in property subject to the court's control and other types of interest. The former distinction has been modified by the recent amendments and had previously been blurred by some appellate decisions that had strained to find a basis for review and reversal of a lower court's denial of intervention. The latter distinction, absent in the present version of Rule 24(a), lost its usefulness when several courts expanded the idea of property beyond all definable boundaries.

Recognizing that any effort at classification is a highly risky venture, and that my final category is little more than a catchall, I suggest that the interests the courts consider sufficient to warrant intervention fall into five general groupings.[42]

1. *Judgment Will Have a Binding Effect on the Applicant.* The first grouping consists of cases in which the prospective intervener may be bound by the judgment — may lose a legal claim or defense — under a governing contract or statute or under the principle of res judicata. Since it is unusual for a person who is not a party to an action to lose a legal claim or defense as a result of that action, these cases are rare. One example is a true in rem proceeding in which a claimant must intervene now or remain forever silent.[43] Another example is a class action. (It is noteworthy that, in those class actions falling within the scope of amended Rule 23(b)(3), a member of the class may either exclude himself from the judgment or enter an appearance through counsel. If the right to "enter an appearance" falls short of a right to intervene, presumably the application of a member of the class to intervene will be denied only if his interests are represented adequately by existing parties.) A third example is a suit brought by a corporation: loss of the action by the corporation will bar a subsequent derivative action on the same claim by the shareholder — thus his claim to intervene should be made contingent only on the adequacy of the corporation's representation of his interests. As a final example, one may be obligated by contract or statute to pay the winner or reimburse the loser of a particular lawsuit.

2. *Effective Loss of Claim or Defense.* Another category of cases embraces those in which the prospective intervener may, as a result of the judgment, be "left with a claim [or defense?] against one of the parties in the . . . action which, although technically unimpaired, is practically and factually worthless." Some of these cases, though not all, fell within the terms of former Rule 24(a)(3) — for example, a case in which the only source for satisfaction of a claim is a fund within the court's control that is insufficient to satisfy all existing claims against it. Similarly, one may be asserting a lien against the proceeds of a judgment or other property and have a legitimate fear that if intervention is not permitted the property may be dissipated before the lien can be enforced in another suit.

If this category is not to blur into the next, it is important to exclude those cases in which the claim or defense may be rendered worthless simply because the court in the second action is almost certain to follow the prior decision on the basis of stare decisis or,

42. These categories do not purport to cover all instances in which there is a specific statutory right to intervene as, for example, under the Miller Act, 40 U.S.C. §276a-2(b) (1964), or the Interstate Commerce Act, 49 U.S.C. §17(11) (1964).

43. . . . Many cases involving intervention in receivership, reorganization, and bankruptcy proceedings . . . would appear to fall into this general category.

if the jurisdiction is a different one, as a matter of comity. The worthlessness of the claim or defense must result from the limited source of satisfaction or from the likelihood that the property in question will be dissipated before it can be reached.

3. *Claim or Defense Related to the Subject Matter of the Action.* A third grouping consists of cases in which the prospective intervener has a claim against one of the parties, or a defense to a claim that might be made by one of the parties, which is related to the subject matter of the action. While the claim or defense will still be available in a separate action if not asserted in the present one, intervention may have several evident advantages. It can insure against inconsistent results[52] and avoid multiplicity of litigation. It can give the prospective intervener a crack at the initial judgment of the court on questions of law and law application; in subsequent litigation he will have to contend with stare decisis in the same jurisdiction, or comity in another. On the other hand, intervention may unduly complicate the proceedings and introduce issues plainly extraneous to the original action.

Although this category appears to be an elaborate statement of the permissive intervention provisions of Rule 24(b)(2), there are instances when such cases have been squeezed into the mold of Rule 24(a) to facilitate reversal of a district court denial of intervention.

Some cases of intervention by the government, or by private persons in government litigation, fit this grouping. As an example of the former, the Government has, with varying success, sought to intervene in patent litigation to assert a claim that the patent in issue had been used in violation of the antitrust laws. And *El Paso* itself may be an example of the latter, at least in part. Had the California utility not become a party to the suit, it might in theory have had a private claim against El Paso, arising out of the acquisition, for which it could have sought injunctive relief going beyond the scope of the decree it was attacking. Such a claim, of course, would not have been worth much as a practical matter since it is highly unlikely that any court would use the existing decree simply as a springboard for the grant of additional relief, even if the requisite private injury could be established.

4. *Government Intervention to Represent the Public Interest.* Clearly deserving a category of their own are those cases in which an agency of government, although it has no claim or defense that could be

52. . . . One possible disincentive to intervention in cases within this category is the growing tendency of courts to permit offensive as well as defensive use of collateral estoppel by a nonparty, who still remains immune from any adverse use of the doctrine. . . .

asserted in a separate action, seeks to intervene to represent the public interest in a particular controversy. Such intervention has grown in importance as the amount of private litigation raising significant issues of public interest has increased, though it does not approach the practice in France, where the local delegate of the Ministry of Justice may intervene in virtually any case which he believes will affect the public interest. . . . Section 2403 of the Judicial Code confers on the Government a right to intervene when the constitutionality of a federal statute is challenged. . . . And Rule 24(b), as amended in 1946, permits intervention by an officer or agency when a party is relying for claim or defense on a statute, executive order, or regulation administered by that officer or agency. . . .

5. *Limited, Identifiable Interest Differentiating Intervener from Ordinary Member of the Public.* A final category consists of those cases in which a private person seeking intervention has no legal claim that can be independently asserted against any of the parties and is subject to no claim that may be asserted against him, but nevertheless has an identifiable interest — usually but not always economic — that sets him apart from an ordinary member of the public. Since Rule 24(b) requires a claim or defense, it would appear that such persons could intervene in a federal proceeding, if at all, only under Rule 24(a), yet some courts have stretched Rule 24(b) to accommodate them.

The cases coming under this heading are of such extraordinary variety that it is probably bootless to attempt to break them down further. But some illustrations of cases in which intervention has been allowed may be helpful.

> *Atlantic Refining Co. v. Standard Oil Co.*[75] A large refining company brought an action against the Secretary of the Interior attacking certain oil import quotas that allegedly favored the smaller refiners. The court of appeals, reversing a district court judgment, held that several smaller refiners must be allowed to intervene. The opinion noted that those refiners would suffer direct and immediate injury if the plaintiff prevailed and that they proposed to add several defenses to those raised by the Secretary. . . .
>
> *Justice v. United States.*[77] In an action brought by the United States to enforce a summons of the Internal Revenue Service seeking documents in possession of a bank and involving transactions between appellant taxpayers and the bank, appellants were denied intervention in the district court. The court of appeals reversed, saying that appellants should be allowed to protect their interests and might be "bound" by the judgment.
>
> *Textile Workers Union v. Allendale Co.*[78] Certain manufacturers brought an action against the Secretary of Labor to review a determina-

75. 304 F.2d 387 (D.C. Cir. 1962).
77. 365 F.2d 312 (6th Cir. 1966).
78. 226 F.2d 765 (D.C. Cir. 1955), *cert. denied,* 351 U.S. 909 (1956).

tion fixing a nationwide minimum wage for an industry under the Walsh-Healey Act. The district court's denial of intervention by a competing manufacturer (who was paying wages above the minimum) and by a union representing textile workers was reversed on appeal under both subsections (a) and (b) of Rule 24.

United States v. Terminal Railroad Association.[79] Certain private companies were permitted to intervene to seek modification of a decree approved by the court in an antitrust action brought by the United States. The companies contended that a provision of the decree prohibiting the defendant carriers from engaging in certain types of transportation would cause them great injury.

A few observations can be made about this final category. First, it is clear from the wide range of situations that have arisen, and from a comparison of cases going different ways, that considerable discretion is being exercised in determining whether, under all the circumstances, intervention is warranted. Second, a factor that is sometimes articulated by the courts . . . is the extent of the contribution that the prospective intervener can make to the understanding of the case by the adjudicator. . . . The factor is explicitly recognized . . . in Rule 24; subsection (a) refers to the adequacy of representation by existing parties and subsection (b) to the relevance of undue delay to the exercise of the court's discretion. . . .

. . . The range of possible interests may defy adequate classification, spreading over a spectrum that is extremely hard to chart. Whether a sufficient interest exists to make intervention appropriate calls for considerable and careful judgment, and perhaps a little faith as well, with attention to such factors as the legal and practical availability of other remedies, the contribution that the prospective intervener can make to the litigation, the immediacy and degree of the harm threatened, and the advantages of avoiding multiplicity of actions. Further, the range of possible interests indicates the propriety of regarding interveners as not necessarily possessing all the litigation rights of the original parties to the action.

C. *Adequacy of Representation*

The issue of the adequacy with which the prospective intervener's interests are being represented by existing parties is often as troublesome as the determination of those interests. . . .

What, then, makes for inadequate representation? If we look for guidance to the *El Paso* decision, we come away puzzled, at best. The Court was evidently dissatisfied with the terms of the decree formulated by the Justice Department, as well as with the performance

79. 236 U.S. 194 (1915).

of the district court judge, and the Court's sympathy with the views of the prospective interveners on the merits was apparently the basis for its conclusion on the issue of adequacy. . . .

Mr. Justice Stewart's dissent points out that the majority's rationale appears to permit a process of second-guessing by the appellate court on the basis of what happened below after intervention was denied. But his summary of the existing state of the law on this issue may have painted a picture of somewhat greater uniformity than the decisions warranted. Inadequacy of representation had been found under Rule 24(a)(2), he stated, only when there was a conflict of interest, a complete failure of representation, or collusion attributable to the party who was supposed to be representing the prospective intervener. Certainly there are many cases granting intervention on these grounds, and others denying it when no such claim could be sustained. Moreover, several decisions have indicated that the showing must be especially clear when it is the adequacy of representation by the government that is challenged. But there are also decisions that implicitly or explicitly reject such limiting standards. One such case, given a "but cf." reference by Mr. Justice Stewart, is Ford Motor Co. v. Bisanz Brothers,[101] a suit in which a group of property owners sought to enjoin a railroad from maintaining and operating storage tracks in a residential neighborhood. Ford, a manufacturer who relied heavily on the use of this trackage, sought to intervene to protect its interest. A denial of intervention below was reversed on appeal, the court noting that the interest of the railroad as a carrier was somewhat different from the interest of Ford as a shipper. Although both were eager for the same result, there was no conflict between them, and the railroad had raised the interests of shippers in its pleadings, "it cannot be said with certainty" that the railroad would adequately bring forth all the evidence and arguments bearing on those interests. The criteria for intervention of right were therefore held to be satisfied.

It is hard, at least for me, to disagree with the decision allowing intervention in this case, although the matter might better be viewed as one of discretion than as one of absolute right. Yet there was no conflict of interest, collusion, or failure of representation on the part of the railroad. The point was simply that Ford's interest was perhaps greater than the railroad's and at least was sufficiently different in character to suggest that it might be able to contribute additional data and arguments to the proceeding.

If there are occasions when a flexible view of adequacy is warranted in private litigation, should courts adhere to a more rigid

101. 249 F.2d 22, 28 (8th Cir. 1957). . . .

standard when it is the adequacy of representation by the *government* that is in question? A number of decisions prior to *El Paso* did not, but the tendency, particularly in antitrust cases, has been to deny intervention by private parties. The Antitrust Division has argued forcefully that this strict policy is essential if its consent decree program is to accomplish its objective. Perhaps the answer to this question, at least in antitrust cases, cannot be given without a full analysis of the underlying substantive issues of economic and legal policy embodied in the antitrust laws. . . .

It is true that interveners are motivated by their private interests, and sometimes their principal goal may be to delay or to block settlement, no matter how desirable. But the very fact that the intervener — from the vantage point of his own interest — sees the case with a perspective and perhaps an intensity different from that of the agency charged with the protection of the public as a whole may indicate that he can in fact contribute to the court's total understanding. Indeed, without him there may be no one to question what the parties have done. That some applicants may be seeking only to delay and obstruct suggests not that the courts should consistently deny intervention but rather that they be vested with discretion to decide both whether intervention should be allowed and, if it should, the extent of the intervener's participation. . . .

The fear that a permissive approach to intervention would lead to a flood of interveners in every case is, I think, unfounded. A state decision, Roosevelt v. Beau Monde Co.,[116] may provide a helpful illustration. The plaintiff brought an action against the municipal authorities to compel the issuance of a building permit for a shopping center, and a number of persons who owned adjoining property, some within the town and some in a neighboring town, sought to intervene. The state supreme court reversed the trial court's refusal to allow either group to intervene. Even the former group, the court reasoned, might not be adequately represented by the municipality, not because of bad faith, collusion, or incompetence, but because the interests of the town as a whole in having the shopping center might not fully coincide with the interests of these residential property owners. Accordingly, their positions and presentations might vary, and the court was entitled to hear from all who had something to offer. Of course, if other adjoining residential property owners had subsequently sought to intervene through their own counsel, a very different issue would have been presented. The interests of these persons would in all likelihood exactly coincide with the interests of those who had already been admitted. Under these circumstances

116. 152 Colo. 567, 384 P.2d 96 (1963). . . .

the court should require a strong showing of inadequacy in the sense of bad faith or incompetence before allowing the proceeding to become more complicated. . . .

This discussion demonstrates, I think, that adequacy of representation is a very complex variable indeed. At one extreme, when the applicant is seeking to assert his own separate claim for relief against one of the parties, it is not really an issue at all. At the other extreme, when the applicant is making no claim of his own but is seeking to assert the same position as one who is already a party and whose interests precisely coincide with his, the issue of adequacy should be, as Mr. Justice Stewart suggests, limited to questions of competence, collusion, and bad faith. But between these poles lies a substantial area where the question of adequacy is closely tied to that of interest. In these cases the applicant wants not to make his own claim but to support or supplement the position of one of the parties whose stake in the proceeding differs from his, though there may be no conflict of interest between them. The court's judgment in such cases should be influenced in part by the extent of the applicant's interest — do considerations of fairness strongly suggest that he be heard on a matter of this importance to him? — and in part by the contribution that he can make to the court's understanding of the case in the light of his knowledge and concern.

D. Appealability of a Denial of Intervention

One of the most fertile sources of difficulty in this field is the question of the appealability of a denial of an application to intervene.[121] Generally an appeal from [a] district court determination will lie only from a "final" decision or order. The prospective intervener, however, does not want to wait until the completion of the case on the merits before appealing from a denial of intervention; thus the question arises whether such a denial is a "final" decision from which an appeal can be taken while litigation is in process. A refusal to allow intervention is not a final decision with respect to the controversy as a whole since the proceeding is still pending, but the decision is certainly the end of the line for the intervener since he can take no further part except perhaps as an amicus curiae.

Courts faced with this dilemma have neither spoken with one voice nor offered very satisfactory solutions. If the trial court errs in denying intervention — whether the error involved an intervention as of right or an abuse of discretion in denying permissive interven-

121. No instances have been found in which an effort has been made, prior to final judgment, to obtain review of a *grant* of intervention.

tion — the time to reverse is when the decision is made so that the intervener will be able to participate in the original trial. Yet some courts, for purposes of appeal, have treated the two types of intervention differently. . . .

Some courts have stated that if the application was addressed to the court's discretion — that is, if the applicant was not entitled to intervention as of right — no appeal will lie from a denial before the litigation is concluded, even if the denial was an abuse of discretion. This approach has led a number of appellate courts, confronted with a denial they believe to be unjust, to squeeze the case into the mold of Rule 24(a), thus avoiding the question of appealability under Rule 24(b). This process, however, has had the undesirable consequence of clouding the distinction between the two types of intervention in situations where that distinction may be valuable.

Other courts have avoided this pitfall but have introduced another questionable limitation on the appealability of a denial of a motion to intervene: if the prospective intervener has some other means of protecting his interest, the denial is not final as to him. . . . The availability of alternative protections should, at most, be a relevant factor in assessing the nature and extent of the applicant's interest. . . . [I]t would be better to hold merely that a denial of intervention is a final decision — permitting any applicant for intervention to appeal from such a denial — but that it can be reversed only if there was a right to intervene or an abuse of discretion.

E. Variations on the Theme: Degrees of Intervention . . .

A variety of procedures short of intervention, generally involving an appearance as an amicus curiae, have been successfully used to allow a person to make his views known in the proceedings. These range from permitting only the submission of a brief, to permitting extensive participation in the trial, including the introduction of evidence or the right of cross-examination. . . .

Another area of potential limitation is on the injection of new issues or the addition of parties by the intervener. Here again the administrative agencies have acted with some success in limiting intervention to particular issues and in resisting undue expansion of the proceedings. Certainly a court may do the same when intervention has been granted as a matter of discretion; indeed, to allow the injection of new, unrelated issues by way of defense, cross-claim, or counterclaim may in itself be an abuse of discretion. But Professor Moore urges that if intervention is a matter of right the intervener cannot be prevented from asserting counterclaims or cross-claims, even if they may unduly complicate the proceeding, provided there is no jurisdictional obstacle. In this situation he suggests that the only recourse of the court is to separate trials under Rule 42(b). Yet it should not follow from the right to intervene on a given issue that the intervener obtains all the rights of a party with respect to every issue. If, for example, the Government exercises its right to intervene in private litigation involving the constitutionality of an act regulating commerce, it should not be able to assert an unrelated contract claim. . . .

III. Some Proposals

A. *Civil Litigation in the Federal Courts*

Throughout this discussion, several express and implied criticisms have been made of the rules governing intervention in federal courts — rules which have a substantial impact on intervention practice in state courts as well. . . .

In light of these comments, I tentatively propose several changes in the rules governing intervention in civil litigation in the federal courts. . . .

First, I recommend that Rule 24 be amended to provide:

> (a) *Intervention of Right.* Upon timely application anyone shall be permitted to intervene in an action: (1) when a statute of the United States confers an unconditional right to intervene; or (2) when the applicant is a member of a class by or against which an action has been brought under Rules 23, 23.1, or 23.2, or is a person as described in Rule 19(a)(2)(i), unless in either case it is clearly established that the applicant's interest is adequately represented by existing parties.
>
> (b) *Permissive Intervention.* Upon timely application anyone may be permitted to intervene in an action: (1) when a statute of the United States confers a conditional right to intervene; or (2) in any other case in which the applicant's intervention is appropriate.
>
> (c) *Same; Factors to be Considered.* The factors to be considered by the court in exercising its discretion under subdivision (b) hereof include, where relevant: (1) the nature and extent of the applicant's interest in the subject matter of the action and the degree to which the disposition of the action may as a practical matter impair or impede his ability to protect that interest; (2) the adequacy of the representation of the applicant's interest by existing parties; (3) the relationship of the applicant's claim or defense, if any, to the subject matter of the action; (4) the avoidance of multiplicity of actions; (5) whether the intervention will unduly delay or prejudice the adjudication of the rights of the original parties; and (6) the contribution the applicant may make to the just determination of the issues.
>
> (d) *Limited Intervention.* In any action in which intervention is granted under this rule, the court, in the interest of just and expeditious

adjudication, may impose reasonable conditions or restrictions on the extent of the intervener's participation in the proceedings, including restrictions on the filing of counterclaims, cross-claims, or additional claims, and on the joinder of additional parties. . . .

(f) *Finality of Denial of Intervention.* A denial of intervention under this rule shall be entered as a final judgment as to the applicant for intervention. An appeal by the applicant for intervention shall not stay proceedings in the district court unless the district judge or the court of appeals or a judge thereof shall so order.

Second, a change should be made in the statutory provisions governing diversity jurisdiction, to remove some or all of the jurisdictional obstacles to intervention in diversity cases.

Class Actions: Efficiency, Compensation, Deterrence, and Conflict of Interest *

Kenneth W. Dam

One of the most controversial recent developments in the law of federal procedure is the growth of the class action. The crucial event was the amendment in 1966 of Rule 23 of the Federal Rules of Civil Procedure. Because of the burdens imposed on the federal court system by class actions and because of their limitations, interest has been growing in the possibility of creating alternative procedures, such as *parens patriae* actions.

The purpose of this article is to examine some of the major choices that must be made in administration of the class action and in the development of alternatives to it. . . .[2]

The discussion is limited to class actions for damages. Class actions seeking equitable relief raise additional issues beyond the scope of this paper and are, at the same time, in some ways simpler for courts to administer.

* *Source:* 4 J. Legal Stud. 47, 47-73 (1975).

2. . . . I shall ignore the restrictive effect on class actions of the recent Supreme Court decision in Eisen v. Carlisle & Jacquelin, 94 S. Ct. 2140 (1974). By requiring individual notice to class members whose names and addresses are easily ascertainable, the *Eisen* decision placed a financial burden on the representative plaintiff that will discourage many class actions. If that decision can be read to rest solely on the wording of Rule 23, then the notice requirement can be reduced or eliminated either by amendment of the rule or by legislation. However, to the extent that the *Eisen* decision rests on the Due Process Clause of the Fifth Amendment, then either there will be a constraint on the use of the class action device or the conception of the class action embodied in the 1966 amendment must be abandoned in favor of a conception based on collateral estoppel. . . .

I. An Introduction

Much of the confusion to be found in the judicial opinions and secondary literature on class actions can be traced to a failure to be explicit about the underlying conflicts in objectives and values created by the vast expansion in the scope and frequency of such actions. Not everyone appreciated at first the extent to which the 1966 amendment would upset the existing balance between plaintiffs and defendants in several important areas of federal regulation. It upset that balance by expanding the number of claimants whose claims were likely to be satisfied and by greatly enlarging the potential liability of defendants. The amendment created a dilemma for judges who were torn between a desire to vindicate all substantive claims, however small, and a fear of the effect of massive class actions on already overcrowded dockets. The developing practice under the rule also raised troublesome questions about the entrepreneurial role of the representative plaintiff's counsel in bringing and settling class actions.

In order to examine these underlying conflicts in objectives and values more explicitly, it will be helpful to isolate four concepts that play a prime role in thinking about class actions: (1) efficiency; (2) compensation; (3) deterrence; and (4) conflict of interest.

Efficiency must be a goal of any system in which resources are scarce. Since scarcity of resources characterizes both the economic system and the court system, both must be concerned with efficiency. Indeed, efficiency in the administration of the court system, where judges and facilities are in short supply, is only a part of the larger goal of efficiency for the economic system as a whole. In administering the legal system, the reduction of the direct costs of resolving disputes (or an increase in the number of disputes resolved with a fixed budget) as well as the reduction of the losses from socially harmful behavior are matters of concern. I shall use the term "administrative efficiency" to refer to efficiency in administration of the court system and the term "overall efficiency" to refer to efficiency in the economic system as a whole. Unless the context requires a different interpretation, "overall efficiency" will include "administrative efficiency."

Unlike the case for most other scarce resources, there is no attempt to charge a market-clearing price for the services of courts. Hence, the class action issue cannot be approached independently from the question how access to courts is rationed in order to clear the market. Class actions are often more efficient administratively than multiple independent actions. But one may properly be puzzled as to the direction administrative-efficiency considerations point where the availability of the class action makes possible litigation that would not be in the courts at all if individual actions were required.

A principal purpose of most actions for damages is *compensation* to a victim of a wrong. Compensation was selected by the Congress as a principal goal of private actions in the antitrust field, one of the fields where class actions have been most popular. A key feature of the class action is that it holds the potential for making feasible the compensation of the victims of mass wrongs even though each victim has a loss that is too small to justify an individual action.

Every substantive rule of law, or at least those where an action for damages for violation will lie, is intended, to a greater or lesser extent, to affect behavior. In that sense its purpose can be said to be *deterrence*. The availability of the class action, by permitting the cumulation of individual damages into a sizable sum, may strengthen the deterrent effect of the substantive rule. The strengthening can be especially dramatic where, because of the small size of the individual claims, no action is likely to be brought in the absence of a class action. If the underlying substantive rule promotes overall efficiency (as does, for example, the antitrust rule against price-fixing), then the enhanced deterrence arising from the availability of class actions contributes to overall efficiency.

Two different *conflicts of interest* should be considered. The first involves the representative party, who is a volunteer not normally chosen by the class members to act on their behalf. The representative plaintiff may have interests that are not in all ways congruent with those of the members of the class. The second, and for the analysis here more significant, conflict is faced by counsel representing the class. In particular, his decision calculus as to settlement versus continued litigation may be sharply different from that of the class.

II. Administrative Efficiency and Compensation

Where the choice is between a class action and a series of individual actions, the class action will often be the more efficient administratively. With a class action certain issues need be tried only once. Even if some of the issues must be tried separately, a class action may nonetheless be more efficient administratively. For example, in antitrust price-fixing litigation, the issue of liability is often treated as an issue for class treatment, and the issue of damages is left for separate determination. Where each member of the class is injured in the same way and damages can be calculated by application of a formula (for example, a certain dollar amount per unit of product), the class action presents great administrative-efficiency advantages for the court in disposing of claims.

On the other hand, even where the alternative would be a series of individual actions, a class action may present no significant administrative efficiency gains. An illustration would be in securities fraud cases where each defrauded purchaser must show reliance on fraudulent misrepresentations.[5] In such cases not only damages but also the most difficult of the substantive factual issues may have to be resolved individually whether or not class action treatment is permitted. Nevertheless, there might be some administrative-efficiency gains from class treatment. Alternatively, the presence of so many individual issues in one action might lead to administrative efficiency losses. The administrative-efficiency outcome may be indeterminate *ex ante.*

Thus far I have discussed the administrative-efficiency question under the assumption that every member of the class would individually litigate his claim in the absence of class treatment. In the overwhelming number of class action cases actually faced by the judiciary, this assumption is unrealistic. At the limit there may be no individual claims pursued because the cost of bringing them individually would exceed the return for each class member. How should we then assess the administrative-efficiency consideration? . . .

At any given time the judiciary has a given output capacity, much like an industry. . . .

The judge can, of course, reduce the quality of his product by skimming rather than reading briefs, coercing settlements and the like, but this cannot be considered to be an increase in the capacity of the court system. Rather, it is a trading of the quality dimension for the quantity dimension. Quality has two aspects. The first is control of judicial error. The greater the percentage of cases decided "correctly," the higher the quality. The second involves the public's sense of justice. An evidentiary hearing or oral argument may be accorded not because it will shed light on the subject or change the judge's mind but because we attach value to the opportunity to be heard. In part, the opportunity to be heard is safeguarded in order to reduce legal error, but it is hard to deny that behind the courts' thinking on due process is the belief that the opportunity to be heard has a value even where the possibility of affecting the result would not alone justify it. . . .

Today a judge's decision on an issue affecting his workload or his rate of disposition must be taken in an environment characterized by what are regarded as lengthy backlogs and, usually, heavy workloads. . . . One likely explanation is that court services are a scarce

5. In that particular situation some courts have sought to change the substantive law by watering down the reliance requirement in order to facilitate class actions. See Note, The Impact of Class Actions on Rule 10B-5, 38 U. Chi. L. Rev. 337 (1971), and authorities cited there.

resource for which, minor court costs aside, no price is charged. In those circumstances the market does not clear, and some form of rationing is necessary. Since the typical trial court (unlike, say, the Supreme Court with its certiorari practice) does not directly control its docket, rationing takes the form of queues — that is, backlogs. Backlogs lengthen until such point as they in effect tax away the gains from free court services.

In the context of rationing by backlog, a judge is bound to be troubled by the typical class action. To him, the class action is usually not an alternative to individual actions by each of the members of the class. At most, a few of the claimants will proceed individually, and in a substantial number of the cases, if not in the majority, no individual actions will be pursued if class treatment is not accorded. At the same time the class action is likely to be burdensome for the court. . . .

In such situations the judge may understandably view the class action not as saving court time but as consuming it. If he accords class treatment, then, to the extent that he takes a short-run view of the matter and does not assume that more judges will be made available, one of two adjustments must be made: (1) quality must decline; or (2) some further rationing will be required, presumably by a lengthening of the backlog.

The backlog may not actually lengthen to a corresponding degree; rather, the implicit tax imposed by the backlog may discourage actions that would otherwise be brought. In short, there is only an incipient lengthening of the backlog, and a new equilibrium — with little or no lengthening — is achieved as the otherwise anticipated number of actions is not filed. Hence, the claims that may be cognizable under the class action, but would not be brought individually, may merely substitute for other claims that will not be asserted as a result of the incipient overcrowding.

If the judge thinks even implicitly in these terms, as it seems likely that he will with the current emphasis on court management and docket control, how should such thoughts influence him in deciding whether or not to certify the marginal class action? The judge will not only regard compensation as a goal of the system but, given the traditions of the common law, he is likely to regard compensation (as opposed to deterrence) as the principal goal of the private damage action. From the compensation viewpoint, he will want to vindicate the substantive rights of the members of the class. But his analysis of administrative efficiency will lead him to realize that he may not be increasing the number of claims vindicated since the claims of the members of the class may come at the expense of claims that will not be asserted, or of claims (already filed or potential) for which vindication will be delayed as a result of the time consumed by the class action. He will be led to weigh not only the administrative-efficiency gain from class treatment of the claims before him but also the administrative-efficiency effects on all of the other cases already filed and that may be filed in the future. It is this broader calculus that judges probably have in mind when they dismiss class actions as "unmanageable." Surely it would be the rare case that would be unmanageable as such. It is only a question of how much court time the judge is willing to devote to the case and what he judges to be the value of vindicating the claims of the class as against other claims that could otherwise be vindicated.

This way of looking at the issue leads one to conclude that the compensation principle adds no new criteria for judgment beyond those inherent in the administrative-efficiency principle. The claims with which the class claims compete are also claims for compensation. There is no reason to prefer one claim for compensation over another.[11] . . .

III. Deterrence . . .

The question for the judge in the class action is whether the deterrence concept adds anything to his calculus based on compensation and administrative efficiency. It is difficult to see that it adds much in the typical case. First, the overwhelming number of the claims that he must face in the class action, in other cases already filed, and in those that may be discouraged by the lengthened-backlog effect will present a deterrence element. In each case the legislature (or, in common-law cases, a prior court establishing the substantive rule) has decided on the remedy. That remedy may be treble or single damages or, in cases where only equitable relief is possible, no damages at all. The judge may properly take those legislative judgments as binding on him as to the optimal amount of deterrence. Only where he has the discretion to give exemplary damages is he invited by the legal system to determine the appropriate amount of deterrence. Consequently, there is no apparent reason for him to favor vindication of claims in antitrust actions by according class relief at the expense of failing to vindicate other claims. He may properly

11. . . . [N]ot all matters before the court are claims for compensation. Aside from equitable actions, there are criminal actions. When one considers that the impact on criminal actions of accepting more class actions is likely to be — in the short run at least — a decline in quality, the argument against accepting more class actions is at least as weighty as if all other matters before the court were claims for compensation.

treat all claims as being created equal from the standpoint of deterrence.[17]

Perhaps, however, one might place deterrence on the scale favoring class treatment in the massive class action regulatory cases precisely because the total amount in controversy is so large. The theory would be that in such cases the harm to the economy from the violation was presumptively large and hence the deterrent effect should be correspondingly large. In short, the amount of compensation is the best indicator of the deterrent effect. Such an approach might make sense if it were part of a broader calculus. A court concerned with deterrence might be led to weight large claims more heavily than small claims in deciding upon priorities in handling cases. If claims are to be weighted, both the size of the claim and the time required for disposition should be taken into account. Such a weighting system would constitute a more sophisticated set of administrative-efficiency criteria than simply treating all claims as of equal value, but it would not give any weight to deterrence as such in the calculus for decision.

We are led then to ask whether there are any situations in which the broader concept of overall efficiency implied in the concept of deterrence adds anything to the narrow concept of administrative efficiency used in the discussion thus far. The conclusion arrived at in the next section is that deterrence can substitute for compensation where compensation is not practicable. But an understanding of that point requires a discussion of conflict of interest in class actions.

IV. Conflict of Interest

In moving to conflict of interest one confronts a different kind of principle from that presented by efficiency, compensation, or deterrence. The existence of conflict of interest in a class action need not enter the judge's calculus in any direct way. But it may color his view of the merits of particular class actions.

The conflict of interest problem derives in the first instance from the representative character of the action. Not only is the named plaintiff a representative, but he is also a volunteer. He chose himself.

17. An interesting class of cases in which the courts have been concerned with the possibility that deterrence might be excessive arises under the Truth-in-Lending Act, 15 U.S.C. §1601 et seq. (1970). The statute provides that each borrower shall have a right to a $100 recovery per transaction even though that amount exceeds his injury. Some classes composed of credit-card holders and credit purchasers from mass merchandisers have been so large that the courts have been concerned with the impact of the resulting damages on the financial viability of the defendants. In some cases they have reasoned that Congress did not intend the $100 individual minimum and class action treatment to be conjoined. . . .

His interests may not be identical with those of the class. At the limit he may, in collusion with the defendant, be seeking a determination that will, by binding the class under res judicata principles, limit the defendant's liability exposure.

A more subtle, though by no means less important, conflict of interest is that faced by the lawyer for the class. His personal interest may be different from that of either the representative plaintiff or the class as a whole. His interest is in his fee. If he does not obtain either a settlement or a judgment for the class, he will not receive any compensation.

The class attorney's conflict of interest derives not from that fact alone, for the plaintiff's lawyer in a personal injury action or, more generally, in any contingent fee arrangement is similarly dependent for his fee on a favorable judgment or settlement. The principal difference lies in the fact that in a substantial number of class action cases the lawyer will be more prone to settle than would the class, whereas in other contingent fee situations such a difference of view between client and lawyer is less likely. It would be difficult to summarize the practicalities of the situation from the class attorney's viewpoint better than has Judge Friendly:

> There can be no blinking at the fact that the interests of the plaintiff in a stockholder's derivative suit and of his attorney are by no means congruent. While, in a general sense, both are interested in maximizing the recovery this is only a half-truth. Even apart from special considerations which . . . may cause special divergence of interest in cases where extremely large amounts are at stake . . . there is a difference in every case. The plaintiff's financial interest is in his share of the total recovery less what may be awarded to counsel, *simpliciter;* counsel's financial interest is in the amount of the award to him less the time and effort needed to produce it. A relatively small settlement may well produce an allowance bearing a higher ratio to the cost of the work than a much larger recovery obtained only after extensive discovery, a long trial and an appeal. The risks in proceeding to trial vary even more essentially. For the plaintiff, a defendant's judgment may mean simply the defeat of an expectation, often of relatively small amount; for his lawyer it can mean the loss of years of costly effort by himself and his staff. In this respect a derivative action is in a quite different posture from a personal injury action conducted on a contingent basis. We say this not in criticism but in simple recognition of the facts of class action life.[20]

To these considerations must be added the special proclivity of the class lawyer to settlement where the proposed settlement runs into the millions, as is the case in many class actions. Here again Judge Friendly, in a stockholder's derivative action, summarized the viewpoint of the class attorney:

20. Saylor v. Lindsley, 456 F.2d 896, 900-901 (2d Cir. 1971). . . .

> The plaintiff stockholders or, more realistically, their attorneys have every incentive to accept a settlement that runs into high six figures or more regardless of how strong the claims for much larger amounts may be. The percentage allowance in stockholders' actions is "reduced as the amount of recovery passes the million dollar mark," . . . the income tax also plays a role; and a juicy bird in the hand is worth more than the vision of a much larger one in the bush, attainable only after years of effort not currently compensated and possibly a mirage.[21]

Unfairness to the class arising out of resulting bias toward relatively small settlements (plus large fees) in class actions is controlled to a certain extent by a series of special rules. The court must approve the settlement and fees, and members of the class are given notice and permitted to assert their views at a hearing. But the lawyer's discretion remains great.

A related difference between class actions and the normal individual action lies more in the client than in the lawyer. A lawyer is rarely a perfect agent of his client, if for no other reason than that the lawyer's own interests will normally diverge somewhat from those of his client. But the client usually is able to supervise at least the objectives of the lawyer in the litigation. And since the client's stake in a lawsuit will be a multiple of the stake of the lawyer, the client will have an interest in exercising such supervision.

In the class action, however, the representative plaintiff's stake will typically be much smaller than that of the lawyer. In many cases the representative plaintiff's stake will be so small that he could not afford to invest any time in supervising the lawyer. Moreover, the institutional arrangements in the class action are such that for many questions the lawyer has no greater responsibility to the representative plaintiff than to any other member of the class. Though subject to whatever controls the court may impose, the lawyer loses the constraints on his actions normally imposed by the existence of a client. The lawyer can, for example, settle the class action over the objection of the representative plaintiff.[23] To be sure, the class members could join together to supervise the lawyer, but in the typical case the transaction costs in doing so would be too high to make such a course feasible.

For all of these reasons any bias toward settlement that the class lawyer may have is not easily corrected through the normal interaction of client and lawyer. Moreover, the bias toward settlement in class actions may be exaggerated in some fields, such as antitrust, by the

21. Alleghany Corp. v. Kirby, 333 F.2d 327, 347 (2d Cir. 1964) (dissenting opinion). . . .

23. Such settlements are, of course, subject to judicial supervision. For an example, see Saylor v. Lindsley, 456 F.2d 896 (2d Cir. 1972).

defendant's fear of a catastrophically large judgment after trial as well as by the great expense of trial. This aspect of the class action, which led Professor Handler to label the antitrust class action as "legalized blackmail,"[24] is independent of any conflict of interest. Unlike the class attorney's propensity for settlement, which tends to work to the disadvantage of the class, the defendant's propensity toward settlement tends to favor the class.

The peculiar calculus of the class attorney may affect the judge's view of a class action in two ways. The first effect derives from the fact that the class action rarely goes to trial. It is normally settled. While no statistics are available as to the proportion of class damage actions settled before trial relative to the number of other damage actions settled and therefore one cannot be certain that class actions are for this reason less burdensome, nonetheless the judge certifying a class action may comfort himself with the high likelihood that he will never have to try the case. Still, the class action normally spawns a large number of pretrial motions, conferences, and other burdens on the judge's time.

The second effect of the attorney's position on the perspective of the judge stems not solely from any conflict of interest but more broadly from the reality that in most class actions the attorney has a larger stake in the lawsuit than any member of the class. The attorney is an entrepreneur. But for his initiative the action would never have been brought. That fact alone will trouble only the more traditional judge; today it is widely appreciated that private enforcement requires for its efficacy a highly motivated plaintiffs' bar. But where the lawyer's stake is large and the stake of each class member is small, it is unlikely that any members of the class will actually receive compensation. For example, the amount of compensation to each class member might be so small that it would be exceeded by the costs of administration or, what is really the same thing, it would not be worthwhile for a class member to go to the expense and bother of claiming his aliquot portion of the class recovery. In *Eisen III* the Second Circuit estimated that the average recovery, after trebling, would be $3.90, and noted that "[n]o claimant in the 6 years of the action had shown any interest in Eisen's claim."

24. Milton Handler, The Shift from Substantive to Procedural Innovations in Antitrust Suits — The Twenty-Third Annual Antitrust Review, 71 Colum. L. Rev. 1, 9 (1971). See also Judge Medina's comments in Eisen v. Carlisle & Jacquelin, 479 F.2d 1005, 1019 (2d Cir. 1973), *aff'd*, 94 S. Ct. 2140 (1974): "There is reason to believe that the practical effect of these procedures, and the fact that possible recoveries run into astronomical amounts, generate more leverage and pressures on defendants to settle, even for millions of dollars, and in cases where the merits of the class representative's claim is to say the least doubtful, than did the old-fashioned strike suits made famous a generation or two ago by Clarence H. Venner."

How is the judge to regard such a case? If he looked only at administrative efficiency and compensation, he might be led to conclude that to the extent that there would be no compensation, class action claims were not as worthy of vindication as other claims and hence, at the margin, decisions should go against class treatment. The Second Circuit in *Eisen II*, for example, was "reluctant to permit actions to proceed where they are not likely to benefit anyone but the lawyers who bring them."

The absence of actual compensation, however, is not dispositive. Here the concept of deterrence has its true role. Deterrence substitutes as a justification for compensation where compensation is not feasible. The principle of deterrence requires that the wrongdoer pay, but says nothing about who shall receive the payment. Hence the argument for nevertheless favoring the class action even though compensation can never be paid is that if class treatment is not accorded, the deterrent effect of the substantive rule will be forfeited. . . .

V. Alternatives to the Class Action

In this part I shall examine some of the more promising alternatives to the class action to see whether the legal system could not devise some better scheme for achieving the laudable goals of proponents of class actions, with fewer of the attendant costs and limitations. . . .

A. *The Fluid Class Action*

One alternative explored in the *Eisen* litigation was an approach to the distribution of damages referred to as a fluid class action or as fluid recovery. The essence of this approach is that it places the emphasis on making the defendant pay damages and does not place much importance on who receives the damages.

Under a fluid class approach class damages would first be fixed. For example, in a price-fixing case class damages would be set by calculating the difference between the collusive price and the competitive price and by then multiplying that amount by the number of units sold. The fact that this method of calculating total damages has been used even where no fluid class alternative was contemplated underscores the point that fluid recovery has to do primarily with the distribution of the total damages rather than with their calculation. In any event, under the fluid class alternative, no attempt would be made to arrive at the total by adding up the sum of the individual injuries, and hence it would not be necessary to have the individual claimants before the court. Nevertheless, any individual claimant would presumably be entitled to come forward to establish his right to his portion of the fund. It is doubtful whether, in view of the Due Process Clause, the individual claimant could be precluded from seeking his compensation, at least without an extensive legislative restructuring of the theory of class actions.

How then is the residue to be distributed? Presumably the judge will seek to identify a group that corresponds as closely as possible to the quiescent claimants. Let us call this group the "surrogate class." Following the approach of the District Court in *Eisen*, it is usually assumed that where the class members are purchasers, the defendant should reduce his price below what he would otherwise charge until such time as he has "worked off" the residue. Thus, future purchasers will be the surrogate class as long as the residue lasts. Such a formula will not work well in nonpurchase cases, such as environmental litigation, and will not even work in some purchase cases, such as stock fraud litigation. In such cases distribution to the surrogate class may present as many problems as compensation to the original class.

Even where distribution to the surrogate class by reduced future prices is feasible, it may be subject to a number of objections. First, to the extent that some of the new purchasers have already recovered their aliquot portion of damages as class claimants, they will enjoy double recovery. Second, under general principles of public finance, some may object to courts rather than legislatures redistributing funds derived from a measure that resembles a tax, albeit of the penalty variety. When the wrongdoer compensates a victim, the transfer does not so clearly constitute redistribution of income by the government. Third, to the extent that the price is reduced below what would otherwise be charged, some will be induced to purchase who would not otherwise have purchased. In the price-fixing cases the base from which the reduction will be made is presumably the competitive price. Some will thus become members of the surrogate class even though they would not have purchased even at a competitive price. Their resemblance to the actual class is rather pale. Fourth, the reduction of price below what would otherwise be charged will tend to increase the quantity demanded and reduce the quantity supplied. An excess demand (that is, a shortage) will be created, and some kind of rationing by the sellers or the court, however informal, will be necessary. The problem created where the judgment is large relative to the size of the industry may be analogous to the problems facing the administrators of a price control scheme. Finally, if the judgment is large enough to require some time to be worked off, the court will have considerable difficulty in determining the price that would otherwise be charged — that is, the base from which the reduction is to be taken. Here too the analogy to price control is suggestive.

These last two points lead to the conclusion that, whatever the impact on the economy, the administration of the distribution to the surrogate class will put some burden on the court, and this burden must have at least some weight in any administrative-efficiency calculus.

Although the normal conception of the fluid recovery involves transfer of damages to a surrogate class, a similar deterrent effect could be achieved by payment of class damages into a fund, followed by escheat of the unclaimed residue to the appropriate state. Use of the escheat power by a state in this manner raises the question whether it would not be more appropriate for a state to bring the action in the first instance. This is what happens in a *parens patriae* action.

B. Parens Patriae Actions

Any evaluation of the seriousness of the objections to fluid class treatment must take into consideration the utility and practicability of other alternatives. One alternative is to allow public officials to sue for damages on behalf of residents of their jurisdictions. . . .

The concept of *parens patriae* actions has a worthy lineage. It has been extensively used in environmental injunction suits[36] and was the basis for an antitrust injunction in *Georgia v. Pennsylvania Railroad Co.*[37] But in *Hawaii v. Standard Oil Co. of California*, the Supreme Court rejected a *parens patriae* treble damage action on behalf of all Hawaiian purchasers of price-fixed refined petroleum products.[38]

The Court's view was that, at least in antitrust litigation, class actions were "definitely preferable" to *parens patriae* actions. Its prime practical objection to *parens patriae* damage actions was that since Hawaiian citizens could also sue for damages (presumably by way of class action), to authorize the *parens patriae* action "would open the door to duplicative recoveries." This objection could be handled by legislation. A Congress that can authorize treble damages can doubtless authorize two parties to recover for the same wrong. In any case, Congress could establish a priority rule to favor either the private action or the *parens patriae* action where there would be overlapping recoveries. . . .

More far-reaching *parens patriae* legislation would abandon compensation as a goal. Such abandonment might be limited to situations where compensation was impracticable or thought not to be worth the effort. For example, the legislature could arbitrarily choose a figure such as the jurisdictional amount figure of $10,000, relegating all claims below that amount exclusively to the *parens patriae* channel.

36. E.g., Georgia v. Tennessee Copper Co., 206 U.S. 230 (1907).
37. 324 U.S. 439 (1945).
38. 405 U.S. 251 (1972).

The advantage of such an approach would be twofold. First, it would reduce the burden on the court system of small claims and make clear that deterrence was the prime objective. Second, resources would not be consumed, either by public officials or by private claimants and their lawyers, in administering individual small claims. The *parens patriae* action would become a relatively efficient penalty tax. It would resemble, to take an example, the effluent tax favored by many economists as a deterrent to uneconomic pollution.

The fundamental objection to the *parens patriae* approach is that it is simply public enforcement decentralized to the fifty states. Each state attorney general would be imposing, in effect, a fine for illegal activity within the state. So long as the substantive rule was federally created, it is not apparent why, once such quasi-public enforcement was chosen over private enforcement for deterrence purposes, the public enforcement should not be in the hands of a federal agency. . . .

If one is led to abandon compensation and if federal enforcement is preferred, why should the entire problem not be handled by higher fines and by civil penalties rather than by civil damages paid to the public treasury? There is no effective difference between a civil penalty and such civil damages so long as the manner of calculating the amount is the same.

C. *Improving Public Enforcement*

Today there is no federal civil penalty for most federal violations. In the antitrust field, where so many of the problems discussed in this article have arisen, only criminal penalties are possible. Aside from imprisonment for not exceeding one year, a sanction that prosecutors are reluctant to seek and courts to impose, the only criminal sanction is a fine of not more than $50,000.

As a maximum $50,000 is absurdly low. It cannot be considered a realistic deterrent to most antitrust violations. Moreover, the fact that it is a criminal rather than a civil penalty leads the Antitrust Division to restrict prosecution to "hard-core" violations where the Division considers the evidence to be unambiguous. The consequence is that today the treble-damage action is the principal deterrent to antitrust violations. To be sure, many, perhaps most, major treble-damage actions come on the heels of an Antitrust Division civil or criminal action. But it is the treble-damage award that is the important sanction and hence the important deterrent. . . .

The literature on optimum deterrence leads to the conclusion that the penalty for law violation should be a multiple of the social cost of the violation; the appropriate multiple would be based on the likelihood of detection. Any attempt to move toward an optimum penalty in public enforcement leads to the question how the public penalty is to be meshed with the private treble-damage penalty. To allow both may result in overdeterrence and, on a more pragmatic level, may create a series of potential problems. Among these problems may be a reluctance of judges to impose the optimum public penalty when they know treble damage actions are pending. Another might be financial difficulties in major industries resulting from the pyramiding of liability, with the prospect of the government's being pressed into a bail-out operation. Therefore, if we are to move to optimal public deterrence, one of two steps will be necessary. Either private enforcement should be abolished or a rule should be established to determine when private enforcement must make way for public enforcement.

The choice between these two ways of resolving the conflict should turn on the relative merits of the two forms of enforcement. Even assuming that public enforcement is in general superior, the public enforcement agency is subject to a budget constraint. . . . [W]hen the budget is determined by the political process, there is no reason to believe that the rate of enforcement would be economically optimal. It might be more or less than optimal. I should suppose that most students of antitrust believe that the present budget of the Antitrust Division is less than optimal. If that is true, then private enforcement provides an important supplementary form of enforcement.

A second possible justification for private enforcement lies in its diversity. There may be some kinds of violations that private enforcers are better situated to uncover and to prosecute than are public enforcers. An example might be found in small industries where the scale is too small to attract public enforcers. Another example might be found in arcane technology industries where an understanding of industry dynamics would require a disproportionate investment of resources for the public enforcers, but where private competitors would already possess that understanding and would have an incentive to enforce some antitrust rules.

Private enforcement has relatively little to commend itself if it merely involves collection of treble damages after public enforcement agencies have established the violation. Then private enforcement only substitutes for an adequate system of public penalties. Even this substitution is fraught with problems where the individual claims are too small to justify actual compensation or where economic knowledge does not permit ascertainment of who in fact suffered injury.

The resolution of the conflict between public and private enforcement thus lies in imposing optimal penalties in any civil or criminal public enforcement proceeding. Once a public proceeding was under way, private actions would be barred. A private action, on the other hand, could proceed so long as it was filed before the public action. A prior private action would not bar the public action, but any private recovery could be credited by the defendant against the public penalty. In this way one could obtain the benefits of both private and public enforcement without risking overdeterrence.

With this resolution of the conflict between public and private enforcement, the class action problem that has bedeviled the courts becomes of lesser importance. Where a public action had been commenced, the class action would be barred. So long as a public action could thereafter be brought, deterrence would not require that class actions be maintained even though no compensation to injured parties was likely to occur. Public enforcement would become a realistic alternative. Indeed, even where compensation was possible, the courts might in good conscience (assuming appropriate legislative authority) decline to proceed with especially burdensome class actions on administrative-efficiency grounds once a public action had been commenced. The judge could then weigh the benefits of according compensation to the class against the costs of denying compensation to other claimants (through the backlog-lengthening effect) and against the costs of reduced quality. In doing so, the judge would be secure in the knowledge that the deterrence function would be discharged in the public action.

The problem would still remain that the judge might not be assured that a public action would be forthcoming. The failure of the public authorities to proceed would be ambiguous. The public authorities might be constrained by their budget or, alternatively, they might be convinced that no violation had occurred. I see no way in which this ambiguity can be resolved by the judge. One could imagine a ruling procedure in which the public enforcement agency would express an opinion on the merits of the private claim, but such a procedure would be fraught with procedural and constitutional problems. But once a system such as I have suggested was in force, the political decision as to the budget of the enforcement authorities would represent the polity's judgment as to the appropriate rate of enforcement. In these circumstances, the judge need not agonize over the possibility that there might be an occasional case where optimal deterrence had not been achieved. After all, deterrence has its costs too, and by hypothesis we are dealing with a situation in which the costs to the judiciary of administering the class action are especially high.

Nonetheless, a "deterrence gap" would remain. Therefore, it is worth considering whether a system could be devised in which any claim for compensation, however small, could be vindicated. If every claim were compensable in fact, then the system would provide deterrence for all large harms however widely spread. If the private enforcement system could be expanded to achieve that level of deterrence, an attractive by-product would be that the efforts of the public enforcement agencies would be supplemented to the fullest degree by the talents and energies of the private bar.

D. *Improving Private Enforcement*

At the outset let us recognize that a private party who is being injured by a violation of a regulatory law, such as the Sherman Act, can protect himself by bringing an action for an injunction. The force of the injunction as to him, once obtained, does not require that it be obtained on behalf of a class. This is deterrence for the future, but in a situation where deterrence failed in the past.

Moreover, the doctrine of collateral estoppel may give a single plaintiff's action for damages a transcendent effect. Under this doctrine, as interpreted in the modern cases, once an issue has been fully litigated between one plaintiff and the defendant and the issue has been resolved in favor of the plaintiff, the defendant is estopped from contesting that issue in actions brought by other plaintiffs. For example, once an antitrust defendant had lost on the basic issue of liability for price fixing, new plaintiffs could take advantage of the court's price-fixing finding and would not have to establish the existence of the price fixing anew.

The single antitrust plaintiff does not receive the benefits that flow to others similarly situated and hence he will not bring some actions that would be beneficial to the class of those similarly situated. One way to offset this "externality" would be to subsidize his litigation. And the natural party to pay for the subsidy would be the unsuccessful defendant. In short, the regulatory statute could provide that the plaintiff's attorney's fees and other litigation costs were to be paid by the unsuccessful defendant. Then the successful plaintiff would be made whole. This is essentially what one finds in private treble-damage litigation, where the unsuccessful defendant must pay "the cost of suit, including a reasonable attorney's fee."

It is ironic that a right to recover fees and costs has been accorded in antitrust, one of the central areas of the class action controversy. It is assumed in those cases that where the representative plaintiff's claim is small, the action must either go forward as a class action or not go forward at all. But why should this be so if the successful plaintiff will be made whole?

Several factors may explain this puzzle. First, counsel for the class may prefer the class action rather than the individual action because the courts, in determining a reasonable attorney's fee, grant fees that rise with the size of the recovery, whether or not the amount of attorney's effort rises. Where counsel for the class is acting as an entrepreneur, he will clearly prefer the class approach and may even spurn a "reasonable attorney's fee" as being unreasonably low for him. But this does not mean that some other competent attorney will not be available to the representative plaintiff if he should decide to pursue his claim individually.

Second, even under the "cost of the suit" formula, not all costs are recompensed. For example, the opportunity costs of the plaintiff's own time are not awarded, even though such costs will be an important factor in deciding whether to assert small claims. Perhaps a perfect system would reimburse all opportunity costs.

Third, the plaintiff must assess the risk that he may fail and hence will have to bear the attorney's fee and other costs. In a complicated case these costs would be very high compared to the value of the claim. Litigation is risky. Where the cost-recovery ratio is high, it is the risk factor that is perhaps the most important factor in discouraging the assertion of small claims.

In attempting to construct an improved system of private enforcement, how should this risk factor be treated? One possibility would be to take the *ex ante* risk into account when setting the *ex post* reasonable attorney's fee in order to make the plaintiff's wager a fair one. Under such a system the expected value (here, the costs awarded multiplied by the *ex ante* probability of success) would equal the actual costs of suit. Then, leaving aside questions of risk aversion or risk proneness, the plaintiff would be in a position equivalent to the position where success was certain.

When one considers the implications of attempting to assure that every claim, however small and however risky, could be asserted without cost to the plaintiff, it becomes apparent that such universal vindication of claims cannot be a goal of the legal system. In the first place, such an approach would lead to an absurdity. Although all lawsuits are risky, some are much more risky than others, and an approach which would offset the risk would lead to subsidization of widespread assertions of frivolous actions by the occasional unlucky defendant in such actions. Yet *ex ante* this defendant had an excellent case, and so it is particularly unjust to saddle him with costs of many lawsuits. Second, this approach focuses on justice to the plaintiff alone. We not only want to encourage the assertion of valid claims, but we also want to discourage invalid claims. Hence, we should consider awarding to the successful defendant, as well as the successful plaintiff, the costs of litigation, including fees. But such a system of awarding costs to the successful party would decrease, not increase, the willingness of the small claimant to resort to the courts.

The fact of the matter is that litigation is costly and these costs must be borne by someone: the plaintiff, the defendant, or the society through taxation. Litigation consumes real resources. Universal assertion of claims is not cost-justified from the standpoint of the society.[61] In the category of cases here under discussion, where claims are small though the harm (and therefore usually the complexity of the case) is large, an individual action involves high costs compared to the possible return. Where the costs of suit exceed the value of the claim, then it is axiomatic that the resources consumed in processing the claim exceed the resource gain derived from increased overall efficiency via deterrence. Were it not for the fact that many other potential claimants stand in the same position as the actual claimant, one would have no difficulty in concluding that society is better off not vindicating the claim than it is vindicating it. If we could combine all of the claims into a single lawsuit, there would be gains in administrative efficiency, and the vindication of the claims jointly might become cost-justified on an overall efficiency basis. But whether the court system gains or loses in administrative efficiency turns on the effect of the class action on other unrelated claims, as it has been the burden of this article to show.

We are thus left with the conclusion that although private enforcement could be improved by providing for recovery of fees and other costs by the successful party, such a system cannot plug the deterrence gap created by the resources consumed in compensating small claimants. Deterrence, however desirable from the standpoint of overall efficiency, may consume more resources within the court system than it saves outside the court system.

VI. Summary

The principal virtue of the class action lies in increasing the efficiency of the court system. Not every class action does so. It is rational for

61. . . . One may properly question whether this analysis does not leave out the question of justice. Is not the vindication of claims a matter of justice that is not captured by efficiency concepts? Aside from the counter-question whether justice can be defined sufficiently to be a useful analytical tool for the procedural questions under discussion, several other responses are possible. First, even if the justice derived from satisfying claims has a value above and beyond the worth of the claims themselves, at some point even justice is not cost-justified. Second, even granting that considerations of justice lead us to want to vindicate more claims than efficiency considerations alone would dictate, there is always the question of who is going to pay for this justice — the party on whom the costs fell in the first instance, the plaintiff, the defendant, the unsuccessful party, the successful party, or the taxpayer?

judges in assessing whether there is any administrative-efficiency gain to consider the impact of class actions upon the ability of the court to vindicate the claims of other users of the court system and upon the quality of judicial work. Where the individual claims are too small to make actual compensation of the class members financially feasible, then the importance of the class action for deterrence, and hence for overall efficiency, must be assessed. But only in that situation does the concept of deterrence add anything to the concepts of administrative efficiency and fairness.

Even in the situation where no compensation would be feasible, there are alternatives to the class action as a means of achieving deterrence. One alternative that has been considered by the courts, converting the conventional class action into a fluid class action, is subject to a number of objections. The *parens patriae* action is an attractive alternative, but neither the fluid class action nor the *parens patriae* action are as desirable as improved public enforcement. Improvement in public enforcement lies primarily in adoption of optimal penalties, which in general would be much higher than present penalties. Even with optimal penalties one cannot assure that the political process will result in an optimal rate of public enforcement, and so there is still a role for private enforcement and hence for the class action. With optimal public penalties, private actions (including class actions) could be made subordinate to the public action, and a rule of priority is suggested in this article to accomplish that result. Under such a system the need to burden the court system with class actions that do not promote administrative efficiency simply in order to achieve deterrence would be largely eliminated.

From Group Litigation to Class Action, Part II: Interest, Class, and Representation *

Stephen C. Yeazell

We operate the modern class action backwards, leaving undone those things which we ought to do and doing those things which we ought not. The difficulty flows from our having inherited two incompatible theories of litigative representation, both of which we have cheerfully embodied in the same procedural rule. To make matters worse, we have applied each theory in just those circumstances in which it makes least sense. The confusion goes back 300 years.

The modern class action can trace its roots to a procedure invented

* *Source:* 27 U.C.L.A. L. Rev. 1067, 1067-1073, 1075-1082, 1084, 1107-1116, 1119 (1980).

by Chancery in the seventeenth century to cope with disputes between rural tenants and landlords, parishioners and parsons. If the origins lie so far back, however, the path of development has taken such sharp turns that resemblances between early and modern group litigation are deceptive. But there are some resemblances, less in form or function than in characteristic tensions and problems. As the first part of this essay suggested, group litigation underwent a fundamental transformation in the early industrial era.[1] Between 1700 and 1850 Chancery adapted to new groups a procedure originally developed to deal with the problems of small, cohesive rural communities. Confronting groups with quite different characteristics, the judges of Chancery encountered a central problem of the modern class action — the question of what circumstances justify treating a collection of people as a single litigative entity. More specifically, the question is when an active litigant may represent other, passive persons in a lawsuit. In the past few centuries two theories of litigative representation have arisen, one permitting an active litigant thought to represent the *interests* of the rest to proceed on their behalf, the other requiring the would-be representative to obtain the *consent* of the represented.

The nineteenth century, working with a limited number of social groupings, hit upon interest representation as its solution. The modern class action, though rooted in this doctrinal development, has superimposed on it — at least some of the time — the additional requirement of consent, thereby creating some splendidly baffling problems. Yet modern scholars looking at the history of group litigation have been distracted from the significance of nineteenth-century developments because they have been looking for the answer to a different question. These scholars have seen Chancery's problem in the old cases as that of justifying the binding effect of group litigation: how could persons not controlling litigation be bound by it? These writers have assumed the existence of some form of group litigation, and they have puzzled over the nineteenth-century courts' failure to discuss the preclusive effect of such litigation. Nineteenth-century judges saw a different problem; they were less concerned with justifying the binding effect of group litigation than with finding a rationale that would permit such litigation in the first place. The rationale they developed, one we have inherited with all its warts, was a theory of litigative representation.

A. *The Problem*

In group litigation, as in government, *A* may have good or ill visited upon him because of actions taken on his behalf by *B*. The

1. See generally Yeazell, From Group Litigation to Class Action, Part I: The Industrialization of Group Litigation, 27 UCLA L. Rev. 514 (1980). . . .

B's of the political realm are generally government officials — either legislative or executive — acting in the name either of the political unit as a whole or of that part to which *A*, the constituent, belongs. In group litigation *B* is the active litigant, conducting the lawsuit in the name of *A*. In either case *B* may make choices that significantly affect *A*.

Both these situations pose serious problems in modern ideology, for in general we deny that any but the individual soul can define the circumstances that will most tend to his well-being. Capitalism responds to this proposition by celebrating the free market, in which individuals exercise sovereignty to the extent of their resources, and the aggregated desires of many individuals making such choices control the conditions of production. In government the problem takes on a more complex aspect, for it is the nature of collective choice that the group as a whole rejects the wishes of some of its members. . . . Representation is the great practical and theoretical invention, enabling at least a pretense of democracy in mass societies. It guards, in theory and sometimes in fact, the power of the individual to be heard on matters affecting him and his society while permitting a manageable number of citizens to reach public decisions as the rest go about their business.

In group litigation the theory of representation performs a similar function. It permits, in theory, a lawsuit involving what Zechariah Chafee called "the multitude" to go forward because what would otherwise be an impracticably large number of people is represented by the active litigant, who protects their interests while guarding his own. Many of the most intense battles in modern class actions are fought over the adequacy of the representative and the representation. Historically, the transition in the eighteenth and nineteenth centuries between two conceptions of representation created the theoretical justification for the modern class action, a litigative justification that emerged even as the political doctrine of representation was debated and reformed. Group litigation moved from consent to interest as the basis of litigative representation; in political life an analogous transition occurred, but in the opposite direction, as political representation moved from interest to consent as its legitimizing basis.

Today we live with an uneasy and in some respects illogical melding of both theories of representation. . . . On one hand, in modern class actions of the sort represented by Federal Rule of Civil Procedure 23(b)(1) and (2), the court may permit the action to proceed once it has found that the interests of the representative class are congruent. In Rule 23(b)(3) actions, on the other hand, for the suit to proceed on a class basis, not only must there be an identity of interests, but in addition the members of the class must consent to the representative and the suit — at least to the extent of being permitted to withdraw from the class after receiving individual notice.

Since the revision of the Federal Rules in 1966 much judicial and scholarly blood has been spilled over the discrepancy between the two procedures. Writers initially focused on the desirability of individual notice and consent in (b)(3) actions, more recently some have suggested that in fact we have it backwards and that it is in the (b)(1) and (b)(2) actions that consent ought to be required. If we do have it backwards, it may be because we have not fully resolved a debate that occupied Britain for much of the nineteenth century.

B. *The Political Tension*

In 1832 Parliament passed the Reform Bill, which broadened the electoral franchise and redesigned the geographic and demographic bases of parliamentary representation. The changes wrought by the bill resulted from years of intermittent national debate. . . .

. . . The adversaries reached for two theories of representation, both of which still uneasily coexist in political theory and group litigation.

The more radical position insists on the complete subjectivity of individual interest and hence, logically, on the notion of the representative as an agent — a simple transmitter of the desires of the constituent to the legislative assembly. Perhaps some of those arguing for the ratification of the American Constitution came closest to adopting such a position politically; for Madison representation was the "pursuit of [the constituents'] interests in accord with their wishes.". . .

. . . [In England] the Utilitarians furnish the prime modern example of those who would root legitimate political representation in the approval of the governed populace, whose interests could finally, in the long run, be known only by themselves and whose consent was accordingly necessary for legitimate government.

Opposed to this tradition, which has become the foundation for much modern political theory, stood a brilliantly articulate defender of the older order, Edmund Burke. . . . He began by insisting that citizens were entitled to have their interests represented in Parliament. In so doing he rejected a vision of Parliament as a convocation of the Crown's chief landholders — a vision that had become untenable after the revolutionary settlement of 1688. But having rejected this vision, he was equally clear about his abhorrence of the notion that electors were entitled to representation in proportion to their numbers or that the representative was in any sense the agent of the voters.

He solved the apparent paradox by positing a definition of "interest" as detached and abstracted from the interest of any particular person or group. . . .

. . . For Burke the elected member of Parliament represented not the particular electorate but its "interest." That interest, as Burke made clear in his speech to the Electors of Bristol, consisted not of the particular electors' wishes but of the representative's soberly considered views of what arrangements would best serve the long-term, worthy aims of the *sort* of persons who made up the Bristol electorate. . . .

. . . [T]he Burkean representative was not the "agent" or "ambassador" of the electorate; he was rather its trustee, charged always with the guardianship of its interests, but — far from being bound by its views of how best to protect those interests — positively charged to seek them by his own means. . . .

Such a vision of legitimate electoral representation rested on a number of factual and ideological assumptions that modern observers might question. First, it assumed social stability; it was a vision in which interests were not shifting aims of the moment but long-term tendencies of permanent social groups. Today those who speak of social or political "interests" generally allow for more flux in those goals than did Burke. The modern class action, in looking to the "interests" of the represented absentees, does not search for those concerns in an invariable social catalog as Burke might have. Rather it selects such interests from among those hypothesized in the actual circumstances giving rise to the litigation. Even for Burke the notion of fixed interests may have had elements of wishful thinking. His vision of interest was born of a wistful backward look into a society that was disappearing even as he enunciated the political theory that would preserve it for a few more decades.

Such a stable social vision . . . shades off into an ideological stance; the interests to be represented are those of the propertied class, to be sure not exclusively the landed gentry, but a class of substance and with a stake in the nation. He would have denied that there could be any essential conflict between such persons and those of the lower orders. . . .

C. *Representation in Group Litigation*

The struggle over parliamentary reform forced the English to articulate ideas about representation. In the process of doing so both sides of the debate were forced to decide what role consent should play in defining interest. Neither side was unequivocal; while the Utilitarians shied away from a scheme that required advance consent and binding instruction of representatives, Burke somewhat erratically insisted that over the long run representation required some link to a group of actual voters. We have not done much to resolve the issue in the years since the debate over the Reform Bill; both contemporary political theorists and politicians waver in their views. Where perhaps they have advanced beyond the state of contemporary class action doctrine, however, is in their clear understanding that there *is* a problem and that at various points one must make choices between alternatives. Present class action rules, by contrast, offer little more than a cursory explanation of why sometimes congruity of interest but other times consent is required for class representation. . . .

Shortly after the enactment of the Reform Bill, Frederick Calvert published a remarkable short treatise unpretentiously titled Parties to Suits in Equity. In it Calvert undertook to explain and rationalize all equity parties law in terms of representation. . . .

. . . Calvert seems to have assumed . . . that interests can be inferred from circumstances, given a modicum of experience and some working hypotheses about how people generally behave.

Once Calvert had ascertained the interests of the active litigant, he could move to the second step, the requirement that there be some community of interest between the active litigant and the members of the represented group. By linking the self-interest of the active litigant to the interests of the passive ones, Calvert had articulated the theoretical justification for group litigation. . . . Calvert neatly concluded that "when a large number of persons have a common interest in the entire object of a suit in its nature beneficial to all, one or more of them may sue on behalf of all."

III. The Paradox of Representation in the Modern Class Action

. . . Modern class actions have eliminated the shadowy categories of the original Rule 23, but the present rule continues to reflect the tension between two conceptions of interest, one based on specific, individualized consent and the other on plausible social assumptions. In litigation involving the first conception, the class representative acts as a volunteer agent for the consenting group; in those of the second sort, he functions as the trustee of a constructive spendthrift trust. In one version of interest the active litigant asks the class where its interest lies; in the other he tells it. Yet we have embodied both versions in the same procedural rule. . . .

A. Interest in the Modern Class

. . . Rule 23 takes the form of a threshold from which two relatively distinct paths depart. The threshold is Burkean, as is one of the paths; the other requires a second, individualized consent to representation after the initial Burkean determination of interest. The threshold is section (a) of the rule, which provides that an active party "may sue or be sued as representative . . . on behalf of all" if, in addition to the requisite numerousness and common questions, "the claims or defenses of the representative . . . are typical . . . and . . . the representative . . . will fairly and adequately protect the interests of the class." The court must determine whether the litigative candidate for class treatment meets these requirements before considering any other issues.

Section (a) of the rule thus requires a court in all class actions to determine, without knowledge of the actual wishes of the members of the group, what their interests are and whether they will be adequately represented by the champion who now presents himself. It bears emphasizing that the rule requires this determination even if the court will subsequently ask the class members to consent to being included in the group.

The judge can make such determinations because all of us make them every day; they are part of the ideological baggage of every member of a society. We constantly act on assumptions about the interests of individuals and groups — taking for granted that home buyers will not desire the end of mortgage-interest deductions, that welfare recipients will favor increased benefits, that public employees will want higher salaries, taxpayers lower taxes, and that litigants will want to win their lawsuits. . . .

Once it has determined the interests of the class and concluded that the would-be litigant shares them, the court, following Rule 23, must decide whether such an identity of updated Burkean interests is sufficient or whether, in addition, the representative must obtain the consent of the group. And it is at this point that Rule 23 seems to stand the world on its head, requiring assent when one would be most confident that there was no arguable question about interest, and dispensing with it just when the coincidence of interests is most debatable. Rule 23 suffers from an ideological schizophrenia, adopting at one moment a theory of representation based on the most radical form of individual consent, and at the next ignoring divided interests that might have given even Burke pause.

This split occurs when the court advances to the second stage of the class certification, the stage at which it must determine into which of the three classifications the action falls. The first two classifications are rather specifically tailored; one provides for a mass-production solution to necessary-parties problems and the other for class treatment when, even without a class action, relief would be "appropriate . . . with respect to the [affected] class as a whole." The third category is cast in much broader terms; intended as a residual provision, it permits a class action when "the court finds that the questions of law or fact common to the members of the class predominate over any questions affecting only individual members, and that a class action is superior to other available methods for the fair and efficient adjudication of the controversy." Whether individual notice and assent are required turns on how the action is classified, for only if the case falls into the last, the notorious (b)(3) category, must the court "direct to the members of the class the best notice practicable under the circumstances, including individual notice to all members who can be identified through reasonable effort." Such notice must give each person the opportunity to withdraw from the class already identified by the court; it gives each class member a last chance to decide for herself whether the action in question serves her interests.

Yet Rule 23's requirement of individual notice in such cases has a paradoxical quality about it. For the rule requires notice just when discrepancy of interest among absentee members of the group is least likely. Many Rule 23(b)(3) actions involve an active plaintiff seeking monetary recovery on behalf of some group which, it is alleged, the defendant has bilked. Under such circumstances the absentees may be quite concerned that the active litigant (and his lawyer) have the same financial stake in the suit as they, that the active litigant will press the suit vigorously, and that the counsel representing them are competent. The threshold inquiries of Rule 23(a) are directed to just such questions. What is not likely, however, if such conditions are fulfilled, is that the absentees would prefer not to sue. It is an axiom of modern social and economic life that we all wish to command more of the world's wealth; there is not much sense in asking someone whether he would rather have one dollar or two. . . .

If the treatment of (b)(3) actions seems to demonstrate overprotectiveness of individual autonomy, the treatment of the other two kinds of class actions seems equally inappropriate for the opposite reason. Class actions falling into the (b)(1) and (b)(2) categories do not require notice, but rely entirely on the threshold findings of common interest and adequate representation — yet here it is realistically possible that the interests of the group's members will conflict and will be least capable of abstract assessment.

An exemplary case may make the point. The Boston school integration case [246] has attracted a good deal of interest in the past few years, for it has dramatically posed issues of school segregation in

246. Morgan v. Hennigan, 379 F. Supp. 410 (D. Mass.), *aff'd sub nom.* Morgan v. Kerrigan, 509 F.2d 580 (1st Cir. 1974), *cert. denied*, 421 U.S. 963 (1975).

the North and of judicial capacity and willingness to face those issues. Such substantive and remedial questions are for my purposes less important than those posed by the class aspects of the case. Managed by the Legal Defense Fund of the NAACP, the plaintiff's suit alleged numerous discriminatory acts by the Boston School Committee and sought a widespread integration decree that involved busing black children into the schools of South Boston, where they encountered strong hostility.

Professor Derrick Bell has reported that many of Boston's black parents, on whose behalf the case was brought, would have preferred a remedy that did not require their children to attend school in a section of the city with poor schools and a tradition of violence; indeed, one can imagine that some of them might have preferred to forgo entirely the legal vindication of their rights if such was the only foreseeable remedy. Under such circumstances, Bell argues, some more searching assessment of interest than the one called for by Rule 23(a) is necessary. Professor Bell is surely right if one grants his premise — that the cognizable interests of the group of represented parents and children are the same as their desires. When members of a group have multiple relations with each other, when the remedy sought is not purely material, and especially when it involves judicially decreed changes in the affective content of people's daily lives, it will be perilous to assume that they desire the same ends. And if interest and desire do coincide, one cannot assume that the active litigants will represent the unitary interests of the group. Nor can one fall back on the assurance present in cases like *Ben-Hur*[252] that the adversary will represent any group members not represented by the class representative. For cases of the type we are considering frequently have more plausibly assertible interests than can be represented by just two sides. For example, in the Boston school case one can easily imagine parents of black schoolchildren wishing to establish that the school board had pursued unconstitutional policies — but wishing to do so only to increase their power in bargaining with the school board over increased funding for black schools, not to win a busing order. In such circumstances neither the plaintiffs, seeking an integration decree, nor the school authorities, denying any liability, would represent the position described.

When classes are also groups that exist independently of the litigation, when foreseeable decrees will involve changes in social behavior, when the stakes are not immediately and directly financial — under such circumstances in everyday life we tend most to insist that only the individual can define his own good. We do so

252. Supreme Tribe of Ben-Hur v. Cauble, 255 U.S. 356 (1921).

because we are unsure where the individual's good lies. Just when, that is, modern class actions most resemble the earliest cases of group litigation, our normal social intuitions require that interest flow from consent. But it is just in such circumstances that Rule 23 moves away from our everyday intuitions, dispensing with the requirement of consent. . . .

By dispensing with the inquiry into individual desire that might reveal fragmented classes in Rule 23(b)(2) situations, the rule permits the assertion of claims by sizable groups seeking redress of social wrongs. It achieves, for such purposes, a kind of ad hoc political organization. Moreover, the arrangement virtually assures that such claims will be effectively asserted by putting their control largely in the hands of experienced institutional litigants, be they the NAACP or the National Association of Manufacturers. This situation comes about because, by definition, Rule 23(b)(2) suits do not involve claims for damages;[259] thus they offer no damage awards from which attorneys can claim fees on a "common fund" theory and are unlikely to attract the group of litigative entrepreneurs that 23(b)(3) actions bring forth.[260] The commencement and guidance of such litigation will therefore lie with such institutional litigators. With them rests the power to define the "interest" of the groups they represent; so long as their articulation of that interest does not strike the court as entirely bizarre, it is likely to be sanctioned by class certification.

The roots of this judicial acquiescence in the active litigant's definition of interest lie far deeper than procedural technique, for such a stance expresses fundamental values dictated by substantive law. If federal civil rights legislation proclaims it a violation of national policy to discriminate in education on the basis of sex, and an active litigant presents herself, alleging that she belongs to a definable group suffering from such discrimination, the court may feel itself hard pressed to deny that it is in the "interest" of the group's members to seek redress for such discrimination. National law has, in effect, proclaimed a national interest in eliminating such discrimination, and the edges of public and private law begin to blur. . . .

Reinforcing such substantive considerations are the procedural requirements for settling class actions. Such settlements require judi-

259. The rule limits suits in this category to actions "making appropriate final injunctive relief or corresponding declaratory relief with respect to the class as a whole." Fed. R. Civ. P. 23(b)(2).

260. . . .To be sure, many suits brought as 23(b)(2) actions fall under statutes entitling prevailing litigants to attorney fees under certain circumstances. E.g., 42 U.S.C. §1988 (1976). The lawyer who brings and wins such actions is therefore unlikely to go unpaid; but such court-awarded fees, however important as an instrument for encouraging meritorious litigation in such cases, do not hold forth the promise of the multi-million dollar jackpots of which lawyers bringing 23(b)(3) actions dream.

cial approval. The obvious ground for requiring court approval is to protect the absent members of the class from a settlement whose advantages accrue primarily to the active litigant or his lawyer rather than to the group as a whole. In (b)(2) suits, however, this purpose blends insensibly with another: the court must protect not only the absentee class, but also the goals of the substantive law giving rise to the plaintiff's claim. These two purposes may come into conflict, as an example will show.

Imagine a plaintiff suing on behalf of a class of women allegedly suffering from a university's acts of sexual discrimination in hiring and admissions. Imagine further that the plaintiff has demonstrated such acts and established substantive liability. If at that point the parties present to the court a settlement that does not address the acts giving rise to liability, but instead proposes greatly increased funding for a Women's Studies Center at the university, the judge might well have doubts about whether he could approve the settlement. I submit that those doubts might persist even if the judge had obtained — as Rule 23 does not require — the consent of each member of the represented group. The doubt would, in such a case, be a product not of questions about whether the "true" interests of the group had been advanced but about whether the true "interests" of the state, defined by the substantive law in question, had been served. . . .

. . . By blinding ourselves to the variety and arbitrariness of individual desires we achieve for this peculiar kind of litigation what we have done, equally imperfectly, for government: we legitimize a regime that organizes the affairs of large groups.

Class Conflicts in Class Actions *

Deborah L. Rhode

A fundamental premise of American adjudicative structures is that clients, not their counsel, define litigation objectives. Thus, the American Bar Association's current and proposed ethical codes both emphasize that an attorney must defer to the client's wishes on matters affecting the merits of legal action. However, by presupposing an individual client with clearly identifiable views, these codes elide a frequent and fundamental difficulty in class action proceedings. In many such cases, the lawyer represents an aggregation of litigants

* *Source:* 34 Stan. L. Rev. 1183, 1183-1193, 1197, 1207-1212, 1214-1226, 1228-1235, 1237-1239, 1241, 1247-1256 (1982).

with unstable, inchoate, or conflicting preferences. The more diffuse and divided the class, the greater the problems in defining its objectives.

This article examines those problems in one selected context: plaintiff class actions seeking structural reforms in public and private institutions. Such cases merit special attention on two grounds. First, the often indeterminate quality of relief available makes conflicts within plaintiff classes particularly likely. Most school desegregation, employment discrimination, prison reform, and related cases present no obvious single solution flowing ineluctably from the nature of the violation. Nor will all class members alleging unlawful conduct agree on what should be done about it. Moreover, the prominence of institutional reform litigation vests these intra-class cleavages with particular significance. Such cases account for a high percentage of all class suits and an even greater proportion of legal claims attracting widespread societal concern. Thus, institutional reform litigation provides a useful paradigm for analyzing some of the most vexing issues in class representation.

In exploring these issues, this article takes one central proposition for granted. On the whole, institutional reform class actions have made and continue to make an enormous contribution to the realization of fundamental constitutional values — a contribution that no other governmental construct has proven able to duplicate. . . . Thus, the following discussion should not be taken to suggest that institutional reform class actions are misused or misconceived, or that there are preferable alternatives. The point, rather, is that the framework in which such actions proceed could benefit from both conceptual and mechanical refurbishing. . . .

I. Intra-Class Conflicts and Disclosure Obligations

A. *A Taxonomy of Conflicts*

For those seeking structural reforms, class actions afford a number of obvious advantages over suits involving individual plaintiffs. By definition, class proceedings force focus on institutional practices rather than isolated grievances. Also, if a variety of allegedly unlawful practices are at issue, it can be cumbersome to seek out separate plaintiffs with standing to challenge each violation. Representing individual plaintiffs also entails some risk of mootness. School children graduate, prison inmates obtain transfers or paroles, and individual employees are subject to temptation by generous settlement offers. By contrast, once the court certifies a suit as a class action, the proceedings can continue despite the termination of individual claims, and any settlement must obtain judicial approval. Thus, class representation obviates the continual need to substitute plaintiffs, and minimizes the allure of proposed settlements benefiting only named litigants. Moreover, compared with individual suits, class litigation may promise counsel greater bargaining leverage, larger attorneys' fees, and enhanced access to funding sources. . . .

The importance, complexity, and protracted character of these lawsuits create opportunities for conflict at every stage of litigation. Class members who prefer the certainty of the status quo to the risks of judicial rearrangement may oppose litigation from the outset. For example, some parents who anticipate busing or closure of institutional facilities as a consequence of legal intervention will prefer to never initiate proceedings. So too, minority employees have feared retaliation by coworkers and management, or loss of job-related advantages in the aftermath of Title VII actions. And some inmates of state institutions have proven reluctant to antagonize their custodians by filing suit.

Disputes can also arise during the liability phase of litigation over which parties to join or where to concentrate scarce resources. Thus, in employment discrimination cases, litigants have differed about whether to sue a union as well as an employer, whether to pursue claims of women and seasonal employees as well as full-time minority workers, and whether to focus on entry level as well as advancement opportunities.

Far more common, however, are schisms that surface during settlement or remedial deliberations. Often when a suit is filed, plaintiffs will not have focused on issues of relief. The impetus for the action will be a general sense that rights have been infringed or needs ignored, rather than a shared conviction about the appropriate remedy. . . . However, once it becomes clear that some relief will be forthcoming, factions emerge. Also, where proceedings are protracted, changes in legal doctrine, contested practices, or plaintiff preferences can create new sources of dissension.

School desegregation cases provide the most well-documented instances of conflict. . . . Dispute has centered on the relative importance of integration, financial resources, minority control, and ethnic identification in enriching school environments. Constituencies that support integration in principle have disputed its value in particular settings where extended bus rides, racial tension, or white flight seem likely concomitants of judicial redistricting. Some minority administrators, teachers, and parental organizations have opposed inter-district remedies that would close minority schools or dilute minority control. . . .

Comparable cleavages arise in various other institutional reform contexts. Parents challenging the adequacy of existing bilingual or special education programs have differed over whether mainstreaming or upgrading separate classes represents the better solution. Suits involving rights of the disabled have divided their families over whether to demand institutional improvement or creation of community care alternatives. . . .

Moreover, as with any form of collective litigation, parties often differ in their amenability to compromise and their assessment of particular proposals. Given the uncertainty of outcome and indeterminacy of relief in many institutional reform class actions, risk-averse plaintiffs will often be prepared to make substantial concessions. Other class members will prefer to fight. . . .

B. The Requirement of Adequate Representation

Prevailing legal doctrine offers strikingly little guidance to courts and counsel who confront intra-class schisms. . . . Among the primary questions left unaddressed is whether interest ever means more than preference and, if so, when and what. Do the named representative and counsel serve primarily as "instructed delegates," pursuing objectives to which a majority of class members subscribe? If so, how are those objectives to be identified, particularly if the class comprises a diffuse and changing constituency of past, present, and future claimants? Alternatively, does the representative role track Edmund Burke's notion of an "enlightened trustee," who makes an independent assessment of class concerns? Under that advocacy model, what recourse is available to individuals who do not share their trustee's vision? . . .

C. Disclosure Mandates and Process Values

. . . [T]wo fundamental threshold inquiries are to what extent disclosure of conflicting preferences really matters and whether it matters more in class than individual adjudication. . . .

Apprising the court of class sentiment serves a number of fundamental due process values. Although empirical foundations are lacking, much of our procedural jurisprudence rests on the assumption that an opportunity to be heard increases the rationality and perceived legitimacy of decisionmaking. Disclosure of the full range of class concerns reduces the chance that courts will overlook, undervalue, or otherwise misconstrue relevant considerations. Parties who believe that their perspectives have been fairly presented may also display more confidence in the judicial process and greater willingness to abide by its results. Moreover, quite apart from the effect on particular outcomes or parties' perceptions, recognition of a right to be heard serves certain broader societal values. Respect for individual dignity, autonomy, and self-expression demands that those with rights directly at risk have an adequate means of registering their concerns.

To be sure, those same heuristic and participatory interests are implicated in much private-law litigation, as the frequent involvement of intervenors and amici curiae attests. Yet sensitivity to process values is of particular importance in institutional reform class actions, given the nature of the underlying disputes. Such litigation tends to involve complex indeterminate remedies, fundamental personal values, nonapparent preferences, and politically vulnerable forms of intervention, all of which counsel special concern. . . .

Much institutional reform litigation presents opportunities for dispute that are less easily identified than in other class actions or individual suits. Where a claim is for monetary damages alone, the interests of various plaintiff subgroups are readily apparent. An adequate working assumption is that for any faction, more compensation is better than less. So too, in much private-law litigation with broad precedential impact, the court can predict the preferences of those not present. Tort victims will generally wish the broadest possible liability and damage rules; insurer's interests are to the contrary. But when remedial choices involve complex forms of injunctive relief, with many opportunities for tradeoffs among subgroups within a plaintiff class, prediction becomes far more difficult. Thus, reported decisions reflect a broad variety of circumstances in which courts and counsel failed to appreciate the nature and intensity of class concerns until after entry of a decree.

That sort of failure is troubling in several respects. Most obviously, it will increase the expense and delay of proceedings, if disaffected parties subsequently challenge the adequacy of their representation and attempt to reopen matters already resolved. Moreover, misperceptions about party preferences may unnecessarily diminish the efficacy of judicial intervention. . . .

. . . Restructuring a school district, prison, or promotion system often demands considerable cooperation from the affected constituencies. Yet the further the judge strays into social planning, the greater his difficulty in commanding the moral force of adjudication. Under such circumstances, maintaining the credibility of judicial office requires special solicitude for process values. . . .

II. The Participants' Roles in Disclosing Conflict: Rules and Realities

Formal mandates governing class adjudication assign responsibility for ensuring adequate representation to three quarters: the named plaintiffs, their attorneys, and the court. In practice, opposing parties and dissenting class members also play a role in exposing conflict. Frequently, however, none of these participants has sufficient incentive or information to respond adequately to class schisms.

A. The Named Plaintiffs

As state and federal courts have repeatedly emphasized, "class actions involve the delegation of authority to a named representative to pursue a common goal. In this pursuit, it is . . . the duty of the class representative to ensure that the absent members' interests are adequately protected. . . ." Yet as a practical matter, once a class is certified, named plaintiffs generally are neither highly motivated nor well situated to monitor the congruence between counsel's conduct and class preferences. . . .

. . . At best, the named plaintiffs may attempt to confirm that counsel is pursuing their own interests, and that any proposed settlement comports with their remedial preferences. Especially where the objectives of nominal representatives are realized early in the litigation, their interest in subsequent proceedings may waver. Absent some external pressure, the objectives of fellow litigants could well remain uncertain and unarticulated.

In any event, since counsel's fiduciary obligations run to the class as a whole, the litigation directives of nominal plaintiffs are not of controlling significance. . . . Particularly where the class membership is diffuse, the issues complicated, or the proceedings protracted, the function of nominal plaintiffs may be no more than what the label implies. . . .

B. Class Counsel . . .

1. PRUDENTIAL INTERESTS

An attorney active in institutional reform class actions is subject to a variety of financial, tactical, and professional pressures that constrain his response to class conflicts. . . .

The most patent of these interests arises from the financial underpinnings of institutional reform litigation. Support for such cases derives largely from limited public interest funding and from court-awarded counsel fees to prevailing parties. Among the factors affecting the attorney's fee award are the relief obtained, the costs of attaining it, and the number of other counsel who have contributed to the result. Given the expense of institutional reform class actions, few litigators can remain impervious to fee-related considerations or organizational budget constraints. And flushing out dissension among class members can prove costly in several respects.

For example, opposing parties often seek to capitalize on class dissension by filing motions for decertification. If such efforts prove successful, class counsel may lose a substantial investment that he cannot, as a practical matter, recoup from former class members. At a minimum, such motions result in expense, delay, and loss of bargaining leverage, and deflect resources from trial preparation. Certification disputes may also trigger involvement of additional lawyers, who would share the limelight, the control over litigation decisions and, under some circumstances, the resources available for attorneys' fees.

Exposing conflict can also impede settlement arrangements that are attractive to class counsel on a number of grounds. As in many other litigation contexts, attorneys often have a bias to settle not shared by their clients. Since institutional reform plaintiffs generally do not underwrite the costs of litigation, their primary interest is in the result attained; the time and effort necessary to attain it are of less concern. Yet from the attorney's perspective, a modest settlement may generate a result "bearing a higher ratio to the cost of the work than a much larger recovery obtained only after extensive discovery, a long trial and an appeal." For example, if the prospects for prevailing on the merits are uncertain, some plaintiffs will see little to lose and everything to gain from persistence. That viewpoint may be inadequately aired by class counsel, who has concerns for his reputation as well as competing claims on his time and his organization's resources to consider.

The potential for attorney-client conflicts is compounded when a proposed settlement makes extremely generous, or totally inadequate, provision for class counsel. . . .

. . . By accepting a liberal reward for his services, the attorney may in fact or appearance be recouping his own investment at his clients' expense. Thus, no matter what course he elects, counsel will have difficulty preventing fee-related considerations from affecting his assessment of settlement opportunities and his willingness to expose contrary views.

A final set of problems emerges in test-case litigation. In some instances, counsel may be reluctant to espouse positions that are at odds with those he has taken or intends to take in other proceedings or that could establish an unwelcome precedent. Moreover, test-case litigation often generates settlement biases directly converse to those discussed above. Once a lawyer has prepared a claim with potentially significant impact, he may be disinclined to settle. He almost certainly would not share some plaintiffs' enthusiasm for pre- or post-trial agreements promising generous terms for the litigants but little recognition and no precedential value for similarly situated victims. Few professionals, class attorneys included, can make decisions wholly independent of concerns about their careers and reputations among peers, potential clients, and funding sources. Litigating well-publicized institutional reform cases can provide desirable trial experience, generate attractive new cases, legitimate organizational objectives in the eyes of private donors, and enhance attorneys' personal standing in the legal community. Where such rewards are likely, counsel may tend to discount preferences for a low-visibility settlement, particularly if it falls short of achieving ideological objectives to which he is strongly committed.

2. IDEOLOGICAL INTERESTS

Almost two decades ago, Justice Harlan's dissenting opinion in NAACP v. Button [105] expressed concerns about ideological conflicts between civil rights lawyers and litigants. . . .

. . . Although there was no evidence in *Button* that any plaintiffs opposed NAACP objectives, more recent desegregation suits suggest that Justice Harlan's concerns were not entirely unfounded. Relying on case histories from Boston, Atlanta, and Detroit, Derek Bell submits that NAACP attorneys' "single-minded commitment" to maximum integration has led them to ignore a shift in priorities among many black parents from racial balance to quality education.

Similar indictments have been leveled against attorneys in other civil rights contexts. For example, in 1974, a number of parents and guardians brought suit in behalf of all present and future residents of Pennsylvania's Pennhurst facility for the retarded. Class counsel took the position that his obligations ran solely to the residents, and that their interests dictated Pennhurst's closure and replacement with community facilities. Accordingly, counsel made little effort to expose or espouse the views of parents and guardians preferring institutionalization. Indeed, according to one of the lawyers subsequently involved, class counsel sought to avoid "stir[ring] people up" by deemphasizing the possibility of Pennhurst's closure in his out-of-court statements. After the district judge ordered removal of Pennhurst residents to community facilities, a systematic survey of their parents and guardians revealed that only 19 percent of respondents favored deinstitutionalization. Accounts of other civil rights litigation suggest that *Pennhurst* is not an isolated example.

It does not follow, of course, that attorneys in these and comparable cases failed to represent class interests. Much depends on who

105. 371 U.S. 415, 448-470 (1963).

one views as appropriate spokesmen for the class and how broadly one defines "interest.". . . [P]arents are often poorly situated to speak for all children who will be affected by judicial decree. But neither is an attorney with strong prudential or ideological preferences well positioned to decide which class members or guardians deserve a hearing and which do not. . . .

3. DISCLOSURE OF ATTORNEY INTERESTS

. . . The profession's customary mechanism for coping with counsel's self-interest — disclosure and informed client consent — is simply not a workable approach in class adjudication. . . .

A threshold difficulty is whose assent suffices. Once the class reaches a certain size, obtaining informed consent from all members is simply infeasible. And neither law nor logic suggests that named representatives can waive remedial alternatives for the full membership. Those representatives will often have preferences shared by counsel but not by the class in its entirety. . . .

So too, the informed-consent model is ill-suited for circumstances where plaintiffs' identities as well as preferences are likely to change over time. Classes in institutional reform cases will typically encompass future victims of allegedly unlawful conduct, whose interests are not coextensive with those of current plaintiffs. If, for example, all past and incumbent employees agreed to forego certain prospective relief in exchange for greater compensation, their consensus would not necessarily be determinative of the "class interest.". . .

C. *Dissenting Plaintiffs and Opposing Parties*

By default rather than formal allocation, the burden of representing some class interests often rests with disaffected plaintiffs or opposing litigants. Adversarial norms may reinforce the sense that those unhappy with existing representation should bear the burden of coming forward. The difficulty, however, is that often neither dissenting plaintiffs nor opposing parties have sufficient information or incentive to do so.

Frequently, until a decree is actually entered or a settlement reached, non-named class members have little appreciation of the likely consequences of litigation, let alone the extent to which their particular concerns have been addressed. . . . Even when informed, dissenters frequently face the very common action problem that class procedures seek to address: No single individual perceives a sufficient stake in the outcome to warrant the expense of organizing a constituency and obtaining separate representation. Also, the less celebrated the case and the less certain the availability of adequate attorneys' fees, the greater the difficulty dissenters confront in finding a qualified advocate.

Similarly, opposing parties at times lack the facts or inclination to challenge the adequacy of class representation. To prevent misleading or coercive communication, prevailing doctrine severely limits opposing counsel's contact with class members, thereby restricting his ability to document disaffection. Even where the likelihood of schisms is patent, defendants may have insufficient evidence of opposition to force decertification or disaggregation of the class. . . . [I]n many instances, opposing parties may see little long-range benefit from exploiting conflicts if the likely consequence is not decertification but only a slight delay, a narrower class definition, or more attorneys. Particularly where defendants have established good relationships with current class counsel or are concerned about their probable liability for attorneys' fees, they might prefer dealing with one rather than multiple adversaries.

If defendants are government employees operating on inadequate budgets, they may also prove sympathetic to the named representatives' objectives. In some desegregation and deinstitutionalization cases, defendants have depended on lawsuits to compel what they "would *like* to do but lack the political courage to accomplish on their own." When a broad remedial order would give them desired bargaining leverage with funding sources, these parties will be unwilling to ferret out conflicts that could jeopardize a mutually desired result. . . .

Moreover, if litigation is bound to proceed in some form, defendants may prefer the largest possible class in order to secure the broadest possible res judicata effect, or to discourage Solomonic compromises. . . .

D. Courts

Both Rule 23 and the due process clause vest ultimate responsibility for ensuring adequate representation in the trial judge. . . .

Despite the judiciary's formal responsibilities, constraints of time and role militate against an active oversight posture. In this context, departures from the courts' traditional umpireal stance often seem a thankless enterprise. Effectively monitoring class counsel's representation could require more personal innuendo and factual investigation than many trial judges are disposed to supply. . . .

Moreover, many trial courts face staggering caseloads and seemingly interminable claims on their time. Where the pressures to clear dockets are substantial, the costs of smoking out conflict may seem prohibitive. For if finding one set of class representatives and their counsel inadequate does not terminate proceedings, it will likely prolong them. From a trial court's perspective, more is seldom merrier. Multiple representation multiplies problems, both administrative and substantive. More parties means more papers, more scheduling difficulties, and more potential for objection to any given ruling or settlement proposal. Increasing the visibility of class cleavages may also increase their intensity, thereby reducing the possibility for settlement or exposing the trial court to greater risks of reversal on appeal. . . .

Appellate court oversight of class conflicts has been similarly myopic. Recognition of trial judges' difficulties, together with the press of other business, have generally inhibited searching review. District court decisions concerning the adequacy of representation are subject to reversal only for an abuse of discretion. As a practical matter, the unavailability of interlocutory review also insulates many certification orders from effective consideration. . . .

III. Procedural Mechanisms for Coping with Conflicts: The Practical Limits of Theoretical Alternatives . . .

A. The Pluralist Approach: Separate Representation

Once significant class cleavages become apparent, the conventional judicial response is to divide by decree classes that are divided in fact. To ensure adequate representation of each constituency, a court may create subclasses, grant mandatory or permissive intervention, or permit amici participation. Subclassification is the preferred alternative if the class divides into discrete groups, each having some "ascertainable characteristic" that explains its distinctive concerns. . . . Separate counsel for each subgroup is usually desirable, since whatever facts would justify subdivision would also reflect a need for independent representation. Absent separate attorneys, subclassification is likely to prove a taxonomic gesture with little practical significance.

Where conflicts arise from divergent preferences that do not correspond to identifiable constituencies within the class, the court might grant some form of intervenor or amici status as an alternative to subclassing. Federal rules governing suits for injunctive or declaratory relief provide for intervention either as a matter of right or discretion, and allow courts to limit intervenors' roles as the interests of justice require. What status dissenting class members enjoy has certain practical consequences. Full intervenors may have some rights — to take discovery, cross-examine witnesses, or appeal adverse decisions — that are denied to partial intervenors or amici curiae, who may only attend hearings or submit briefs. For present purposes, however, what merit attention are less these distinctions than the common advantages and disadvantages that separate representation entails.

The potential benefits attending independent advocacy are readily apparent. Constituencies whose concerns are antithetical or peripheral to those of the class representatives receive a hearing. Such participation may assist courts in formulating remedies that best accommodate all interests affected by judicial decree. Since many civil rights litigators operate under severe resource constraints, the inclusion of additional advocates with separate funding sources could often improve factual deliberations. . . . And insofar as dissenters believe their values have been forcefully advocated, they may be more supportive of both the process and result of judicial deliberations.

How frequently separate representation will in fact improve or legitimate particular decisions is, however, open to question. In this as in other decisionmaking contexts, problems of bias, timing, manageability, and expense all render the pluralist model less attractive in practice than in theory.

As long as a given constituency's views are still mediated through self-appointed representatives and their counsel, the potential for biased advocacy remains. Certainly the pluralist approach cannot fully redress difficulties arising from attorneys' prudential or ideological concerns. . . .

Similarly, adding attorneys can be counterproductive if it generates a more distorted account of membership concerns than that emerging from a single advocate's presentation. Like other interest groups, each litigant faction is likely to overstate the extent and intensity of its support. Since would-be intervenors or amici need not voice interests other than their own, their involvement may distort the trial court's perception of aggregate class preferences and skew settlement negotiations accordingly. As one experienced public interest litigator has observed, it does not help to have "lawyers representing ten different interest groups objecting to ten different aspects of a proposed decree, if the court has no sense of how substantial a constituency each represents.". . .

Related difficulties with the pluralist strategy involve issues of timing. To avoid unnecessary expense and complication, courts certifying diverse classes may resist subdivision at the outset but reserve it as an option should schisms later develop. Yet the extent of conflict frequently will not be apparent until the parties propose a settlement or the court enters a remedial order. At that point, defining subclasses whose separate counsel could upset the proposed disposition will be costly to all concerned. Precisely when conflicts are most concrete, the pressures on the parties and courts to overlook them are most intense.

Requests for permissive intervention can pose analogous problems. Under the federal rules, trial judges may deny untimely requests, and appellate courts are reluctant to find such denials an abuse of discretion. Given the protracted character of structural reform litigation, a factual predicate for timeliness objections is frequently available. . . . Yet for courts to deny intervention on grounds of timeliness disserves constituencies that did not appreciate the need for full participation until remedial terms became apparent.

Even where provision of separate counsel presents no difficulties of timing, it may raise questions of manageability. Especially in celebrated cases, extending subsidized opportunities for participation to any disaffected class members could generate a host of applicants. With complex litigation involving diffuse classes, how many overlapping interests warrant independent advocacy? . . .

. . . Full participation in institutional reform litigation can be extremely costly. It took the ACLU years to locate volunteer counsel willing and able to bring the Los Angeles school case, a commitment that ultimately spanned a decade. In less celebrated cases, it frequently will prove impossible to attract qualified counsel on a pro bono basis. Despite its professed commitment, the private bar contributes a very small percentage of volunteer time to civil rights cases, and public interest organizations have extremely limited litigation resources.

Doctrinal and practical constraints on court-awarded compensation further compound the problems of locating legal assistance. Application of federal attorneys' fees statutes to counsel for dissenting class members presents several difficulties. To qualify for fees, the client must be a "prevailing party," a term subject to varying interpretations. Some courts have construed the standard to require "success" on the merits of an "important" issue in litigation, and have restricted fees to work performed on those issues. Other decisions reflect a more permissive approach; participants making a significant contribution to the proceedings have received awards, even with respect to matters on which they did not "prevail" in a technical legal sense. Of course, even under the latter approach, what constitutes a sufficient contribution will often be open to debate, particularly if independent counsel has opposed much of the relief ordered or if a large number of attorneys have participated. Thus, the availability of fee awards may be difficult to predict at the time when class members are seeking an attorney to intervene on their behalf.

If no class member comes forward with separate counsel, a second set of difficulties arises. The circumstances under which trial judges may appoint, and award fees for, counsel representing disaffected plaintiffs remain unsettled. . . . Once courts have found, for purposes of certification, that the named parties' counsel "adequately represents" the class, they may be disinclined to find separate advocates necessary. And, depending on the opposing party's financial circumstances, some trial judges will have reservations about how many sides of the same lawsuit defendants should have to underwrite. . . .

. . . As in other contexts, the pluralist approach biases decisionmaking in favor of those with the organizational acumen and financial resources to make themselves heard. Obvious as this deficiency appears, it receives little attention among defenders of the pluralist faith in class adjudication. Yet to accept their solution as appropriate in theory implies a strong indictment of class representation in practice. If separate interests warrant separate voices, it is hard to justify a structure that supplies them only to those willing and able to pay.

Of course, on one level, that objection simply expresses a problem with civil adjudication generally — a hearing is available, but only at a price. Yet the critique assumes special force in institutional reform litigation, where most class members are involuntary parties to actions of considerable personal significance and indeterminate doctrinal outcome. Adequate decisionmaking under those circumstances requires information about the full spectrum of plaintiff concerns. Such information will not be forthcoming in a system heavily dependent on class members' own resources and initiative.

Thus, what is ultimately most troubling about the pluralist response to class conflict is its failure either to identify limiting principles or to confront the manner in which information, incentive, and cost constraints combine to skew representation. In many instances, no participant will have sufficient reason, knowledge, or resources to voice interests other than those of named plaintiffs or their counsel. In other, usually well-publicized cases, any number of interested parties might wish a role, although their participation could impede or distort decisionmaking. Although these deficiencies are by no means unique to class adjudication, their presence counsels some attention to majoritarian alternatives.

B. *The Majoritarian Response: Direct Participation Through Plebiscites and Public Hearings . . .*

As a means of conveying information to the court and a sense of participation to class members, majoritarian strategies seemingly offer several advantages over pluralist devices. The first is economic. Relatively speaking, talk is cheap, at least when it occurs among class members rather than through separate counsel. Even with large classes, trial judges can often minimize notice and processing costs through reliance on nonindividualized methods of communication and information from court-appointed experts. Moreover, soliciting class preferences directly, rather than through the mediating influence of attorneys or named representatives, may reduce distortion and enhance individuals' sense of efficacy and confidence in the decision-making process. In practice, however, this approach is vulnerable to three serious objections, largely overlooked by advocates of enhanced client control in class proceedings. Absent extraordinary expenditures, the views elicited from notice and hearings will frequently be unrepresentative, uninformed, and unresponsive to a range of concerns particularly significant in institutional reform litigation.

To provide meaningful evidence of class preferences, responses to written notices or attendance at open meetings must reflect a fair cross section of the class as a whole. The scant empirical data available raise significant doubts about how frequently this condition could be met. Even in cases affording strong incentives for written response, where class members are notified that they can recover damages merely by mailing a single proof of loss, only 10 percent to 15 percent have done so. Absent some efforts to ascertain the representativeness of respondents — efforts that are rarely if ever undertaken in injunctive class actions — the reliability of survey replies is questionable. . . .

Reliance on views expressed at public meetings or settlement hearings presents similar difficulties. Interviews with class action litigators confirm the difficulty of convincing a representative sample of the class to attend. Attorneys who have held open meetings in school desegregation and employment cases generally report poor attendance. Judicial decisions that disclose the percentage of class members present at settlement hearings reflect equally low turnouts, even when there is evidence of strong opposition to a proposed decree. That community organizers generally experienced comparable attendance rates at the height of the War on Poverty suggests that the problems of mobilization are deep-seated if not intractable.

Although class members' failure to register dissent has often been taken to denote satisfaction, such inferences are troubling on several grounds. Rarely will class members have sufficient understanding of the meaning of notice, the positions of counsel, or the remedial alternatives available to make informed decisions about whether or how to respond. . . .

Analogous problems arise when class sentiment is gauged by votes at public meetings. . . .

These considerations, coupled with problems of timing and expense, militate against soliciting class sentiment during the negotiation process. Yet if, as is often the case, class members are invited to register preferences only after agreement is reached, they will have too little appreciation of plausible alternatives to make independent and informed evaluations. Some individuals may miscalculate the likelihood of obtaining a more attractive remedial package after trial, appeal, or further bargaining. Others might too readily accept counsel's less than disinterested assessment of particular proposals. And of course, simple plebiscites cannot adjust for differentials in voter comprehension, acuity, or intensity of concerns. Thus, as political theorists remind us, the more technical the issue, the less the point in counting noses.

In some circumstances, class members are uninformed in a still more fundamental sense. Individuals who lack experience with a controversial remedial option may have a distorted view of its probable consequences. Those plaintiffs might fear the worst and vote accordingly. For instance, several studies indicate that black families subject to metropolitan busing programs are far more supportive of the concept than the black population generally. Similarly, surveys of individuals involved in the *Pennhurst* litigation found that family members became significantly more positive about community placement after they witnessed it, and that the vast majority have been pleased with the result. As this and comparable research also discloses, much parental opposition to deinstitutionalization arises from concerns that adequate community-based alternatives will never materialize, and that the programs which are established will not guarantee necessary support services and trained personnel. If experience is likely to allay such fears, there is reason to discount family members' *ex ante* preferences.

Moreover, these same illustrations point up a final problem with relying on majoritarian methods in institutional reform litigation. Often, those eligible to vote are not reliable spokesmen for the entire class affected by judicial decree. For example, actions against facilities for the retarded typically proceed on behalf of all current and future institutionalized patients "speaking through" their parents or legal guardians. In reality, the latter are often speaking for other personal and family interests as well. . . .

These considerations undoubtedly account for many judges' reluctance to demand systematic evidence of class sentiment, or to view it as controlling. . . .

IV. Alternatives and Apologia . . .

B. Possible Prescriptions . . .

1. INFORMATION AND INCENTIVE BARRIERS

A central anomaly of Rule 23(b), as currently construed, stems from its notice provisions. In suits requesting money damages, where plaintiffs' preferences are generally self-evident, notification of individual class members is required. Yet in claims seeking structural relief, where class sentiment is less readily apparent, notice is discretionary, except with respect to settlements. All too often, when courts do order notification, it occurs either at the certification stage, before disputes over relief have crystallized, or else after the named parties and the court have agreed on settlement terms, at which point opposition will rarely have much impact. The result may be costly, ineffectual appeals, or a decisionmaking process that in fact or appearance is insensitive to the full range of class concerns.

As with most other issues in class adjudication, the problem is far more easily defined than regulated. Given the enormous variation in pace and subject matter of institutional reform cases, as well as all the communication barriers discussed in Part III, it would be impractical to mandate any uniform method or time for providing notice. Since the need for broad trial court discretion is inescapable, the most sensible strategy may simply be to encourage closer scrutiny of the issue. To that end, courts should be required to make a factual record concerning notice. More specifically, the trial judge should be obligated to specify, before entering any remedial order or consent decree, the nature and timing of information provided to class members and why the court found it adequate in the circumstances. Among the factors relevant to that determination would be the probable intelligibility and expense of various forms of communication, and the likelihood that responses would significantly inform the decisionmaking process. For the vast majority of cases, those factors would militate against any individualized communication. Some combination of public announcements, postings at central locations, open meetings, insertions in regular mailings, or contact with court-appointed experts should suffice to apprise the court of significant unrepresented constituencies. However, where those options are unsuitable or the court requires more accurate information about aggregate preferences, the expense of sampling or individual notice may be warranted.

Given that possibility, some attention to allocation of costs is in order. If a court orders notice after finding defendants liable, they would bear the expense under existing federal statutes. Where the judge mandates an expensive form of notification prior to determining liability, he should have discretion to charge such expenditures to defendants *pendente lite* unless the plaintiffs' claim appears insubstantial. Although in Eisen v. Carlisle & Jacquelin,[253] the Supreme Court rejected the possibility of shifting expenses to defendants in damage suits under Federal Rule 23(b)(3), that holding should not foreclose a different result in (b)(2) structural relief cases. . . .

253. 417 U.S. 156 (1974)

A second means of enhancing judicial sensitivity to conflicts would be to require that trial courts make a factual record on the adequacy of representation before entering a remedial or consent decree. . . . Before entering any consent or remedial decree, the judge should have to determine that a fair cross section of class views has been presented, and that no significant constituency has been excluded.

To assist its determination, the trial judge should require plaintiffs' counsel or a court-appointed expert to submit statements detailing contact with class members and any nonprivileged indications of substantial dissension within the class. In addition, the trial judge's findings should explore any significant divergence between plaintiff sentiment — as expressed in responses to notice or presentations at settlement hearings — and the views espoused by class representatives. Where substantial conflict is apparent, the court should be obligated to specify what steps were taken to ensure representation of dissenting viewpoints. . . .

Finally, to minimize the potential for financial bias, trial judges should enjoin counsel from negotiating fees pending settlement of substantive issues, absent explicit court approval. At present, defendants may proffer generous attorneys' fees in tacit exchange for remedial concessions, or alternatively, condition an otherwise attractive settlement on counsel's reduction of claims to compensation. Despite concerted efforts at objectivity, a lawyer may have difficulties keeping fee-related concerns from affecting his assessment of particular settlement offers or his willingness to expose views that could jeopardize a desirable disposition. . . .

2. RESPONSES TO CONFLICT

A second set of procedural reforms should focus on legal standards and practical techniques for coping with intra-class cleavages that are in fact disclosed. . . .

Many of the difficulties with prevailing intervention analysis stem from insensitivity to the special procedural concerns at issue in institutional reform litigation. Decisions denying intervention as untimely have often seemed unresponsive both to the information structures that made earlier participation unlikely and to the remedial dynamics that make even belated involvement desirable. . . . Given the distinctive pace and participatory character of structural reform litigation, traditional biases against belated intervenors require reassessment.

Decisions denying intervenor status on the theory that defendants have adequately presented dissident plaintiffs' views are similarly unsatisfying. . . . [M]inority parents who wish to preserve certain racially-identified schools can often provide additional evidence or credibility on arguments relevant to remedial choices. Since such parents are unlikely to perceive a defendant school board as an effective advocate for their concerns, foreclosing participation on that ground impairs the legitimacy of judicial resolution. Overlap in argument should be tolerated, absent a more convincing basis for exclusion. . . .

. . . Within an adjudicative framework, we cannot indefinitely increase access without diminishing capacity. When the cacophony of separate counsel precludes effective decisionmaking, or belated intervention requires extensive reopening of issues, participatory values may have to yield. Although there is obviously no magic tipping point uniform for all cases, the costs of additional participants at some stage become prohibitive.

Thus, intervention analysis in institutional reform adjudication should reflect a more broad-gauged inquiry into the potential contribution of intervenors and a more particularized assessment of its expense. Concern should focus less on the timing of the dissenters' request or the partial redundancy of their views, and more on the direct administrative costs that their involvement would entail. Especially if remedial processes are still fluid, courts should make maximum efforts to accommodate new entrants in some capacity. . . .

The committee mechanism could prove useful in a variety of settings. Parental groups have played an official advisory role in implementing school decrees, and elected negotiating committees have helped formulate remedial proposals in employment discrimination cases. Although those who serve may not always reflect a representative sample of class views, experience suggests that they will often articulate a broader range of concerns than named plaintiffs, while lending greater credibility to remedial decrees.

In addition, clearer standards are needed for appointing and compensating separate counsel. Reported decisions reflect no consensus on the circumstances justifying fee awards for court-appointed or privately-selected representatives of dissenting plaintiffs. The result is an adjudicative structure that too often conditions participation on willingness and ability to pay. . . .

Of course, neither should courts grant carte blanche recoveries for all participants in institutional reform litigation. Without question, the costs of underwriting separate counsel for all class constituencies that might desire it would be prohibitive. . . .

Absent circumstances warranting separate counsel, trial judges could make greater use of expert witnesses, special masters, and magistrates for surrogate representation functions. Especially where the objectives are primarily majoritarian — to obtain information about aggregate plaintiff preferences or to give class members some direct participatory role — neutral court-appointed advisors could play a more prominent role. . . .

Given the values at issue in institutional reform cases, conflicts are an ineradicable feature of the legal landscape. Virtually all of the pluralist and majoritarian deficiencies that impede judicial management of such conflicts would arise with equal force if the underlying issues were addressed in legislative or bureaucratic settings. Indeed, one of the strongest justifications for those governance structures is equally available to class actions: While we cannot depend on disinterested and informed judgment by any single group of decisionmakers, we can at least create sufficient procedural checks and balances to prevent the worst abuses.

NOTES AND COMMENTS

As Rhode points out, if a court declines to certify a class in an institutional reform case, the action may still be carried forward by an individual member of the putative class. Moreover, she says that if liability is established the scope of relief may be fully as broad as if the case had been litigated as a class action: "Under prevailing doctrine, a single schoolchild who proves intentional district-wide segregation could force dismantling of an entire dual school system." To the extent this is so, why should plaintiffs seek to litigate institutional reform cases as class actions? If the defendant wins a case tried as a class action, then presumably the class is bound, assuming there has been adequate representation. If the case is tried as an individual action, a defeat for the individual plaintiff does not preclude relitigation of the same issues by other members of the plaintiff's group. On this view shouldn't it be defendants in institutional reform cases who want class actions and plaintiffs who resist them? Could it be argued that where a self-appointed representative of a plaintiff class suffers an adverse judgment, the very fact that he brought the case as a class action demonstrates inadequate representation?

Like Chayes, Rhode describes institutional reform (or public law) litigation as characterized by a degree of separation of right and remedy, or remedial indeterminacy. Remedies are seen as not clearly defined by the violation of the right that establishes liability. For Rhode this makes relevant, though not necessarily determinative, the preferences of individual class members. Does it also make relevant, and legitimate, the interests of third persons who will be affected by the action — for example, staff members of a defendant prison or mental hospital, or white or male employees of a defendant employer in an employment discrimination case? Doesn't the Shapiro article on intervention (*supra* this chapter) provide arguments supporting intervention by people who stand in this kind of relation to institutional reform litigation? On the other hand, wouldn't this often greatly complicate an already difficult case?

Chapter 5

Preclusion

A Single Package for Multiparty Disputes *

John C. McCoid

The problem itself is straightforward enough. The answer, too, is relatively simple. Its implementation, however, is more complex.

Increasingly in our society human behavior affects multiple parties. New methods of marketing and transportation, contemporary consumer concerns, and growing government contribute to the fact that when injury occurs, or is thought to occur, there are multiple victims, or multiple perpetrators, or both. And when those injuries lead to litigation, they regularly yield multiple suits involving the same issues.

If the several suits are dealt with independently, if each is handled as if the others did not exist, one serious consequence is repetitious litigation. The resources devoted to any lawsuit, the efforts of judges, clerks, witnesses, and others, are scarce. Spending them in repeated examination of the issues raised by a single transaction is a waste. Either repetitive litigation requires the expenditure of additional resources on adjudication, or, if expenditure remains constant, it diverts those resources from resolution of other controversies of significance. That diversion may appear as delay; or it may be a reduction of the time given to examination of any or all controversies presented, with resulting loss of quality. Another product of multiplicity is inconsistency. The spectre of public dismay over a system that decides like cases differently is a disturbing one. Perhaps that concern is overrated, but it is easy to see that different triers of law and fact, responding perhaps to slightly different evidence or presentation at different

* *Source:* 28 Stan. L. Rev. 707, 707-721, 723-728 (1976).

times or places, might well reach different judgments on the same transaction.

Provident Tradesmens Bank & Trust Co. v. Patterson,[4] which has become a leading casebook decision, provides a suitable example of these dangers. A car owned by Dutcher, driven by Cionci, and carrying Lynch and Harris as passengers, collided with a vehicle driven by Smith. Cionci, Lynch, and Smith were killed; Harris was seriously injured. Lynch's estate sued Cionci's in the federal court. Smith's estate and Harris each brought an action against Cionci's estate, Lynch's estate, and Dutcher in the state court. Dutcher's insurer, Lumbermens, refused to defend Cionci's estate in the action in the federal court, and Lynch's estate got an uncollected $50,000 judgment. Lynch's estate, claiming that Cionci operated the car with Dutcher's permission and was therefore an insured, then sued Lumbermens, again in federal court.[5] There you have it: three tort suits and one insurance action plus the prospect of two more. The problem could have been worse; Smith's estate and Harris at least joined three defendants in their state court suits.

The problem is not new. Rather, it is an old one grown worse with time. Because it is old, it has been addressed before, and the sensible answer has been to put the transaction, or at least its common issues, before a court only once for final resolution. This Article explores three possibilities — expanded collateral estoppel, compulsory intervention, and broadened mandatory joinder — and concludes that

4. 390 U.S. 102 (1968).

5. Thereafter, on Lumbermens' motion Smith's estate and Harris were joined as plaintiffs. At trial, Dutcher was allowed to testify against Harris but not against the estate plaintiffs under a state dead man's statute which forbade testimony against an estate by one with interests adverse to the estate. Because there was no other evidence on the permission issue, the Lynch and Smith estates won directed verdicts based on a presumption that a driver (Cionci) operates a borrowed vehicle with permission. Harris won a jury verdict on the permission issue. Provident Tradesmens Bank & Trust Co. v. Lumbermens Mut. Cas. Co., 218 F. Supp. 802 (E.D. Pa. 1963). On Lumbermens' appeal, the Third Circuit, holding Dutcher indispensable, reversed. 365 F.2d 802 (3d Cir. 1966). The Supreme Court, responding especially to the fact that the victims had won judgments against Lumbermens, refused to regard Dutcher as indispensable. 390 U.S. 102, 108 (1968). On remand, the Third Circuit found no other error; it remanded the case to the district court to see whether the three victims would agree to restrict the total of their claims to the policy limit; otherwise execution was to be stayed until Dutcher had an opportunity to protect his interest. 411 F.2d 88 (3d Cir. 1969). The assumption of both the Supreme Court and the Third Circuit was that Dutcher was threatened by exhaustion of the policy limit on behalf of Cionci's estate. Professor Kaplan has asked, however, whether Lumbermens might not be subjected to a payout in excess of that limit. Kaplan, Continuing Work of the Civil Committee: 1966 Amendments of the Federal Rules of Civil Procedure (I), 81 Harv. L. Rev. 356, 374 (1967) (critically discussing the first Third Circuit opinion). If so, the threat was to the insurer, but it had not complained in timely fashion so dismissal for indispensability should not have been granted.

the last is superior to the others. First, however, a brief description of the existing approaches will establish a necessary perspective.

I. Existing Approaches

A. *Res Judicata*

One of the important existing approaches to implementing the single-adjudication answer is res judicata. Merger and bar, twin doctrines of claim preclusion, produce economies in litigation by prohibiting a second suit on the same cause of action where the first resulted in a final judgment on the merits. A shift in the definition of a cause of action from conceptual to transactional terms has expanded the reach of those doctrines. Only rarely, however, are they of much utility in multiparty contexts because, in the main, multiple claimants or defendants by definition produce multiple causes of action.

More useful in the multiparty area is collateral estoppel, or issue preclusion, which prevents relitigation of issues actually litigated and decided in a way that is both identifiable and essential to the judgment in the first suit. Even application of that doctrine is limited where the parties to the two suits are not the same. Two concepts, mutuality and privity, are material to the utility of collateral estoppel where different parties are concerned.

Mutuality restricts estoppel. Mutuality means that one may not invoke a judgment in his own favor unless an adverse judgment could have been used against him. Thus passenger Harris, if not a party, could not rely on a judgment against Lumbermens and for passenger Lynch's estate on the permission-to-drive issue because Harris, not having had his day in court, would not have been bound if no permission to drive the car had been found in the first proceeding.

Increasingly, however, courts have stopped requiring mutuality as a prerequisite for collateral estoppel. The most influential opinion has been Justice Traynor's in Bernhard v. Bank of America National Trust & Savings Association.[13] The nub of his argument there was that the significant question is whether the party *against* whom the judgment is invoked has had his day in court. There is debate about how far the *Bernhard* doctrine should be carried — principally whether it may be used offensively, that is, to establish liability. Obviously, the wider its reach the greater the apparent reduction of repetitive litigation. I say "apparent" because the doctrine can be counterproductive. For example, Harris might have preferred to stay out of the

13. 19 Cal. 2d 807, 122 P.2d 892 (1942).

Lynch-Lumbermens suit in the hope that Lynch would establish permission and that he could then rely on that finding. If Lynch failed, Harris would not be bound but could relitigate the issue. Thus, if necessary, Harris could have two bites at the insurance apple.

Where applicable, the concept of privity makes mutuality immaterial and collateral estoppel a two-way street in the multiparty situation. If there were privity between Lynch's estate and Harris, then Harris would be bound if Lynch's estate lost and could invoke the judgment if Lynch's estate won. Like "indispensability," privity is a label for a result rather than its rationale. That label comprehends a variety of relationships that have sustained subsequent preclusion of nonparties to the first action. One of these is representation. An expanded view of res judicata privity on a representation theory is currently the subject of substantial debate, and is one of the packaging possibilities to be explored here.

B. *Joinder*

Modern permissive joinder devices have allowed substantial packaging of multiparty interests in a single action.

Several such devices are available to plaintiffs. The most liberal of these is the rule which allows several claimants to join in asserting their separate claims against a defendant. All three accident victims might have joined in suing driver Cionci's estate and/or his insurer Lumbermens, although they did not do so. Or a single plaintiff may join claims against several defendants. Smith's estate and Harris did do this.[21] Or multiple claimants can sue multiple defendants. That too was a possibility in *Provident Tradesmens.* Federal Rule 20, with same-transaction and common-question requirements only, is a good example of this packaging device for plaintiffs.

Other devices perform a similar function for other parties. One such device is impleader, which allows a defendant to assert a claim against a third party who is liable to the defendant if the defendant is liable to the plaintiff. Cionci's estate probably could have impleaded Lumbermens. Interestingly, federal impleader once had broader scope than it does today. It allowed the defendant to implead a third party directly liable to the plaintiff. This aspect was dropped in 1948, perhaps restricting packaging to some extent. Intervention, based largely on common questions, allows a nonparty to enter an action between

21. Both victims sued Cionci's estate, Lynch's estate, and Dutcher; the latter two, presumably, were alleged to be vicariously liable. Pennsylvania had no statutory liability of the owner for negligence of a permittee, so that the basis of such claims must have been common law agency.

others. A significantly modified form of intervention is the second of the three packaging innovations examined by this Article. Interpleader, which may be offensive or defensive, is still another device. It allows a stakeholder to obtain judicial resolution of the demands of competing claimants; it may be extended as well to cases where the stakeholder denies an obligation to any claimant. Not as broad as permissive joinder, it is nonetheless a valuable packaging tool when allowed in cases where the stakeholder is not threatened with double or multiple liability. Insurers in Lumbermens' position have made increasing use of the device.

The common element of all these devices is that they are permissive and depend on assertion by an interested person. One might expect that mandatory joinder would play a substantial role in packaging multiparty litigation. My impression is that it has not, that mandatory joinder usually has been employed only where there was a threat to an interested person, whether it was lack of complete relief to the plaintiff, double liability or inconsistent obligation of the defendant, or impairment of the interests of a nonparty. Use of mandatory joinder as a packaging tool is the third proposal examined here.

C. *Consolidation*

Finally, packaging of litigation involving common issues has been achieved by consolidation. This device, which can extend to some or all of the issues and to some or all stages of the proceedings, merges actions, usually only those before the same court, which have been separately instituted. Although consolidation is frequently triggered by the parties, the court can consolidate on its own initiative. In this respect the device, although it does not create new parties, permits an appraisal of the possibly competing interests of litigants and society, an evaluation more likely to result in a sound judgment.

II. The Variables

Two variables emerge from examination of the existing tools for packaging: the character of the package and who controls it.

First, the package has to be either inclusive or preclusive. A suit is inclusive when all those with interests at stake become parties. All of the joinder devices, as well as consolidation, are inclusive. On the other hand, a preclusive suit determines the rights of those having interests without their participation, for example, through res judicata privity.

Historically, the preclusive model has been disfavored. The due process guaranty of an opportunity to be heard is a formidable obstacle to foreclosure of one's rights without one's participation. Any proposal enlarging preclusion therefore must be carefully scrutinized.

On the other hand, the preclusive model offers several advantages. Stripped of multiple parties with varying views of the controversy, the preclusive suit is cleaner and simpler; it seems less likely to present management problems.[38] Moreover, reducing the number of parties promises to create a package less subject to jurisdictional and venue problems. Thus the new Restatement of Judgments states that, where there is representation, privies need not be given notice nor be subject to the court's process power. Freedom from such jurisdictional constraints may be implicit in many res judicata decisions not addressing such issues. One old Supreme Court case, Bigelow v. Old Dominion Copper Mining & Smelting Co.,[41] indicates the contrary, and I am persuaded that it is sound. It makes no sense to me to say that a court without authority to adjudicate directly against one as a party has authority to bind him indirectly as a nonparty. And if the response is that the court has jurisdiction over one with whom the nonparty is in privity, then the scope of privity becomes doubly suspect: authority to adjudicate and opportunity to be heard, both governed by due process, are at stake.[42]

The second variable is whether control of packaging is lodged with a party or with a court. Control has two components: initiation and acceptance.

It is fair to say that ultimate acceptance almost always lies with the court. Permissive joinder decisions of parties may be rejected outright by the court in some instances; in others the power of severance has comparable effect. Res judicata pleas can also be rejected

38. Adding Smith's estate and Harris to the tort suit against Cionci's estate, for example, probably adds the issues of vicarious liability of Lynch's estate and Dutcher as well as additional damage questions. Even as to the common issues growing out of the alleged negligence of Cionci, new plaintiffs may have different factual or legal theories. Moreover, presentation of witnesses and their examination may be different even in the framework of shared theories.

41. 225 U.S. 111 (1912). In a Massachusetts suit Bigelow, the defendant, pleaded as an estoppel a New York federal court judgment rendered in favor of his New York associate who had been separately sued there. Because of mutuality, res judicata depended on whether Bigelow, who was not amenable in New York, would have been bound had the New York suit gone the other way. The Supreme Court held that lack of jurisdiction over Bigelow would have prevented binding him as a matter of due process. It distinguished cases in which stockholders were bound by judgments against corporations as being justified by privity.

42. In *Bigelow*, decided before Erie R.R. Co. v. Tompkins, 304 U.S. 64 (1938), privity between joint tortfeasors was a matter of "general law" to be decided independently of New York precedents. Bigelow v. Old Dominion Copper Mining & Smelting Co., 225 U.S. 111, 130 (1912). Authorities are divided as to whether federal or state law governs on res judicata issues in diversity cases. . . .

on policy grounds, though such decisions are relatively rare. Consolidation and severance decisions rest with the court.

Initiation, on the other hand, for the most part is in the hands of a party. Courts can and do consolidate actions or compel joinder sua sponte, but whether a permissive joinder device is invoked is the option of those interested in the transaction. Res judicata pleas, too, rest with the parties rather than the court. Although it is a rare litigant who, aware of a final judgment in his favor, does not invoke it, the phenomenon of litigant choice not to initiate joinder is very common. This happens, for example, where the potential plaintiffs are competing for a limited pot, such as the amount of an insurance policy. Thus in *Provident Tradesmens,* Lynch's estate may well have concluded that its interest dictated besting the others in a race to judgment against Lumbermens. Or, as already discussed, abandoning mutuality in collateral estoppel may result in some plaintiffs choosing not to initiate action until other plaintiffs' cases are decided. In such cases the public interest against multiplicity is simply ignored. Sometimes choice not to join is prompted by concerns which reflect values of sound judicial administration but conflict with efficiency and consistency. Fear of delay or prejudice, for instance, may prevent a party from choosing to join. Even here the presence of competing values requires a weighing process that, in the hands of one whose decision is colored by self-interest, may be highly suspect. In short, devices dependent on party initiative lack the balance of neutral evaluation.

History might be said to favor party over judicial control. The basis for this preference is, I believe, our tradition of adversary presentation. Initiatives are for the litigants; judges are accustomed to a reactive posture. Whether the legal system can afford to indulge that posture is an issue lurking behind evaluation of packaging choices.

III. Res Judicata Privity and Adequate Representation

The most widely discussed possibility for reducing multiplicity is to enlarge the range of collateral estoppel by expanding privity on a theory of adequate representation. Elaborated, the theory is that preclusion is justified when the interests of the nonparty and of the party-representative are substantially identical; in that confluence vigorous litigation by the representative sufficiently protects the interests of both. Thus, under this approach, the results of Lynch's suits in *Provident Tradesmens* against Cionci's estate and Lumbermens, whether favorable or unfavorable on the fault and permission issues, would have been binding on the other accident victims. . . .

Although privity based on representation is by no means confined to the class action, much of the theoretical support for the proposal to expand the privity concept is drawn from that area, perhaps because of its contemporary popularity. Consequently, comparison of the proposal and class actions is instructive. Both the privity proposal and the class action carry a built-in problem. If preclusion is to be based on representation, according to the new Restatement the representation must be "adequate." Inadequate representation may be narrowly confined to collusion with an opponent, conflicting interests, or failure to fulfill a duty of representation. More indeterminate guides such as quality of counsel, the financial stake of the representative, and degree of identity of the legal and factual positions taken also may be deemed material, especially where the nonparty and the putative representative are strangers. Whatever the tests, the class action has features which ameliorate the adequacy problem. At least in the federal system, the court makes the adequacy determination at the outset. Thereafter representation is monitored, and class action status may be lost if inadequacies appear. In contrast, under the privity proposal the adequacy issue can only arise collaterally. Thus the appraisal must always be from a distance, in a different proceeding at a different time. And it will always be based on hindsight. Perceived inadequacies in representation cannot be corrected; they can only defeat privity.

Moreover, it is misleading to say that the binding force of a class action is premised simply on identity of interest plus vigorous advocacy. Necessity plays a part, as does the fact that the class action is inclusive as well as preclusive. A prerequisite of the class action is that the class be so numerous as to make individual joinder impracticable. Indeed, many of the earlier cases really focus on the class action device as a means of going forward with suits which otherwise would have to be dismissed for want of indispensable parties. In other words, preclusion in class actions is supported by the need to proceed. The class action is inclusive at least in the sense that a class member, informed of the proceeding, may intervene to protect his interests. When he elects not to intervene, he consents to representation.

I believe that consent and /or necessity are the principal supports of all res judicata privity categories based on representation, a concept that covers a number of quite different relationships, including trustee-beneficiary, administrator-estate beneficiary, and present interest holder-unborn remaindermen. The diversity revealed by even this brief listing argues for further inquiry into the *why* of representation privity. Several of the relationships, such as trustee-beneficiary and agent-principal, are contractual, and the role of one party is understood to include representation in litigation. Even where there is no prearrangement there may be a subsequent assent, such as accepting the representation of a personal representative, which amounts to the same thing. In these cases representation is supported by consent. In still other cases representation flows from necessity. This factor itself is a broad one covering a variety of exigencies such as incompetency (guardian-ward), need for marketable title (unborn remaindermen), and need for unified estate administration (administrator-estate beneficiary). The common element is the need to go forward with litigation which will be effective.

Consent and necessity are significant especially because of the due process problem. Historically, knowing consent, or waiver, has been a complete answer to due process objections. And the demands of necessity have frequently qualified due process rights in important respects. It is not surprising that representation grounded in the need to proceed warrants preclusion.

Is there consent or necessity in cases covered by the privity proposal? Perhaps consent can be inferred fairly from the activities of a nonparty in some instances. I see no grounds, however, for concluding in our example that Harris or Smith's estate consented to representation by Lynch's estate. Caution should be exercised here. If the person to be precluded did not in fact agree to representation, consent should not be fictionalized to achieve preclusion. A claim of necessity, of course, might be founded on the multiplicity problem. I would urge caution here as well. Equating efficiency and necessity is debatable. Moreover, the concept of representation based simply on substantial identity of interest and vigorous advocacy is open ended, and the preclusion consequence is a drastic one. In my opinion the necessity argument is not persuasive enough to warrant this extension of preclusion, at least not until less stringent measures have been exhausted. A *Provident Tradesmens* situation can be packaged without going so far.

IV. Compulsory Intervention

The second proposal falls in the twilight zone between preclusion and inclusion with characteristics of both: one with an interest in a transaction which is the subject of pending litigation of which he has been notified must intervene and there assert his claim or defense. Whether he does so or not, he is bound by the judgment. The consequence of the rule, then, is packaging that is inclusive or preclusive at the option of the nonparty. If it is assumed that Lynch's estate was the first victim to sue both Cionci's estate and Lumbermens, under this proposal the other two victims, if notified of the suit, would have the choice between intervention and res judicata.

An obvious historical counterpart is the compulsory counterclaim rule, which requires the defendant to assert any claims against the plaintiff which arise from the same transaction as plaintiff's claim or forfeit them. The counterclaim rule, of course, applies to claim joinder rather than party joinder and, accordingly, speaks only to one who is already a party.

Application to a nonparty may be a significantly different matter. The Supreme Court in Chase National Bank v. Norwalk,[76] speaking through Justice Brandeis, ruled in 1934 that: "The law does not impose upon any person absolutely entitled to a hearing the burden of voluntary intervention in a suit to which he is a stranger." This cryptic statement did not explain why intervention should be permissive only and it is unclear from the opinion whether the announced rule was thought to be constitutionally mandated or was based only on the absence of authorizing legislation.

In any event, there are recent decisions to the contrary. In 1968 the Supreme Court ruled, over vigorous dissent by Justice Douglas, that a Pennsylvania town whose Pennsylvania proceeding had been stayed and which had been given an opportunity to intervene in a New York suit was precluded from challenging Interstate Commerce Commission (ICC) merger and inclusion orders there upheld.[78] Preclusive effect was to be limited to issues passed upon in the prior action; claims for specific relief from specific curtailments were left open. But the rights of a nonparty were affected. There are similar holdings with regard to agency proceedings in the public interest in antitrust, Federal Trade Commission, and labor matters.

These cases and the proposal can be distinguished. The cases all involved multiple suits seeking judicial review of an agency decision rather than litigation separate from the outset. In other words, these cases essentially involve separate appeals by different parties from a single trial-level decision.

Only a week after the ICC case, in litigation involving purely private rights, Justice Harlan suggested in *Provident Tradesmens* that a nonparty who had "purposely bypassed an adequate opportunity to intervene" might be bound by the findings underlying the judgment in the proceedings he had avoided. As in the ICC case, the idea was stated in preclusive terms. Directed to the problem posed by

76. 291 U.S. 431 (1934) (holding a mortgagee not bound by a judgment against his mortgagor obtained after the mortgagee's interest was acquired).

78. Penn-Central Merger & N&W Inclusion Cases, 389 U.S. 486, 505-506 (1968). . . .

omitting Dutcher, the owner, from the suit against his insurer, the suggestion was not pursued, perhaps because his intervention would have posed difficulties under a complete diversity requirement[82] or perhaps because a res judicata determination would have been premature.[83] Certainly, however, it implied a common law rule of compulsory intervention.

"Mandatory intervention" legislation has been proposed as an alternative to expanding res judicata privity based on adequate representation. This proposal, also stated in terms of preclusion, is especially valuable for its listing of both the prerequisites and limitations of the concept. The prerequisites are (1) same transaction, (2) interests not adverse, (3) notice to the nonparty, and (4) substantial saving of time and expense. The first and last of these identify the presence of the problem and the advantages of packaging. The second prerequisite (interests not adverse) approaches, but falls short of, adequate representation. Presumably it justifies preclusion, though it also avoids a prejudice factor which would argue against inclusion. The third, notice to the nonparty, is the central requirement in my view.

Notice is an essential step in affording the opportunity to be heard required by due process. The case for compulsory intervention, simply stated, is that it provides both notice and an opportunity to be heard, thereby leaving the nonparty without a basis for complaining of preclusion.

This argument does not deal satisfactorily with a companion requirement, personal jurisdiction over the nonparty. Ordinarily, intervention does not pose a problem of personal jurisdiction over the intervenor because it is voluntary; any objection by the intervenor based on lack of personal jurisdiction is waived. But it is not enough to say that jurisdiction over the person of an intervenor is not required for compulsory intervention because nonintervention under the proposal has a price. In reality the nonparty is required to choose between preclusion and intervention. I have stated already my view that per-

82. Adding Dutcher, a citizen of Pennsylvania, as a defendant would have destroyed diversity where the three plaintiffs were citizens of Pennsylvania. The idea that his citizenship would not prevent intervention depends on the proposition that intervention of right comes under ancillary jurisdiction. It is not clear, however, that the requirement of complete diversity may be thus circumvented. If the absentee-intervenor is indispensable, there is no proper action before the court to which his claim or defense can be attached. . . . If, on the other hand, he is not indispensable, i.e., if the action could proceed without him, then ancillary jurisdiction can apply. Obviously, if indispensability turns on his opportunity to protect himself by intervention, analysis is circular.

83. Justice Harlan seemed to contemplate a subsequent proceeding against Dutcher in which an estoppel would be asserted against him in response to his defense that money paid by the insurer on behalf of Cionci should be credited against Dutcher's liability. . . .

sonal jurisdiction is required for preclusion. Clearly it is required for involuntary inclusion. It follows that it is required for compelling a choice between the two.

Were personal jurisdiction the only issue, compulsory intervention would still have great utility, for in many, perhaps most, cases the nonparty is subject to the court's jurisdiction. The question then becomes a different one: must the court's process power be exercised, that is, must the outsider be made a party, or do notice and opportunity to be heard suffice to compel an outsider's choice between inclusion and preclusion? . . .

The inconclusive character of the precedents suggests that whether the law should insist that the outsiders be subjected to process before being required to choose between participation and preclusion should depend on whether process is more than a formality. It seems to me that process does offer values that may justify requiring it. Process includes notice, or at least the use of means reasonably calculated to give notice, and it avoids the difficult factual issue whether the outsider knew of the proceeding, implicit in some of the compulsory intervention formulas. And if I am correct in concluding that compelling choice between intervention and preclusion requires personal jurisdiction, process provides an opportunity for direct challenge on that score that seems missing by definition in the compulsory intervention model. Finally, process brings home more vividly the fight-or-default choice. One can imagine a layman ignoring litigation in which he is not a party as none of his affair. Indifference to process is less likely. It should be stressed that the preclusive sanction behind compulsory intervention will deny the nonintervenor a hearing. Even if justified by a waiver theory, it remains a harsh measure. Preclusion imposed on a defaulting party is more palatable than preclusion based on failure to intervene. Process invites participation as the compulsory intervention model does not.

V. Mandatory Joinder

The value in making the outsider a party leads clearly to the third possibility, mandatory joinder of nonparties with an interest in the transaction which is the subject of litigation. Smith's estate and Harris, for example, might have been joined as plaintiffs when Lynch's estate sued Cionci's estate, as they were in the suit against Lumbermens. It seems to me an additional advantage that joinder may be either voluntary (triggered by the defendant) or imposed (required by the court).

Most contemporary mandatory joinder seems to be premised

on potential double liability or other inconsistent obligation of the defendant or on impairment of a nonparty's interest. Although these appear to be narrow premises, threat to the defendant may have broader scope than has been supposed. Perhaps it is only a matter of time until a defendant convinces a court that losing a suit, which in the world of *Bernhard* may preclude him as to all future claimants though he can win only against the current plaintiff, constitutes a threat to him that warrants compelling the joinder of nonparty claimants.[110] That argument aside, the question remains whether joinder can be compelled on the simple ground of multiplicity. It is a ground that a defendant might assert as a matter of self-interest or that the court might raise in the public interest. Simple multiplicity surely should have concerned both Lumbermens and the court in *Provident Tradesmens.* The historians tell us that multiplicity was one of the grounds for requiring joinder in equity, and at least a few cases today respond to the argument. No better example can be found than Davila Mendez v. Vatican Shrimp Co.,[115] where on defendant's motion in a wrongful death action the personal representative of another victim of the same accident was joined to prevent multiplicity.

What I have said thus far reveals, perhaps, a judgment that the multiplicity ground for compelling joinder is not as weighty as the threat of double liability to the defendant or some impairment of an absentee's interest. If joinder is opposed, the case for it must be weighed against other interests, such as complexity, prejudice, or delay. This weighing, very like that involved in dealing with consolidation and severance problems, gives mandatory joinder the advantage of direct examination of competing considerations and response to them. In contrast, res judicata privity and compulsory intervention at worst simply reject conflicting values and at best address them only after it is too late for interested persons to alter their positions. For example, in some cases a nonparty claimant may object that mandatory joinder lodges his claim in an inconvenient forum.[118] The

110. Hindsight tells us that Lumbermens could have made such an argument for joining Smith's estate and Harris. By losing to Harris in the original trial, where Dutcher's testimony was admitted, it lost to the Lynch and Smith estates as well when, on remand from the Supreme Court, the Third Circuit held the insurer collaterally estopped on the permission issue. Provident Tradesmens Bank & Trust Co. v. Lumbermens Mut. Cas. Co., 411 F.2d 88 (1969).

115. 43 F.R.D. 294 (S.D. Tex. 1966).

118. Tooker v. Lopez, 24 N.Y.2d 569, 249 N.E.2d 394, 301 N.Y.S.2d 519 (1969), a well-known choice-of-law case, provides a good example. There a New York accident victim (actually the victim's estate) sued a New York defendant (the owner of the vehicle in which the victim had been riding) in a New York court. The accident had occurred in Michigan, and there was a second, Michigan passenger-victim. Should the Michigan claimant have been compelled to travel to New York to litigate?

issue can be adequately addressed by the principles that fashion the doctrines of *forum non conveniens* and, in the federal court, interdistrict transfer. Multiparty cases certainly complicate the problems of location of litigation but [such cases are] not beyond the reach of those doctrines. The idea that every claimant has a right to choose his forum makes no more sense than conferring similar control on a defendant. Whether one agrees with this or not, mandatory joinder provides a vehicle for examination of the problem. Presumably, the two preclusion devices — res judicata privity and compulsory intervention — would prevent multiplicity without regard to inconvenience to the nonparty. . . .

If joinder is to be compelled, then some means of identifying those who ought to be joined is necessary. Federal Rule 19(c), which requires the plaintiff to list nonparties who should have been joined under Rule 19(a) but could not be, points the way. Identification of those with an interest in the transaction being litigated should come from the parties — the defendant as well as the plaintiff — in their pleadings. It is difficult to ascertain the effectiveness of such a provision, though my hunch is that compliance under the present rule is rare. It could be reinforced by the Rule 11 certificate. Judicial inquiry on the subject at the first opportunity would also be useful.

VI. Conclusion

A *Provident Tradesmens* transaction should not be allowed to clog busy courts with multiple suits in the absence of significant countervailing circumstances. While it is tempting to seek to package litigation into a single suit by means of preclusive devices, provision of the opportunity to be heard guaranteed by due process argues that an inclusive device ordinarily is superior. Moreover, because a policy against multiplicity is not the only value at stake in cases of multiparty litigation centering on a single transaction, an inclusive device that permits weighing of competing values at the outset is highly desirable. Mandatory joinder offers both kinds of advantages, along with the power of courts to insist upon it when the parties are indifferent or even opposed to it.

What I have said here goes to the relative merits of the devices considered. Beyond that, I must acknowledge the real possibility that all of them may carry evils worse than the problem to which they are addressed. Use of any one of them may foment assertion of claims that otherwise would never be litigated and thereby increase the adjudication burden of courts. That risk is obvious where compulsory intervention and mandatory joinder are concerned. When the consequences of expanded res judicata privity are perceived, I believe that the device might produce a similar result; interested persons may be prompted to participate in one way or another in judicial resolution of the transaction. Even if the devices do not generate additional claims, they may deter settlement of existing ones. Moreover, they may increase the expenses of the parties, for example, by increasing recovery.

I do not know how to assess those risks, but their presence argues for caution in developing a response to the multiplicity problem. Further experimentation in all three directions by courts alert to these dangers therefore seems desirable to me. It is as well, perhaps, that the responses thus far have been ad hoc and tentative. The remedy is sometimes worse than the disease.

NOTES AND COMMENTS

Kaplan objects to a class action rule that allows persons to join as members of a plaintiff class after a judgment of liability against the defendant. The latecomers had taken no risk of defeat, and yet they shared the benefits of victory. Such "one-way intervention" was argued to be unfair, and Rule 23 was revised so as to make the risks of litigation run against a class as well as for it. However, in the period leading up to and following the 1966 revision of Rule 23, the requirement of mutuality as a condition of preclusion was progressively repudiated. That is, where two successive actions shared common issues, a nonparty to action one was allowed the benefit of preclusion in action 2 against an adversary who had been on the losing side in action one.

Isn't the abandonment of mutuality the equivalent of one-way intervention? In both situations a person who took no risk of loss nevertheless gains the benefit of success. On one level, opposition to mutuality seems inconsistent with opposition to one-way intervention in class actions. On another level, however, both positions are consistent: both reduce the risk of inconsistent results and increase efficiency by preventing repeated litigation of the same issues.

These themes of increasing efficiency and preventing inconsistent results run through much analysis of procedure. A difficulty with dropping the rule of mutuality is that persons may be motivated to stay outside an action; under current doctrine "bystanders" can't lose by a judgment in the case, but may gain by it. McCoid's article explores ways of solving this difficulty and, more generally, of preventing repetitious litigation by compelling joinder. The following selection by George moves in the opposite direction; it borrows from the class action's reliance on adequate representation to suggest extending the preclusive effect of judgments to nonparties. This proposal dissolves the anomaly of insisting on mutuality in the context of class actions while abandoning it elsewhere: given adequacy of representation, similarly situated persons are precluded from relitigating issues decided in an earlier action, whether or not it was a class action.

Sweet Uses of Adversity: Parklane Hosiery *and the Collateral Class Action* *

Lawrence C. George

In Parklane Hosiery Co. v. Shore,[1] the United States Supreme Court completed its rejection of the long-criticized but relatively well-settled collateral estoppel doctrine of "mutuality." Under the doctrine of collateral estoppel, a judgment on the merits precludes the parties to a suit (S-1) from relitigating in a subsequent suit (S-2) issues which were actually litigated and which were necessary to the outcome of the judgment in S-1. The effect of collateral estoppel, however, is limited by the twin concepts of mutuality and privity. Under the limiting constraint of mutuality, a party in a later action cannot demand preclusion of an issue on the basis of an earlier lawsuit unless he or she would also have been precluded by a contrary judgment in the earlier suit. And under the further constraint of privity,[8] a party to a subsequent suit cannot be precluded on an issue by the loss of that issue by a different party in an earlier suit. The joint operation of privity and mutuality, therefore, prevents both the *defensive* use of collateral estoppel — where defendant precludes plaintiff from asserting claims that plaintiff had previously litigated and lost against a different defendant — and the *offensive* use of collateral estoppel — where plaintiff precludes defendant from relitigating issues which the defendant previously litigated and lost against a different plaintiff.

In recent years, however, the mutuality doctrine has been eroded, first by the state courts, and more recently by the federal courts. In

* *Source:* 32 Stan. L. Rev. 655, 655-676, 684-686 (1980).

1. 439 U.S. 322 (1979).

8. "Privity" is the due process requirement that a party precluded from relitigating an issue must have had a day in court on the merits of that issue. The authority cited in *Parklane* for this requirement was Hansberry v. Lee, 311 U.S. 32, 40 (1940), cited in 439 U.S. at 327 n.7. . . .

Blonder-Tongue Laboratories, Inc. v. University of Illinois Foundation,[10] the Supreme Court abandoned the requirement of mutuality when a defendant uses collateral estoppel defensively. And despite several important differences between the offensive and defensive uses of collateral estoppel, the *Parklane* Court rejected the requirement of mutuality for offensive collateral estoppel as well, leaving it to the broad discretion of trial courts to determine when to permit collateral estoppel.

The most immediate effect of *Parklane* and *Blonder-Tongue* is to extend the scope of a federal civil judgment to affect interests beyond those of the immediate parties to a particular lawsuit. Although subject to the court's discretion and to the continuing requirements that an issue be actually litigated and necessary to the earlier judgment before it may become preclusive, after *Blonder-Tongue* and *Parklane* a previous victory by an unrelated plaintiff over the same defendant or by an unrelated defendant over the same plaintiff may well be decisive in later litigation, when the issue reappears.

In this article, however, I will explore a less obvious implication of the rejection of mutuality: the convergence of collateral estoppel doctrine and doctrines concerning representation in class actions. After the Court's decisions in *Blonder-Tongue* and *Parklane*, the victory of an unrelated plaintiff or defendant — a "stranger"[18] — opens up two "classes"[19] of beneficiaries: an offensive class of "other plaintiffs"[20] who can share in an earlier plaintiff's victory over a common defendant, and a defensive class of "other defendants"[21] who can share in an earlier defendant's victory over a common plaintiff. Moreover, as I will argue below, the Court, having freed itself from the requirement of mutuality, should further rid itself of the constraint of privity and recognize two other classes — a defensive class of "other plaintiffs" who must share in an earlier plaintiff's *loss* to a common defendant, and an offensive class of "other defendants" who must share in an earlier defendant's *loss* to a common plaintiff. The resulting

10. 402 U.S. 313 (1971).

18. "Stranger" is used in a special sense to denote a known person — one of the parties to S-1 — who opposed the "common plaintiff" (*Blonder-Tongue*) or the "common defendant" (*Parklane*) in S-1. There is no privity between this unmysterious party and the class member(s) he or she represents through a victory in S-1.

19. "Class" is used in a sense apart from its use in procedural law, and includes classes with unique or null membership, as well as those numerous enough to require special handling under Fed. R. Civ. P. 23.

20. "Other plaintiffs" and "offensive estoppel class" refer to the group of indeterminate size entitled by *Parklane* to claim the benefit of a stranger's victory in S-1 over the common defendant in S-1 and S-2.

21. "Other defendants" and "defensive estoppel class" refer to the group of indeterminate size entitled by *Blonder-Tongue* to claim the advantage of a stranger's previous victory in S-1 over the common plaintiff in S-1 and S-2.

4-class structure would closely resemble the configuration of parties and preclusion established by the class action. In the class action, privity is of no concern — subsequent plaintiffs are bound by the defeat of the plaintiff class, just as subsequent defendants are bound by the defeat of the defendant class. To the extent that a great deal of turbulent debate presently surrounds the role of the class action, equally fundamental disputes can now be anticipated from the Court's general reappraisal of the formal structure of fairness in the ordinary civil trial.

In the interests of efficiency and consistency, the new model of judgments and due process which follows from *Parklane* permits "issues" to emerge as free-floating, independent entities, and views trials as experiments concerning the merits of the "issues" they comprise. Yet the legal change which follows from the Court's new approach has not yet been embodied in a more general theory of judgments. By continuing to insist on the requirement of privity, the Court itself has recognized only the two classes who are able to share in a stranger's victory, rather than the four classes inherent in the logic of *Parklane* and *Blonder-Tongue*.

In this article, I will argue that the lines drawn in *Parklane* and *Blonder-Tongue* attempt to limit the emerging conception of trials, issues, evidence, and justiciability by preserving the "day in court" shibboleth of procedural due process as a barrier against further extension of preclusion. The Court has turned the guarantee of a day in court into a fundamental right, without carefully and systematically considering the events that occur in court, and the participants in those events. For reasons which are the subject of the following reflections, if the participatory and legitimizing values of due process require privity to be a precondition of preclusion, incantation of the "day in court" slogan will not accomplish the task. The analytical advantages of this article's concept of post-*Parklane* collateral estoppel will emerge as the discussion progresses, although ultimately my emphasis will be placed not upon purely formal legal analysis, but upon the advantages and disadvantages of trials as experiments, of classes as legal constructs, and of parties as the fungible carriers of abstract interests.

I. Collateral Estoppel and the Bootstrap Classes

By breaking away from the requirement of mutuality, the *Parklane* Court recognized the existence of two classes — what I will call "estoppel classes" — of other plaintiffs and other defendants. In this part, I will argue that the Court's continuing allegiance to the privity requirement is compelled by neither due process nor policy, and that the Court thus should recognize all four of the estoppel classes which follow from the logic of *Parklane.*

An "estoppel class" is a hybrid formed by combining the concepts of issue preclusion and classness, and follows from the reasoning of *Blonder-Tongue* and *Parklane.* A party in S-2 who was not involved in S-1, and who successfully invokes a stranger's victory in the earlier lawsuit — or conversely, points to the common party's adverse result in S-1 — thereby becomes a member of the estoppel class of "other plaintiffs" or "other defendants" by prevailing on the preclusion issue. The class member, linked to the first lawsuit only by his or her opposition to a common party, wins preclusion by showing that the issue in S-2 is identical or sufficiently similar to the issue in S-1 to be treated as conclusively determined vis-à-vis the common party. *Parklane*'s complete abandonment of mutuality means that all other strangers similarly situated to the victorious movant in S-2 can claim the advantage of a conclusive — because preclusive — determination that: (1) the winner of the motion in S-2 was similarly situated to the winner of the issue in S-1; and (2) the issue in S-1 and S-2 is legally identical. In considering motions identical to that offered by the winner in S-2, courts in S-3 to S-n must take the class definition established in S-2 as settled by the principle of res judicata — a basis as strong as any class certification in advance could be. I will refer to this phenomenon as "bootstrap estoppel."

The *Parklane* Court implicitly rejected two of the possible four estoppel classes that might logically exist. Complementing the class of "other plaintiffs" who might share in a stranger's glory is a class of "other plaintiffs" who could share the ignominy of the stranger's loss. Besides the class of "other defendants" who shelter behind a stranger's protective judgment is a class of "other defendants" who will suffer summary judgment because the outcome of a crucial issue is established already, through the loss by a stranger of a parallel defense. The Court rejected the extension of its logic to these two classes of plaintiffs and defendants who would be forced to share in the losses of others, finding that binding a party to a judgment to which he or she was neither a privy nor a party violated due process.

The due process argument for treating the two potential estoppel classes bound by an earlier party's loss differently from the classes created by *Parklane* and *Blonder-Tongue* is not that the litigant who unsuccessfully seeks preclusion in S-2 was not a party to S-1 — that consideration is irrelevant. After all, the victorious members of the estoppel classes created by *Blonder-Tongue* and *Parklane* were not parties to S-1, while the litigant unsuccessfully seeking preclusion in

S-2 may have been victorious in S-1 against a different defendant or plaintiff. Rather, the argument rests on the belief that, if a party who had not participated in S-1 were precluded in S-2, such a preclusion would violate the due process requirement that a precluded issue have been fully and fairly litigated in S-1. In order to assure the precluded party of this due process requirement, the Court deems it essential to be able to tell the precluded loser in S-2: "You (or your privy) have had your day in court in S-1." But although privity may be a very important consideration in assessing the fairness of preclusion, its absence does not necessarily mean that a party is deprived of due process. Even if "privity" were to be demoted to the same inconclusive but weighty status as "mutuality," it would remain both possible and desirable to retain the fundamental safeguards that a precluded issue in S-2 was necessary to the determination of S-1 and fully and adequately litigated during S-1. From this point of view, privity is but an additional requirement of due process not necessitated by the other two more basic requirements. A fully and fairly litigated issue need not always be litigated by the very person who is subject to estoppel by the result.

This flexible view of privity finds support in the *Parklane* Court's citation of Hansberry v. Lee [41] for the proposition that privity is an essential element of issue preclusion. In *Hansberry*, the Court held that the plaintiff could not be bound by a prior determination of the legality of a racial covenant. Illinois law allowed a previous "class" of plaintiffs to be defined by residence in the affected neighborhood, rather than "interest." The collusive class "representative" who lost in S-1 had interests adverse to the plaintiff in S-2, and may have served no function except to lose the material issue in S-1. The Court found that the Illinois definition of a class by a criterion other than "interest" divested the plaintiff in S-2 of valuable legal rights protected by due process. This narrow but classical interpretation of *Hansberry*, as a due process case which justifies a requirement of adequate representation to serve the purpose of privity, carries different implications than those drawn from it in *Parklane*. "Representation" under *Hansberry* excuses a lack of privity by assuring that the representative will pursue the same ends as the virtual representee, and will do so with equal or greater fervor, derived from the fiduciary obligations of the representation status, as a matter of equity. This reading of *Hansberry* not only permits but requires the recognition of two more estoppel classes following the logic of *Parklane*. It is quite easy to imagine and to give precise legal definition to the circumstances which would allow a court to tell another defendant: "Your issue has had

41. 311 U.S. 32 (1940).

its day in court, and it lost after the fullest exposure of its merits by a party as interested in the outcome as you are now."

Indeed, if privity is not an absolute requirement of due process, a blanket insistence on privity can lead to the same evils which the Court sought to avoid when it broke through the mutuality barrier. By insisting on privity, the courts may subject the common opponent to the vexation of repetitive law suits while creating the risk of embarrassment to the system that essentially like cases will be decided in different ways. These evils are most clearly seen in the context of the bootstrap classes, where the policies no more logically support granting preclusion motions for permissible bootstrap classes of winners than they support barring impermissible classes from suffering vicarious defeat by the day-in-court requirement. For example, assume that the movant in an S-2 preclusion motion, the decision which defines the bootstrap class, claims that his or her situation concerning the common issue is identical to that of the plaintiff who won the issue in S-1. Although the Court agrees that the issue itself is redundant, it determines nevertheless, under the discretionary powers accorded to the courts by *Parklane,* that it would not be just and proper to give the second plaintiff a free ride. A literal insistence upon privity as a precondition for the preclusion of absentee losers will encourage the repetition of the same preclusion motion before other courts, so long as separate members of the estoppel classes are available to try and try again. Inconsistency and thus embarrassment to the judicial system, as well as waste and vexation to the common opponent, would ensue if privity were allowed to bar the opponent's use, defensively, of his or her victory on the preclusion motion, when a person juridically identical to the defeated "free rider" repeats the S-2 preclusion motion in S-3. True, the opponent of the estoppel class has already lost the substantive issue in S-1, and won only the right to relitigate the issue in S-2. Also, it is hypothesized that the losing member of the "other plaintiffs" estoppel class in S-2 has no privity relationship with the plaintiff in S-1 and no fiduciary duty to plaintiffs in actions S-3 to S-n. Still, the S-2 plaintiff's juridical circumstances and interests are assumed to be precisely comparable to those of his nonprivies in S-3 to S-n. The S-2 court's negative decision on the preclusion motion therefore ranks as a very attractive candidate for universal treatment "in rem" against the whole world, without regard to privity.

The same reasoning applied to the failure of a defendant in S-2 to demonstrate his or her eligibility for preclusion as a member of the *Blonder-Tongue* "other defendants" estoppel class makes a similar, possibly even stronger, argument for ignoring the privity limitation. Again, our hypothesis is that the losing movant in S-2 is not related to the stranger who defeated the common plaintiff in S-1. One may persuasively argue that the S-2 court's refusal to give this second defendant a free ride entitles the persistent plaintiff to a blanket exemption from the further annoyance of dealing with the "same" preclusion motion every time he or she sues another defendant. The common plaintiff in S-1 was saddled with the burden of proof in that case, and a court might easily find that his loss in S-1 was caused by a lack of sufficient preparation, discovery, or ingenuity to overcome the burden of proof in the earlier action. Given a finding in S-2 that it would be unfair to preclude plaintiff by granting defendant's *Blonder-Tongue* motion, a refusal to extend defendant's defeat on his preclusion motion to the whole world merely subjects plaintiffs and the courts to additional burdens. On the other hand, lifting the privity requirement in such cases would do no damage to defendants' rights.

Thus, neither due process nor the policies underlying collateral estoppel in general and *Parklane* in particular argue for the retention of an absolute privity requirement. Privity should not, therefore, stand in the way of extending the analogy between collateral estoppel and true class actions. But since the foregoing analogy is neither perfect nor complete, we now turn to survey the distinctions which need consideration before the day-in-court exception can be discarded and the full force of estoppel by class adopted as the basic logic of the law of judgments.

II. Scope, Scale, and Fairness Problems of Estoppel Classes

Even if the logic behind the *Parklane* abandonment of mutuality supports the assimilation of collateral estoppel into class action doctrine, several formal objections to this assimilation must still be answered. First, free riding, which has been found unjust under class action procedure, may also attend the creation of estoppel classes. Second, the morality of law generally prohibits retroactivity. The lack of notice to the class opponent, while S-1 is pending, of the likely scope of S-1 may violate this principle. Third, while the *party* analysis underlying class actions ensures that individual rights are given due process protections, the focus on *issues* in collateral estoppel may not provide the same protections.

A. Free Riding

The most prominent distinction between postjudgment issue preclusion and class actions, as noted by the *Parklane* Court and commentators on collateral estoppel, is that class actions do, and *Parklane* issue preclusion does not, expose potential parties to future actions to risk. Although the risk may be more theoretical than real, class certification binds the class to the judgment in S-1 no matter how it turns out. In contrast, the two estoppel classes of *Parklane* and *Blonder-Tongue* are basically defined by free riding — they are "bound" only by the victories of earlier parties. Yet, if this element of free riding is unfair either to the class opponent who does bear the risk of loss and preclusion or to the class representative who risks his or her individual claim, the solution is surprisingly simple. By adopting the full 4-class scheme of estoppel classes, free riding is ended in one fell swoop: The estoppel classes bear the brunt of defeat just as they enjoy the fruits of victory.

B. *Retroactivity*

The collateral estoppel doctrine following *Parklane* and *Blonder-Tongue* effectively prevents individuals from keeping the scale of their controversy within the age-old limits of a private binary dispute between present parties. Under the class interpretation of *Parklane,* a lawsuit can have consequences far beyond those contemplated by the original parties. And these consequences pose problems of notice and retroactivity not experienced in the true class action.

The theory behind Federal Rule of Civil Procedure 23 is that "classness" can be determined even before the court has much more than an inkling of the merits of the self-styled representative's claim. In contrast, the theory behind collateral estoppel is that a court can best resolve the problems of typicality, identity of interest, and competency of representation — the factors relevant to "classness" — by looking retrospectively to see what occurred in S-1 before ennobling it to the awesome status of a judgment against the world. But this potentially large scale for private suits after *Parklane* raises notice problems. The backward-looking nature of the decision in S-2 concerning the "class" could deprive the estoppel class opponent of timely notice in S-1 that he or she is faced with a lawsuit which is sufficiently representative of recurrent issues to carry the force of true class consequences. The only creature worse than a Rule 23(b)(3) certified class action is a minor case that looks big in retrospect, when collateral estoppel is applied on behalf of *Parklane* or *Blonder-Tongue* class members in S-3 and later suits.

The fear of unfairness to the class opponent, however, may be more theoretical than real. It does not follow that simply because the parties in S-1 did not realize the class implications of an otherwise fairly litigated issue, resolution of it should not later be given preclusive effect. Moreover, even if notice is not essential to fairness, it would appear that the common class opponent is effectively on notice after *Parklane* and *Blonder-Tongue,* such that the argument in S-2 by the class opponent that he or she did not realize the "classness" inherent in S-1 appears rather lame. The Court has now defined the stakes of S-1 clearly enough to satisfy the due process rights to notice and a day in court of the class opponent. These cases teach that no litigation is so private or parochial that the interests of others similarly situated may be totally ignored by the parties.

Indeed, it is the parties' very awareness that any pending case could carry legions of others on its coattails that raises an additional question about the fairness of estoppel by class. The threat of later preclusion, like the threat of class certification, may deny economically rational actors the opportunity to exercise their constitutionally protected procedural rights to fully litigate each case, because the stakes are simply apt to be too high. Many litigants would settle simple, private controversies before the day of judgment to avoid the collateral consequences of a formal determination of a contested key issue.

But the pressure on litigants to forego trial, unlike the problem of notice, does not distinguish estoppel by class from the traditional class action. The drastic revision of the balance of power between plaintiff classes and their singular targets implicit in the Rule 23(b)(3) class action also applies to the class interpretation of collateral estoppel doctrine. And in both cases, the revolutionary change is justified by a principled consideration of the courts' institutional stake in efficiency and the interests of the parties as juridical entities. A simple case with a large estoppel class obviously lurking behind it may be settled to avoid the risk of exposure to preclusion, but that contingency is not a decisive argument against the fairness of rules aimed at divesting individual parties of the exclusive power to define the stakes of private litigation.

Thus, neither the absence of notice nor the presence of pressure to settle indicates that estoppel by class is any less fair than the traditional class action. Rather, both estoppel by class and the class action rely on judicial discretion to ensure fairness. A court in S-2 determining a fair scale to give a private controversy in S-1, like a court deciding the scale to give a Rule 23 class action, must balance the equities of the disadvantages suffered by the class or its opponent(s), such as their exclusion from the primary trial of the issue, lack of initiative in bringing the action, or lack of opportunity to use discovery effectively. Losers in S-1 may assert principally two types of justification regarding the quality and intensity of trial in resisting claims in S-2 that the loss of an issue in S-1 is preclusive: (1) that the record does not adequately support the conclusion that an issue was "necessary" to the determination of S-1, and was fully and fairly tried on the merits; and (2) that the loser in S-1 was advised by counsel that it was "safe" to expose the merits of an issue in S-1, since a legal analysis of the structure of S-1 indicated that the issue would not be treated under *Parklane* and *Blonder-Tongue* as "common."

Trial courts following *Parklane* also will be faced with an irresolvable tension between formal and excessively functional definitions of the fully tried issue in S-1, as viewed in the context of a preclusion motion. Courts may find it increasingly difficult to maintain and defend the *Parklane* and *Blonder-Tongue* doctrine's oblivious disregard of the reality of contemporary civil procedure, which permits, invites, and depends upon a multitude of pathways and practical alternatives to exploring the merits of an issue without triggering the legal consequences of "trial" as a term of art derived from the Restatement of Judgments.

Administering a system of two or four estoppel classes will require courts to undertake subtle and searching reviews of earlier judgments and their circumstances. It will always be possible for the parties in S-1 to manipulate the proportions and formalities of their dispute with preclusion in mind. The indeterminacy of the *Parklane* equitable standards, and the backward-looking nature of the preclusion hearing, will introduce a disruptive element in S-1 that will profoundly alter assessments of risk by the parties. The spirit of equitable preclusion will transform "winning" into a subtle term of art, and an especially elusive one, during the period of "winners only" asymmetry following *Parklane* and *Blonder-Tongue*. A deeper appreciation of the ubiquity of preclusion will require a new orientation on the part of courts reviewing records of S-1. Instead of the customary deferential appellate attitude toward factfinding, a new type of scrutiny can be expected to be focused upon the kinds of consideration that flow inside or outside the record, above the table or below it.

C. *Fairness to Nonparties . . .*

. . . [P]rivity in a class action is achieved by the creation, in formal legal terms, of a fictitious party comprised of the class representative and his or her virtual representees. Rule 23 accomplishes this fictitious amalgamation by considering the common and divergent interests among the members of the potential class in S-1. Since the court looks for internal conflicts among the membership proposed for class designation, the certification issue depends on the typicality of the claim of the representative in relation to those he or she hypothetically represents, instead of the "identity" of issues required by the issue-oriented doctrine of collateral estoppel. By the identification and procedural recognition of certain "interests" in defining the class, the party orientation to class issues assures that each member of the class has a common interest and thus a vicarious "day in court." Of course, interests of this sort transcend the individuals who hold them. As we will see in the next part, the theory underlying the class action supports a coercive, collective measure which disregards possibly divergent private utilities of class members, and respects the individual's "right" to pursue or forego personal claims only by retaining the option for potential members to opt out of the class after receiving notice of class certification.

In contrast, an estoppel class member's individual "interest" is always protected by the twofold estoppel class framework created by *Parklane* and *Blonder-Tongue.* Only if an estoppel class member wishes to urge preclusion may he or she exploit the prior resolution of the common issue. But this freedom of estoppel class members to opt in or out would be lost were the Court to adopt the 4-way estoppel class framework suggested by this article. Under such a framework, members would be bound by the losses of prior parties without being able to opt out and without any judicial determination that their interests — as opposed to their issues — are common. Even so, the due process rights of estoppel class members can be protected.

In our earlier discussion of Hansberry v. Lee, we noted that the Court appeared to view privity as one means, rather than the only means, to due process. A case decided by the Fifth Circuit Court of Appeals shows that in practice an absence of privity of the estoppel class member does not mean an absence of due process protections. In Cauefield v. Fidelity & Casualty Co.,[93] the court, applying Louisiana law, approved the use of issue preclusion against a plaintiff who was intimately associated — though not privy — with an earlier plaintiff who had lost his case against the defendant cemetery for desecration of graves. In response to plaintiff's objection that he was not in privity with the plaintiff in the earlier case, the court applied a broad due process analysis. It allowed preclusion since it found no fundamental unfairness in denying a day in court to a plaintiff who was similarly situated to the losing plaintiff in S-1 — e.g., the plaintiffs had the same counsel and the plaintiff in S-2 could not specify the different evidence or legal theory he would advance in S-2. The court weighed the supposed individual right to adjudicate each case against the waste and vexation such piecemeal disposition would impose upon both the courts and the class opponent. Thus, due process did not bar a class opponent from using a judgment defensively against a participating but nonparty class member. The court stressed that all of the similarly situated tort claimants

93. 378 F.2d 876 (5th Cir.), *cert. denied,* 389 U.S. 1009 (1967).

had testified in the lost cause of the claimant in S-1. Literally speaking, each member of the *Cauefield* estoppel class had had a day in court — as a witness!

Thus, the issue-oriented analysis of collateral estoppel can protect members of all four estoppel classes as effectively as the party-oriented class action analysis protects parties there.[98] First, *Cauefield* answers the argument that a court should always require privity when precluding a plaintiff because of a loss by "another plaintiff" in an earlier lawsuit. Representation can be a proxy for privity, and, in fact, it should serve as a proxy whenever the multiple determination of a common issue would be unjust or impracticable. This answer, as well as its rationale, is similar to those provided by class action theory to the objection that inclusion of class members, without their consent, is unfair given the risks of litigation under Rule 23. Second, an issue orientation does not mean that a potentially preclusive issue in S-1 which becomes actually preclusive in S-2 must become determined in rem against the world. Although bootstrap preclusion of issues might often be desirable, discriminating equitable qualifications may be interposed in *S-2* when the in rem consequences of S-1 are being claimed by a worldly classmate of the winning or losing party in S-1.

In sum, neither a fear of free riding, nor retroactivity, nor fairness to nonparties stands in the way of adopting the 4-way estoppel class framework and the class action analogy. . . .

III. A Substantive Approach to the Scope of Judgments

. . . Does any theory as powerful as the substantive theory supporting class actions support the 4-class estoppel framework?

A. Solving the Mass-Tort Anomaly: Solidarity

The substantive theory behind the true class action requires the coercive amalgamation of claims in order to prevent the unjust enrich-

98. Ironically, if the Court should ever use *Cauefield*-type reasoning to breach the *Hansberry* barrier against recognition of further estoppel classes, it will undoubtedly express its conclusion in the rhetoric of mutuality. "Despite your due process arguments," the Court might say, "we rule in favor of preclusion because it is fundamentally fair that your class should be bound whether they win or lose. If your 'representative' had won, you would be before us citing *Parklane*. If the trial judge had been alert to the estoppel potential of S-1, he would have certified, see Fed. R. Civ. P. 23(c), or consolidated, see 28 U.S.C. §1407 (1976), the case or ordered you joined as a party under Fed. R. Civ. P. 19. As it is, you did not intervene, see Fed. R. Civ. P. 24; Restatement (Second) of Judgments §88(3) (Tent. Draft No. 2, 1975), or show any other manifestation of solidarity with other persons similarly situated. Thereby you forfeited your asserted right to a *subsequent* bite at what is after all the same cherry.". . .

ment of a party who might otherwise violate legal norms because transaction costs prevented individual suits from being an effective sanction. It is more difficult to find a corresponding rationale for extending to others the effects of the determination of an issue which a court has allowed an individual (however representative) to assert in S-1. The very existence of a determination of the issue in S-1 establishes that the matter can be resolved through individual litigation, which most courts administering Rule 23 would regard as a reasonable alternative pathway to a class action. Thus, presumably all preclusion classes are uncertifiable under Rule 23. What we seek is a different, but equally cogent, substantive justification for 4-way collateral estoppel. . . .

The mass-tort anomaly suggested by Professor Brainerd Currie [105] provides a simple and powerful argument for holding the preclusion line where it was before the Court's decision in *Parklane*. I shall therefore use it to analyze the substantive problems of 4-way collateral estoppel, in the hope that by considering the strongest case against estoppel, the underlying rationale for expanded collateral estoppel will emerge.

Professor Currie raised the fear that an extension of preclusion in S-2 to S-n on an issue such as negligence would mean that S-1 in a mass-tort situation — e.g., a great number of passengers injured in a train wreck — would determine all later lawsuits. Thus, if the plaintiff in S-1 won, so would all subsequent plaintiffs, even though the victory was but the result of a race to the courthouse. Moreover, if, for example, the first five plaintiffs lost but the sixth won, then all later plaintiffs would triumph, despite defendant's prior victories. Any one of these results appears capricious — certainly unfair to defendant, but also to those early plaintiffs, if any, unable to reap the benefits of a later triumph.

The case of a mass-tort claim is anomalous because we lack a criterion for deciding how to extend preclusive effects from a representative case to other cases that are distinguishable from the first only by the procedural and temporal differences caused by the separate and autonomous assertion of individual claims. Professor Currie sought to avoid capriciousness in the mass-tort context by arguing against the offensive use of collateral estoppel generally. But despite Professor Currie's fears, the *Parklane* Court rejected his argument by granting preclusion where the loser in S-1 was the party precluded from relitigating the issue in S-2. And while the *Parklane* Court rejected the offensive/defensive distinction as the method by which to avoid

105. See Currie, Mutuality of Collateral Estoppel: Limits of the *Bernhard* Doctrine, [9 Stan. L. Rev. 281 (1957)].

the capriciousness of "Currie-unfairness," it has been my constant theme that the *Parklane* Court's privity/no-privity line in turn does little in itself to assure fairness. Indeed, the party considerations which underlie *Parklane*'s adherence to privity are simply irrelevant to "Currie-unfairness," because the mass-tort anomaly is an argument about indeterminacy and irregularity rather than about the identity of postures or temporal priorities of contestants.

Thus, neither the privity/no-privity line nor the offensive/defensive distinction provide a way to extend preclusion while avoiding "Currie-unfairness." But the unfairness recognized by Professor Currie suggests that another principle might more effectively illuminate the plight of persons similarly situated by reason of involuntary involvement in a common disaster — a principle that might justify estoppel by class in the way that "desperate necessity" justifies the class action. That principle, as suggested by the preference in federal law for unitary disposition of common transactions like mass torts, is solidarity — a legally ordained systematic preference for equality of treatment among *all* persons similarly situated. . . .

D. The Future of Collateral Estoppel: A Look to Stare Decisis

Since the problems addressed by the expansion of collateral estoppel have a number of striking parallels with 19th century developments in the doctrine of stare decisis, those developments may provide insights into the direction and proper scope of that expansion. Stare decisis demands that the application of the same legal provisions to like cases should produce like results. Under stare decisis, case law provides a detailed definition of settled areas of law, so that citizens have notice of, and can claim reliance on, these settled areas. Parties can use settled law, like collateral estoppel after *Parklane,* offensively or defensively.

Although the analogy between collateral estoppel and stare decisis is imperfect, certain lessons carry over to the search for uniform treatment of factual issues. The very purpose of stare decisis is to establish legal norms which control similar fact situations. While individual cases arising from a common accident traditionally have been entirely matters of unique historical occurrence, *Parklane* and *Blonder-Tongue* exemplify the modern perception that there should be some "lawlike" finality in the resolution of a factual dispute whenever it matters more to be treated alike, to the many persons interested in the determination of a fact, than it does to individually contest the outcome. . . .

. . . Lying beneath the complexity and the apparent technicality of the doctrinal changes are transformations at a deeper level, the end result of which may be noted some day as the transformation of litigation into administration as the paradigm for conflict resolution in modern American jurisprudence.

Note, A Probabilistic Analysis of the Doctrine of Mutuality of Collateral Estoppel *

Introduction

Traditionally, the preclusive effect given a judgment has been limited by the doctrine of mutuality of collateral estoppel: A party to litigation may not invoke the benefits of a prior judgment to preclude an opponent unless that party would have been bound had the prior judgment gone the other way. The mutuality doctrine has for some years been the subject of sustained and vigorous attack from both courts and commentators. The leading case advocating abandonment of mutuality is Bernhard v. Bank of America National Savings & Trust Association [4] (so much so that the abandonment of the mutuality requirement is often referred to as the *Bernhard* doctrine). Though the case might easily have been brought within one of the established exceptions to the mutuality doctrine, Justice Traynor, writing for the California Supreme Court, seized upon *Bernhard* to "extirpate the mutuality requirement and put it to the torch.". . .

. . . Certainly the courts have been moved to abandon mutuality at least partly by the embarrassment of obviously inconsistent findings made possible by more than one trial of the same issue. But the primary motivation has been a concern for judicial economy offset by no perceived reason for maintaining mutuality. In the absence

* *Source:* 76 Mich. L. Rev. 612, 612-619, 640-642, 644-645, 653-655, 659-661 (1978).

4. 19 Cal. 2d 807, 122 P.2d 892 (1942). In *Bernhard*, Clara Sather authorized Charles Cook to issue drafts against her Los Angeles bank account. Cook opened an account on her behalf with the Bank of America in San Dimas. Upon Clara's death, Cook was appointed executor of her estate and failed to account for the San Dimas monies. The beneficiaries, including Helen Bernhard, filed objections, but the probate court held that Clara had made a gift of the funds to Cook.

Following Cook's discharge as executor, Helen Bernhard was appointed administratrix. Claiming that Clara had never consented to the withdrawal of the San Dimas monies, she proceeded, in her new capacity, to sue the bank on the theory that it remained indebted to the estate. 19 Cal. 2d at 809-810, 122 P.2d at 893-894.

On appeal from a judgment favorable to the bank, the California Supreme Court, in an opinion written by Justice Traynor, held that the matter was res judicata. 19 Cal. 2d at 812-814, 122 P.2d at 895-896. Bernhard, having litigated and lost the gift question in the probate court, was estopped to relitigate against the bank even though the bank had not been a party to the probate proceedings and would not have been bound had the judgment of the probate court gone the other way.

of any apparent justification for mutuality, critics have attributed the requirement to vague notions of equality and justice, an overzealous devotion to formal symmetry rather than to substantial justice, and, as Jeremy Bentham suggested, the importation to the bench of notions appropriate only to the "gaming-table." At best, the critics concede that the mutuality doctrine may, on occasion, achieve some desirable results, almost as if by accident. Ultimately, the arguments against the mutuality doctrine amount to little more than a single rhetorical question: Why, other than the "sterile prating of the requirement of mutuality," should a party who has had a "full and fair opportunity to litigate" be permitted to reopen a question once decided merely because he has found, or been found by, a new adversary? . . .

It is the thesis of this Note that the function of the mutuality requirement is the fair allocation of litigation risks. Although other commentators have recognized that the abandonment of mutuality alters litigation risks, they have not attached enough weight to this fact to conclude that it warrants the retention of mutuality. . . . [T]he Second Restatement of Judgments, for example, treats the results dictated by the *Bernhard* doctrine as presumptively correct, to be rejected if required by the consideration of a number of factors, only one of which is the distribution of litigation risks. This Note concludes that mutuality is qualitatively different from the other Restatement factors. Mutuality is the equitable norm for the distribution of litigation risks. . . .

Perhaps more significantly (at least to the judicial economists), the dollars saved by the *Bernhard* doctrine are purchased at the price of a real although previously unnoted degradation of the other product of judicial enterprise — deterrence. If the sanctions which the law imposes are to effectuate the substantive policies which justify their invocation, the imposition of the sanction must be seen to follow from the prohibited conduct. If sanctions are seen as randomly imposed they lose all deterrent effect. The *Bernhard* doctrine weakens this crucial link between the theory of liability and the sanction by interjecting an irrelevant and capricious criterion for decision — the number of litigants on a given side of a question.

Using probability theory as an aid to analysis, this Note will demonstrate that the mutuality doctrine is designed to allocate trial risks in a manner consistent with the burden of persuasion in civil litigation. Thus, the abandonment of mutuality strikes at the heart of the trial process. Where a single party (hereinafter the "common party") faces multiple opponents on a common question, the abandonment of mutuality can significantly alter the common party's probability of success. *Bernhard* thus amounts to little more than an instruction to the trier of fact to find against the common party simply because he is the common party, a fact entirely unrelated to the merits of the case. . . .

B. *A Probabilistic Analysis of the* Bernhard *Doctrine*

1. THE ABANDONMENT OF THE MUTUALITY REQUIREMENT

The central theme of mutuality is the fair apportionment of trial risks. By potentially precluding either party (if both would have been bound) or neither party (if either party would not have been bound), mutuality allows litigation risks to reflect only the merits of the cases. The abandonment of mutuality alters the litigation risks by forcing only one party to face the potential of preclusion in subsequent litigation, thus shifting additional risks to that party. In addition to altering the distribution of risks between the parties, the *Bernhard* doctrine affects the measure of trial efficacy by generally increasing the error rate.

To see more clearly and to what extent mutuality and *Bernhard* affect the allocation of litigation risks, consider the result in two hypothetical multiple litigation situations that differ only with respect to the presence or absence of the mutuality requirement. . . . [I]t will be assumed in both hypotheticals that a common party plaintiff seeks to assert related claims against a series of defendants. . . .

Assume also that the plaintiff has a fifty percent probability of winning his case, that is, that if the case were tried indefinitely, the plaintiff would be successful fifty percent of the time. The general result reached in this analysis is independent of the particular probability selected — the fifty percent figure is employed for ease of calculation and because under such an assumption no single outcome is anomalous in the sense that it is contrary to the majority verdict. Initially, the significance of the total number of cases will be ignored. It is assumed that the plaintiff has ten claims, each liquidated in the amount of $100. As with the probability of a verdict for the plaintiff, the amount of the claim has no bearing on the general conclusions of the analysis.

The impact of a full and fair opportunity to litigate will be analyzed separately in a subsequent subpart. For present purposes, the fifty percent probability of a verdict for the plaintiff common party is taken to be the result of all causes, including those that might lead a subsequent court to conclude, under a full and fair opportunity analysis, that preclusive effect ought to be denied a prior judgment for one of the defendants. Thus, the rule of collateral estoppel will be treated as operating mechanically.

Finally, assume that no defendant is in privity with any other defendant, so that under the traditional mutuality doctrine, as well as under *Bernhard,* the common party plaintiff will not be able to use a favorable judgment against one defendant to preclude any other defendant from relitigating the common issue. Given this set of assumptions, if each case is tried separately and preclusive effect is denied for lack of mutuality, all ten cases will be litigated. By hypothesis, the plaintiff can expect to win fifty percent of his cases for a total expected recovery of $500. This result is illustrated in the mutuality column of Table 5-1.

On the other hand, under *Bernhard,* once the plaintiff loses one case, he will be precluded from litigating the remaining cases. While the probability of winning any single case that is litigated is still fifty percent, the preclusive effect of a single loss makes the probability of ever litigating a case dependent upon the outcome of previous cases. This cumulative effect reduces the common party's expected recovery from $500 to $100, as illustrated in the *Bernhard* column of Table 5-1. . . .

. . . Since the existence of subsequent claims does not affect the expectation value of preceding claims, the expectation value of the second claim is the same whether there are two claims or ten. Thus, the situation in which there are only two claims is not fundamentally different from that in which there are ten. The total expectation value of two claims is simply the sum of the expectation values of the first claim and of the second claim. This sum is $100 under mutuality and only $75 under *Bernhard.* While the decrease in total expected recovery is not as spectacular when there are two suits rather than ten, the effect of the *Bernhard* doctrine is hardly insignificant.

Although the common party in the preceding analysis was a plaintiff (for the purpose of demonstrating that the multiple-claimant anomaly is not limited to the case in which the common party is the defendant . . .) the conclusions reached were without reference to the trial role of the common party. If the common party were defending, the only difference in the hypotheticals would be that the recovery would become the loss avoided. Where, as here, the *Bernhard* doctrine diminishes a common plaintiff's expected recovery from $500 to $100, it would increase a common defendant's losses from $500 to $900. Thus, except to the extent that the initial trial posture bears on whether the common party has had a full and fair opportunity to litigate, trial posture is irrelevant to the alteration of litigation risks attributable to *Bernhard.* . . .

If, in the hypotheticals, all defendants were joined in a single suit so that each would be bound by an adverse judgment as well as benefitted by a favorable one, the plaintiff's expected recovery

TABLE 5-1

		Mutuality			Bernhard		
Trial	*Recovery if win trial*	*Probability of winning trial*	*Expected recovery*	*Cumulative expected recovery*	*Probability of winning trial*	*Expected recovery*	*Cumulative expected recovery*
1	$100	.5	$ 50	$ 50	.500	$ 50.00	$ 50.00
2	100	.5	50	100	.250	25.00	75.00
3	100	.5	50	150	.125	12.50	87.50
4	100	.5	50	200	.063	6.30	93.80
5	100	.5	50	250	.031	3.10	96.90
6	100	.5	50	300	.016	1.60	98.50
7	100	.5	50	350	.008	.80	99.30
8	100	.5	50	400	.004	.40	99.70
9	100	.5	50	450	.002	.20	99.90
10	100	.5	50	500	.001	.10	100.00
Total expected recovery			$500			$100.00	

would be $500. Thus, the expected recovery when all of the defendants are joined in a single action is the same as it would be if the suits were tried separately under mutuality, but it is not the same as it would be if they were tried under *Bernhard*. There is a vast difference between compelling a litigant to accept an all-or-nothing bet with even odds, as joinder rules do, and weighting the odds heavily in favor of his opponent, as the *Bernhard* doctrine does. . . .

2. FULL AND FAIR OPPORTUNITY TO LITIGATE

The unqualified abandonment of mutuality causes intolerable inequities and diminishes the accuracy of the trial process. Does the full and fair opportunity test ameliorate these problems? Critics have complained that the mutuality doctrine is too mechanical a rule, that it denies courts needed flexibility. Commentators have proposed that the flexible tool which modern justice requires would be a rule that precludes a party who has litigated and lost unless, by design or circumstance, that party has been denied a full and fair opportunity to litigate. . . . In assessing the effect of the *Bernhard* doctrine on the distribution of risks, it was initially assumed that the full and fair opportunity test is always satisfied. The conclusions reached under this assumption are sufficient to demonstrate the flaws in *Bernhard* even when the full and fair opportunity test is incorporated in that doctrine. As long as there are some cases in which the test will be met and in which the common party has some chance of winning on the merits, *Bernhard* will reduce that chance by precluding the common party after just one loss. Thus, unless the *Bernhard* supporters are prepared to maintain that all inconsistencies in outcome are attributable to the lack of full and fair opportunity (i.e., that the evidence itself is never ambiguous), so that a party who loses after a full and fair opportunity to litigate would never have won the case even if it were relitigated indefinitely, *Bernhard*'s supporters must concede that preclusion will alter the common party's risks. . . .

[Another] possibility, however, is that a determination of full and fair opportunity is somehow related to the merits of the case. The full and fair opportunity doctrine might be employed to deny preclusive effect whenever the prior judgment is unrepresentative in the fullest sense of the word — that is, whenever the judgment does not accord with the majority view. . . .

If . . . a judge faced with a plea of collateral estoppel were actually capable of discerning the majority view by reviewing the prior action for full and fair opportunity, the *Bernhard* doctrine would be wholly unobjectionable. . . . Although the recovery for common parties with better than 50 percent cases cannot be increased beyond what it would be under mutuality, the common parties estopped to relitigate are those who, ideally, should not recover at all. Thus there is a decrease in the rate of error.

But the full and fair opportunity test cannot be administered so as to reflect the merits of the case. . . . On its face, the test purports to concern itself with purely procedural matters — randomizing errors and biases — the elimination of which cannot raise the recovery of a common party with better than a 50 percent case under *Bernhard* to the level achieved under mutuality. . . . For a trial judge to relate full and fair opportunity to the merits of the preceding case is for him to make his own decision on the merits and then to invoke the prior judgment to justify his usurpation of the jury's function in the second case.[118] Thus, unless it is expanded to unrealistic and unintended dimensions, the full and fair opportunity element of *Bernhard* does not meet the objections to the abandonment of mutuality.

NOTES AND COMMENTS

If the foregoing "probabilistic analysis" is correct, is there any other choice than restoring the rule of mutuality?

118. Where mutuality has been abrogated, courts are probably manipulating full and fair opportunity to reflect their view of the merits of the case. Courts are able to do this because there are no articulated criteria for such judgments and because it is carried on sub silentio. . . .

Chapter 6

Appeal

Trial Courts and Appellate Courts — Fact-Finding *

Martin Shapiro

In the United States the distinction between questions of fact and questions of law which is supposed to be the key to the limits of appellate jurisdiction, is a notoriously slippery one. It is so slippery that a whole new category, "mixed questions of fact and law," has been invented. In reality that category defines the huge number of instances in which appellate courts have refused to accept trial court findings of fact and substituted their own fact-finding under the guise of law finding. As we have noted, the Supreme Court has long held that it will make its own findings of "constitutional fact." But constitutional facts are often the same routine facts that the trial court has already decided. For instance, let us suppose a trial court has determined that a given speech did incite a riot and so convicts a speaker of incitement to riot. The Supreme Court will, under the constitutional fact doctrine, redetermine exactly the same factual question. For it will decide the constitutional issue of whether the speech constituted such a clear and present danger of serious social evil that its repression might be justified in the face of the First Amendment's guarantees of free speech.

This pull of appellate courts toward the facts can also be seen in the endless proliferation in the United States, Great Britain, and on the Continent of statutes, rules, and practices about how much evidence a trial court or administrative agency must have to support its decisions. Typically there has been pressure from the legislature or the courts themselves to keep appellate courts from substituting

* *Source:* Courts: A Comparative and Political Analysis 41-44, 49-56 (1981).

their own fact-finding for that of the decisionmaker who hears the evidence in the first instance. Two basic rationales underlie this pressure. One is that the first-instance trier actually sees and hears the witnesses, examines the physical evidence, and is simply closer in space and time to the disputed events than the appeals court that sees only a printed record. The second, particularly important where administrative agencies are the first-instance trier, is that the agencies are more competent to find facts in the highly specialized areas of their expertise than are appeals courts staffed by nonspecialist judges. This pressure manifests itself in various rules requiring appellate courts to pay various degrees of deference to initial fact-finding by others. In the United States there are generally three grades of deference, although similar standards in different verbal formulations are to be found in other countries. Indeed the verbal formulations are far from uniform even in the United States. The strictest standard of deference is the "no evidence" rule used by the Supreme Court in review of state court fact-finding and the "some evidence" rule involved frequently where courts are reviewing agency fact-finding. The Supreme Court announces that it will reverse state courts on the facts in criminal cases only when the state record contains "no evidence" supporting conviction. While in theory this would mean that the presence of even a single bit of evidence tending to show guilt would be sufficient to obviate review, in practice the court has sometimes found that what others would consider quite a bit of evidence turns out to be "no evidence." Similarly, courts frequently say that they will not reverse on factual grounds an agency's decisions in areas of its peculiar expertise unless the record is totally devoid of agency fact-finding supporting its decision. In other words so long as the agency can show some evidence in support of its decision, the court will not make its own judgment on where the preponderance of evidence lies.

The next lower standard of deference is the "substantial evidence" rule. In various verbal formulations and degrees of severity, this rule has become the most typical rule of judicial review of agency fact-finding throughout the Western world. The court will look to see if an administrative agency has developed a substantial body of evidence in support of its decision. If it has, the court will not weigh the evidence of one side against that on the other and substitute its own judgment for the agency's about where the preponderance of evidence lies.

The lowest standard of deference is a "preponderance of evidence" rule. Under such a rule appellate courts generally purport to give great weight to first-instance fact-finding but nonetheless strike their own final balance of the weight of evidence on each side. Of course legislatures may seek to prevent court review of agency fact-finding altogether by providing that their decisions are final and unreviewable. As we shall see . . . courts tend to resist such limitations on their review power.

But why does this whole body of jurisprudence arise in legal systems that employ the general rule that appellate courts should not redetermine facts? Obviously, because there is such a strong thrust in appellate courts toward fact-finding that it cannot be contained by the general rule. And that thrust occurs because, while the principal job of appellate courts is lawmaking, they continuously seek to reiterate their connection with the basis of all judicial legitimacy, conflict resolution. So long as appellate courts do their lawmaking under the guise of doing substantial justice between man and man in particular cases — and they must do this if they are to be perceived as and supported as courts — they will keep clawing their way back toward the facts. For disputes about the facts are at the root of a large proportion of the conflicts to be resolved.

This point is well illustrated by the evolution of "jury instructions" in the United States where, as we have seen, the tradition of the writ of error and the employment of juries severely limits review. Trial courts need not write lengthy opinions. The jury's deliberations are oral and secret and thus cannot be reviewed at all. The appellate court may conduct only an extremely limited review of the trial transcript because it is almost entirely devoted to the presentation of factual evidence and trial court findings of fact are not appealable. About the only thing in the record that is reviewable by an appellate court is the instructions given by the judge to the jury. These instructions are technically the judge's explanation of the relevant law to the jury. In reality they tend to be a review of both the facts and law by the judge indicating what verdict the jury ought to bring in if it believes one or the other of the two versions of facts offered by the parties. Thus criticism of the instruction becomes the vehicle for appellate court intervention against the trial court's findings of both fact and law, even though technically appeal is limited to issues of law. Nearly everything in the instruction is a "mixed question of fact and law" subject to review.

Instructions thus become a crucial intersection between trial court and appellate court power. As a result they tend to become a highly complex and technical legal ritual in which the trial judge seeks to protect himself against appellate reversal by carefully quoting various verbal formulae that previous appellate opinions have announced to be the proper ones. A conscientious trial judge, therefore, tends to write instructions that bounce back and forth between legal statements so technical that they can be understood only by those who know the appellate precedents and simple explanations designed for jurors. What began as a message from trial judge to jury has become a defense by trial judge against appellate judge.

At the very opposite pole of appellate fact-finding lies the distinction between judicial and legislative fact. In theory courts are supposed to confine themselves to the particular facts of the particular case. And because they are supposed to follow adversary proceedings, they are supposed to limit themselves to consideration of the facts presented by the two parties rather than ranging broadly over social data in a way permissible to legislatures drafting new laws. These limitations, rooted as they are in the conflict resolution aspect of judicial activity, work in a rough and ready way for trial courts. Where appellate court lawmaking is involved, they hardly work at all. Whether it be dressed in the language of American sociological jurisprudence, Continental free decisionmaking, or a tribal chief's common sense concern with preserving his authority, it is clear that where an appellate body seeks to formulate a legal rule, it must consider the fit of that rule to the society at large, not just to the two contending parties. In most societies the arguments presented to courts have either presumed or injected a great deal of general knowledge of the operation of the society. Courts usually hold that even the adversary model does not require them to be blind to what any fool can plainly see just because neither party got it into evidence. Doctrines like judicial notice have allowed either one of the parties or the judge himself to assume widely known social facts without proving them.

In the United States the "Brandeis brief," first invented for the special purpose of defending state regulatory statutes against constitutional attack, has now blossomed forth in nearly every instance in which an appellate court is in reality being asked to make new law. Today's brief on an environmental, desegregation, apportionment, or welfare issue frequently contains exactly the same data in exactly the same format as would a presentation to a congressional committee. The United States no doubt represents the extreme case. But on narrower fronts, for instance in the willingness of English and Continental courts to hear evidence on general commercial practices, most courts find some way of touching base with general social reality. Of course this is as true of trial as appellate courts, but the issue of just what range of facts a court may hear arises most dramatically at appellate levels. For appeals court lawmaking in rivalry to legislatures is much clearer than that of trial courts. . . .

The Uses of Appeal

As we noted earlier, one of the principal virtues of a trial is that it provides an official termination to conflict, relieving the disputants of the necessity of further reciprocal assertions or retributions. But too much finality may be disturbing to the losing member of the triad. One of the functions of a "right of appeal" may be to provide a psychological outlet and a social cover for the loser at trial. For appeal allows the loser to continue to assert his rightness in the abstract without attacking the legitimacy of the legal system or refusing to obey the trial court. Indeed the loser's displeasure is funnelled into a further assertion of the legitimacy of the legal system. Appealing to a higher court entails the acknowledgment of its legitimacy.

We also noted earlier that the principal problem of the triadic form of conflict resolution was keeping the loser from perceiving the final situation as "two against one." Appeals mechanisms are devices for telling the loser that if he believes that it did turn out two against one, he may try another triadic figure. Perhaps just as important, the availability of appeal allows the loser to accept his loss without having to acknowledge it publicly. The purpose of a trial is to effect a termination of conflict. But too abrupt a termination may be counterproductive of true conflict resolution. Appeal, whether actually exercised, threatened, or only held in reserve, avoids adding insult to injury. The loser can leave the courtroom with his head high talking of appeal and then accept his loss, slowly, privately, and passively by failing to make an appeal. We often see appeal principally as a mode of ensuring against the venality, prejudice, and/or ignorance of trial court judges and of soothing the ruffled feelings of the loser. Appeal does indeed serve these functions, but it does so by the imposition of hierarchical controls on trial court behavior. A great deal of interest to political scientists lurks in that hierarchical element.

We have already noted that in a predominant share of the governing systems that have existed in the world, judging is either a facet of administration, or is closely aligned with it. It is a commonplace of administrative lore that no matter what the theory, Weberian hierarchies do not give the top or center adequate control over rank and file administrators in the field. Such control will not occur unless a number of alternative channels of information are available that can be cross-checked at or near the top. The best-known modern example is obviously the Soviet Union, with its trade union, government, party, control commission, and police hierarchies superimposed on one another. When administrators hold courts, appeal becomes such a mechanism of control. A "right" of appeal is a mechanism providing an independent flow of information to the top on the field performance of administrative subordinates.

It is not only an independent flow, but one highly complementary to the normal administrative reporting. Such reporting usually takes the form of summarization. Each field administrator handles hundreds of thousands of bits of information about local affairs and his own performance. Let us suppose that each passed everything he knew along to his superiors. Each superior supervises a number of subordinates. Each would be flooded with millions of bits of information — far more than he could handle. So normally each field administrator passes to his superior only a summary of the information he has developed. And each superior passes on only a summary of those summaries to his superior. In the process much information is necessarily lost. And not unnaturally, what tend to get lost most easily are those instances in which the subordinate has done badly. The superior never sees the full details of any specific things his subordinates have done. The summaries he sees tend to emphasize his subordinates' successes and leave out the failures. ("Last year this office handled over three thousand claims of which 91 percent were settled within forty-eight hours.")

The appeals process cuts across this summarization because the unit of appeal is a single case, in all its details, rather than a summary of overall performance. It is not a single instance chosen by an administrator to illustrate his success, but an instance chosen by a consumer of administration who feels that the administrator has failed. Finally, not only is the appeals case a detailed sample of administrative work product, but it is a partially random sample. The distribution of cases appealed is not determined by either the goals of the administrative subordinate or his superior but by the nonadministrative motivations of individual litigants. Let us suppose that a chief engineer wishes to check the performance of his auto assembly line. His normal mechanism is to check the statistics reported by his foremen on the number of engines mounted, doors attached, and so on, including the final figures on cars produced. Or alternatively, he could look at every hundredth car. Appeal would allow him to check in yet another way. The customer who got the "lemon" would bring the car in and insist that the chief engineer take it all apart to see exactly what things had been done wrong on the line.

Thus, on the one hand, while appeal is a partially random sample, it is one loaded toward administrative failure. It will not be every fifth car or every green car that is sampled, but some of the worst cars and very, very few of the best. On the other hand, the administrative superior may impose some patterning by making it known what kinds of appeal are most likely to be successful. We have already seen that English appeals courts at one time said they would listen to appeals on questions of law but not of fact. Thus they got to see cases in which trial courts had made mistakes of law, but not those where the court had done bad fact-finding. Field administrators can also partially control the pattern of appeals. . . . [A] Chinese local magistrate who did not wish his superiors to know about his performance in a particular dispute could pressure the parties to settle by mediation. A mediated settlement could not be appealed.

At the opposite extreme, it is possible to run an appeals system that takes 100 percent or at least a very full sample. In Tokagawa, Japan, every opinion of a trial court was prepared as only a draft of an opinion by the higher authorities. Each draft went forward and came into legal force only after the higher authorities had approved it. In this system, then, all cases are appealed. Most American states provide one appeal in criminal cases as a matter of right. The common practice of the defense bar in many of those states is routinely to file an appeal for every losing defendant. Some states have mandatory first appeals for all cases in which the punishment is severe. These state systems approach 100 percent appeal. Whenever a central government seems to be attempting 100 percent sampling, however, the reality will usually turn out to be otherwise. Thus in states where a first appeal is routine, the intermediate appellate court that hears such appeals will usually deny 90 percent of them in one-line orders that show that they were given only a cursory glance. The appellate court will decide the other 10 percent. And of those only a very few will move on to a further appeal to the state supreme court.

Of course, where there is a separate judicial hierarchy, appeal is typically the central mode of supervision by higher courts over lower, and reversal on appeal a central form of administrative sanction. In such instances the need for multiple channels of information and control leads the top to demand other institutions in addition to appeal, such as judicial conferences, centralized personnel systems, and administrative reporting, to increase their control over their subordinates.

The insistence, so frequently encountered, that the chain of appeal eventually arrive at the chief, the king, or the capital, instead of stopping at some intermediate level, is difficult to explain except in terms of centralized political control. If the only function of appeal were to ensure against corruptness or arbitrariness on the part of the trial judge, then appeal to anyone even a single step higher in the scale of authority would be sufficient. In the American states we have just discussed, for instance, appeals could all stop at intermediate appellate courts. Why should any go on to a state supreme court? Its justices are really no more capable of righting the injustices done to the loser in the trial court than are the appeals court judges who first heard the appeal. The top insists on being the ultimate level of appeal because it serves its purposes, not those of a losing disputant.

Of course, just as one of the functions of any appeal may be to reduce the psychic shock to losers, so the right to "take the case all the way to the Supreme Court" provides even greater catharsis for the loser whether he employs it only rhetorically or actually does it. Yet even at this personal level, and quite apart from the question of hierarchical control, the top is likely to see advantages in preserving a right of ultimate appeal. . . . [T]he extension of judicial services outward and downward is a device for wedding the countryside to the regime. So the preservation of appeal to the chief-king-emperor-capital is a device for keeping the strings of legitimacy tied directly between the ruled and the person of the ruler or the highest institutions of government. In the imperial Chinese legal system . . . cases involving capital punishment were automatically appealed from local courts through intermediate appeals courts and ultimately to the emperor himself. The accused was shipped along with his appeal up the appeals ladder. When the death sentence was ultimately commuted, the commutation was ceremonially delivered to the prisoner in the capital and depicted as the personal mercy of the emperor. When the death penalty was confirmed, the prisoner was shipped back down the appeals ladder. He was dispatched on the local execution ground of the trial court that had convicted him initially. No clearer declaration of the political purposes of appeal could be made.

Conversely, the ability to reach down occasionally into the most particular affairs of the countryside provides an important means of reminding the rank and file that the rulers are everywhere, that no one may use his insignificance or his embeddedness in the mass to hide from central authority. Thus the personal ruler, be he Zulu war chief or medieval monarch, rarely totally gives up his personal participation in appeals. Nor do modern central governments often provide that there be only a single appeal from trial court to regional appeals court without any opportunity to go on to a central appeals court.

Thus appellate institutions are more fundamentally related to the political purposes of central regimes than to the doing of individual justice. That this is true is evidenced by the nearly universal existence of appellate mechanisms in politically developed societies, even those whose governments place little or no value on individual rights. . . .

Even if judges did nothing but conflict resolution, appeal would be an important political mechanism both for increasing the level of central control over administrative subordinates and for ensuring the authority and legitimacy of rulers. When we enter the realms of social control and lawmaking, the multiple functions of appeal are even more apparent. When trial courts or first-instance judging by administrators is used as a mode of social control, appeal is a mechanism for central coordination of local control. The "questions of law" passed on to the appeals courts are in reality requests for uniform rules of social conduct and indicators of what range of case-by-case deviation from those rules is permissible by first-line controllers.

A partial breakdown of this supervisory mechanism is largely responsible for the wave of discontent with American criminal courts. In most Western criminal law systems there can be no appeal after a plea of guilty. Something over 90 percent of American criminal cases are settled by a guilty plea or its equivalent, frequently as a result of specific or tacit plea bargaining. As we have noted, appeals courts do not normally consider questions of fact. In the United States "disposition," or sentencing, that is, the decision about what to do with the person of the convicted criminal, is not normally reviewable by appellate courts.

These three factors combine to create a major anomaly, at least within the Western political and administrative tradition. The basic business of American criminal courts is not the triadic resolution of disputes cast in the form of the People v. John Doe. And this is quite apart from the point that casting criminal law enforcement in this ritual form of conflict between individual and the state is a transparent fiction. Most American trial courts rarely bother even with the ritual of trial. Their time is spent disposing of the bodies of those who have pleaded guilty. Thus they are clearly administrators distributing the scarce sanctioning and rehabilitative resources of society among a mass of "applicants." In this sense trial courts have ceased to be courts.

This absorption of "courts" in administrative tasks is not particularly surprising or alarming in view of the natural affinities between judging and administration. . . . The anomaly arises precisely because we persist in formally viewing these administrative tasks as judicial. As a result we get an enormous volume of particularized administrative discretion without any of the hierarchical supervision we normally exercise over low-level administrators. In short, what trial courts really do, sentence, is not subject to appellate court review. And because trial courts are *courts* in a political system that endorses judicial independence, they are not subject to any other form of hierarchical supervision. Thus they are one of the few agencies of government in which rank-and-file operators are subject to almost no supervision at all in the wielding of enormous discretion. Imagine the loss in legitimacy that any bureaucratic agency would suffer if the clients were told that the clerks at the windows had broad discretion and their decisions were not reviewable by their superiors.

This American situation is an example of the need to focus clearly on appeal as a mode of hierarchical political management, as well as a guarantee of fairness to the accused, if we are to understand the actual operation of real political systems.

In this context social control and lawmaking are usually intimately connected. Appeal is not simply a device for ensuring a certain uniformity in the operations of rank-and-file social controllers. It also ensures that they are following rules or laws or policies of social control acceptable to the regime. Indeed, appeal is a key mechanism in injecting centralized social control into the conflict resolution activities of courts. For appeal is the channel through which the central political authority assures itself that its rank-and-file conflict resolvers are applying legal rules that resolve conflicts in the desired directions. . . . [T]he substitution of legislated law for rules created by the mutual consent of the parties introduced a third set of interests into two-party litigation, whatever interests were embodied in the legislation. At least in large and complex societies, trial courts are too many and too localized to articulate this third set satisfactorily. Appellate courts are more suitable.

Tort serves as a good example. When social policy is stable, trial courts will finally dispose of most tort cases. The "reasonable man" doctrine applied by juries will impose sanctions on those who deviate from commonly accepted standards of conduct. The parties will see their conflict as existing within fairly clearly pre-established rules enunciated in the pattern of previous cases. It will be resolved by a judgment of their peers about who was at fault or more at fault. However, when new social and economic policies are to be introduced, appellate courts will become active, enunciating new tort doctrines, or theories, and creating or plugging exceptions to existing rules. Thus, during the rapid industrialization of the United States in the nineteenth century, when allocating the costs of industrial accidents became an important economic issue, the high courts of the states created or expanded the contributory negligence and fellow-servant rules and the doctrine of assumed risk. Trial courts still resolved conflicts between employer and injured worker and controlled deviations from accepted standards of proper industrial conduct. But they did so within a set of overarching doctrines that injected the national interests in industrial growth as a counterweight to the interests of injured workers. We have already noted the role jury instructions can play in the relations between trial and appellate courts. When appellate courts are striving to impose centrally determined uniform policies, such instructions will serve as a battleground where, no matter what he says to the jury, the trial judge is threatened with reversal if he does not achieve outcomes satisfactory to the central authorities.

On the broadest scale, of course, constitutional review by the highest appeals courts in federal systems has been a principal device of centralized policymaking. A good example is school desegregation in the United States. And appeal has been used in highly centralized political systems such as that in France as one of numerous routine mechanisms for controlling and coordinating government agents in the field. Appeals courts can and do act in this capacity whether they are themselves doing a great deal of lawmaking or acting as enforcers of law made by others. An interesting variant is the sending of trial judges on "circuit" from the capitol or the insistence that suitors travel to the capitol for trial — both important tactics of the medieval English monarchs for centralizing political authority. . . . It is because England had this special overlay of national trial courts, above the essentially local county and baronial courts, that a large proportion of English common law has been made by what are technically trial courts, while most of American judicial lawmaking occurs in appeals courts. Far more typical are the arrangements of the nineteenth- and twentieth-century European-based empires, all of which provided for appeal either to a high court sitting in the metropolis or a territorial high court employing metropolitan law and/or staffed by judges trained as imperial servants. The British system of appeal to the Privy Council is the best-known example.

Quite obviously, if there is any judicial lawmaking within a territorially dispersed system of courts, then a pyramid of appeal is necessary in order to assure that any central body of law is relatively uniformly administered throughout its domain. For instance, in spite of its onerous constitutional duties, the United States Supreme Court devotes about 40 percent of its opinions to creating uniform interpretations of federal statutes among the intermediate federal courts of appeal. In a unitary (as opposed to federal) noncommon-law state, in which courts do not enjoy the power to declare laws unconstitutional and in which intermediate appellate courts exist, about the only legal rationale possible for the existence of a high court of appeal is the need for uniformity of statutory interpretation. . . .

Earlier we noted that even if all courts did was conflict resolution, appeal would serve the regime's purposes of hierarchical control by providing a sample of low level administrative performance. When we focus on the lawmaking activities of courts, we can see that appeal is a mechanism that sorts out unresolved issues of public policy and moves them toward the top for decision. In some cases the questions of law appealed from trial courts represent instances in which the trial court has deviated from the uniform national rule and will be brought back into line by an appeals court. In others the question of law arises because there is no national rule and the appeals court is being asked to make one. This is why appeals courts inevitably become lawmaking bodies even in legal systems that denigrate judicial lawmaking.

To emphasize this function, however, is to assert that most high courts of appeal are barely courts at all. That is, while in form they may be engaged in finally resolving one particular dispute between two particular litigants, their principal role may be to provide uniform rules of law. Naturally such rules must be based on considerations far broader than the concerns of the two litigants, essentially on considerations of public policy that may have little to do with the particular litigation. At worst the litigants are irrelevant; at best they are examples or samples of the general problems to be solved.

Political scientists and lawyers concerned with the legitimacy of courts have tended to concentrate on appellate courts. Appellate courts are the furthest removed from the basic social logic of courts. As a result courts appear far more problematic to scholars than they do to the citizenry. Nevertheless, the study of appellate courts makes clear that courts always exist in a state of tension between their basic source of legitimacy as consensual triadic resolvers of conflict and their position as government agencies imposing law on the citizenry. To put this matter somewhat differently, the social legitimacy of courts as a universal social device for conflict resolution and the political legitimacy of courts as a particular segment of a particular political regime are sometimes additive and mutually supportive and sometimes quite the contrary.

Note, The Finality Rule for Supreme Court Review of State Court Orders *

A fundamental institutional concern in multitiered judicial systems is the establishment of a procedure for regulating access by litigants to appellate review. Subsumed under this concern are a number of questions, including whether appeals are to be permitted at all in particular types of cases, and if so, whether they are to be mandatory or discretionary. But the central question, assuming a decision to permit appeals, is the one of timing: When can an appeal be taken? The answer given by the English common law, and generally adopted in the United States, was that an appeal could be taken only after a final judgment had been rendered. Congress, in enacting

* *Source:* 91 Harv. L. Rev. 1004, 1004-1017, 1019-1026 (1978).

the Judiciary Act of 1789 to establish a federal judicial system, included this final judgment principle among the rules circumscribing the jurisdiction of the federal courts. Although statutory exceptions to the principle of finality have been created for appeals wholly within the federal court system, the finality rule remains the statutory basis for appeal from state courts to the United States Supreme Court. But in the application of this statutory limitation upon its appellate jurisdiction over state courts — now embodied in 28 U.S.C. §1257 — the Supreme Court has in many cases entertained appeals from state court decisions that are not strictly final. The cumulative effect of these ad hoc exceptions to the rule of finality is a rather confusing common law of appellate jurisdiction. Further complicating the application of section 1257 are the special concerns of federalism and comity that result from the interplay between two independent, although not equal, judicial systems. . . .

I. Approaches to Appealability

There are two paradigmatic approaches to the regulation of appellate jurisdiction. One requires that review be predicated upon the trial court's disposition of the entire case; the other permits appellate consideration of each issue in a case as it arises. Under the "entire case" paradigm, appellate jurisdiction is extended only to completed cases, in which a final decision has been rendered; the "individual issue" model, on the other hand, permits the appeals court to consider interlocutory rulings immediately.

The entire case approach — with its corresponding finality rule — rests in part upon the supposition that efficiency is best served by restricting appellate interruptions of the trial process to an absolute minimum. By preserving the integrity of the trial, the rule of finality under the entire case model obviously facilitates continuity and results in a speedier disposition of the case. The finality rule also finds support in considerations other than efficiency. The interests of litigants in securing justice is served when controversies are resolved in the most expeditious fashion consistent with preserving the requirements of due process. Significantly, from the standpoint of fairness to the parties, the prohibition of interlocutory appeals prevents dilatory tactics by those litigants who can afford to subject their adversaries to attrition or who have an interest in delaying completion of the trial. Traditional notions of deference to the trial judge, which suggest that he ought to be permitted to proceed without the intrusion of intermittent reconsideration of his rulings by a higher court, provide further support for a finality rule.

Appellate tribunals also benefit from a finality principle. Completed cases can be submitted for review within the context of a developed factual record and the articulated reasoning and legal conclusions of the trial judge. Where several grounds for the decision on appeal are presented, the reviewing court is able to avoid unnecessary lawmaking by choosing the narrowest ground for affirming or reversing the trial judge's decision. Indeed, postponing appellate consideration increases the possibility that challenged rulings will not be appealed because subsequent events at trial remove the incentive for one or more parties to press for review.

The individual issue model and its concomitant interlocutory appeal principle flow from very different assumptions about the most efficient and just arrangement of judicial procedures. Advocates of this model may contend, for example, that interlocutory appellate reversal of denials of motions for dismissal or summary judgment permit some cases to be terminated quickly, thus conserving judicial resources that would otherwise be expended during a lengthy trial. Yet, because such terminations by appellate courts are rare, it is highly unlikely that the savings in time and resources yielded by the early resolution of cases on appeal will compensate for the systemic delays resulting from widespread interruption of trial court proceedings. The case for interlocutory review must therefore rest on other considerations — reasons which outweigh the inefficiencies of piecemeal adjudication. Arguably, one such reason is that appellate resolution of legal issues is improved when the issues are abstracted from the complicated network of legal and factual challenges that is often presented when a fully adjudicated case is submitted to an appellate court. More compelling, however, is the fact that interlocutory review permits the immediate correction of highly prejudicial legal error; this is especially important when the harm flowing from the error may not be susceptible to later repair, as, for example, damage caused by an arguably improper denial of the protection afforded against strike suits by a procedural requirement.

In enacting the statutes regulating appellate jurisdiction in the federal courts, Congress apparently opted for the "entire case" model and the principle of finality. As provided for under 28 U.S.C. §1257, Supreme Court review of state court decisions — both on direct appeal and by writ of certiorari — is limited to "final judgments or decrees rendered by the highest court of a state in which a decision could be had." [23] Appeals from federal district court to the United States Court of Appeals under 28 U.S.C. §1291 are similarly limited to "ap-

23. 28 U.S.C. §1257 (1970). The "highest court of a state in which a decision could be had" may be a lower court in the state system. . . . The benchmark for decision is whether further appellate review within the state system is possible. Where the only further review possible within the state court system is a discretionary appeal, a litigant must attempt to invoke it before he can secure Supreme Court review. . . .

peals from . . . final decisions,"[24] although other jurisdictional provisions also authorize appellate review of certain interlocutory orders.[25]

Rigid adherence to the rule of finality does, however, entail certain costs. Insistence on the formalistic application of the rule can lead to inefficient results — for example, where it would require the remand, for further proceedings, of a case whose outcome has been effectively determined by the lower court ruling that is being appealed. In other circumstances, denial of interlocutory appellate review may result in the loss of a right which by nature demands immediate protection. Cases of this sort might be expected to generate pressures on appellate courts to create exceptions to the finality rule. It is therefore not surprising that the actual application of the jurisdictional rules under the statutes regulating appealability in the federal courts sometimes departs from a strict rule of finality. In some instances, the departure from the finality rule is in form only; as a practical matter, the litigation is complete. On other occasions, however, appellate jurisdiction over genuinely interlocutory orders has been justified by the court's articulated concern that postponing review could result in a miscarriage of justice. As applied, therefore, appealability rules in the federal system are to a degree poised between the "entire case" paradigm apparently mandated by the statutes and the interlocutory model that may be perceived as more responsive to the demands of justice in particular cases.

However, permitting exceptions to a strict finality rule — especially in an ad hoc fashion — introduces an element of uncertainty that may undermine the efficiency benefits of the entire case model even when it is followed in the majority of cases. Imprecision in the rules of finality governing appealability can have untoward results:

24. 28 U.S.C. §1291 (1970).

Appeals from decisions of three-judge district courts may be had directly to the Supreme Court under 28 U.S.C. §1253 (1970).

Supreme Court review of decisions by the courts of appeals is provided for by 28 U.S.C. §1254 (1970). This provision does not limit the Court's appellate jurisdiction to final decisions, and the Court has on several occasions reviewed interlocutory decisions. . . . The Court has power under §1254 to grant certiorari before judgment by the court of appeals, so long as the case has been docketed in the intermediate appellate court . . . but the exercise of this power has been limited to cases involving important constitutional questions or matters of great national significance in which a speedy decision from the Supreme Court is important. . . .

25. Principal among these is 28 U.S.C. §1292(a) (1970), which authorizes appeals from interlocutory orders (1) dealing with injunctive relief, (2) issued in connection with aspects of receivership proceedings, (3) determining rights and liabilities in some admiralty cases, or (4) issued in civil actions for patent infringement where only an accounting remains to be conducted. . . . Under 28 U.S.C. §1292(b) (1970), a district court may certify, and the court of appeals may thereupon permit, appeals from interlocutory orders which involve a "controlling question of law as to which there is substantial ground for difference of opinion" and the immediate review of which "may materially advance the ultimate termination of the litigation."

either litigants will forfeit their rights to appellate review because their appeals or petitions for certiorari are not timely filed, or, as is more likely, they will be overly cautious and seek review at every possible stage of the litigation. Not only would this increase the sheer volume of appeals, but the time and energy consumed in determining whether in each case an exception indeed applies would produce the very delays and inefficiencies which the finality rule is designed to avoid. Exceptions to the finality rule should therefore be defined as clearly and precisely as possible.

In addition, the scope and number of any exceptions to the generally applicable finality rule must be limited if the systemic benefits of the finality principle are not to be undermined. Because the premise of the finality paradigm is that the claims of individuals to special interlocutory review should be subordinated so that all parties can enjoy the systemwide advantages which finality confers, exceptions to finality should be restricted either to circumstances so extraordinary and compelling that they cannot justifiably be sacrificed for the common good or to situations in which insistence on finality would be sheer formalism.

The appropriate scope of finality exceptions can be illustrated by contrasting two Supreme Court decisions under section 1291, which regulates appeals from federal district courts to the courts of appeals. In Cohen v. Beneficial Industrial Loan Corp.,[35] the Court declared that nonfinal orders could be appealed immediately where (1) they were unrelated to an ingredient of the cause of action — and hence collateral to the merits — and (2) they affected important rights that might be irreparably lost were interlocutory review denied. This "collateral order" doctrine is consistent with the principles that justify a departure from the finality rule despite some efficiency costs. The requirement that the claims asserted for interlocutory review be collateral and important conforms to the need to confine the ambit of the exception to a "small class" of cases. At the same time, the fact that the issue reviewed is not an ingredient of the cause of action insures that matters considered upon interlocutory appeal will not overlap with issues to be considered should the merits of the case be presented for review after final judgment. Thus, judicial resources are, to some degree, conserved. Most importantly, the circumstances of the interlocutory ruling in *Cohen* were sufficiently compelling to warrant an exception to the general rule. The defendant corporation in *Cohen* sought review of an order denying its motion to compel the plaintiff in a derivative suit to post a bond for costs as required

35. 337 U.S. 541 (1949).

by state statute. The purpose of the bond requirement was to deter "strike" suits; essentially, therefore, it protected the corporation from the burden of defending against nuisance claims. To be sure, many individuals must suffer the costs of frivolous suits, and these hardships are not deemed sufficient to warrant granting interlocutory appeals from every denial of a motion to dismiss. The right asserted by the defendant in *Cohen*, however, was more than a general interest in freedom from the burden of litigation — it was a specific statutory right to be free of "strike" suits. And, as the Court pointed out, the nature of the right was such that to postpone review of its denial would have been tantamount to a deprivation without review.

So understood, the *Cohen* collateral order doctrine exemplifies a precisely contoured exception to the finality rule that minimizes systemic efficiency losses while responding to the concern for justice in compelling and unusual cases. But other exceptions developed by the Court have been inconsistent with the general applicability of a finality principle. In sharp contrast to *Cohen* is the Court's decision in Gillespie v. United States Steel Corp.,[43] where it approved the grant of an interlocutory appeal from a district court order dismissing a pendent state claim. Justice Black, writing for the majority, acknowledged that interlocutory review would create some delay in the trial process, but reasoned that such an intrusion was justified by the harm that would result to the appellants from having their claims for recovery "cut off so long as the District Judge's ruling stands." But such reasoning fails to differentiate between the burden suffered by appellants in this case and the burdens suffered whenever a motion for summary judgment is denied or a motion to dismiss one of several claims is granted. Since no particular right to avoid such a burden could be invoked on behalf of the appellants in *Gillespie*, there was no compelling reason to accord them treatment distinct from that applied generally to litigants. Moreover, as Justice Harlan pointed out in dissent, the dismissed claim "would have merged in the judgment" — it related to the merits of the case and could have been presented for review upon appeal from a final judgment. Finally, the ad hoc balancing approach employed by Justice Black in *Gillespie* — comparing the advantages of finality with the concern for justice in the particular case — introduces an unacceptable degree of indeterminacy into the general finality principle. If the systemic benefits of the entire case paradigm are not to be undermined, any accommodation between the principle of finality and special concerns of justice

43. 379 U.S. 148 (1964).

must be accomplished through the formulation of clearly and narrowly defined categories of exceptions.

II. Section 1257 and Federalism

Since a requirement of finality is embodied in both section 1291 and section 1257, the appropriateness of any exception to either jurisdictional provision must be tested against the same standard — whether the form and content of the exception are consistent with the systemic benefits of the entire case paradigm. Unlike section 1291, however, appeals brought to the Supreme Court under section 1257 involve the transmission of cases or issues between separate judicial systems. Thus, the invocation of section 1257 not only requires attentiveness to the functional concerns underlying the congressionally mandated principle of finality; it also implicates the relationship between the states and the federal government, and hence the special concerns of federalism and comity.

One manifestation of these federalism concerns is the notion that the Court, in deciding whether to hear an appeal brought under section 1257, should exhibit a heightened solicitude for the integrity of the trial process because of possible state sensitivity about interlocutory supervision by the federal judiciary. A more important feature of the federal context in which section 1257 appeals arise is the independent and adequate state grounds doctrine, which imposes limitations on the types of state cases the Supreme Court may hear on appeal. Under that doctrine the Court may not review state court determinations of federal law in cases in which there exist adequate and separate state law grounds to sustain the judgment. In part, the doctrine rests upon the Court's construction of its jurisdictional statute as precluding its power to review state court determinations of state law; review of any issues of federal law which, in light of the determinations of state law, are not necessary to the disposition of the case is therefore prevented by the constitutional prohibition of advisory opinions. But the doctrine also reflects a keen respect for the semi-independent role of the state courts in our federal system. Although the doctrine often is not applicable when a case is presented on interlocutory appeal, since there has not yet been a full opportunity to articulate any state grounds, respect for the state courts and the desire to avoid unnecessary adjudication militate in favor of postponing appellate review until state court proceedings have been completed and any possible independent and adequate state grounds have been developed. By facilitating the development of alternative grounds for the disposition of cases, the rule of finality under section

1257 permits the Court to avoid unnecessary decisionmaking — particularly important when state statutes are challenged under federal law.[55] The principle of finality is therefore a vital counterpart to the independent and adequate state grounds doctrine.

It may be argued, however, that finality rules should be interpreted so as to preempt the operation of the independent and adequate state grounds doctrine. Specifically, it might be contended that more aggressive interlocutory supervision of state court decisions on federal questions is warranted where an erroneous or hostile decision of federal law may be insulated from later Supreme Court review by the adequate state grounds doctrine. Quite apart from the fact that it is somewhat incongruous for the Court to hasten to circumvent a doctrine to which it otherwise adheres, this reasoning is inconsistent with the thrust of other doctrines developed by the Court to maintain harmonious federal-state court relations. For example, the Court's recent elaboration of the *Younger* doctrine — requiring the federal judiciary to decline jurisdiction to enjoin state criminal proceedings involving federal constitutional rights — illustrates an increasing sensitivity to perceived concerns of federalism and comity. And under the rubric of the abstention doctrine, federal courts are required to refrain from deciding cases challenging state actions on federal constitutional grounds in which there are questions of state law that may prove dispositive. Finally, and most significantly, the independent and adequate state grounds doctrine and the rule of finality are of equal authority as limitations on the jurisdiction of the Supreme Court; since both have the same statutory source, there is no principled reason for compromising one out of a desire to avoid giving effect to the other.

III. Cox Broadcasting Corp. v. Cohn: Four Categories of Exceptions to Finality

Cox Broadcasting Corp. v. Cohn [59] arose out of a suit in state court brought by the father of a murdered rape victim who sought damages under a Georgia statute for the telecast publication of the victim's name. The trial judge rejected the defendant's claim that the telecast was privileged under the first amendment and granted summary

55. Where the challenge to the state statute is on federal constitutional grounds, the desire to avoid unnecessary adjudication derives additional force from the doctrine of reticence in constitutional adjudication, most commonly associated with Justice Brandeis' *Ashwander* concurrence. See Ashwander v. Tennessee Valley Auth., 297 U.S. 288, 346-347 (1936) (Brandeis, J., concurring).

59. 420 U.S. 469 (1975).

judgment for the father on the issue of liability; the issue of damages, however, was reserved for a trial by jury. On appeal, the Supreme Court of Georgia upheld the trial judge's ruling denying the claim of constitutional protection, but reversed on other grounds and remanded the case for trial on the merits. Despite the fact that further proceedings in the trial court were contemplated, the United States Supreme Court ruled that the Georgia Supreme Court's decision was an appealable final judgment.

The majority took the opportunity to restate and rationalize the doctrine of finality as it applies to appeals from state court judgments. Justice White's opinion elaborated four categories of situations in which the Supreme Court will review state court decisions before a final judgment is rendered. The first two categories consist of cases in which the "federal issue would not be mooted or otherwise affected by the proceedings yet to be had" after the state court's decision of the federal question presented for interlocutory review. The latter two categories comprehend situations in which the federal issue may yet be mooted by further proceedings but in which "there is nevertheless sufficient justification for immediate review."

A. *Category 1: Practical Finality*

The first category of exceptions delineated by the Court is composed of cases in which the federal claim to be reviewed on interlocutory appeal is, as a practical matter, conclusive of the case because the party asserting the claim has no other grounds upon which to rest his case. In Mills v. Alabama,[65] for example, the state brought a criminal prosecution against the defendant for publishing an editorial on election day concerning an issue that was to be decided that day at the polls. The defendant's sole defense on first amendment grounds was sustained on demurrer by the trial court, but the state supreme court reversed and remanded for jury trial. The Supreme Court took the appeal, noting that since the defendant had conceded violation of a statute whose constitutionality had been upheld by the highest state court, proceedings in the trial court would be mere formal "gestures" leading inevitably to a conviction.

Cases in which "practical finality" had been achieved at the time appeal is presented constitute the least problematic category under the finality doctrine because the departure from the "entire case" paradigm is merely technical. Although the steps between substantial and formal completion of the trial may be few, forcing the appellant to await the official conclusion and to bring his appeal once again

65. 384 U.S. 214 (1966).

through the state court system entails the expenditure of both judicial and litigants' resources not in the consideration of substantive issues, but in the sterile exercise of satisfying the formal indicia of finality.

Nonetheless, it may not always be easy to establish the existence of practical finality. Because the designation given a judgment by state practice is not controlling, the Court must examine the opinion, the record, and possibly questions of state law to determine whether the federal question is dispositive. To avoid further demands upon the Court and the risk of imprecision and unpredictability in applying this exception, the Court must be free from the need to undertake an examination in every case of the possibility that appellant will raise additional claims in further proceedings. The proper solution to this problem is for the Court to predicate interlocutory appeal under this category upon the appellant's renunciation of any additional claims and defenses and to insist that this stipulation be binding in the absence of extraordinary subsequent developments.

B. *Category 2: Survivable Federal Claims*

The second category of exceptions defined in *Cox* embraced those cases in which "the federal issue, finally decided by the highest court in the State, will survive and require decision regardless of the outcome of future state-court proceedings.". . .

. . . [T]hat category does initially commend itself as a theoretically proper exception to the rule of finality. The Supreme Court sacrifices none of the benefits that accrue to it from strict adherence to the entire case model if it accepts jurisdiction of cases in which the only federal issues have already been determined by the highest possible state court and will definitely not be mooted by subsequent proceedings. By definition, if the Court accepts such a case for interlocutory review, it will not have to reconsider the case at a later date because the predicate to the exception is that no federal issues remain to be raised. It is therefore likely that all the facts and judgments relevant to the federal issue are present at the time of appeal and that any alternative grounds for decision have been developed. Furthermore, implicit in the notion of survivability is the nonexistence of any independent and adequate state ground; there is no danger that the Court will be evading that doctrinal restriction.

The major drawback to this exception is the difficulty of determining whether the federal issue would in fact survive further state court proceedings. The Court must ascertain not only that no additional federal claims will be raised — as it does under category 1 — but that subsequent state proceedings, which will be no more than perfunctory, will not as a practical matter nullify the federal claim.

. . . Moreover, there is no counterpart under the survivability exception to the stipulation forgoing additional claims that aids predictability in category 1. Since clarity and predictability should be the prerequisites for adopting any categorical departure from the statutory finality policy, the difficulties in ascertaining in many instances whether category 2 applies suggest that survivability is an inappropriate basis for a general exception.

C. *Category 3: State Barriers to Review of Final Judgments*

This category of exceptions encompasses cases in which subsequent review of a fully adjudicated federal claim will be impossible regardless of the ultimate outcome of further proceedings on the merits still to be conducted in the state courts. As Justice White explained, "in these cases, if the party seeking interim review ultimately prevails on the merits, the federal issue will be mooted; if he were to lose on the merits, however, the governing state law would not permit him again to present his federal claims for review.". . .

The precise content of this category is difficult to delineate. Read broadly, the category would authorize the Court to circumvent the independent and adequate state grounds doctrine completely by reviewing, on interlocutory appeal, federal questions that might, after final judgment, be insulated from review by an independent ground of state *substantive* law. But . . . a central function of the section 1257 finality requirement is to facilitate the development of independent and adequate state substantive grounds, thereby enabling the Court both to avoid unnecessary lawmaking and to accord the deference to state courts required by federalism and comity. It is improbable, then, that the *Cox* Court, in formulating category 3, was concerned with any barriers to subsequent review that might be posed by a rule or decision of state substantive law.

By "state law," the operation of which would preclude Supreme Court review after full proceedings on the merits, the Court must therefore have meant something in the nature of state *procedural* law. But the independent and adequate state grounds doctrine also applies to rules of state procedure, and the Court will generally give effect to reasonable rules of state procedure, even though a party's failure to comply with such rules bars Supreme Court review of federal questions. Category 3 may be seen as reflecting the Court's reluctance to accord state procedural barriers to the review of federal issues the same weight it must accord state substantive barriers. But since the independent and adequate state grounds doctrine as applied to state procedural law rests primarily upon considerations of comity—

as opposed to a congressional statute, which underlies the doctrine as applied to state substantive law — the Court need not observe state procedural law as scrupulously as it must state substantive grounds. As a rule, then, any clash between the comity concerns underlying the Court's solicitude for state procedural rules and the statutorily based finality principle should be resolved by making adjustments in the former rather than the latter. . . .

D. *Category 4: Important Federal Rights*

Of the four categories of exceptions articulated by the *Cox* Court, this is the most far-reaching; it is also the category found applicable to the *Cox* case itself. Under this exception, interlocutory review is permitted (1) when "reversal of the state court on the federal issue would be preclusive of any further litigation on the relevant cause of action," and (2) when failure to consider the state court decision immediately "might seriously erode federal policy.". . .

. . . [T]he nature and scope of the category are fundamentally at odds with the finality principle that governs appeals generally. Category 4 is susceptible of virtually limitless expansion. The Court's language does not clearly describe the ambit of the exception because it fails to delineate precisely which federal policies and what degree of erosion will trigger interlocutory review. It is, for example, difficult to imagine any federal issues of greater significance than those arising under the Constitution; category 4 as defined would seem to counsel that all constitutional questions be resolved on an interlocutory basis. Not only would this substantially expand the number of exceptions to finality, but it would vitiate one of the chief benefits of the finality principle in the section 1257 context — the opportunity to avoid striking down state statutes on federal constitutional grounds by permitting states to develop adequate state grounds.

Further, the imprecise manner in which the scope of the category is defined invites litigants to seek review in all cases in which even arguably significant federal rights are asserted. There is, for example, no clear principle for distinguishing labor injunctions — which are not of constitutional magnitude and yet are of sufficiently important federal interest to warrant interlocutory Supreme Court review — from other important statutorily based federal rights. Even if the Court denies review of many of these interlocutory orders, the unpredictability of the exception disrupts the state court proceedings in general and forces the Court itself to evaluate an increased number of petitions for interlocutory review, thereby nullifying the efficiency advantages of the finality principle.

. . . [T]he finality paradigm is the polar opposite of the model in which interlocutory review is extended on an issue-by-issue basis. The latter model rests upon the premise that systemic benefits of a finality rule should be forfeited to allow important issues to be resolved immediately. Having embraced this rationale to a considerable extent in establishing category 4, the Court seems to have moved in a direction incompatible with the overarching orientation on appellate jurisdiction prescribed by Congress.